## BRAZIL

# Anthropological Perspectives

Essays in Honor of Charles Wagley

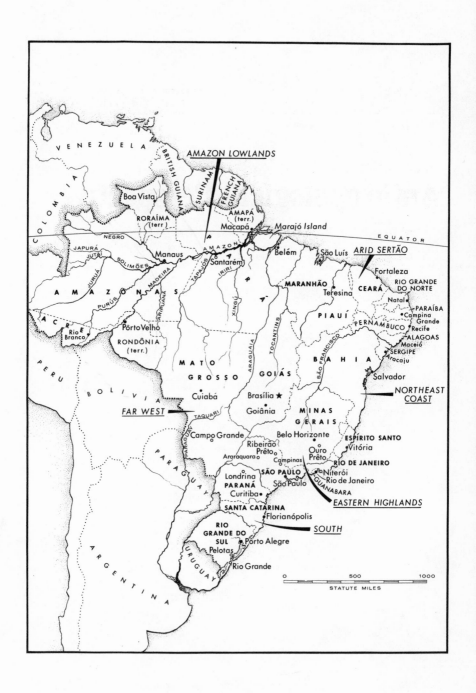

VENEZUELA

COLOMBIA

BRITISH GUIANA

SURINAM

FRENCH GUIANA

AMAZON LOWLANDS

Boa Vista

RORAÍMA (terr.)

AMAPÁ (terr.)

Macapá

Marajó Island

EQUATOR

NEGRO

Manaus

AMAZON

Belém

São Luís

ARID SERTÃO

JAPURÁ
JUTAÍ
SOLIMÕES

Santarém

TAPAJÓS

IRIRI

Fortaleza

MARANHÃO

Teresina

CEARÁ

RIO GRANDE DO NORTE

JURUÁ

A M A Z O N A S

MADEIRA

TAPAJÓS

XINGÚ

P A R Á

Natal

PARAÍBA

PURÚS

ARIPUANÁ

PIAUÍ

PERNAMBUCO

Campina Grande

Recife

ACRE

Rio Branco

Pôrto Velho

RONDÔNIA (terr.)

ALAGOAS

Maceió

SERGIPE

Aracaju

PERU

TOCANTINS

ARAGUAIA

B A H I A

SÃO FRANCISCO

B O L I V I A

MATO GROSSO

GOIÁS

Salvador

Cuiabá

Brasília ★

NORTHEAST COAST

FAR WEST

TAQUARI

Goiânia

MINAS GERAIS

PARAGUAY

Campo Grande

Belo Horizonte

ESPÍRITO SANTO

Vitória

Ribeirão Prêto

Araraquara

Ouro Prêto

Campinas

RIO DE JANEIRO

SÃO PAULO

Niterói

Rio de Janeiro

GUANABARA

PARAGUAY

Londrina

PARANÁ

Curitiba

São Paulo

EASTERN HIGHLANDS

SANTA CATARINA

Florianópolis

SOUTH

RIO GRANDE DO SUL

Pôrto Alegre

Pelotas

ARGENTINA

URUGUAY

Rio Grande

0        500       1000

STATUTE MILES

# BRAZIL

## Anthropological Perspectives

### Essays in Honor of Charles Wagley

**Maxine L. Margolis and William E. Carter
Editors**

COLUMBIA UNIVERSITY PRESS-NEW YORK-1979

The generous support of the Tinker Foundation has made possible the publication of this book.

Library of Congress Cataloging in Publication Data
Main entry under title:

Brazil, anthropological perspectives.
    Bibliography: p.
    Includes index.
    1. Ethnology—Brazil—Addresses, essays, lectures.
2. Indians of South America—Brazil—Addresses,
essays, lectures.   3. Brazil—Social life and customs—
Addresses, essays, lectures.   4. Wagley, Charles,
1913–    —Addresses, essays, lectures.   I. Wagley,
Charles, 1913–    II. Margolis, Maxine L., 1942–
III. Carter, William E., 1927–
GN564.B6B7        301.29′81        79-11843
ISBN 0-231-04714-2

Columbia University Press
New York      Guildford, Surrey

ečemano
iečopa
ečerā nenopa, doto kalo. . . .

lie quietly
in your hammock
listen to your story, Doctor Carlos. . . .

-Tapirapé song

# CONTENTS

# Preface
# and Acknowledgments

IT IS NOT fortuitous that all of the contributors to a volume on the anthropology of Brazil are former students or colleagues of Charles Wagley. Of all anthropologists, he has long been the one most closely associated with that country. His former students, both inside and outside the discipline, dominate Brazilian studies today.

In spite of such preeminence with regard to a single country, Wagley's influence reaches far beyond. Throughout his career he has trained students and encouraged research for a variety of Latin American settings. Mexico, Guatemala, Central America, the Caribbean, the Andes, and the River Plate countries all have received students and researchers that he either influenced directly or supervised. Nevertheless, the most appropriate focus of a volume in his honor is Brazil.

Charles Wagley began his distinguished career as a student of anthropology at Columbia University, where he received both his undergraduate and graduate degrees. He was a member of Columbia University's anthropology faculty for over twenty-five years, becoming Franz Boas Professor of Anthropology in 1965. He founded the university's Institute of Latin American Studies and served as its director from 1961 to 1969. In 1971 he moved to the University of Florida as Graduate Research Professor of Anthropology and Latin American Studies.

The recognition and honors given Wagley over the years are many. In 1945 he received the Cruzeiro do Sul from the Brazilian government—the highest honor accorded to foreigners—in recognition of his work in public health in Brazil during World War II. His contributions to Brazilian studies were similarly recognized in 1962 when he was awarded a Doctor Honora Causa degree from the Universidade Federal da Bahia, and again, in 1964 when he received a Doctor of Laws from Notre Dame University. In 1957–1958 he was a fellow of the Center for Advanced Study in the Behavioral Sciences. He also served as president of the American Ethnological Society in 1957–1958 and as president of the American Anthropological Association in 1970–1971. In addition, he has held various positions on the National Research Council, the Social Science Research Council, and the Inter-American Foundation, and he is a member of the American Philosophical Society, the Council on Foreign Relations, the American Academy of Arts and Sciences, and the Center for Inter-American Relations.

In cooperation with a handful of other outstanding scholars of his generation, Wagley helped lay the basis for the professionalization of Latin American studies in the United States. He contributed significantly to the recognition of the importance of Latin America, and has played a key role in the development of fellowship programs for the support of training and research in that region. If area studies today continue to receive federal and foundation support, it is in no small part due to the efforts of Charles Wagley.

Wagley's publications on Brazilian topics have been very well received and widely read. A glance at the references at the end of this volume will reveal the duration and scope of his interests, even though these references represent only a part of his scholarly production. Within Brazil his interests have included Indians, peasants, community studies, race relations, social structure, culture change, and applied studies. Special mention should be made of two of his most important works: *Amazon Town* (1953), and, most recently, *Welcome of Tears* (1977). These are not only excellent examples of anthropological research; they are also models of clarity in style and give ample evidence of his humanistic approach to his subjects. His collection of essays *The Latin American Tradition* (1968) demonstrates once again that his interests go far beyond Brazil, while his widely acclaimed *An Introduction to Brazil* (1971) is recognized as *the* introduction to Brazilian society and culture, and is required reading for anyone with even a passing interest in that country.

Those who have studied under Charles Wagley remember him most for his personal support and encouragement. At both Columbia University and the University of Florida his relationship with his students went far beyond what would be expected professionally. One of the editors of this volume (Carter) would not have been an anthropologist had it not been for Wagley's special interest and practical encouragement. At a time when Carter was only a part-time student with no financial resources and no hope of working full-time toward a doctorate, Wagley assured him that, if he made a professional commitment to the discipline, financial support would be forthcoming. Needless to say, it was. Other former students of Wagley will well recall this sort of deeply personal encouragement and generous support. It has been the rule rather than the exception, and it by no means ends with the student's receipt of the graduate degree. Wagley always has been concerned and has actively labored so that his students would be well placed professionally, and would continue to rise, as each merited, throughout his or her career. It is these rare qualities that most distinguish Chuck as mentor, colleague, and friend.

The pages that follow are the result of the combined efforts of many people over a lengthy period of time. Contributors to the volume have spent years conducting research in Brazil, and many are recognized as outstanding scholars in the fields of Brazilian ethnology, sociology, and archaeology. We thank them, first and foremost, for their generous cooperation in developing this volume.

Much work is always needed even after manuscripts are received. In editing the contributions and typing the final draft we are greatly indebted to the personnel of the Center for Latin American Studies at the University of Florida. We wish to acknowledge in a very special way the patient careful efforts of Melanie Aultman, Sue Callaway, Lydia Gonzalez, Vivian Nolan, and Sarah E. Roberts in typing the various versions of the manuscripts. In addition, we would like to thank the translators of several of the papers within the volume: Cecilia Roxo Wagley, Susan Poats, Darrel L. Miller, and Linda Hahn Miller.

Finally, we would like to express our special thanks for the support of the Tinker Foundation. Through a generous grant to Columbia

University Press, the Foundation moved the entire project from
dream to reality.

M.L.M.
W.E.C.
March 1979

# About the Contributors

**Thales de Azevedo** is Professor Emeritus of Anthropology at the Universidade Federal da Bahia in Salvador. He has done field research in various parts of northeastern and southern Brazil. Among his numerous publications are *Les Elites de Couleur dans une Ville Brésilienne, Social Change in Brazil* and, most recently, *Italianos e Gauchos*.

**Diana Brown** received her Ph.D. in anthropology at Columbia University and was Assistant Professor of Anthropology at Lehman College-CUNY until 1978. She has carried out research on Umbanda in Rio de Janeiro and on folk medicine in Campinas, and has taught at the Universidade Estadual de Campinas in São Paulo.

**William E. Carter** was Professor of Anthropology at the University of Florida and Director of its Center for Latin American Studies from 1968 to 1977. He is currently Chief of the Hispanic Division of the Library of Congress. He has done research in Bolivia, Guatemala, and Costa Rica and is the author of *Bolivia: A Profile, New Lands and Old Traditions,* and *Aymara Communities and Bolivian Agrarian Reform.*

**William H. Crocker** is Curator for South American Ethnology at the Smithsonian Institution. He has carried out extensive field work among the Canela Indians of the Central Brazilian Plateau and has published numerous articles on various aspects of Canela life.

**Clifford Evans** is Curator and Supervisory Archaeologist at the Smithsonian Institution. In collaboration with his wife, Betty J. Meggers, he has done archaeological excavations at the mouth of the Amazon, in lowland Ecuador, and in Guyana, and co-authored *Early Formative Period of Coastal Ecuador,* and *Archaeological Investigations at the Mouth of the Amazon.*

**Florestan Fernandes** is widely recognized as the "dean" of Brazilian sociology. For many years he was Professor Catedrático at the Universidade de São Paulo, and is the author of numerous books and articles, among the most recent, *A Revolução Burguesa no Brasil* and *A Sociologia no Brasil: Contribução para o Estudo de sua Formação e Desenvolvimento.*

**Shepard Forman,** Associate Professor of Anthropology at the University of Michigan, is currently Social Science Program Officer at the Ford Foundation in Rio de Janeiro. He has carried out research in northeastern Brazil and Portuguese Timor and his works include *The Raft Fisherman* and *The Brazilian Peasantry* as well as a number of journal articles.

The late **Eduardo Galvão** was Director of the Division of Anthropology of the Museu Paraense Emílio Goeldi in Belém. Galvão's research interests focused on culture change among Brazil's indigenous populations. He co-authored *The Tenetehara Indians of Brazil* (with Charles Wagley) and wrote *Santos e Visagems: Um Estudo da Vida Religiosa de Itá, Amazonas.*

**Sidney M. Greenfield** is Professor of Anthropology and Sociology at the University of Wisconsin in Milwaukee. His field work in Brazil investigated the nature of patron-clientship and has resulted in numerous articles dealing with that topic. He is co-editor (with Arnold Strickon) of *Structure and Process in Latin America.*

**Thomas Gregor,** Associate Professor of Anthropology at Vanderbilt University, has done field work among the Mehinaku Indians of the Upper Xingu. This research has resulted in a number of publications, the most recent of which is *Mehinaku: The Drama of Daily Life in a Brazilian Indian Village.*

**Daniel R. Gross** is Associate Professor of Anthropology at Hunter College-CUNY. His research includes work among sisal cultivators in northeastern Brazil and among various Gé speaking groups in central Brazil. He is the editor of *Peoples and Cultures of Native South America* and has authored a number of significant journal articles.

**Marvin Harris** is Professor of Anthropology at Columbia University. He has done research in Brazil, Ecuador, and Mozambique. He is the author of a number of books including *Town and Country in Brazil, Patterns of Race in the Americas, The Rise of Anthropological Theory, Culture, People and Nature, Cows, Pigs, Wars and Witches* and, most recently, *Cannibals and Kings.*

**Conrad P. Kottak** is Professor of Anthropology at the University of Michigan. His research interests have taken him to northeast Brazil and the Malagasy Republic. He is the author of *Anthropology: The Exploration of Human Diversity* and a number of recent articles on American culture.

**Maxine Margolis** is Associate Professor of Anthropology at the University of Florida. She has carried out field work in northeastern and southern Brazil and is the author of *The Moving Frontier: Social and Economic Change in a Southern Brazilian Community,* as well as articles on contemporary sex roles in the United States.

**Betty J. Meggers** is research associate at the Smithsonian Institution. She has done archaeological investigations in the Amazon region, Ecuador, and Guyana. She co-authored a number of books with her husband, Clifford Evans, and co-edited *Tropical Forest Ecosystems in Africa and South America.* Among her other works are *Amazonia: Man and Culture in a Counterfeit Paradise* and *Prehistoric America.*

**Charlotte I. Miller** received her Ph.D. in anthropology from the University of Florida. She carried out field work among the urban middle class in Belo Horizonte, and is currently doing an investigation of rural health practices in Peru.

**Emilio F. Moran** is Assistant Professor of Anthropology at Indiana University. His field work has focused on the ecological aspects of Amazonian development and he has published a number of articles dealing with that topic. He is the author of *Human Adaptability: An Introduction to Ecological Anthropology.*

**Robert F. Murphy** is Professor of Anthropology at Columbia University. He has conducted field work among the Mundurucú Indians of Pará and among the Tuareg of North Africa. His publications have included *Mundurucú Religion, Headhunters' Heritage, The Dialectics of Social Life,* and with Buell Quain, *The Trumaí Indians of Central Brazil.*

**Joyce F. Riegelhaupt** teaches on the anthropology faculty of Sarah Lawrence College. Her research has taken her to northeastern Brazil and Portugal, and she has published a number of articles on peasant politics and rural marketing systems.

**Judith Shapiro** is Associate Professor of Anthropology at Bryn Mawr College. She has done field work among the Tapirapé and Yanamamö Indians of Brazil, and has written a number of articles in academic journals dealing with social organization and sex roles.

**Robert W. Shirley** is Associate Professor of Anthropology at the University of Toronto. His field work in Brazil has focused on various aspects of the legal system and he is author of *The End of a Tradition: Culture Change and Development in the Município of Cunha, São Paulo.*

**Charles Wagley:** see Preface.

# BRAZIL

# Anthropological Perspectives

Essays in Honor of Charles Wagley

# INTRODUCTION

# Anthropology and Brazilian National Identity

## Charles Wagley

ANTHROPOLOGY HAS BEEN directly relevant to the way that modern Brazilians think about themselves. Today Brazilians have enormous pride in themselves as a people and as a nation, and they aspire to becoming a world economic and political power. Brazilians are proud of their recent industrial development, their gigantic hydro-electric plants, their new highways, and other indicators of material progress. They are proud of their "racial democracy" with its assimilation of people of different races and tolerance of phenotypical differences. They are proud of their poets, novelists, architects, composers, scientists, cinema directors, soccer players, and popular music. This has not always been the case. On the contrary, until about the third decade of the twentieth century, Brazilians were often dubious, sometimes downright pessimistic, about the future of their vast country. "Brazil is rich but Brazilians are poor" was a commonly used adage. It is the theme of this paper, written as an introduction to a volume on Brazil by anthropologists,[1] that their discipline has played an important role in providing Brazilians with a basis for an objective and optimistic view of themselves.

Ever since the sixteenth century, Brazil has been a natural laboratory for the study of human society. In Brazil, the European encountered the Amerindian and learned from them the basic knowledge with which to adapt to the new tropical and semi-tropical

1

environment. Soon, the Amerindian and the European were joined by literally millions of African slaves torn from their native societies to operate the sugar plantations, the mines, and other economic enterprises of the colonial society. Then, with miscegenation, new Brazilian physical types appeared whose ancestry derived from three racial stocks. Although the Portuguese imposed their formal institutions such as government, religion, and the like upon the colony and later on the new nation, each of these peoples contributed important elements of Brazilian national culture. Brazil became both physically and culturally a mosaic of three continents. But rather than being a source of pride, this physical and cultural diversity of origins in a new tropical environment plagued the thinking of Brazilians about themselves and about the future of their great nation. The powerful and educated Brazilian elite wanted to be considered European albeit deriving their position and wealth from the New World. They were often ashamed of the "mongrel aspect of their people" and of the non-European aspects of Brazilian cultural life.

Following the prevalent "scientific thought" of nineteenth and early twentieth century Europe and the United States, it seemed clear to Brazilian intellectuals (and to many not so intellectual) that Brazil was doomed to an inferior status among nations by two immutable conditions. These were the racial inferiority of the Negro and the Indian, and of the mixed offspring of these darker races with the European. Even the darker European Mediterranean from which the Portuguese derived were considered inferior to the lighter Nordic northern European. Furthermore, this nineteenth-century "scientific thought" which carried over into the twentieth century stressed the enervating influence of the tropical climate. In the tropics, the white man was doomed to disintegration—to disease, to low productivity, to alcoholism, and to general depression. Brazilian intellectuals had read the racist theories of Comte de Gobineau, Houston Chamberlain, Madison Grant, Gustave Le Bon, and others; they were also familiar with the environmental determinist theories of Ratzel and Ellsworth Huntington. Both racial origin and climate seemed to condemn Brazil to second-rate status.

Thomas E. Skidmore in his book *Black into White: Race and Nationality in Brazilian Thought* (1974) has shown how the concept of the inferiority of the Negro, the Amerindian, and even of the southern European prevailed in Brazilian thought through the nineteenth century and well into the twentieth century. Even such astute and otherwise objective Brazilian writers such as Silvio Romero, Nina Rodrigues, and Oliveira Vianna were taken in by European and North American racial doctrines. Euclides da Cunha, the author of the Brazilian masterpiece *Rebellion in the Backlands* (*Os Sertões*) which was first published in 1902, ascribed to racist doctrines. In this book, a defense of the small band of religious fanatic followers of Anthony the Councilor who rebelled against the new Republic and who held off the attacks of the Brazilian army at Canudos in Bahia until they were finally massacred, da Cunha shows his basic confusion about the concept of race. At times, he wrote proudly of the intelligence, the energy, and the adaptability of the simple Northeastern rustic. But at times he apologizes for their mixed racial ancestry and condemns them to moral and intellectual inferiority. *Os Sertões* was widely read and was without doubt the most influential book to appear in Brazil around the turn of the century. In the next two decades, only a few writers such as Manoel Bomfim, Alberto Torres, and Edgar Roquette-Pinto (an anthropologist) challenged the negative view of the potentialities of the Brazilian people (Skidmore 1974:113–23). Others took refuge in a peculiar Brazilian concept of "whitening" the population. This concept, based upon the premise of racial inferiority of the Negro and the Amerindian, stated that the future of Brazil lay in the progressive genetic domination of the Caucasoid elements in the Brazilian population over the Negroid. Through a lower birth rate and lower survival rate, the percentage of the black population would become progressively smaller. Miscegenation would speed the whitening process because people would choose partners lighter than themselves. This "whitening theory" was at least one reason for the fact that Brazil actively sought German, Italian, and Polish immigrants during the nineteenth and early twentieth centuries. Following this whitening theory of a future for the Brazilian people, even Teddy Roosevelt, after his visit to Brazil in 1913–1914, wrote an article (promptly translated into Portuguese) in which he predicted: "The Brazilian in the future will be in blood more European than in the past. . . ." (quoted in Skidmore 1974:68–69). Yet, many Brazilians continued to worry. Would Brazil remain tainted by the mixed ancestry of its people for many generations, for centuries, or even permanently?

As Brazilians held to a racist doctrine, they also held in dispraisal customs and institutions which derived from Africa and the Amerindian—even those created by their mixed cultural heritage in the new tropical world. The Brazilian writer Vianna Moog calls the predominating intellectual attitude *mazombism*. By this term he characterizes those who were spiritually Europeans and were critical of all that was Brazilian (Vianna Moog 1964:107–10). At the beginning of the nineteenth century, these *mazombos* imitated Portugal and, by the end of the century, they looked to France and were "irritated with Brazil because Brazilian culture was not an exact projection of French culture." (Vianna Moog 1964:108). Thus, Brazilians tried to write like Europeans, paint like Europeans, compose music like Europeans, and, as far as possible, think like Europeans. Such people seemed to deny the way of life and the culture of the people among whom they lived.

Brazilian thinking about their country and its people began to change during the first decades of the twentieth century. Credit for this change cannot be claimed by anthropologists nor by any brand of social scientists. Change seems to have come first from the field of literature and the arts. Novelists and artists began to discover Brazil and Brazilians. Ironically, many of them were stimulated by Euclides da Cunha who, although he had been taken in by racist doctrines, sympathetically described the simple *sertanejo* (or backlander). And equally ironically "it began with the attempt of some younger poets to introduce the latest European literary fashion into Brazil" (Skidmore 1974:178). It was a revolt against the conservative and formalistic style and content of the Parnassians who controlled the Academy of Letters in favor of a new Brazilian style and new Brazilian subject matter. A testimony to this movement was the "Week of Modern Art" held in São Paulo in 1922 during which Brazilian writers and artists declared their intent to write in the Brazilian vernacular about Brazilian subjects and to paint in a modern style what they saw in Brazil. One well-known Brazilian literary scholar states that this Modernist movement was a declaration of Brazilian artistic independence. "Everything that made up the 'pastism' patrimony was rejected: oratorical emphasis, eloquence, Parnassian hieraticism, the cult of rich rhymes, perfect and conventional meters, classic and lustyfying [sic] language; it advocated a greater faithfulness to Brazilian reality" (Coutinho 1969:220). This modernist movement produced in the next ten years a series of novels (and other literary forms) which treated Brazilian subjects. Mario de Andrade, a folklorist and poet, published his well-known *Macunaíma* (1928) written with vocabulary from various regions of Brazil and crammed with folklore of African, Amerindian, and Portuguese origin. In fact, his satirical tale follows vaguely the outlines of a classical Tupí Indian myth in which a culture hero, Maíra, travels with his twin brother in search of their supernatural father. Andrade's hero is also an Indian of supernatural birth and magical ability; but he is a white Indian who travels with his brothers Jiguê and Mawape, one of whom is bronze and the other black. They visit a strange tribe living in a large village called São Paulo where the people are bilingual. They speak in a rich vernacular, but to learn their written language one must resort to "bilingual books" called "dictionaries." To understand Mario de Andrade's prose one had to be a Brazilian and, even more, a Brazilian versed in regional vocabulary and folk belief.

Almost simultaneously, out of the Northeast of Brazil came the so-called "regionalist" writers such as José Americo de Almeida, Rachel de Queiroz, José Lins do Rego, Graciliano Ramos, Jorge Amado, and others who wrote about the miseries caused by the land tenure system, the class system, and the frequent droughts in the arid backlands; they also wrote about the plantation system (now in decline), the life of the poor blacks in the cities, and the violence of the bandits and the fight over land on the cacao frontier of southern Bahia. It was the novelists of Brazil more than writers in any social science discipline who brought to the public consciousness just those aspects of Brazilian life which the mazombos of the past would hide or even deny.

It was not until about the 1930s that a modern concept of culture and an outright denial of the deleterious influence of climate and racial determinism was introduced broadly into the intellectual currents of Brazil. As stated previously, isolated individuals had already denied these out-moded concepts. One writer, Gilberto Freyre, must be given credit for disseminating the concepts of the equal intellectual potential of people of all racial groups, the influence of culture and social conditions on human behavior, and the error of viewing climate as a factor limiting economic and cultural development. His first important book, *Casa Grande e Senzala* (translated into English as *The Masters and the Slaves*), was published in 1933. This book quickly caught the imagination of the Brazilian reading public. It has gone through numerous Brazilian editions, three editions in English, and has been translated into several other languages. The impact upon Brazil was strong and immediate. It was almost as if the intellectuals of Brazil, who were becoming increasingly nationalistic and proud of their achievements and ready to face the realities of Brazilian life, had been waiting for a book of this kind. *Casa Grande e Senzala* is not an uncritical book for it often portrays the plantation aristocracy of Northeastern Brazil as indolent, syphilitic, and subject to a variety of vices, but it places the cause squarely on the plantation and the slavocrat culture and, in addition, it attempts to treat the positive contributions of the Indian and the African to Northeastern Brazilian culture. Gilberto Freyre is not an anthropologist. He can perhaps best be described as a social historian, but he brought modern anthropological concepts to bear on his studies of Brazilian society. As Freyre states in the Preface to the second English edition to *The Masters and the Slaves:* "It was my studies in anthropology under the direction of Professor (Franz) Boas that first revealed to me the Negro and the mulatto for what they are—with the effects of environment or cultural experience separate from racial characteristics. I learned to regard as fundamental the difference between *race* and *culture,* to discriminate between the effects of purely genetic relationships and those resulting from social influences, the cultural heritage and the milieu. It is upon the criterion of the basic difference between race and culture that the entire plan of this essay rests as well as the distinction to be made between racial and family heredity" (Freyre, 1956:27. Freyre's italics).

*Casa Grande e Senzala* relieved Brazilians once and for all of feelings of inferiority on the basis of race and climate and it soon became a Brazilian and international classic. But it was somewhat of a shocking book to many Brazilians. Although it perhaps painted an overly mild picture of Brazilian slavery and over-emphasized the special tolerance of the Portuguese to miscegenation, it was a critical book on the influence of the plantation and slave system. It called attention to just those aspects of Brazilian culture which the racists and environmental determinists would have hidden—the influence of the African on Brazilian cuisine, on family life, on religion, on music, and on folklore. Freyre also described the extent of miscegenation in Brazil not only among the lower classes but in the aristocratic families. Although Freyre worked mainly in the field of social history, he continued to express his debt to anthropology and urged Brazilians to study the *caboclo* (the peasant of mixed racial origin), the Negro, and other neglected aspects of Brazilian culture. More than anyone else, Freyre opened the door to modern anthropology in Brazil.

Freyre's book, as brilliant and idiosyncratic as it is, was a reflection of a more general trend in the 1930s in Brazil. It was in the 1930s that the first Brazilian universities were established, bringing together what had been previously isolated faculties of higher education. In Rio de Janeiro and in São Paulo, faculties of philosophy were established as part of the newly formed universities and there were chairs of sociology and anthropology. In Rio de Janeiro, at the newly founded University of Brazil, Arthur Ramos held the chair in anthropology. Ramos was a physician who followed in the footsteps of Nina Rodrigues in the study of the African in Brazil. But unlike Nina Rodrigues, Ramos had read modern social science and especially contemporary social and cultural anthropology. He was, of course, free of racist theories. Ramos had visited Europe, lectured at Louisiana State University where he came to know T. Lynn Smith, and was a visitor at Northwestern University where he entered into close contact with Melville Herskovits who gave him direction in his reading about Africa and the background of the Brazilian Negro. He did considerable field research on Afro-Brazilian cults in Bahia and in Rio de Janeiro. It was Ramos who wrote the first synthesis of Brazilian anthropology, *Introdução a Anthropologia Brasileira* (2 vols., 1943 and 1947) in which he describes the Indian, the African, and the European cultures of Brazil and the fusions of these three heritages into contemporary Brazilian culture. Ramos was a pioneer in modern Brazilian anthropology, but he did not create a group of students to continue his work. In 1948 he moved to Paris as director of social sciences for UNESCO and died there in 1949.

In São Paulo, modern social sciences were developing even more rapidly. In 1933, the Escola Livre de Sociologia e Política was established as an independent faculty and one year later the Faculty of Philosophy of the University of São Paulo was founded. The Escola Livre offered courses in anthropology and sociology almost at once and it soon offered a master's degree in social sciences. At first, anthropology and sociology were offered at the University of São Paulo only as part of a wider curriculum, but by 1947 specialization in these fields was officially recognized (Fernandes 1958:27). Both institutions recruited an amazingly talented faculty from Brazil and from abroad. At the Escola Livre, Herbert Baldus, who was German by birth but living in Brazil, taught ethnology. He had studied anthropology in Germany under Thurnwald and had carried out field research in the Gran Chaco and among the Kaingang and Tapirapé Indians of Brazil. Donald Pierson, a sociologist trained at the University of Chicago by Robert Park who had done pioneer research on race relations in Bahia, taught sociology and became Dean of Graduate Studies. Samuel H. Lowrie, a sociologist, and Alexander Kafka, an economist, also taught at the Escola Livre. They were later joined by Kalervo Oberg and other Brazilian and foreign social scientists.

At the University of São Paulo, Emilio Willems, trained in Germany but who had emigrated to Brazil, taught anthropology. The University of São Paulo soon contracted a group of professors from France, many of whom established their international reputations through their research in Brazil. Among them were Claude Lévi-Strauss, Pierre Monbeig, and Roger Bastide. The members of the so-called "French mission" not only taught and trained Brazilian students, but all of them carried out research of their own during their Brazilian sojourn. Lévi-Strauss undertook field research among the Bororo Indians, among the Nambikwara and the Tupi-Kawibib (Lévi-Strauss 1936 and 1948). In his well-known book, *Tristes Tropiques* (1961), Lévi-Strauss describes his experience in Brazil as a teacher and a field researcher. Pierre Monbeig, a human geographer, did research that resulted in his *Pionniers et Planteurs de São Paulo* (1952) and other more general works. Roger Bastide produced a large number of articles and books, but his *Les Réligions Africains au Brésil* (1960) sums up his many years of research on Afro-Brazilian religious cults. The combined efforts of the Escola Livre and the faculty of philosophy of the University of São Paulo established the basis for what has often been called the "São Paulo school" of sociology and anthropology. The first students at these institutions included Florestan Fernandes, Egon Schaden, Lucila Hermann, Gioconda Mussolini, Antônio Rubbo Müller, Fernando Altenfelder Silva, Esdra Borges Costa, Oracy Nogueira, Darcy Ribeiro, and others who became leaders in modern sociology and anthropology in Brazil. Some of them, such as Oracy Nogueira, Octavio da Costa Eduardo, and Antônio Rubbo Müller, continued their studies abroad but most were Sâo Paulo trained.

Beginning in 1938, the Museu Nacional in Rio de Janeiro sponsored the research in Brazil of a small group of young anthropologists from Columbia University. In this program, Buell Quain undertook research among the Trumai Indians of the Xingu headwaters (Murphy and Quain 1955), William Lipkind studied the Carajá of the Araguaia River (Lipkind 1940 and 1948), Ruth Landes studied Afro-Brazilian cults in Bahia (Landes 1947), and Charles Wagley began his field research among the Tapirapé Indians in 1939. Almost simultaneously, Luis Castro Faria joined the staff of the Museu Nacional and took part in the expedition led by Claude Lévi-Strauss to the Nambikwara. This program was not as productive for Brazilian students as programs underway in São Paulo but, in 1941, Charles Wagley returned to Brazil to teach at the Museu and to lead a group of students in field research among the Tenetehara Indians of Maranhão (Wagley and Galvão 1949). One of these students, Eduardo Galvão, later came to Columbia University where he took his doctorate under Julian Steward and Charles Wagley. This program formed the basis for modern anthropology at the Museu Nacional which, in later years under the leadership of Luis Castro Faria, Roberto Cardoso de Oliveira (who had studied in São Paulo), and Roberto da Matta, became a leading center for graduate study in Brazil.[2]

By about 1950 a new group of Brazilian sociologists and anthropologists had appeared. No longer was Brazilian anthropology and sociology the domain of foreign scholars, self-trained intellectuals, and armchair theorists. It was a discipline manned mainly by Brazilians who were well-trained scholars fully aware of the trends, methods, and theories current in France, Great Britain, and the United States. Some of these new Brazilian social scientists called themselves anthropologists and others identified themselves as sociologists. But in the 1950s there was little to distinguish one from the other. At first, they were so few in number that everyone felt a sense of unity. Both sociologists and anthropologists were interested in studying the same neglected aspects of Brazilian culture and society—the Indian, the African, and the rural peasant—and they focused upon problems relating to rural life and relations between the people of different races. Furthermore, they all tended to work with a generally similar methodology. Their anthropological and sociological mentors from France and from the United States tended to favor an ethnographic and historical approach rather than a quantitative survey method.

Donald Pierson, in his study of race relations in Bahia (1942) and later in his study with his students of the small community of Cruz das Almas (1952), used basically an ethnographic method. Herbert Baldus was an anthropologist and thus ethnographic and historical in his methods. Claude Lévi-Strauss, also contracted as a professor of sociology, was already a confirmed ethnologist when he left France. He seems to have been converted to anthropology by reading Robert Lowie's *Primitive Society* (1920) and came to Brazil hoping to do studies among Indian groups (Lévi-Strauss 1961:63). Emilio Willems, although he identified himself in his studies of Brazil as an anthropologist, was in Florestan Fernandes' words "perhaps the principal figure of this stage in the transformation of sociology in Brazil and possessed the great merit of having combined field work with research into historical reconstruction" (Fernandes 1977:42, translation my own). His pioneer study of Cunha, a small community in São Paulo, was definitely an ethnographic study[3] (Willems 1947). Roger Bastide's studies of Afro-Brazilian cults were basically ethnographic (cf. Bastide 1944, 1945, and 1960). It is little wonder, then, that the first studies by this early group of modern social scientists were basically ethnographic and historical whether the authors called themselves anthropologists or sociologists. And of primary importance was the fact that their studies were based upon field research and the use of historical documents. Furthermore, these first studies were in the fields of the neglected "grass roots" aspects of Brazilian society.

Florestan Fernandes (who studied with Herbert Baldus, Donald Pierson, Claude Lévi-Strauss, and Roger Bastide), who later became the leader of a new generation of Brazilian sociologists, did his first studies in the field of folklore and indigenous ethnology. His first contributions concerned the extinct Tupinambá Indians of the Brazilian coast. With an intimate knowledge of the historical sources left by the chroniclers of the sixteenth and seventeenth centuries, Florestan Fernandes used a functionalist methodology to interpret Tupinambá social organization and warfare. These studies stand today as masterpieces of Brazilian social science (Fernandes 1949a, 1949b, and 1952).

In the years that followed, numerous Brazilian anthropologists turned to the study of indigenous cultures. Egon Schaden, who became a leader of São Paulo anthropology, took up work with the southern Guaraní of Brazil (cf. Schaden 1962). Eduardo Galvão published work on the Tentetehara in collaboration with Charles Wagley (Wagley and Galvão 1949) on the tribes of the Xingú headwaters (Galvão 1953), and the indigenous groups of the upper Rio Negro. Darcy Ribeiro did important research on the Kadiweu of southern Brazil (Ribeiro 1950 and 1951) and among the Kaapor (Urubú) Indians of Maranhão (Ribeiro 1955) as well as publishing important historical and synthetic studies of Brazilian Indians (Ribeiro 1962 and 1970). Roberto Cardoso de Oliveira wrote on the Terena of southern Brazil (Oliveira 1960) and on the Tukuna of upper Amazonas from the point of view of their contact with Brazilian society and inter-ethnic relations (Oliveira 1972). Others, such as Fernando Altenfelder Silva, Harald Schultz, Protásio Frikel, Carlos Moreira Neto, Julio Cezar Melatti, Roque de Barros Laraia, and Roberto da Matta have made major contributions to indigenous studies. They were joined by a host of foreign anthropologists such as Simone Dreyfus, Robert Murphy, William H. Crocker, David Maybury-Lewis, Terence Turner, Jean Carter Lave, Joan Bamberger, Christopher Crocker, Thomas Gregor, Judith Shapiro, and others too numerous to list. Each year the bibliography of Brazilian indigenous cultures grows almost geometrically as Brazilians and foreign scholars contribute to it.

Studies of Brazilian Indians during recent years have emphasized two major preoccupations in modern socio-cultural anthropology, namely social structure and cultural ecology. Nimuendajú's studies of the Gê-speaking tribes had provided data on the extraordinary complexities of Gê social life. Claude Lévi-Strauss' *Les Structures Elémentaires de la Parenté* (1949) opened up new vistas in the interpretation of social structure particularly pertinent to Gê groups who emphasize moieties and duality. It is not surprising that the "new" anthropology of Brazil focused upon kinship and social structure; in doing so, it corrected and extended the data of Nimuendajú and contributed to contemporary theory.

It is also not surprising that so much research on Brazilian aboriginal and peasant groups is concerned with cultural ecology. Most of Brazil is tropical or semitropical in environment and yet there is a wide range of ecological adaptation among the indigenous peoples and among the peasant societies that took form after 1500. There are still many unresolved problems in tropical ecology. How large a population can be supported, and for how long, by a system of horticulture with manioc as a principal crop? What is the relationship between social structure and primitive warfare? How have indigenous and peasant ecologies responded to world economic demands (i.e., rubber and coffee)? How did tropical forest horticulturalists meet nutritional needs such as protein? Often these studies in cultural ecology have provided information important for national policy (cf. Moran 1976a). Brazil provides a wonderful natural laboratory for cultural ecology and such studies are directly relevant to national development.

Similarly the new group of Brazilian anthropologists and their foreign colleagues continued the tradition of Afro-Brazilian studies. As stated earlier, Nina Rodrigues, Manuel Querino, and Artur Ramos had devoted themselves to the study of Afro-Brazilian cults and the contribution of the African to Brazilian culture. In 1934 and 1937 "Afro-Brazilian Congresses" were held in Recife and in Bahia and these resulted in the publishing of ethnographic and historical data as well as calling this field of study to the attention of the intellectual community. In 1939, Ruth Landes undertook the research in Bahia which led to the publication of her *A City of Women* (1947). Landes worked closely with Edison Carneiro who published a number of important historical and ethnographic studies of blacks in Bahia and Rio de Janeiro (Carneiro 1937 and 1948, for example). Soon afterwards René Ribeiro (1952) and Octávio da Costa Eduardo (1948), both of whom had studied at Northwestern University with Melville Herskovits, undertook important studies of Afro-Brazilian life in Recife and in Maranhão. And, as mentioned earlier, Roger Bastide had already begun his studies of Afro-Brazilian religions. In more recent years, anthropologists have turned to the study of Umbanda, a new syncretic religion founded in the early 1920s which combines African elements, European spiritism, and Christianity and is followed by literally millions of Brazilians (cf. Brown 1974).

The new Brazilian anthropology also turned very early to the study of the little community following the lead of anthropologists in other parts of the world. The pioneer study of this kind was Emilio Willems' *Cunha: Tradição e Transição em uma Cultural Rural do Brasil* (1947). Willems' study of Cunha was quickly followed by a study of another São Paulo community by Donald Pierson and his students in a small community which they called by the fictitious name of Cruz das Almas (Pierson et al. 1952). In 1953, I published a book on a small Amazonian community (Wagley 1953) and Eduardo Galvão published a study of the religious life of the same community in 1955 (Galvão 1955a). These early studies of small communities, made up of peasants and small town people, were followed by a long series of similar studies in different regions of Brazil. Some of these studies, such as those by Marvin Harris (1956) and Harry W. Hutchinson (1957), were part of a larger research program undertaken by the State of Bahia (Fundação para Desenvolvimento de Ciências) and Columbia University (Department of Anthropology) directed by Thales de Azevedo and myself. Others were part of a research program directed by Donald Pierson for the São Francisco Valley Authority (Fernando Altenfelder Silva 1955; Alceu Maynard Araujó Lima 1961; Esdra Borges Costa 1960; and Alfonso Trujillo Ferrari 1960). Still others, such as Antonio Candido's study of rural São Paulo society (1964), Allen Johnson's study of sharecroppers in Ceará (1971), Shepard Forman's study of raft fishermen on the northeastern coast (1970), Oracy Nogueira's study of family life in Itapetininga, São Paulo (1962), and Maxine Margolis' study of a community on the Paraná coffee frontier (1973), were individual undertakings. All of them taken together, however, provided a picture of Brazilian rural and small town society never before recorded in such detail. And, it should be noted that these community studies, focusing as they generally did on rather small and often isolated population units, followed a pattern set earlier by anthropological studies of indigenous cultures and Afro-Brazilian institutions. They focused upon aspects of Brazilian society and culture previously ignored by other social scientists studying Brazil. They all were concerned with what Robert Redfield called the "Little Tradition" of a complex society—that is, those aspects of a culture carried by the peasant, the urban poor, and the illiterate worker—in contrast to the "Great Tradition" which is the literate culture of the dominant class. In other words, anthropologists worked toward describing and analyzing the so-called "grass roots" of Brazil rather than the formal system of government, the nationwide economic institutions, or the literary movements. As a discipline, anthropology uncovered the reality of Brazilian life which had so often been overlooked or even denied.

A review of the development of anthropology and its role in changing Brazilian identity would be incomplete without some mention of the UNESCO supported project on the study of race relations in Brazil. In 1950, Alfred Metraux, director of a UNESCO program of race relations studies, stimulated a series of studies in various parts of Brazil—in the rural zones throughout north Brazil, in São Paulo, Rio de Janeiro, Bahia, and Recife. The research was conducted by anthropologists and sociologists. Thus, Marvin Harris, Harry W. Hutchinson, Ben Zimmerman, and I reported on race relations in four different little communities located in different cultural regions of Brazil (Wagley ed. 1952). Thales de Azevedo, the leading anthropologist of Bahia, studied the problem of race and social mobility in the city of Salvador (Bahia) (Azevedo 1953). Luis Costa Pinto, a sociologist, wrote on the situation of the Negro in Rio de Janeiro (Costa Pinto 1953). René Ribeiro studied the relationship of religion to race relations in Recife (Ribeiro 1956), and Roger Bastide and Florestan Fernandes produced their monumental study of racial contact in the city of São Paulo (Bastide and Fernandes 1955). These studies, although motivated by an effort to depict a positive picture of race relations in Brazil as compared to the United States and South Africa, for example, actually uncovered considerable "race" prejudice. They found that, although there was generally considerable tolerance of phenotypical physical appearance, that the rigid class structure of Brazil relegated most blacks and people of mixed ancestry to the lower class; and they found that African ancestry was a definite barrier to social mobility. These studies helped to bring objectivity to the "myth of racial democracy" and perhaps in the process helped somewhat to ameliorate the situation of people of color in Brazil.

In the 1960s and 1970s when anthropologists entered the field of urban studies in Brazil, as they did in other parts of the world, the same preoccupation marked their studies. The traditional research methods of anthropology, which took form in the study of small communities, were hardly adaptable to large metropolitan agglomerations. The anthropologists thus searched for social units within the city which lent themselves to their anthropological methods. Since anthropologists had already studied rural peasants and small town dwellers, they first turned to the study of *favelas* (shantytowns) within the great cities. These settlements had a spatial dimension, and at first it seemed that they were made up of peasant migrants to the city. Anthropologists thought that they were following the rural peasant into the city. They soon found, however, that they were wrong, for these favelas contained people already born in the city, people from nearby smaller cities, as well as people from nearby rural zones. Anthropologists (and sociologists) who studied these favelas found also that they functioned like communities; they had an internal organization, leadership, and community identity; they were far from being marginal to the city. They performed an important role in city life and their inhabitants were fully aware of the complex legal and political mechanisms of urban life (cf. Leeds 1969, Perlman 1976). Again, anthropologists focused upon a neglected segment of Brazilian society, namely the urban poor.

In the move to the city as a site of research, anthropologists did not limit themselves to shantytowns. They also undertook studies of other small groups and traditional institutions such as the Umbanda cults mentioned earlier. Two outstanding examples will suffice. During 1973 and 1974 the anthropologist, Maria Julia Goldwasser, studied the "Escola de Samba" (literally "Samba School") called Mangueira which is one of the best known and most traditional clubs in Rio de Janeiro which organizes group presentations at the annual Carnaval. She was able to study this Carnaval club, founded in 1928 and originally made up of residents of the favela of Mangueira as a community, because it "emerged as an ordered social group fixed in a determined space, and regulated by a definite pattern of social relations" (Goldwasser 1975:10). Her study shows this social group within the large city as an important institution breaking the anomie of urban life and providing direction to the lives of a large number of people. The other example which I would like to cite is Charlotte Miller's as yet unpublished study of middle class family and kinship in Belo Horizonte, a city of over a million people. Charlotte Miller limited her study to four kindreds or *parentelas*—that is, networks of kinsmen both consanguineally and affinally related living in Belo Horizonte. She found constant interaction and mutual cooperation within these groups who tended to live in apartments and houses within the same neighborhood. Her study provided a different view of urban life than that of isolated nuclear families depending for support on impersonal public and private institutions such as daycare centers and the like. A widespread kinship network gave support to young families often with working mothers and the details of urban bureaucracy were often smoothed by the mutual help of kinsmen (Miller 1975 and Miller in this volume).

Today in Brazil, social science manpower has increased many

fold since the 1930s and 1940s when modern anthropology and sociology dominated and seemed to have a common identity. Today there are numerous centers of social science research, and economists, sociologists, demographers, city planners, geographers, political scientists, anthropologists, and other specialists ply their trade. Likewise, anthropology as a discipline has expanded in its scope and its number of practitioners. At the biannual meeting of the Brazilian anthropological association which took place in Salvador in Bahia in 1974, over three hundred people attended; there are at least that number of foreign anthropologists in Europe and the United States who have done research in Brazil who were not present. Anthropology is today but one of many social science disciplines that attempt to analyze and interpret the complexities of Brazilian society. But anthropology has in this century played an important role in Brazilian society. It described and brought to public attention those aspects of Brazilian life which were, in the past, a source of embarrassment to the mazombists, the racists, and even the middle and upper class of traditional Brazil. Before 1930, Brazilians were often ashamed of the mixed racial aspect of their people and it is said that people of African and mixed ancestry were by common practice excluded from the diplomatic corps and from the Navy, services that represented Brazil abroad. Brazilians were ashamed of the Afro-Brazilian religious cults and practices, of the illiterate *caboclo* or *caipira* (peasants) of the interior and of the nascent favelas in their large cities. These were the aspects of Brazil which anthropologists elected to study and in doing so exposed them in all their ugliness and in their beauty—not as something always to be proud of but to be recognized as essentially unique aspects of Brazilian life.

Thus, today Brazilians have a different picture of themselves. They are a proud and highly nationalistic people; they are proud of their accomplishments within the last two or three decades—the building of their new capital of Brasilia, in the heart of a wilderness; the construction of the Transamazon highway, and of the Brazilian economic "miracle" which was a result of the rapid growth of industry. They are also proud of Brazilian "futebol" (soccer) and their international team which has won the World Cup three times, of Brazilian popular music, of other manifestations of the Brazilian common man such as the Carnaval, the Afro-Brazilian religious cults, the strength and adaptability of the peasant, and the like. Thus, a movie such as *Black Orpheus* might be shown throughout Brazil and around the world depicting life in technicolor of the favelas against the background of beautiful Guanabara Bay. And, another movie, *Pagador de Promessas,* applauded in Brazil and abroad, showed the religious fanaticism of the northeastern caboclo, the Afro-Brazilian cults of Bahia, and the favelas. Mass media magazines report on the raft fishermen of the northeastern coast, the cowboys of the northeastern sertão, and the rubber gatherer and placer miners of Amazonia. Before 1930, these subjects would have hardly interested, perhaps offended, the middle and upper class Brazilian who was eager to project an image of Brazil as a European culture in the New World. Along with writers of fiction, anthropologists have helped Brazilians to discover themselves.

This book is a collection of essays by anthropologists, both Brazilian and North American, who have devoted their research to Brazil. It should be noted that, in keeping with anthropological traditions, many of the authors are concerned with indigenous cultures and societies and often with little communities made up of peasants. On the other hand, some are concerned with other institutions such as family networks in large cities, the anthropology of law, a new religion and class structure, the adaptation of migrants to a new Amazonian environment, and even to political behavior. The essays in this book are representative of both the traditional fields of anthropological research and the new directions that it has taken in the last twenty years. Each of these essays in its way helps us understand Brazil as a nation and each contributes to the view which Brazilians today hold of themselves.

## Notes

1. It should be understood that throughout this essay, I am referring to socio-cultural anthropology, the sub-discipline of anthropology most highly developed in Brazil.

2. It will come as a surprise that in this brief history of Brazilian anthropology the name of Curt Nimuendajú has not as yet been mentioned. Nimuendajú was without doubt the leading anthropologist working with Indians in the first half of the twentieth century. Nimuendajú was German by birth but came to Brazil in 1903 and became a Brazilian citizen in 1922. He soon dropped his German surname, Unkel, in favor of the surname Nimuendajú, given to him by the Apapucua-Guaraní, the first group of Indians with whom he lived and studied. Nimuendajú produced literally

hundreds of articles on Brazilian Indians and Brazilian indigenous languages but his major monographs were written on the Gê-speaking peoples of Northeastern Brazil (Nimuendajú 1939, 1942, and 1946). Nimuendajú was essentially a self taught ethnologist but he had received some training in Germany before coming to Brazil, and in later years he profited by his lengthy correspondence with Robert Lowie who translated his monographs into English. Nimuendajú was a "loner." He had little to do with Brazilian anthropology or anthropologists, except perhaps with Herbert Baldus with whom he corresponded regularly. His most important monographs were first published in German and then English and for a long time were little known in Brazil. His only influence on Brazilian anthropology in its formative years was to have produced "models" for others to follow and to open up problems which attracted others to do research in Brazil. It was Nimuendajú's Gê monographs which attracted William H. Crocker to Brazil to restudy the Northeastern Timbira beginning in 1957 and which lay the basis of the important Gê studies by David Maybury-Lewis and his students and colleagues (cf. Maybury-Lewis, 1979).

3. This same community was restudied over a generation later by Robert Shirley (1971).

# PART II

# Some Perspectives from the Past

ANTHROPOLOGISTS CONCERNED WITH Brazil have long realized that an understanding of contemporary social and cultural institutions depends, in part, on a knowledge of the past. Thus, even though this section deals with a variety of topics from ethnographic, archaeological, and sociological perspectives, they are united by their common interest in history and processes of sociocultural change.

The section also touches upon the recurring question of the "have-nots" of Brazilian society. These are either populations—both past and present—that have not been fully integrated into the national scene, or segments that have been integrated into Brazilian society, but on unfavorable terms. In different regions of the country, and to varying degrees, Indians, people of color, and the rural and urban poor have consistently been forced into an exploited underclass position with extremely limited access to the strategic resources, goods, and services enjoyed by the more fortunate socio-economic groups in this highly stratified society.

The indigenous people of Brazil were the first victims of such exploitation. From the onset of Portuguese colonization, they were varyingly subjected to enslavement, forced missionization and relocation, debt peonage, and land confiscation. Estimates vary as to how many Indians have withstood this onslaught. Today, they almost certainly number less than 100,000, a remnant of a far larger population that inhabited Brazilian territory at the time of Portuguese contact. Yet, despite their diminished numbers, Amerindians still form an important part of what has been called Brazil's "cultural mosaic"; they

**19**

have contributed many elements to contemporary Luso-Brazilian culture (see Wagley 1971: ch. 1).

Galvão briefly outlines the history of the native populations of the Amazon Basin from the time the Portuguese arrived there in the sixteenth century to the mid-twentieth century. By way of illustration, he uses data from the Rio Negro sub-region to detail the processes of assimilation and acculturation experienced by native inhabitants of the Basin as a whole. He clearly demonstrates that the "conquest" of the Amazon is an on-going process; some isolated groups have remained autonomous until well into this century. But the fate of the vast majority of Amazonian Indians has been otherwise. Those along the main courses of the major rivers either rapidly succumbed to European diseases and enslavement shortly after Portuguese contact, or lost their distinctive cultural traditions, and became the core of the contemporary *caboclo* population.*

Perhaps the most significant process noted by Galvão is the inter-tribal acculturation that has taken place among a number of formerly distinct Indian populations. As Brazilians have moved further into the recesses of the Amazon in search of rubber and other extractive products, the region's native inhabitants have been forced into an ever-decreasing area of land. The resulting geographical proximity of a number of once distinct Indian cultures has led to inter-tribal acculturation. Since these inter-tribal amalgams now share a common language (*lingua geral*)† as well as many culture traits, Galvão suggests that they now constitute a new and distinct Amazonian culture area.

The now extinct Taruma of the Guyana-Brazil border, discussed in the article by Meggers and Evans, are but one of many indigenous groups whose cultural heritage can be retrieved only archaeologically. Although Taruma culture ceased to exist long ago, the destruction of Brazil's Indian population is an on-going process. Ribeiro estimates that of the 230 linguistically and culturally distinct Amerindian groups enumerated in various sources in 1900, 87 or about 38 percent had become extinct a mere fifty years later (1967:91). The recent construction of a road network throughout the Amazon Basin and the opening up of previously inaccessible lands for commercial exploitation also has had a devastating effect on the

---

* In the Amazon region the term *caboclo* refers to anyone of Indian-white ancestry, and, by extension, to the rural culture and people of the Amazon.

† *Lingua geral* is an inter-tribal language based on Tupi-Guarani.

indigenous populations of the region, an effect that has been termed "ethnocide" by some observers (Brazilian Studies 1975).

Since so many indigenous groups have become extinct and their cultural heritages at least temporarily lost to history, Meggers and Evans use of archaeological, ethnographic, and historical materials to reconstruct the settlement patterns and social organization of one such group—the Taruma—has wide application. They suggest the benefits that can be obtained in reconstructing cultural histories when anthropologists reach beyond their own specialties and make use of data and methods from other disciplines. This is a particularly valuable approach for archaeologists working in tropical environments, such as the Amazon Basin, where climate and terrain make excavations and data retrieval difficult at best.

Two decades ago it appeared that the fate of the Tapirapé Indians of central Brazil would be that of the Taruma—extinction. But, as Shapiro shows us, the Tapirapé have managed to survive and maintain some semblance of their cultural tradition despite a long period of contact. A series of felicitous and, probably, unique circumstances have allowed the Tapirapé to turn around their sharp population decline and stem the erosion of their traditional domestic and cermonial organization. In part, the Tapirapé's receptiveness to external cultural practices, along with a desire to maintain their distinctiveness, have enabled them to remain economically self-sufficient, while neighboring Indian populations have been caught up by the whims of the local and national economy. Then, too, the Tapirapé's generally benign and often beneficial contacts with missionaries, anthropologists, and local Brazilians have buffered them from the usual harshness of the contact situation, and have given them the information and skills needed to adapt to changing conditions. But unfortunately, as Shapiro makes clear, the Tapirapé experience is all too rare among Brazil's Indian population.

Other segments of what comprises the contemporary Brazilian population have fared better historically in their encounters with national society. During the nineteenth and early twentieth centuries, a massive wave of immigrants from Italy, Portugal, Spain, Germany, Japan, and elsewhere in the Old World came to Brazil, most settling in the southern portion of the country. Thousands worked as *colonos* * on the coffee estates of São Paulo, while others remained in the

* A *colono* is a worker paid on a monthly basis to care for a set number of coffee trees.

cities of the littoral. A fair number settled with their compatriots in agricultural colonies in remote regions where they lived rather insular lives. Retaining their language and many of their customs, they farmed the land using a number of crops and methods brought over from the "old country." These colonies were self-contained, subsistence level communities which, for decades, had little contact with the larger Brazilian society.

Thales de Azevedo provides an account of the history of one such immigrant group—the Italians—beginning with their passage from Europe, through their arrival in Brazil, and their establishment of farming communities in the southern state of Rio Grande do Sul. Here we see a rather isolated people adapting to their new environment, while retaining many of the material items and customs of their homeland. It was perhaps, in part, the very isolation of such colonies that allowed them to continue and, in some cases, prosper without becoming enmeshed in the lower rungs of Brazil's hierarchical social structure.

Other segments of Brazilian society, owing to their poor terms of integration and position at the bottom of the nation's class structure, have not fared as well. There is abundant evidence that a large majority of Brazilians have not benefited from the widely heralded "economic miracle" that has seen Brazil's gross national product skyrocket over the past fifteen years. This "miracle," in fact, has been accompanied by an increasing maldistribution of the nation's income; the share of the wealthiest 3.5 percent of Brazil's earning population increased from one-fourth to one-third of national income between 1960 and 1970, while the share of the poorest 43 percent declined from 11 percent to 8 percent (Fishlow 1972).

The largest "have-not" segment of Brazilian society consists of people of color. While it is true that not all poor people are black, mulatto, or *mestiço*,* it is a fact that a very large percentage of Brazil's non-white population belongs to the nation's underclass. Despite this fact, many Brazilian and North American social scientists have contended that Brazil is a "racial paradise" (Freyre 1963:9), basing their claim on the absence of institutionalized racism of the sort found in the United States. A number of studies have shown that the "racial paradise" view is fiction (see, for example, Degler 1971 and Harris 1974b).

---

* A *mestiço* is a person of Indian-white ancestry.

Florestan Fernades, author of the last contribution to this section, would agree. He argues that "tolerance," combined with a strong system of racial inequality, best describes the Brazilian situation. Nor does he believe that this can be easily changed. Were change to come, it would imply a basic restructuring of Brazilian society. Even in such an affluent and supposedly fluid urban center like São Paulo, racial inequalities continue. Economic development has given a small number of "Negros" the chance to move ahead, but the mass of non-whites in the city have been unaffected.

The system brought to Brazil by the Portuguese was one based on exploitation and rigid social stratification. In the more than four centuries since conquest, affluence has softened some of the rougher edges of the system, but its basic structure remains unchanged. In its encounters with the micro-societies of indigenous groups, it has resulted in suppression, if not actual extinction. In its dealings with blacks, it has forced them first into slavery and subsequently into a relatively powerless labor force. The few who are at the top continue to reap most of the rewards offered by the society. The means by which they maintain their hegemony are various: differential access to strategic resources, patron-client relationships, dominance of the legal system, and outright coercion through military force. All myths notwithstanding, Brazil is not and never was an equalitarian society. To even approach such a state would involve changes far more revolutionary than anything the country has seen to date. Yet changes have occurred and are occurring. The Brazil of the late twentieth century is a nation of divergence, flux, and conflict.

# ONE

# The Encounter of Tribal and National Societies in the Brazilian Amazon

## Eduardo Galvão

DARCY RIBEIRO (1967) POSITS four categories of contact among indigenous Brazilian cultures. These are: isolation, intermittent contact, permanent contact, and full integration. To this could be added total assimilation, distinct from integration in that tribal identity and culture are completely lost. Where this occurs, the Indian is simply transformed into a *caboclo*.[1]

During the Portuguese occupation, which began in the early seventeenth century, the Amazon region was inhabited by several indigenous tribes whose cultures, following Steward's typology (Steward 1949), were of the "Tropical Forest" type, i.e., cultures characterized by subsistence oriented toward manioc cultivation and a more or less sedentary village life. Even though it constituted a social unit based on a shared language, culture patterns, and communal territories, the tribe as a political entity was poorly defined. The villages, inhabited in most cases by a single lineage, were the primary structural units. Some exceptions occurred. Marginal groups living inland

This article is a revised and updated version of a paper, "Encontro de Sociedades Tribal e Nacional," originally published in Portuguese by the government of Amazonas state in 1966. It was translated from the Portuguese by Darrel L. Miller.

25

at the edge of savannas or scattered near rivers had a subsistence based primarily on fishing and hunting.

More complex cultural groups, originating from the slopes of the Eastern Andes and the Circum-Caribbean region, also inhabited the Amazon area in pre-Columbian times. A number of ceramic sites found in the region, which define phases or archaeological traditions, such as those of Marajó, Santarem, Maracá, Itacotoara, Miracanguera, Manaus, and others, have indicated, judging by the elaborate ceramic techniques and the extension of the deposits, the existence of chiefdoms. These ceramic traditions do not seem to have evolved locally. They appear to have developed elsewhere: archaeological evidence suggests their origin in the western and northwestern Amazon area (Meggers and Evans 1958). The time when this occupation occurred is not precisely established because data based on a more accurate chronology, such as that which can be obtained from carbon 14, does not exist. However, analysis of the ceramics from the cultures on the periphery of the Amazon Valley, such as Soladero and Baizo Orinoco, indicates that these cultures probably existed between 950 B.C. and 600 B.C. (cf. Armillas 1957:15). Meggers and Evans place the appearance of the first ceramic cultures of Marajó Island at the mouth of the Amazon River at c.700 B.C. The Marajoara phase, A.D. 120–1450, probably originated in the Napo River region and diffused from there. Both archaeological evidence and historical information indicate that these foci of greater cultural development along the Amazon River died out before the arrival of the first Europeans. One hypothesis holds that the decline of Circum-Caribbean culture patterns was due to the inability of the subsistence base to support a growing population. One of the exceptions would appear to be the Tapajonica culture which survived until the first century of European colonization (Barata 1952).

The Portuguese conquest of the Amazon region started in 1616 with the establishment of the Fort Presépio de Santa Maria de Belém on an estuary of the Amazon River. English, Dutch, and some French preceded the Portuguese in establishing posts up to the Xingu River to trade with the Indians. In 1637, Pedro Teixeira left Belém with "70 Portuguese soldiers and 1,200 Indian oarsmen and riflemen who, with other assistants and women, amounted to more than 2,000 people" (Carvajal 1941:5). They reached Quito, Ecuador a year later. In 1669, Pedro da Costa Favela and Frei Teodoro gathered the Taraumãs Indians together at the mouth of the Rio Negro. The Fort Barra de São José (today Manaus) was erected shortly thereafter. In 1725, Portuguese troops reached Marabitanas, at the upper Rio Negro, and the Cassiquari waterway, which connects the Rio Negro and the Orinoco, was discovered. In 1752 and 1763, forts were built on the upper Rio Branco and Rio Negro, and a new route to the south through the Madeira River was opened.

Colonial villages, which eventually became the urban centers of the Amazon region, were established alongside Indian settlements. Portuguese names, such as Santarem, Ega, Barcelos, and São Gabriel, replaced indigenous ones. A policy of miscegenation was implemented; it granted land, money, and firearms to Portuguese soldiers and colonists who married Indian women (Reis 1940). At the same time, political status was granted to "domesticated" Indians. With the creation of *edilidades* (roughly, town councils), they gained even the right to manage village and settlement affairs (Reis 1940, 1943).

In spite of these steps, the absorption of the Indian population was hardly peaceful. Although protectionist ordinances existed, Indians were obliged to perform compulsory service on ships, in the so-called "fabricas" (workshops), and in public service in the growing urban centers.

Large contingents of Indians were brought down from the river's watersheds for public work in the cities of Belém and Manaus and for the construction of fortresses, such as that at Macapa (Reis 1943:12). The Indian was subjugated by violent means: through "just wars" (*guerras justas*)[2] and through slave raids (*tropas de resgate*).[3] At the Indian missions, regulations were equally severe; the system of the "stick rather than the word" (*pau que a retórica*) was preferred. At the same time, the native populations were decimated by exposure to viral diseases such as small pox.[4]

The Indian reaction was not peaceful. Rebellions sprang up in several parts of the Amazon region. In the Rio Negro region, the Indian rebellions were not only retaliatory, but assumed the characteristics of a messianic movement (Terreiro Aranha 1907:2:86). Often the rebellions were aborted by punitive armed expeditions largely manned by Indians from other tribes. The Mundurucú, for example, became famous for having joined force with the Portuguese in the conquest of the territory lying between the Madeira and Tocantins Rivers.

The result of this type of contact was the disintegration of tribal organization among the more vulnerable groups, especially those inhabiting the banks of the Amazon and the lower part of its affluents. Individuals from different tribes were herded together in villages in missionary settlements, and in the new, sparsely populated colonial centers. Once there, Iberian culture was imposed upon them. A common dialect (*lingua geral*), based on Tupi-Guarani, which was spoken by the coastal tribes and which had been codified by missionaries and colonists, replaced the numerous indigenous languages. Even during the second half of the nineteenth century, travelers and naturalists such as Bates (1864) and Wallace (1899) noted the persistence of lingua geral as a means of communication among the local population of the Amazon region.

One of the major changes imposed was the alteration of the indigenous Amazonian groups, which began in the sixteenth century, and is not yet complete. As a result of the sparse settlement of the Amazon basin, some isolated tribal groups still exist as autonomous entities, speaking their own languages and practicing their traditional cultures. Omitting the more isolated groups, however, an appreciable part of the contemporary tribal population is more an extension of the national frontier than it is a distinctive unit within it (Galvão 1959:55). Many of these groups are engaged in regional production and have lost their self-sufficiency; they now depend on trade and the enticements of extractive industry. Accommodation with the dominant society prevails.

The history of contact between tribal and Luso-Brazilian societies can, therefore, be outlined as follows (Galvão 1955b:179ss): the first period, between 1600 and 1759, took place at the time of the Portuguese expansion and was earmarked by the establishment of trading posts and settlements, by exploratory expeditions, by slave raids, by so-called "just wars," and by the removal and resettlement of up-river Indians in colonial centers. In other words, the process of Indian detribalization and acculturation began at the time of European settlement.

The second period, which lasted from 1759 to 1840, began with two events: the explusion of the Jesuits, an affirmation of commercial secular power, and the onset of a nativistic revolutionary movement, the Cabanda, in which indigenous groups participated with the mestizo population. This period is marked by the integration of the Amazonian population into the national society which then was beginning to take shape as a political unit, independent from metropolitan Portugal. Systems of production, however, remained the same as those of the previous period; emphasis was still on the gathering of natural products along with simple agriculture.

Between 1840 and 1920 the course of the regional economy based on the extraction of native products, such as rubber, became firmly established. This period was marked by an influx into the Amazon region of outside influences other than those of the natives and the Portuguese. Above all, the area attracted Northeastern immigrants, themselves mestizos descended from Portuguese and indigenous populations. The impact of this migration was not felt markedly because the Northeasterners settled in scattered areas and lived in isolation as demanded by an economy based on extractive techniques. It was in this period, however, that the question of assimilation or avoidance of it by the indigenous elements of the population reached a critical point. Those who refused to assimilate or adjust to these new contacts retreated to isolated areas, thus appreciably reducing their absorption by regional society. Others moved into *freguesias* (parish towns), settlements, and urban centers, and became as settled as the local economy allowed.

The region of the Rio Negro illustrates these different processes. It was opened up in the middle of the seventeenth century with the founding of Vila de Barra, today the city of Manaus. The exploration of its headwaters up to Marabitanas in 1725, and the installation of fortresses in Uaupés (today San Gabriel) and on the Rio Branco in 1752 and 1763, guaranteed definite political boundaries and territorial possession to the Portuguese.

The Rio Negro region was inhabited by a large number of tribal groups such as the Tarumãs, Passés, Barés, and Manaos who spoke languages belonging to the Arawak family. Their resistance to the Portuguese invaders was broken by punitive expeditions such as the one led by Belchior Mendes de Morais in 1729, which was said to have been responsible for either the killing or capture of 20,000 Manaos Indians. Another expedition, led by Pedro da Costa Favela, resulted in the destruction of 300 Indian huts on the banks of the

Urubu River, while another, led by Miguel Siqueira, in reprisal for an attack by the Manaos Indians at Mariuá (today Barcelos), turned "the majority of (the Indians) into fodder for their rifles" (Baena 1838:250).

During the first century of colonization the region's indigenous population provided labor for the construction of the villages and towns which were then being established. Indians also participated in expeditions in search of *drogas de sertão* ("drugs of the hinterland"), as wild forest products were called, and in the agricultural experiments introduced into the area in the beginning of the eighteenth century.

The revolutionary movement of the Cabanda, which began in 1834, spread throughout the Rio Negro region and reached the Icana River. Messianic uprisings proclaiming the arrival of a native Christ subsequently took place (Terreiro Aranha 1907: 2:86); Koch-Grunberg 1909). These movements began in the early nineteenth century and still exist today (Galvão 1959:4).

The indigenous peoples on the main course of the Rio Negro were either decimated or assimilated. Today, the remnants of some tribal groups inhabit the Icana and Uaupés Rivers, affluents of the Rio Negro. Other isolated groups, such as the Waiká, who live between the Demeni and Cauaboris Rivers, or those on the Uricoera River at the foothills of the Parima Mountains have had effective contact with non-indigenous peoples for only the last thirty years.

The process of inter-tribal acculturation, which existed prior to the arrival of the Portuguese, was accelerated by territorial restrictions and the prohibition of tribal warfare imposed by missionaries and colonists. Previously distinct tribes, such as the Baniwa, Tukano, and Makus, have become more homogeneous due to cultural exchange, and now can be identified as belonging to a similar cultural sub-area.

From colonial times to the present, the indigenous populations, even those living in isolated villages, have maintained periodic and permanent contacts, and have participated actively in the local economy either in trading agricultural products, such as manioc flour, or in gathering rubber, Brazil nuts, and piassava palm.

Lingua geral has been replacing the prevailing languages of the area, especially Arawak, since the eighteenth century. Lingua geral, based on Tupi-Gurani, was spoken by the colonists in preference to

Portuguese, although it was completely foreign to the original inhabitants of the area.

As in other parts of the Luso-Brazilian Amazon, the economy of the Rio Negro region during colonial times was based on the collection of wild forest products, although there was an agricultural experiment of some importance. This experiment was not begun by the private initiative of the colonists, but by the government: "The officials of settlements and municipal governments should implement intensive farming" (Reis 1943:27). "Each village, therefore, received a number of head of cattle which it was supposed to care for, insuring the increase of the herd . . ." (Reis 1943:28). However, this plan encountered difficulties arising from the fact that many of these administrative units "were staffed by Indians recently elevated to prominent positions in the developing society of the region" (Reis 1943:28). In order to solve this problem an administrative Department of Commerce, Agriculture, and Manufacturing was created.

In addition to the crops already cultivated by the Indian, such as manioc flour which was a staple in the diet of both the native and the colonist, other crops such as corn, beans, coffee, cocoa, sugar cane, indigo, and cotton were added. Reis (1943:33) stresses the importance of the crops which were introduced by citing the fact that by 1785 there were about 220,000 coffee trees in the captaincy (a political unit), and a total of 200,000 cocoa trees in the Rio Negro region alone.

This agricultural experiment reached its peak during the administration of Lobo d'Almada who became governor of the captaincy in 1779. D'Almada's administration reinforced and stimulated the agricultural program and it also focused on increasing the size of the labor force by recruiting recalcitrant Indians into the armed forces. One way this was achieved was to increase the number of Indians brought downriver, a practice which violated the protective Indian legislation enacted by the Portuguese crown.

Local produce was channeled to Belém and Portugal, but it also was used to supply large numbers of Portuguese and Spanish expeditions which were then actively engaged in the struggle to demarcate territorial boundaries.

Barcelos, the old village of Mariuá, the stronghold of the Manaos Indians and site of conflicts between Indians and the armed forces, became the administrative seat of the captaincy and a center for the manufacturing and processing of agricultural products. Its population in 1800 was estimated to have been 3,000.

An administrative crisis took place, however, which the successors of Lobo d'Almada were unable to resolve. The economic center of the captaincy temporarily shifted from the Rio Negro to the Solimões River, causing a decrease in farming and manufacturing. The naturalists Spix and Martius (1824) have given an excellent description and analysis of this period of decline. The captaincy lost its administrative autonomy and came under the jurisdiction of the *comarca* (judicial district) of Pará. Excessive taxation on natural and agricultural products, imposed to save a declining colonial structure, served only to discourage production at the same time that it created restlessness among the mestizos and Indians of the region which culminated in the Cabanda nativistic movement.

The agricultural experiment's failure induced the population to return to the collection of wild forest products. This time an important new product was added: latex rubber, an item used by the Cambevas Indians of the Solimões River. At first, latex was employed as a waterproofing material, but later it became an important industrial product. Between 1870 and 1910, practically the entire economic apparatus of the Amazon Valley was devoted to rubber production. Even after the decline in prices due to competition from plantations in the Far East, rubber persisted as one of the few products for which credit could be obtained.

Rubber attracted to Amazonia large contingents of immigrants from other parts of Brazil and from abroad. Their arrival broke up the relative isolation of the region's population and also affected its regional economy. Most newcomers in the Rio Negro region came from the state of Maranhão. They settled there, becoming a managerial class of overseers administering the rubber fields. As in the past in the Rio Negro region, the gatherers of forest products, now latex, were the Indians. The process of recruiting Indians followed more or less the same pattern adopted in colonial times; the Indians were brought from up river and subjected to compulsory labor through various forms of pressure. Because the low and middle Rio Negro was sparsely populated, labor demands required intensified efforts to lure tribal Indians, such as the Icana and the Uaupés, hidden away on tributaries of the Rio Negro. The domination of these Indians by "civilizados" was hardly a novelty; from the eighteenth century on, the Directorias de Índios e Missões (Indian and Mission Administrations) had regularly served as labor contractors. The means of communication, lingua geral, which had persisted among the mestizo population, was adopted by the immigrants from Maranhão and the new arrivals from Portugal.

The lack of women among the new immigrants helped maintain the old pattern of miscegenation. Liaisons between immigrant men and Indian and mestizo women created a kinship network which facilitated an ongoing paternalistic relationship with the dominant class.

As in other extractive industries, the weakness and inconsistency of the rubber fields' credit and *aviamento* systems (in which goods were furnished in exchange for raw products), impeded the concentration of capital with its potential for generating new enterprises. The sparse urban centers, remnants of the old edilidades, survived only as outposts for the administrative bureaucracy and fiscal agencies. All discretionary income was spent on imported goods. There were no specialists or local industries and, aside from state employees and the small group of traders who remained stable because of their commercial activities, the rest of the population fluctuated in size according to the seasonal extractive activity in which it was engaged.

In short, several historical, cultural, and ecological factors were responsible for acculturation in the Rio Negro region. Detribalization began with initial Portuguese contacts and was facilitated by prior intertribal acculturation. A common language, lingua geral, begun by European missionaries, also aided in the acculturation process both among tribes and between tribal and national cultures. Miscegenation helped to develop kinship ties between tribal groups and immigrant men. The integrative stage was reached through the adoption of trade goods and the absorption of the tribe into the local economy. The boom-bust economic cycles in the Amazon allowed a resurgence of native techniques of adaptation during "bust" periods. This often kept tribal units from total disintegration.

Today, mechanisms of change are beginning to accelerate. New means of communication—the motor boat, airplane, radio, and printed word—have broken the isolation of the region. Government involvement has been strengthened by the establishment of institutions such as the Banco de Crédito da Amazonia (Amazonian Credit Bank) which finances and controls rubber operations and, with less impact, the new health and education programs. In spite of the presence of Servico de Proteção aos Índios (Indian Protection Service), the religious missions retain control over the great majority of the tribal Indian population. Indian villages near commercial exploration routes have become outposts of support for the advancing frontier. A common tendency is for tribal nuclei to fragment into centers with mixed populations, or to diminish in population, becoming *sítios* (small farms) inhabited by a family group.

Today the main tribal centers are located on the Icana and Uaupés Rivers and consist of the Baniwa and Tukano Indians. The Baniwa are divided into two dialectical groups as well as a number of patrilineal sibs (such as the Siuci, Ipeca, Katapolitani, Marakyá, and others) which are described in the literature as separate tribal groups (Koch Grunberg 1909, Goldman 1948, Nimuendajú 1950, Galvão 1959). The Tukano, scattered along the Uaupés River and its tributaries, also are subdivided into several groups such as the Kobewa, the Uanana, and the Sesana. A number of groups referred to by the generic name of "Makus" live along the Inuixí River, a tributary on the south bank of the Rio Negro up to the Uaupés River. They have been influenced by the Tukano, but generally are considered resistent to contact. The Waiká-Xiriana, now living on the north bank between the Demini and Cauaboris Rivers are, according to local information, recent arrivals there who probably came from the north. They remain isolated and have only sporadic contact with missionaries and agents of the Indian Protection Service.

It is important to note that, due to the geographical proximity of all of these groups as well as to the restrictions imposed on their territories by colonial expansion, they have undergone an intense process of inter-tribal acculturation. This acculturation has proceeded to such a degree that these groups now constitute a clearly defined culture area with its own cultural traits. These traits are the same as those already described for the North Amazon culture area (Galvão 1960).

The social structure of the Baniwas and the Tukanos, but not the Makus, was based on a division into localized sibs. The relationship between these two principal groups and the Makus helped create new sibs of mixed origin. Thus, the Wira-miri, mixed descendents of the Warikena, became integrated with the Baniwas as the sib, as did the Kadaupuritana and the Hohodene who, according to Nimuendajú (1950:164–65), were descendants of earlier Makus bands. In the same way, Baniwas groups such as the Querari sibs were "Tukanoi-zed" and today speak a Kobewa language (Nimuendajú 1950:65). A process of tribal reversal occurred among the Djibeia. They pre-viously lived on the Querari River and assimilated the Kobewa lan-guage, but they later migrated to the Aiari River, and reintegrated themselves, socially and linguistically, to the Baniwa Karu of that region. The Tariana, an Arawak-speaking tribe, who migrated to the Uaupés River, "are becoming more and more like the Tukano to the point of having abandoned their own language and adopting Tukano" (Nimuendajú 1950:165).

In spite of the relative isolation of these groups, one of the cumulative effects of the acculturation pressures caused by the ad-vancing colonial frontier were the changes which occurred in the sibs' traditional locations. Some groups, such as the Siuci, Bakuriu, Koati, and the Ipeca who, according to tribal tradition and historical information, inhabited the high waters of the Aiari, today are living along the lower part of the Icana River.

It is my view that the prior experience of these groups with in-tertribal acculturation and cultural exchange facilitated their accul-turation to Luso-Brazilian society. One of the factors which greatly contributed to this process was the diffusion of a common language: lingua geral was the language of communication between not only In-dians and Luso-Brazilians; it was the predominant inter-tribal dialect as well.

As the primary source of labor, indigenous populations had to move near the centers of production. The sibs were forced to abandon their traditional locations, with the result that, in some cases, the traditional rules forbidding their co-habitation in the same village were broken. This has happened in Sant'Ana, the old village of the Marakayá, which today is inhabited by individuals belonging to the Jurapari sib.

Not only are individuals from various sibs now living in the same location; there is also an assembling of people from different tribes in the same locality. In Campinas, near Tapuruquara, a few members of the Baniwa, Tariana, and Tukano sibs live together. They speak lingua geral and, through a process of accommodation, the rule of sib exogamy has been extended to the entire tribal unit. Conscious of their tribal and sib affiliations, individuals will marry only members of other tribes. This process is not a recent innovation;

Wallace (1899) reported its existence in the middle of the nineteenth century. There has been a tendency, however, for it to increase due to the progressive dislocation and growing proximity of local groups which, in turn, is related to the demands placed upon them by the new labor markets.[5]

These changes in the life of tribal society have not come about at an even pace; their rhythm results from the transformations occurring in national Brazilian society. The process of inter-tribal acculturation, which started before the Portuguese conquest, underwent a progressive, but irregular acceleration which depended upon the goals of colonial occupation and the expansion of frontier settlement into Indian territory. At the same time, culture change also was stimulated by the regulation of inter-tribal contacts imposed by the Directoria de Índios, the religious missions and, more recently, the Indian Protection Service. These restrictions outlawed wars and hostilities between neighboring groups.

The acculturation process between tribal and national societies was facilitated by the following factors: the cultural simplicity of the seventeenth-century colonists, their dependence upon indigenous labor, and the Indian's possession of a complex system of adaptation to the new ecological conditions confronting the colonists. The Indians were particularly attracted by the introduction of more efficient tools which aided them in the adaptational process. In this region, secular and religious domination backed by the force of arms was motivated by the desire to integrate the Indian into colonial society.

Early on, however, the acculturative process lost its bilateral character; it changed into another form imposed by the Luso-Brazilian on the Indian. The social cleavage between the two was increasingly stressed, and by destroying tribal self-determination, the dominant position of the colonist was clearly established.

During its process of transformation, the interference of national society with indigenous culture was not uniform. As mentioned previously, the activities of the colonists during some periods resulted in rapid tribal disintegration. The "drugs of the sertão" cycle, agricultural experiments, and intense labor recruitment periods all had enormous impacts on tribal organization and culture. However, there were other periods, usually of briefer duration, such as that following the failure of the agricultural experiments and the one following the decline of the rubber industry, when the frontier receded and the colonial impact on the Indian abated. The preservation of remnant tribal populations and, in more isolated areas, the consolidation of Indian populations was permitted by these periods of colonial withdrawal.

In general, however, changes in the tribal patterns of both the remnant and consolidated Indian populations have been in the direction of accommodation with the values and traits of the dominant society. For example, the basic institution of local chieftainship has come to depend less on lineage and personal status than on the "civilizados" imposition of chiefly status on an individual. In order for a chief's position to be recognized even within his own sib, he has to have a *carta patente,* a written document issued by someone in authority. In addition, chiefly functions have been substantially reduced by the growing independence and importance of the household unit which individually contracts for labor assignments. In such cases, the chief becomes just a middleman in the relationship between the local Indian group and outsiders.

In Barcelos, on the lower Rio Negro near Manaus, a national population with a substratum of caboclo culture, containing a number of indigenous traits, is now in contact with Indian groups who were, until recently, isolated and hostile. The possibilities of assimilation seem to be minimal because of the "cultural distance" between the two societies. As a result of new conditions, the processes which operated in the past do not seem to be functioning in the present.

The situation is somewhat different in Tapuruquara (old Santa Isabel) on the middle Rio Negro. There, a mixed population descended from Indians and whites live near the settlements of "up river" Indians who were settled in the region one or two generations ago. Alongside of them is the village of Campinas with a mixed Indian population from various tribes as well as "wild Indians" (called by the generic term "Makus") who moved into the area only within the last ten years. As in Barcelos, these recent arrivals are resisting assimilation, but are adopting material traits such as tools which will not seriously affect their social structure.

Uaupés, on the site of the fortress of São Gabriel da Cachoeira, and one of the oldest towns in the Rio Negro region, is almost exclusively a commercial and administrative center. It is here that the Indians' "patrões" reside, that is, individuals who contracted Indians from the Icana and Uaupés Rivers and brought them down to the middle Rio Negro for temporary work in the rubber fields. The Indians never became integral parts of town life since they were there only in transit. The whites, on the other hand, rarely go beyond the city limits, but, just as in the vicinity of Tapuruquara, there are a considerable number of small settlements occupied by indigenous families just outside of Uaupés.

In conclusion, through a historical review of acculturation in the Amazon in general, and several communities along the Rio Negro in particular, we have accomplished two goals. First, we have illustrated various stages of acculturation, from the taking on of a few traits to assimilation. Second, we have isolated the cultural, historical, and ecological factors which have characterized and facilitated this process.

The various stages of acculturation are represented by several of the communities we have discussed. Acculturation does not always end in total assimilation. Barcelos, for example, represents a situation which is characterized by semi-permanent contact. Indian families living just outside Uaupés represent, by contrast, virtual assimilation by the caboclo community. These differences in the acculturation process can be traced to the historical, cultural, and ecological factors which have intervened. They have imparted a distinct character to the acculturation of each group.

## Notes

1. In the Amazon region the term *caboclo* refers to anyone of Indian-white descent, and by extension, to the rural culture and people of the Amazon (editor's note).

2. ". . . In 1729, the Portuguese corporal Belchior Mendes de Morais shot 20,800 Indians as he himself reported to the Captain-General and the Governor of Pará" (Reis 1943:2).

3. The tropa de resgate or "rescue mission" was a euphemism for slave raids. In order to circumvent laws prohibiting the enslavement of Indians, the slave hunters claimed that they were "rescuing" Indians captured by enemy tribes and claimed that all of their Indian captives fell into this category (editor's note).

4. "Small pox epidemics from time to time spread through the region killing a total of 40,000 Indians between 1743 and 1749" (Reis 1943:12). Also see Ribeiro 1956.

5. Despite being accustomed to compulsory labor in the rubber fields and other extractive industries, the Rio Negro Indian still prefers agricultural work. The latter activity, however, does not provide him with the credit necessary to buy salt, clothing, firearms, and other acquired needs.

# TWO

# An Experimental Reconstruction of Taruma Village Succession and Some Implications

Betty J. Meggers and Clifford Evans

IN RECENT YEARS, archeologists have increased their efforts to infer the intangible aspects of extinct cultures. This endeavor is a consequence of more sophisticated methods of retrieval and improved techniques of analysis, as well as an incentive for their refinement. The validity of reconstructions based on protohistoric remains can be assessed by ethnographic descriptions or ethnohistoric information obtained before the population became extinct or acculturated. This approach has been employed in several North American areas, but the accelerating disappearance of primitive groups elsewhere makes it urgent that more be done before it is too late. Since this volume will be read mainly by ethnologists, and South America is one of the areas where indigenous cultures have survived, we would like to point out some types of information that might permit archeologists to make more detailed and accurate reconstructions of the community organization and settlement pattern among semi-permanent sedentary groups. We have selected the Taruma Phase of the southern area of Guyana, bordering on Brazil, as the focus for discussion because sufficient archeological and ethnological data are available to show what might be done. Much of the analysis is hypothetical, and we consider it fiction. The purpose is not to establish the validity of the inferences, but to specify some of the advantages of closer collaboration between archeologists and ethnologists concerned with simpler forms of culture.

The problem will be to reconstruct the history of Taruma settlement along the upper Essequibo. We will attempt to infer the number of contemporary villages, to follow the successive locations of villages occupied by the same subgroup, and to estimate the duration of residence. We will base the analysis on the archeological data and then compare the results with ethnographic and historical information to see whether there is any agreement. Finally, we will suggest what types of information are needed to assess the feasibility of achieving valid reconstructions of this type.

## Archeological Evidence

The archeological data was obtained from survey and stratigraphic excavations at twenty-four habitation sites along Essequibo south of the Kuyuwini, a major tributary of the left bank. The absence of accurate maps in 1952–53, when the fieldwork was done, makes it impossible to specify the distance between the northernmost and southernmost sites; instead, a scale phrased in terms of the time required for traveling in a dugout with four or five paddlers was employed. In addition to villages, eleven former field clearings were encountered. Litter obscured surface sherds and the area occupied was defined by testing with a pick. When the depth of refuse exceeded 10 centimeters, one or two stratigraphic tests were excavated at opposite ends of the site. The absence of natural stratigraphy made it necessary to employ arbitrary levels; these were 8 centimeters in thickness. Sites were numbered in order of discovery.

Classification of the pottery provided a basis for construction of a seriated sequence (figure 2.1). Most of the stratigraphic cuts, which are identified by the vertical bars to the left, exhibit similar trends in the two principal undecorated types; Yochó Plain, tempered with coarse grains of decomposed granite, and Kalunye Plain, tempered with fine sand. When the excavated levels and surface collections are interdigitated, Yochó Plain declines from a frequency of 96 percent at the earliest site to about 18 percent at the latest; concurrently, Kalunye Plain increases from about 3 percent to 75 percent. Most of the decorated types are rare and display erratic fluctuations or stable frequencies. Several levels seriating in the middle of the sequence contain large amounts of Mawiká Plain, which is tempered with siliceous particles obtained from burned bark. This reduces the proportions of the major plain types in those samples. Otherwise, the trends are generally smooth, implying absence of significant gaps.

Another reason for believing that few sites were missed is the method by which they were encountered. The absence of surface indications made it necessary to solicit information from older men of the Waiwai tribe, the current occupants of the region. Their identifications of places where "the old people" had lived was based on the ability to recognize secondary forests rather than observation of fragments of pottery in the soil. Other seemingly appropriate high spots that were checked produced no village refuse. When the durations for the periods are considered, however, the unusually brief estimates for Periods 1 and 5 suggest that sites occupied during these times may not be represented in the survey (figure 2.2).

In the original publication (Evans and Meggers 1960:238–41), we attempted to estimate the rate of change in the two major plain pottery types from the historic evidence for the duration of the Taruma occupation of the region. To do this, it was necessary to eliminate contemporary villages. Experimental calculations were made using standard amounts of change in the frequency of the pottery. Beginning at the bottom or early end of the chart and working upward, the lengths of the bars representing Yochó Plain were examined and the locations where the change in frequency reached 5 percent, 10 percent, and 15 percent were recorded. The same criteria were applied to Kalunye Plain. The levels within each of these periods were considered contemporary. The durations of the periods were estimated by applying a sherd-density formula (1,156 sherds per square meter = 100 years) derived from earlier fieldwork (Meggers and Evans 1957:250–57) to each level and then taking the average of the levels included within a period. When the results were compared with the historical information, the 10 percent change was found to agree best. The intervals derived from Yochó Plain and Kalunye Plain showed no significant disagreement; also, the total length of time calculated from the estimates for the two types differed by only 5.2 years.

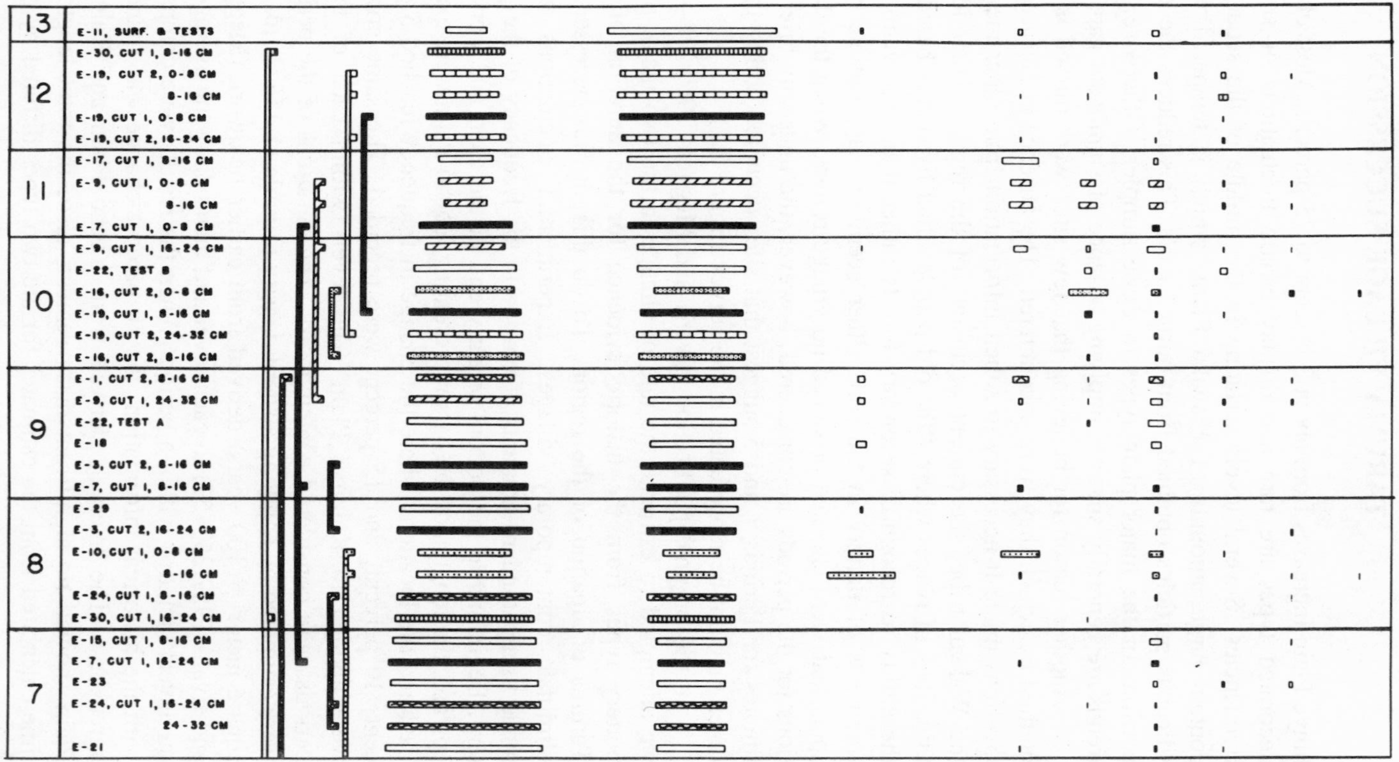
13
E-11, SURF. & TESTS
12
E-30, CUT 1, 8-16 CM
E-19, CUT 2, 0-8 CM
8-16 CM
E-19, CUT 1, 0-8 CM
E-19, CUT 2, 16-24 CM
11
E-17, CUT 1, 8-16 CM
E-9, CUT 1, 0-8 CM
8-16 CM
E-7, CUT 1, 0-8 CM
10
E-9, CUT 1, 16-24 CM
E-22, TEST B
E-16, CUT 2, 0-8 CM
E-19, CUT 1, 8-16 CM
E-19, CUT 2, 24-32 CM
E-16, CUT 2, 8-16 CM
9
E-1, CUT 2, 8-16 CM
E-9, CUT 1, 24-32 CM
E-22, TEST A
E-18
E-3, CUT 2, 8-16 CM
E-7, CUT 1, 8-16 CM
8
E-29
E-3, CUT 2, 16-24 CM
E-10, CUT 1, 0-8 CM
8-16 CM
E-24, CUT 1, 8-16 CM
E-30, CUT 1, 16-24 CM
7
E-15, CUT 1, 8-16 CM
E-7, CUT 1, 16-24 CM
E-23
E-24, CUT 1, 16-24 CM
24-32 CM
E-21

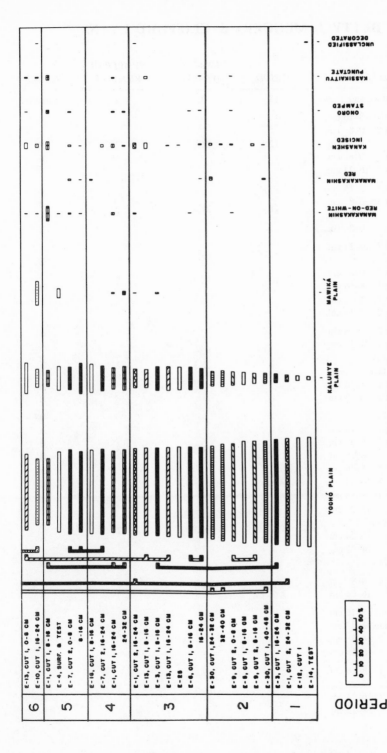

**Figure 2.1.** Seriated sequence derived from trends exhibited by Yochó Plain in stratigraphic excavations at Taruma Phase habitation sites. Vertical bars unite levels belonging to the same excavations; horizontal bars show the relative frequencies of the pottery types on each sample. Periods defined by a 10 percent increase in the relative frequency of Kalunye Plain are identified by number at the left.

43

| SERIATED SEQUENCE | PERIOD | DURATION (YEARS) | NUMBER OF VILLAGES | GROUP |
|---|---|---|---|---|
| E-11, Surface and Tests | 13 | 3.0 | 1 | A and B? |
| E-30, Cut 1:  8–16 cm. | | | | A |
| E-19, Cut 2:  0–8  cm. | | | | B |
| 8–16 cm. | 12 | 21.3 | 2 | B |
| Cut 1:  0–8  cm. | | | | B |
| Cut 2: 16–24 cm. | | | | B |
| E-17, Cut 1:  8–16 cm. | | | | B |
| E-9,  Cut 1:  0–8  cm. | | | | A |
| 8–16 cm. | 11 | 21.4 | 2 | A |
| E-7,  Cut 1:  0–8  cm. | | | | B |
| E-9,  Cut 1: 16–24 cm. | | | | A |
| E-22, Test B | | | | B |
| E-16, Cut 2:  0–8  cm. | | | | A |
| E-19, Cut 1:  8–16 cm. | 10 | 18.4 | 2 | B |
| Cut 2: 24–32 cm. | | | | B |
| E-16, Cut 2:  8–16 cm. | | | | A |
| E-1,  Cut 2:  8–16 cm. | | | | B |
| E-9,  Cut 1: 24–32 cm. | | | | A |
| E-22, Test A | | | | B |
| E-18, Surface | 9 | 21.3 | 2 | A |
| E-3,  Cut 2:  8–16 cm. | | | | A |
| E-7,  Cut 1:  8–16 cm. | | | | B |
| E-29, Surface | | | | B? |
| E-3,  Cut 2: 16–24 cm. | | | | A |
| E-10, Cut 1:  0–8  cm. | | | | B |
| 8–16 cm. | 8 | 21.8 | 3 | B |
| E-24, Cut 1:  8–16 cm. | | | | A |
| E-30, Cut 1: 16–24 cm. | | | | B |
| E-15, Cut 1:  8–16 cm. | | | | A |
| E-7,  Cut 1: 16–24 cm. | | | | B |
| E-23, Surface | | | | A? |
| E-24, Cut 1: 16–24 cm. | 7 | 16.0 | 2 | A |
| 24–32 cm. | | | | A |
| E-21, Surface | | | | B |
| E-13, Cut 1:  0–8  cm. | | | | A |
| E-10, Cut 1: 16–24 cm. | 6 | 16.9 | 2 | B |
| E-1,  Cut 1:  8–16 cm. | | | | B |
| E-4,  Surface and Test | | | | A |
| E-7,  Cut 2:  0–8  cm. | 5 | 11.1 | 2? | B |
| 8–16 cm. | | | | B |
| E-16, Cut 1:  8–16 cm. | | | | A |
| E-7,  Cut 2: 16–24 cm. | | | | B |
| E-1,  Cut 1: 16–24 cm. | 4 | 16.7 | 2 | B |
| 24–32 cm. | | | | B |

| SERIATED SEQUENCE | PERIOD | DURATION (YEARS) | NUMBER OF VILLAGES | GROUP |
|---|---|---|---|---|
| E-1,  Cut 2: 16–24 cm. | | | | B |
| E-13, Cut 1:  8–16 cm. | | | | A |
| E-3,  Cut 1:  8–16 cm. | | | | A |
| E-13, Cut 1: 16–24 cm. | 3 | 17.6 | 2–3 | A |
| E-25, Surface | | | | B |
| E-6,  Cut 1:  8–16 cm. | | | | A |
|            16–24 cm. | | | | A |
| E-30, Cut 1: 24–32 cm. | | | | B |
|            32–40 cm. | | | | B |
| E-9,  Cut 2:  0–8  cm. | 2 | 14.9 | 2–3 | A |
| E-5,  Cut 1:  8–16 cm. | | | | A? |
| E-9,  Cut 2:  8–16 cm. | | | | A |
| E-30, Cut 1: 40–48 cm. | | | | B |
| E-3,  Cut 1: 16–24 cm. | | | | A? |
| E-1,  Cut 2: 24–32 cm. | 1 | 9.2 | 2 | B |
| E-12, Cut 1 | | | | A |
| E-14, Test | | | | B |

**Figure 2.2.** Period divisions, period durations, number of contemporary villages, and group affiliation estimated from the seriated sequence for the Taruma Phase (see Figure 2.1).

## Reconstruction of Settlement History

To reconstruct the pattern of village movements, we have employed the intervals obtained for Kalunye Plain because they are more equal in duration than those derived from Yochó Plain (figure 2.2). Thirteen periods have been distinguished, the longest estimated to have lasted 21.8 years and the shortest 9.2 years (except for the terminal one, which contains a single site). In converting the seriation to a series of maps showing movement from one location to another, several assumptions were made. First, we considered interdigitated levels to indicate contemporaneity and attempted to recognize the number of villages represented. In most periods, there seemed to be two; during Periods 2, 3, and 8, however, there may have been three (figure 2.2). The duration of many villages extends from one period into the next. This reflects the independence of the movements and the arbitrariness of the periods. When successive levels of an excavation are separated by one or more periods, the gap has been interpreted as indicating abandonment of the site. Second, we assumed that if our inference regarding the number of contemporary villages were correct, they represented two lineages and, furthermore, since most Guiana tribes were matrilineal and matrilocal, they corresponded to this kind of kinship group. Third, we assumed that a site "belonged" to the first group that inhabited it; if reoccupied, it was consequently assigned to the same group.

The maps show the pattern of movement resulting from applying these assumptions to the seriated ceramic sequence. The earliest sites, E-12 and E-14, were founded at the southern margin of the area surveyed (figure 2.3). They were not far apart and neither was occupied very long, judging from the sparsity of the sherd refuse. For purposes of identification, the occupants of E-12 were designated Group A and those at E-14, Group B. E-14, being oldest, was probably abandoned first. If the inhabitants moved to E-1, the next site in the seriation, the same logic would assign E-3 to Group A.

Neither E-1 nor E-3 is represented by the levels associated with Period 2. E-1 was abandoned first and the next site in the sequence is E-30, far downriver (figure 2.4). Assuming that Group B made this move, E-9 can be assigned to Group A. The short-term village at E-5 is not clearly affiliated with either group. The occupation at E-9 appears uninterrupted and E-5 is far south of E-30, which remained inhabited until the end of Period 2. Perhaps E-5 represents a temporary schism in Group A, a phenomenon often observed among Tropical Forest households. Period 3 begins with the founding of a village at E-6 and, since E-9 was abandoned first, it can be postulated that the inhabitants were Group A. This makes E-25 available to Group B. The next series of moves is more difficult to decipher. The frequencies of the pottery types in the samples from E-25 and E-6, Cut 1, 8–16 cm. imply that abandonment of these two villages was simultaneous or nearly so. The ratios in the succeeding levels, representing sites E-1, E-3, and E-13, are also almost identical. If we follow the hypothesis of "ownership," E-1 belongs to Group B, which lived there during Period 1. Similarly, E-3 belongs to Group A. This leaves E-13. Since it brackets the single level at E-3 and since a schism in Group A was hypothesized during Period 2, the same explanation may apply.

This type of logic underlies reconstruction of the movements during Periods 4 through 13, delineated on figures 2.5 through 2.10. The terminal site, E-11, is in the southern part of the area, near the initial settlements. The patterning shows a mixture of long and short distance movements by both groups, with a slight tendency for Group B to make longer moves. Eight sites were reoccupied once or twice; of these, E-3, E-9, and E-13 are associated with Group A and E-1, E-7, E-10, and E-19 with Group B. E-30, which has 3 occupations, is the only one that creates a problem when the rule assigning a site to the original founders is followed. Period 12 contains two settlements, E-19 and E-30, both previously affiliated with Group B. If Group B moved from E-30 to E-19, what happened to Group A? Did it leave the area? Did it occupy a site not recorded in the survey? Did it occupy E-19? Or did Groups A and B amalgamate during Period 12 because population decline made the maintenance of two villages impractical? Available evidence does not permit a choice between these possibilities.

A number of locations identified by Waiwai informants as former clearings produced little or no pottery and probably represent gardens. Although these might be expected to be associated with villages of longer duration or possessing multiple occupations, this does not appear to be the case. The number of sherds was seldom sufficient to permit seriation of fields so that their chronological positions are unknown. They are shown on the maps when they are in the vicinity of the villages occupied during the period represented. Several are not close to any village, which may mean either that the Taruma were more willing than the Waiwai to travel to distant locations or that the associated village is missing from the survey.

The historical information permits evaluation of some of these inferences, but before considering it let us see whether there is archeological evidence to support the hypothesis that the sequence represents two autonomous matrilocal residence groups.

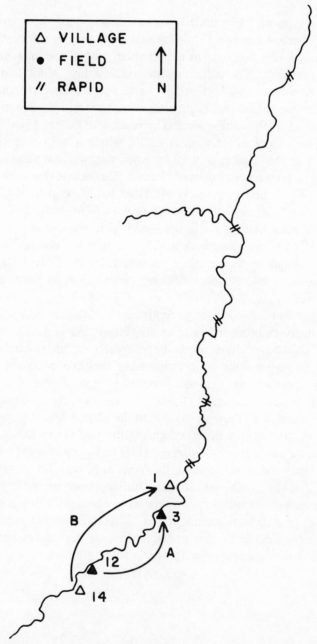

**Figure 2.3.** Villages occupied and abandoned during Period 1. Postulated changes in residence locations are indicated by arrows; site succession follows the seriated sequence.

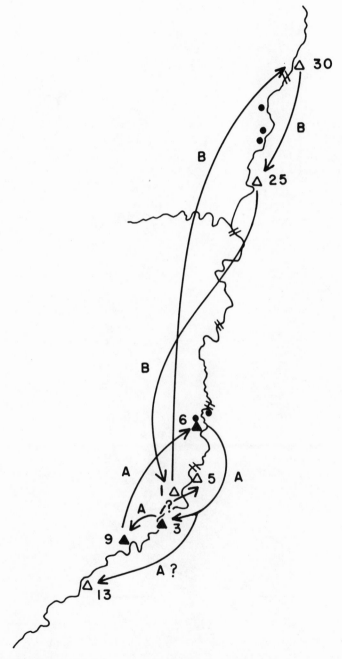

**Figure 2.4.** Villages occupied and abandoned during Periods 2 and 3.

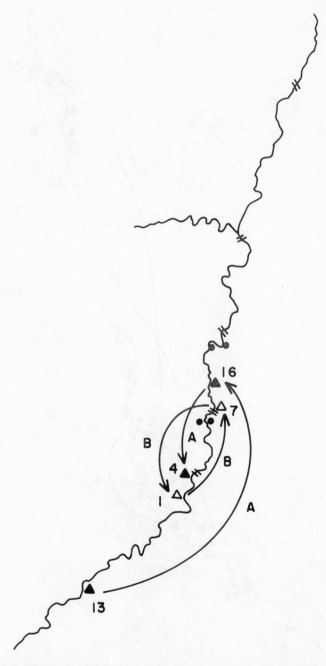

**Figure 2.5.** Villages occupied and abandoned during Periods 4 and 5.

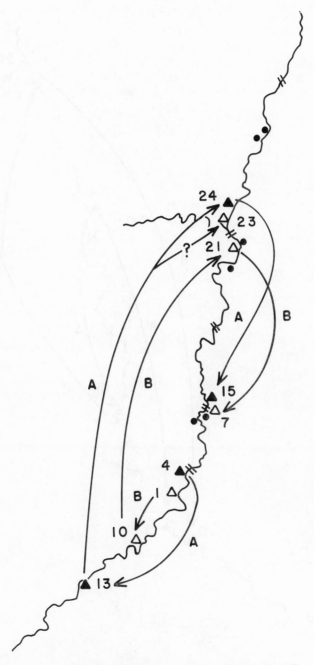

**Figure 2.6.** Villages occupied and abandoned during Periods 6 and 7.

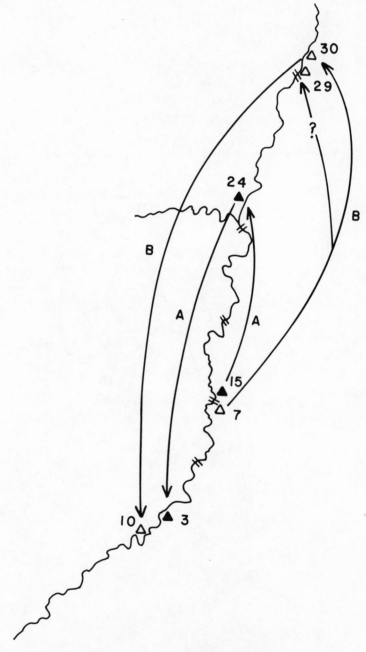

**Figure 2.7.** Villages occupied and abandoned during Period 8.

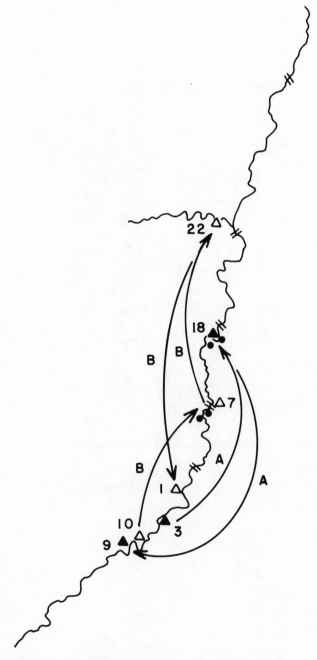

**Figure 2.8.** Villages occupied and abandoned during Period 9.

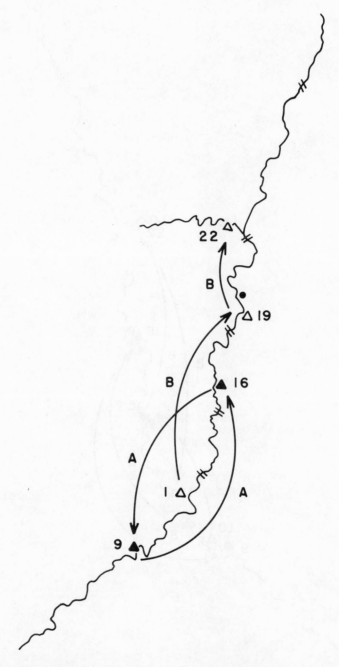

**Figure 2.9.** Villages occupied and abandoned during Period 10.

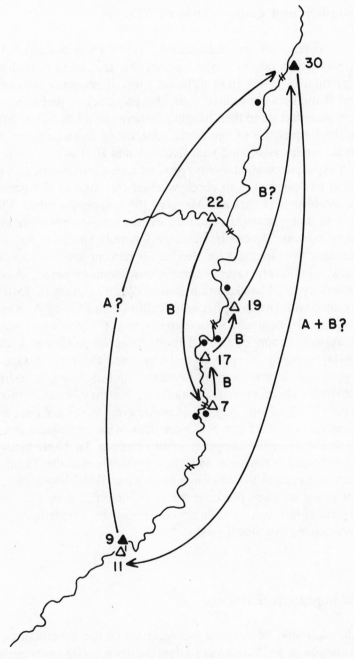

**Figure 2.10.** Villages occupied and abandoned during Periods 11, 12, and 13.

## Number and Composition of Villages

The existence of two contemporary villages was postulated from the similarities in pottery type frequency that frequently caused the inter-digitation of levels from different sites. If residence was matrilocal and if mothers transmitted their idiosyncracies or preferences in pottery manufacture to their daughters, there should be minor differences in the frequencies of rim forms, decorative techniques, or other ceramic modes associated with Group A and B. The tabulations of pottery types, decorative motifs, rim and base forms by site and level offered an opportunity to check whether this kind of distinction could be established (Evans and Meggers 1960, appendix tables 30–35).

In many instances, samples are too small to eliminate the possibility of coincidence. If these are ignored, however, and only differences that approach or exceed 50 percent are considered potentially significant, several correlations seem to occur. Among the pottery types, Manakakashin Red-on-White appears in 15 levels associated with Group B, but only 8 attributed to Group A. Kassikaityu Punctate, by contrast, is correlated almost twice as often with Group A as with Group B. Only 8 levels assigned to Group A contained Onoro Stamped, as opposed to 14 assigned to Group B. One distinctive vessel, a bowl with an interiorly thickened rim, is restricted on Group B. There are only 7 examples, but they occur in two pottery types (Yochó Plain, Form 1, Manakakashin Red-on-White, Form 3). Kanashen Incised Form 3 is more than twice as frequent at Group A sites, but again the sample is small (7 versus 3). These kinds of correlations are compatible with the hypothesis that the Taruma Phase sequence reflects the existence of two matrilocal households, but do not prove it. They illustrate the kinds of differences that should be expected, however, and could be verified by ethnographic observations among matrilocal groups.

*could be particular in intermarrying groups also*

## Ethnographic Evidence

Although little information was recorded on the Taruma prior to their extinction in 1925, there are a few details relevant to the archeological reconstruction. When W. C. Farabee passed through the region in

1914, he encountered two Taruma villages on the right bank of the Essequibo River above a left bank tributary designated as "Duerwau" and below a high hill known as "Kenaimataua" (Farabee 1917). Nearly a century earlier, in 1837–38, Robert Schomburgk had reported three villages on the Essequibo and five on the Kuyuwini (1841:167–69). A map produced between 1771 and 1775 shows the Taruma west of the Essequibo and north of the Tumuc-humac Mountains, which form the boundary between Guyana and Brazil. They were first reported on the Essequibo in 1800 (Farabee 1918:135). Apparently, they had retreated northeastward from an original location near the mouth of the Rio Negro, where a tributary on the left bank continues to bear the name "Taruma." After their departure about 1670, they were believed extinct until they turned up in the central Guiana region.

These dates and numbers of villages can be compared with the inferences based on the seriated sequence. If we consider the river Farabee called "Duerwau" to be the Kassikaityu, the two villages he saw might have been E-17 and E-19. They span the transition from Periods 11 and 12 (figure 2.1). Counting 1925 as the terminal date, the estimated time scale places the occupation of these sites around 1900, slightly earlier than Farabee's visit but remarkably close considering the arbitrary nature of the sherd density formula. A second checkpoint is provided by Schomburgk's report of three villages about 1837. Counting backward from 1925 places this date in Period 8, where three villages seem indicated by the seriation. The entire duration of the phase is estimated at 207 years. Subtracting this from 1925 places the arrival of the Taruma on the upper Essequibo about 1718. Although somewhat earlier than the first report, this date is not necessarily invalid since the people could have been in the area for some time before their presence was recorded.

Other observations made by Farabee are relevant to appraising the accuracy of the durations postulated for the periods and villages. Most of the periods are estimated to have lasted between fifteen and twenty-two years. In terms of the sites and levels included, this implies a residence permanency of a decade or more, somewhat longer than the average for Tropical Forest shifting agriculturalists. Consequently, it is of interest to read Farabee's comment that the Taruma were "the greatest fish eaters of all the tribes" and had "more forest game and pay less attention to growing vegetables"

(Farabee 1918:136). Since soil exhaustion and depletion of game in the vicinity of the village are primarily reasons for abandonment, less dependence on gardens and unusual abundance of wild animals would have permitted longer periods of occupation. The fact that the site did not have to be abandoned on the death of an adult member of the household would also have allowed greater than average sedentariness (p. 142). While these data do not prove the period and site durations are correct, they indicate that some of the factors limiting the permanence of villages among other Tropical Forest groups may have applied less intensively to the Taruma.

## Converting Fiction to Fact

By combining archeological, ethnographic, and historical information, we have produced a hypothetical reconstruction of the settlement history of the Taruma on the upper Essequibo. How much is fact and how much fiction is unknown and it is too late to collect the ethnological evidence needed to make this evaluation for the Taruma. There is still time, however, to secure more complete information from other groups. Ethnologists, it is hoped, will ask the questions and make the observations that might permit transformation of this type of fiction into fact.

The incompleteness and uncertain reliability of much of the Taruma Phase data have made some circular reasoning necessary. For example, a 10 percent change in pottery-type frequency was chosen as the criterion for breaking the seriated sequence into periods because it agreed most closely with the historically reported duration of the phase. The fact that the levels included in Period 8 were inferred to represent three villages and the correlation of the data for Period 8 with Schomburgk's visit may be a coincidence, but is not the result of similar manipulation. Nor was the preference for certain ceramic modes by Group A or Group B anticipated or "built in" to the analysis. Such agreements suggest that this approach might provide useful insights if the hypotheses on which it is based could be substantiated.

Two of the assumptions could easily be checked by ethnographers. One is the "ownership" of a site by the household or lineage that first occupied it. It is generally believed that shifting agriculturalists, in Amazonia at least, are free to settle anywhere within the tribal territory. Is this always true or do some tribes recognize priorities of the kind we have hypothesized? Among the Yukpa, who now live in the Serra de Perijá on the western border of Venezuela, adult males own the cultivable land. Ownership rights are retained even when a plot remains unused for several generations (Ruddle 1974:34). The Tukano of the upper Rio Uaupés also are reported to recognize "exclusive and permanent" rights of a phratry, clan, or lineage to a portion of the tribal territory (Dreyfus 1972:12). This may reflect centuries of European contact, but the possibility that it was an indigenous practice should be checked. Variations in preference for certain ceramic modes by matrilineal households is another aspect subject to verification among living groups. Correlations of this kind proposed by archeologists in North America from clusterings of decorative motifs within sites have been disputed by ethnologists (Allen and Richardson 1971), but these cases involve within-village rather than between-village distinctions. Similar studies are needed among groups such as the Waiwai, where each village is occupied by a single extended family.

Tracing of village succession can be successful only with archeological sequences that are complete or have a minimum of omissions. There are many situations where this goal cannot be achieved. If a river is undergoing channel modification, numerous sites are likely to have been destroyed by erosion or missed because they are far from the present course. Fortunately, the upper Essequibo is a stable river and these variables are not an important source of error. The rolling terrain, which restricted the number of places suitable for habitation, and the qualifications of the informants, whose identifications were checked by testing hilltops where sites had not been reported, suggest that the site inventory for the section surveyed is as complete as possible, given the density of the vegetation. Another potential pitfall is the seriation. The repetition of the plainware trends in numerous stratigraphic excavations suggests they are reliable. The samples are unselected, but do not satisfy the statistical requirements of randomness. How important is this? Another hypothesis that needs evaluation is the rate of ceramic change. There is no reason to presume that the Taruma Phase rate of 1 percent per 3.26 years is a constant. On the contrary, population size, intensity of interaction with other groups, and various other kinds of variables probably cause acceleration or deceleration. Whether archeologists can develop a scale comparable to glottochronology remains to be established. The possibility is worth investigating, however, because of the difficulties in applying other forms of dating to shallow sites in forested regions. Particularly where evidence is reduced to characteristics of the site and the ceramic refuse, as it is in so many parts of tropical America, more reliable methods of extracting a maximum of information from these remains need to be developed if archeology is to advance beyond description and chronology to reconstruction of general patterns of cultural adaptation that prevailed in the past.

*attempt without defining objectives.*

# THREE

# The Tapirapé During the Era of Reconstruction

## Judith Shapiro

THE BRAZILIAN INDIAN has, since Europeans first landed on the eastern coast of South America, occupied a special place in the European world view. More than any other so-called "primitive" or tribal people, the Indians of tropical Brazil have represented to Western civilization its antithesis because the Indians appeared to be living in harmony with nature, sharing the fruits of their labor, and free from the social inequalities of class and structured, centralized systems of political authority. Brazilian national society today, in the quickening pace of its push toward development of the interior, invades those territories where the last autonomous Indian groups had managed to survive and maintain their independence and integrity as a people. As reports by anthropologists, journalists, and other concerned observers chronicle their overnight destruction (or transformation into rural proletarians), international attention has come to focus with a particular urgency on the Indians of Brazil. Few in number compared with the impoverished masses of Brazil's rural backlands and urban slums, the significance of the Indians' plight goes beyond their sufferings as individuals. They stand as an indictment of a system that is not only lacking in social and economic justice for a large proportion of its own members, but inexorable in its appropriation of all that surrounds it, a system that represents the negation of what was for so long the central fact of our species' condition: cultural diversity. In

**61**

terms of Western society's own mythology, which commonly provides a metaphor for accounts of the Brazilian experience, we are witnessing the culmination of man's fall from grace; having been expelled from Eden, he now takes upon himself the project of destroying it entirely.

It is understandable that concern with the fate of the Brazilian Indian currently centers on those groups who are either still relatively isolated (their contacts with non-Indians thus far limited to travelers, anthropologists, Indian agents, or missionaries), or are experiencing their first major shock of confrontation with the expanding Brazilian frontier. It is important, however, not to lose sight of those who, having endured a more prolonged period of contact, are engaged in the struggle to preserve at least some portion of their traditional way of life. The Tapirapé Indians of central Brazil are one such group. Their case is of particular interest because it is unique and at the same time contributes to a more general understanding of the possibilities for cultural survival.

The Tapirapé are one of the best documented Indian groups in Brazil. Their major ethnographers are Charles Wagley and Herbert Baldus. Wagley has been producing publications on the Tapirapé since his first and most extended period of field research in 1939–40. A recent monograph is both an ethnographic summation and a personal memoir (Wagley 1977). Baldus, who first visited the Tapirapé in 1935, continued to concern himself with Tapirapé studies over the succeeding decades, making his most important contributions in the areas of ethnohistory and material culture, and setting the Tapirapé in comparative ethnological perspective; his own monograph appeared in 1970. Other anthropologists who have visited and written about the Tapirapé include Eduardo Galvão, Roberto Cardoso de Oliveira, and myself.[1] Since this research spans a time period of over 40 years, we have material for the kind of longitudinal study that is not often encountered in the anthropological literature on tribal peoples.

The earliest sources on the Tapirapé indicate that they have been living in their present homeland just to the north of the river that bears their name since at least the eighteenth century.[2] They are, however, relative newcomers to an area of central Brazil whose Indian population is otherwise composed of Gê-speaking peoples (the Kayapó to the north and the Sherente and Shavante to the east and south) and Karajá, who inhabit the banks of the Araguaia River. A true tropical forest people who, at some point in their history, moved into a region of savannah and gallery forest, the Tapirapé differ markedly from their Indian neighbors in the degree to which their subsistence revolves around horticulture. Their language is Tupian, of the same family as those spoken by the first encountered and long extinct populations of the Brazilian coast.

The history of the Tapirapé during the twentieth century, particularly since they first began to have sustained contact with outsiders in the 1930s, has been treated in detail in the published work of Wagley and Baldus. I will therefore limit myself to an outline of the facts that form a necessary background to the present discussion, adding in places to the information available elsewhere.

At the turn of the century, the Tapirapé were living in five villages, each with a population of approximately 200.[3] By the 1930s, the *total* Tapirapé population had been reduced to fewer than 200 individuals. A single village, Tampiitawa ("Village of the Tapirs"), constituted the permanent settlement for most of the remaining Tapirapé population. Three villages had become extinct. The other, Chechutawa ("Village of the Fish"), located several days' journey to the north of Tampiitawa and which Baldus believed also to be extinct at the time of his visit to the Tapirapé in 1935, was in 1939 the home of some 40 Tapirapé who left it to move to Tampiitawa during Wagley's stay (Wagley 1977:38). Chechutawa was later re-established and inhabited intermittently by groups of Tapirapé during succeeding years.[4] The Tapirapé population continued to decline during the 1940s. When Baldus returned to Tampiitawa in 1947, there were only 62 Tapirapé living there. He was told that a smaller group were living at Chechutawa and estimated that the total number of Tapirapé could not have been more than 100 (Baldus 1970:75,81).

The year 1947 proved to be a major turning point in Tapirapé history. Described as a "pacific" people as far back as the eighteenth century, the Tapirapé had for some time been suffering at the hands of their more aggressive Kayapó and Karajá neighbors. Shortly after Baldus's departure, Tampiitawa was attacked by the Kayapó, who looted and set fire to the village. Some Tapirapé were killed; others, women and young girls, were abducted. The attack occurred at a time when most of the men were away working in their gardens. As a result of this event, Tampiitawa was abandoned and the Tapirapé became dependent upon outsiders for their continued existence. Those who survived the attack scattered, some taking refuge with a local rancher and others at an Indian Protection Service Post that had been established at the mouth of the Tapirapé River.[5] Their fate from this point on might well have been either gradual extinction or incorporation into the bottom layer of the local Brazilian social order. Instead, after spending two years in this fragmented state, decimated further by disease and hunger, having neither village nor gardens of their own, they were able to re-establish themselves as a community and to rebuild their horticultural economy. Through the efforts of an exceptionally devoted Indian agent, Valentim Gomes, who had served as Wagley's companion during his field research among the Tapirapé and had subsequently joined the Indian Protection Service, the survivors of Tampiitawa were brought together at the Indian post and assisted while they chose a site for their new settlement and began clearing and planting their gardens. This settlement, Tawaiho ("New Village"), has continued to be the home of the Tapirapé up to the present.

In 1952, Tawaiho also became the home of a group of nuns belonging to the Order of the Little Sisters of Jesus, who have maintained a mission there ever since.[6] In 1954, a French priest, Father François Jentel, arrived in the region and spent the next twenty years living and working both with the Tapirapé and with the Brazilian population of the nearby town of Santa Teresinha until his expulsion by the Brazilian government in 1974. The Little Sisters of Jesus and Father Jentel have, as we shall see, influenced Tapirapé life in crucial and complementary ways.

When Tawaiho was founded, there were 54 Tapirapé living there. The population reached a low point of 48 following a measles epidemic in 1955 and has been climbing ever since. There were 55 at the time of Wagley's and Cardoso's visit in 1957, 79 when I arrived in 1966, 81 when I returned the following year, and over 120 by my 1974 visit. According to a Brazilian government report (Wagley 1977:45), there were a total of 136 Tapirapé as of 1976. This figure includes, in addition to the survivors of Tampiitawa and their descendents, remnants of the population that had been living in Chechutawa at the time of the Kayapó attack. The Tapirapé who founded Tawaiho had continued to speak of other Tapirapé whom they believed still to be living to the north and had made some unsuccessful attempts to locate them. In 1963 and again in 1970, small groups of survivors from Chechutawa made their way to Tawaiho after years of living in isolation in the forest. The first, composed of three women and two children, appeared one day in a Brazilian settlement, were recognized as Tapirapé, and sent on to join the others. The group that arrived in 1970 included the last surviving Tapirapé shaman, a powerful man named Kamaira who had led a move to Chechutawa shortly before the Kayapó attack (see note 4). He was encountered in the forest, together with his elderly wife and adolescent son, by a local settler who recognized the language they were speaking. The family had been living alone for many years, fearful of approaching white settlements and believing that they were the only remaining Tapirapé. With Kamaira's return, the Tapirapé saw the possibility of recovering valuable knowledge that had been slipping away from them and reinstituting ceremonies that they had not been able to perform for a number of years. His house became the social center of the village; people would come to ask him about matters of tradition and several Tapirapé showed an interest in becoming apprentice shamans. Kamaira was, however, seriously ill with a tubercular condition aggravated by a chronic grippe and was generally unable to adjust to life in the village. He died in November 1970, four months after his arrival; his wife and son survived, the last of the Tapirapé to become a part of the reconstructed society of Tawaiho.

When Wagley first wrote about the Tapirapé as they appeared to him in 1939–1940, he described them as a people heading toward extinction.[7] He focused on the disruptive effects of drastic depopulation, noting the breakdown of traditional patterns of domestic organization and dislocations in the Tapirapé system of socio-ceremonial groupings. He also analyzed the way in which the Tapirapé, by adhering to their traditional policy of family planning, were conspiring in their own demise. The Tapirapé belief that no family should have more than three children, and no more than two of the same sex had, in former conditions, served to maintain a stable population; given the circumstances in which the Tapirapé found themselves in the 1930s, however, such a policy was demographic suicide.

Upon his return to the Tapirapé after a brief visit in 1953, Wagley found that their cultural repertoire had been reduced in certain respects, most notably by the virtual disappearance of shamanism, but he was nonetheless struck by the degree to which the Tapirapé had been able to reconstitute their traditional way of life (Wagley 1955).

The period since the founding of Tawaiho has, in fact, been one of both physical and cultural vitality for the Tapirapé. The steady increase in their population, noted above, is a result of the medical assistance they have been receiving and the abandonment of taboos on family size and composition. Subsistence needs are plentifully provided for, since the Tapirapé have up to now been able to retain access to sufficient land for extensive and productive horticultural plots. Hunting plays a smaller role in their economy than when they were living in Tampiitawa, but this has been balanced by an increased emphasis on fishing. Dry rice is an important new food source, and chickens, which the Tapirapé already had in Tampiitawa, have, along with eggs, come to play a larger role in their diet. The Tapirapé have become accustomed to various items that they acquire from Brazilians through trade or purchase, including material for the clothes they now wear, kerosene, soap, flashlights and batteries, fishhooks, combs, salt, and rapadura, a molasses-like sweetener. A number of Tapirapé men have spent time working as commercial fishermen. The Tapirapé have, however, largely retained their economic self-sufficiency and are certainly not dependent upon the regional economy for their basic sustenance.

The village of Tawaiho itself is laid out in the traditional manner, with family dwellings forming a circle around a central plaza and men's house. The family houses show the influence of Brazilian styles of building, but the men's house is constructed in the traditional style and continues to serve as the sleeping place for young unmarried men and a social and ritual center for all men in the community. The relationship between the structure of the village circle and the organization of ceremonial events still remains; the sponsors that co-ordinate certain major ceremonies must still come from opposite sides of the village and patterns of dancing between the men's house and family houses have been maintained. The domestic groups that live in these houses are no longer the large uxorilocal extended families of former times and they tend instead to be composed of single nuclear families,[8] augmented in some cases by other unmarried relatives. The principle of uxorilocality persists, however, in the tendency for a couple to reside with the girl's parents in the early period of the marriage, moving out as their own family grows.

The social and ceremonial categories into which the Tapirapé, particularly the males, are divided, and (which Wagley had considered particularly vulnerable to the kind of disruption the Tapirapé had been experiencing in the course of the twentieth century), continue to function in the life of Tawaiho. The most important of these are the men's moieties, each divided into three age-graded groups. At the time of my stay in 1966, there were only three men in the senior age level; since they all belonged to the same moiety, this left the senior age grade of the other moiety, a temporarily depleted category. Membership in the adolescent and mature men's age grades was, however, evenly balanced and served as an ordering principle in various activities that took place during my stay. The formal differentiation of age levels remains an important principle in Tapirapé social life and is reflected in the system of naming, in patterns of body decoration, in the movement of boys into the men's house and their subsequent elaborate initiation into adulthood, and in the common use of age status terms in reference and address.

Another important set of groups are the feasting societies, which involve everyone in the village and meet from time to time throughout the year, either singly or simultaneously in the village plaza, for the purpose of having their members share communal meals. Of the nine named groups that were remembered in 1966, and were considered to constitute the entire set, three were extinct and another, with only two members, seemed on the verge of becoming so. The ideology associated with these groups was passing into the realm of esoteric knowledge, understood by only a small segment of the community; its value for the others, particularly the younger members of the village, was as an enjoyable culinary and social event.[9]

My visits to the Tapirapé in 1966 and 1967 coincided with the height of their ceremonial cycle, which occurs during the dry season. There was dancing and singing almost every night and again at dawn, several major ceremonies were performed, and the feast groups came together for a communal meal. The men's moiety and age grade groupings played a central role in village life during this time, since they determine the pattern of men's activities in a large proportion of ritual events. The female population of Tawaiho was also mobilized for the full range of ceremonial activities. Though women's role in this sphere of life is secondary to that of men, it is still considerable. They take part in much of the singing and dancing that goes on daily, married women participating in accordance with the moiety affiliations of their husbands; unmarried girls play important roles in some rituals; and the entire community of women serves as an active chorus and audience to masked dances performed by the men. The intensity of Tapirapé involvement in ceremonial activities, and the importance of these in the life of their community, can scarcely be exaggerated. Aside from the ceremonies themselves, there are the various preparations that go into them, which include the manufacture of regalia, the execution of intricate body painting, and the preparation of food for feasts and distributions.

Given this focus on ritual, the disappearance of the central institution of shamanism from the Tapirapé cultural repertoire is worthy of some further comment, particularly since other cases of shamanism have been known to survive the breakdown of the kinds of communal ceremonial activities that still form a part of Tapirapé life.[10] Part of the explanation lies, to be sure, in the drastic shocks and dislocations the Tapirapé have suffered, which made it more likely that shamans would die before being able to pass on their special skills and knowledge to others. There is, however, more to the matter than this; it seems necessary also to consider the ambivalence with which the Tapirapé themselves regarded their shamans. While shamans were felt to possess knowledge vital to the continuing survival and well-being of the group and played a central role in what was formerly the most important event in the Tapirapé ritual cycle,[11] they were also feared as sorcerers and commonly executed by the relatives of their alleged victims. During my visits to Tawaiho in the 1960s, I heard several Tapirapé express relief to be free of the fear and violence associated with shamanism. I also became aware that the interest the Tapirapé had in trying to locate Kamaira was tempered by a reluctance to have a man of his powers back in their midst. There were also new factors in their lives that made it easier for them to conceive of being able to manage without their shamans—the medical assistance provided by the Sisters and the possibility of consulting shamans among the nearby Karajá. Karajá shamans could also serve as targets of sorcery accusations, a convenient situation because it allowed these hostilities to be projected outside the village. When Kamaira did rejoin the other Tapirapé, most of them, as we have seen, greeted his arrival with enthusiasm; perhaps they felt that, in their new social setting, the institution of shamanism could be revived selectively, that they could enjoy its ceremonial benefits without being exposed to its dangers. In any event, in considering cases

*Survey of their shamans*

like this one, it is important to keep in mind that people's attitudes toward their own cultural institutions cannot be taken for granted. We are accustomed to thinking of them as varied and complex in our own society, and this perspective must be extended to societies like the Tapirapé as well.

The increased contact that the Tapirapé have had with Karajá, given the proximity of Tawaiho to the Araguaia River, has been an important new feature of Tapirapé social life in recent decades. The Indian Post located at the mouth of the Tapirapé River serves both groups and is the site of a Karajá settlement. During the 1950s and 1960s, there were several cases of intermarriage between Tapirapé men and Karajá women, due primarily to demographic imbalances in the Tapirapé population. Since both groups tend toward an uxorilocal residence pattern, and since Karajá women are not accustomed to performing the kinds of horticultural tasks at which Tapirapé women are proficient, such marriages generally involved the Tapirapé husband's leaving Tawaiho to live with his wife's people. Cardoso de Oliveira commented upon this situation after his 1957 visit, predicting a future of intensified inter-tribal contact, greater dependence of the Tapirapé on the Karajá, and an accelerated rate of culture change (Oliveira 1959). I raised similar questions myself, following my visits in the 1960s, calling attention not only to intermarriage, but to the involvement of young, unmarried Tapirapé men in such Karajá activities as commercial fishing. I felt that these young men would become used to a style of life different from that of Tawaiho and might not want to settle down again in the village (Shapiro 1968a:25–26). I found, however, when I returned in 1974 that all of these young men had married within the village, had cleared large gardens, and had taken on the full social and ceremonial responsibilities of Tapirapé family men. Out-marriage has, in fact, declined in recent years as the Tapirapé population has grown and the sex ratio become more balanced. One Karajá woman who had been living in Tawaiho with her Tapirapé husband in the 1960s was still living there in 1974, with a different Tapirapé husband. As of September 1977, a Karajá couple, related to Tapirapé through marriage, was living in Tawaiho. The couple had gone back to their Karajá village after living for a while in Tawaiho, but were urged to return by the Tapirapé who said they had grown attached to them.[12] Karajá have been attending ceremonies at Tawaiho for some time now and are included in the food distributions that form part of these events. The relationship between the two groups has, in general, been less a matter of the Karajá exercising an acculturative influence over the Tapirapé than of the Tapirapé being able to fit the Karajá into their own social world.

The relationships Tapirapé have had with outsiders have been generally characterized by a receptiveness on the part of the Tapirapé to the cultural practices of others. They have, while maintaining their social and cultural distinctiveness, incorporated a variety of institutions borrowed from their Indian neighbors. Their moiety and age grade system, feasting groups, and various details of ceremonial life are clearly derived from similar patterns found among the Gê-speaking peoples of the region. They have adopted a major Karajá ritual, a masked dance known locally by the term *aruanã*,[13] and integrated it into their own ceremonial cycle and cosmological system. This ritual, like other borrowed institutions, has undergone certain transformations in the Tapirapé context. The elements of sexual opposition and symbolic male dominance, which are central to the Karajá ritual, play a subordinate role in the Tapirapé version; the pairs who perform the dance together are said by the Karajá to represent two male spirits, while the Tapirapé see the spirit couple as husband and wife.

The distinctiveness of the Tapirapé vis à vis other Indian groups is expressed not only in such changes in borrowed practices, but also asserted symbolically by the Tapirapé in ritual enactments of the history of inter-tribal contact. One of the most important annual ceremonies performed by the Tapirapé represents the attacks they have suffered from their more warlike neighbors. The masks that are prepared for this ceremony are the most striking artifacts produced by the Tapirapé.[14] These masks are worn by two male dancers, one of whom represents the Kayapó and the other the Karajá. The Kayapó are also portrayed by a number of young men and boys who dress in what are meant to be outlandish costumes and engage in wild and aggressive behavior. The men who represent the Tapirapé wear the clothing of "civilized" non-Indians and contrast with the others by virtue of their calm and stately demeanor. The various performers, after making a circuit of the village, gather in the plaza to stage a tableau in which the "Tapirapé" impassively sustain the ritual assaults of the "Kayapó" and "Karajá," and then overcome them by leading or carrying them, one by one, into the men's house. This finale not only serves as a reversal in which the victims become the victors, but posits a victory in terms of incorporation: erstwhile enemies are absorbed into the center of Tapirapé social and religious life. The ceremony concludes with a communal meal in the men's house, which male guests are invited to share with the men of Tawaiho. Since Karajá have come to figure prominently among the guests, the ceremony has become a ritual of incorporation on two levels. At the same time, given the presence of Karajá spectators and guests, politeness dictates that overt references to the identity of the "Karajá" masked figure be avoided. I discovered this when I made the mistake of trying to elicit the symbolic significance of the masks during the ceremony. It is possible that changes in the relationship between Tapirapé and Karajá will come to be reflected in a changing interpretation of the ritual.

One of the more intriguing features of this ritual, as it has come to be performed in Tawaiho, is the use of Western clothing as a means of symbolically distinguishing the Tapirapé from their traditional Indian enemies. This may seem, on the face of it, to be merely a reflection of the values and prejudices of the surrounding Brazilian society, an acquiescence to the notion that "civilizados" are superior to Indians. The matter is, however, more complex and requires a consideration of the unusual history of contacts between the Tapirapé and non-Indians. The Tapirapé have generally fared better with non-Indians than with their indigenous neighbors. This is not to say that the Tapirapé have escaped the kinds of threats that have brought about the extinction of other Indian groups. However, the fact that they have been able to survive as a people and to withstand these pressures up to the present is largely due to the help they have had from non-Indian outsiders.

Some of this help has already been described above, including, for example, the role played by a local Brazilian rancher, who supported a large part of the Tapirapé population in the period following the Kayapó attack of 1947. This episode of Tapirapé history stands in sharp contrast to the general pattern of relations between ranchers and Indian groups. The Tapirapé are also one of the few peoples for whom the Indian Protection Service fulfilled its intended function, at least during the time that Valentim Gomes was in charge of the Indian post.

Another unusual feature of Tapirapé history is the extent and variety of their relationships with anthropologists, many of whom have remained in contact with the Tapirapé over long periods of time. The diversity in national backgrounds of these anthropologists has been one factor contributing to the development of a certain cosmopolitanism that characterizes Tapirapé attitudes toward outsiders. In their relationships with anthropologists, the Tapirapé have been introduced to non-Indians who find their way of life interesting, valuable, and enjoyable.

While anthropologists, like other outsiders, have served as agents of social change, they have, at the same time, acted to encourage the preservation of cultural traditions. One example of this traditionalizing effect comes from my own field experience. While I was living in Tawaiho in 1966, the time came for the men to clear plots of land for new gardens. This can be done in one of two ways: either each man works alone to clear his own horticultural plot or the men work communally to clear the plots in succession. In the latter case, the men's moiety system serves to organize labor and each day's work is followed by a communal meal. Of the two methods, the former had come to be the usual one during the decades preceding my own visit. When I heard the men begin to talk about clearing new gardens, I asked the village headman, who was my neighbor, if they were by any chance planning to do so communally. He told me that the Tapirapé were now too "lazy" for that and that each man would just go out to work alone. I must have made my disappointment evident, since that evening there was a general meeting in the men's house and the headman could be heard addressing his fellow Tapirapé at length. Though I could not follow the conversation in detail, I did catch the frequent mention of "Doto Kalo" (Doctor Carlos), the name by which Wagley is known to the Tapirapé. I subsequently learned that the headman's exhortations had taken the form of pointing out that Doctor Carlos had sent his niece from a great distance to come and live with the Tapirapé and that they would be disappointing both of us were they not to do things the "right" way. The next day, and on succeeding days, the men left the village together in the morning, spent the day clearing land, and returned in the early evening. At the conclusion of each day's work, the men would be met outside the village by their wives who brought food for the communal meal. The meal was shared by the men according to moiety and age-grade affiliation. A few hours later, after everyone had had a chance to rest, the night's singing and dancing began.

This departure from what would otherwise have been the normal routine should not be seen as an artifical performance put on for my benefit. I may have served as a stimulus or pretext for the undertaking, but it was clearly something that the Tapirapé carried out to heighten the excitement of village life for themselves. It is commonly the case among the Tapirapé that practices that have been allowed to fall into disuse for a time will be revived when there is some special cause for animation in the community. In 1977, the communal garden clearing and its attendant rituals were performed again just before the arrival of delegates to an inter-tribal meeting that the Tapirapé were hosting.[15] Thus, the best way to understand the decision in 1966 is not that the Tapirapé did something especially for their anthropologist friends, but that relationships with anthropologists had become a factor in their plans.

Another function that anthropologists have filled in the course of their work with the Tapirapé has been to serve as intermediaries between the Tapirapé and members of the local Brazilian population. The most important such case is Wagley's bringing Valentim Gomes with him on his 1939 trip, thereby initiating a relationship that was to be so crucial for the Tapirapé in the ensuing years. When I lived with the Tapirapé in 1966, I was accompanied by a young woman from the nearby settlement of Furo de Pedra. She was at first both shy and fearful of living in Tawaiho, but soon developed easy and companionable relationships in the village. She continued to receive visits from Tapirapé after returning to Furo de Pedra, and her relationship with them seems to have affected the attitudes of others in the town.

The closest and most important relationships the Tapirapé have had with outsiders have been with the Little Sisters of Jesus and Father François Jentel. Contacts with missionaries prior to the arrival of the Sisters and Father Jentel had, for the most part, been limited to brief and intermittent visits from representatives of a variety of different persuasions. The only fairly sustained contact during this time was with the Scottish evangelical missionary F. C. Kegel, who made several visits to the Tapirapé between 1932 and 1935, each of two to five months' duration, and introduced Baldus to the Tapirapé in 1935. Kegel's main activity among the Tapirapé was to teach them songs (Baldus 1970:51). The Tapirapé, who have a strong interest in music that extends to learning any foreign songs they can master, proved receptive to his efforts and still speak of him often.

The role that the Little Sisters of Jesus have played in Tapirapé life from 1952 up to the present has few if any parallels in the history of contact between missionaries and Indians in Brazil. Their efforts were singled out by Brazil's foremost authority on Indian policy, Darcy Ribeiro, who, in an otherwise critical review of missionary activity, held the Tapirapé mission up as a "model" for others to emulate.[16]

The unique quality of the relationship between the Little Sisters of Jesus and the Tapirapé stems mainly from the fact that their order, founded by followers of the French priest Charles Foucault, does not define its purpose in terms of proselytism and the acquisition of converts. The life of each chapter revolves around the dual activities of work and contemplation. The Sisters must, on the one hand, maintain a routine that includes several hours a day spent in silent prayer, and, on the other, seek to adapt themselves to the mode of life characteristic of the community in which they are living. The Sisters at Tawaiho perform many of the same subsistence activities as the Tapirapé, including the cultivation of swidden plots. I have had occasion to visit households of Sisters in one of the hillside slums of Rio, where they had jobs in the factory that employed many of their neighbors, and in a ghetto area of southwest Chicago, where they hold jobs similar to those of the Little Sisters in Rio. The house they live in at Tawaiho, while having certain structural features related to the life of the Order, like a chapel and a private sleeping area, was designed and built to blend in as much as possible with the architectural style of the Tapirapé village.

The Sisters participate to a considerable extent in the social and ceremonial round of village life. They have, like the anthropologists who have lived with the Tapirapé, been incorporated into such institutions as the system of feasting groups. The Sisters have also collaborated in the revival of certain Tapirapé customs. To give an example, the traditional practice of piercing the lower lip of male infants was abandoned at one point when increased contact with Brazilians made the Tapirapé self-conscious about this aspect of their appearance. Three years before my last visit in 1974, the Tapirapé, in a burst of good feeling that followed upon the rebuilding of their men's house and the initiation of a group of young men, decided to revive the practice. There was, however, a problem because the young boys who had not had their lips pierced at birth were fearful of undergoing the operation because of the pain involved. A solution was found when the Sisters offered to provide a local anaesthetic.

An incident that is similarly revealing of the relationship between the Sisters and the Tapirapé in matters of custom and personal adornment occurred during my 1974 visit. I wanted to look at the quartz lip plug worn by a young man during the initiation ceremony. There is only one such plug left and the Tapirapé are no longer able to obtain material to replace it. The Tapirapé have asked the Sisters to keep it in a secluded part of their house, since they consider it the safest place in the village. When the Sisters brought it out to me, I noticed that it was wrapped in a pair of black knit briefs. Since I would not have expected the Sisters to possess an undergarment of this sort, I inquired about it. The explanation had to do with the fact that initiates had become unwilling to appear publicly wearing the penis sheath that constituted the sole item of male clothing in former years, and that the aesthetically unsatisfactory alternative was for them to complete a beautiful and intricate ensemble of regalia and body painting with a pair of baggy khaki shorts. One of the Sisters had, in the course of a trip to Rio, found the briefs in the Brazilian equivalent of a five and ten cent store and it occurred to her that they would be virtually invisible against the black body paint worn by the initiate. The effect, as she had foreseen, was most pleasing to the Tapirapé, particularly to the initiate who could improve his appearance without sacrificing his modesty.

The Sisters have played a central role in the physical survival and well-being of the Tapirapé not only through medical assistance, but also by their efforts in bringing about a change in the Tapirapé system of family planning. They did this in a manner that was both tactful and effective. Rather than attempting to convince the Tapirapé that infanticide was evil, the usual approach taken by missionaries, they instead offered to adopt the unwanted child of any woman who already had 3 children or 2 of the same sex. As it turned out, once the infants were not killed immediately at birth, their mothers were unwilling to renounce them. The first step was for the mother to decide to go on nursing the child until it could be given over entirely to the Sisters' care; the second was for the parents simply to accept the child into their household. The change was effected quite rapidly, requiring only a few precedents to break the taboo. By 1966, large families were common and one couple had six sons.

The Sisters have mediated many of the relationships between Tapirapé and outsiders, including both local Brazilians and representatives of large development companies that have been seeking to establish themselves in the area in recent years. They have served as a buffer against tourists who have been traveling through the region in ever increasing numbers. In 1966, a traveling houseboat had begun making "safari" tours along the Araguaia, docking at the Tapirapé village whence tourists would be flown to Gê villages for sightseeing. Among those who were brought to Tawaiho on this floating hotel during my stay in 1966 was the American novelist John Dos Passos, who subsequently published an account of his visit to the Tapirapé in *Holiday Magazine*. Such tourist traffic, besides being disruptive of village life, posed a pollution hazard to the Tapirapé bathing place and drinking supply, and the Sisters intervened to prevent the boat from coming as far as the village. Since that time the Sisters have continually sought to limit and control contacts between Tapirapé and tourists.

As Christians, the Sisters believe that their faith offers to humankind the greatest opportunity for spiritual fulfillment. However, they tend not to emphasize the exclusivity of their religion and will at times express the belief that God is present in different ways to different peoples. Nor do they consider themselves superior to the Tapirapé with regard to the practice of those virtues defined as "Christian." I have often heard the Sisters remark upon how much they can learn from the Tapirapé about such things as patience, humility, and charity. While their chapel is open to anyone who wishes to enter it, they do not exert any pressure on the Tapirapé to join them. They seem to be aware of what conversion amounts to in situations of social and economic inequality, when the bringers of a new religion are also the providers of desired goods; aware also that the process is usually one in which an intellectually and emotionally rich set of beliefs is replaced by an ill-undertstood approximation of a religious system.

It is interesting to note that the tolerance and degree of cultural relativism that informs the Sisters' view of their work antedates the liberalization of attitudes found among certain missionaries who have more recently been influenced by the social sciences, cultural anthropology in particular, or by the general climate of opinion in their own societies. It seems that the Sisters have found within their own belief system, the same one that has historically provided the rationale for extreme forms of cultural imperialism, a very different and less traveled path.

There are, as of the present, no Tapirapé converts. The Tapirapé do show a certain amount of interest in the Sisters' religious observances, particularly those connected with Christmas and Easter, but the meaning of this interest is open to interpretation. It may be a part of the general curiosity the Tapirapé have for exotic customs, and also a reciprocal return for the Sisters' interest in Tapirapé traditions.

Though the Sisters have sought to impose themselves as little as possible on the Tapirapé, they have, inevitably, affected Tapirapé society in a number of ways. The Tapirapé have come to depend upon the Sisters, not only for medical assistance, but in terms of their social life as well. The Sisters' house has become a focal point of the village, a gathering place that has, to some extent, supplanted the men's house. The change is one that has significant social structural implications, since visits to the Sisters are made by women as well as men, and commonly involve married couples and family groups.

Given the fact that the Little Sisters of Jesus are representatives of a technologically and politically dominant society, their relationship to the Tapirapé is bound to be a hierarchical one. It is important, however, to see this relationship in comparative context, that is, to measure it against other relationships between tribal peoples and Westerners. In this light, the relationship between the Tapirapé and the Sisters is remarkable for its degree of symmetry and mutuality. The Sisters' approach is so different from that of most other missionaries that one wonders if the common label is even appropriate. In matters of religious belief and standards of dress, where missionary interference has been notorious, the Sisters have shown a respect for cultural differences. Where they have intervened to bring about social change, as in the case of the birth policy, they have done so in a nonaggressive manner and, as it turns out, to the advantage of the Tapirapé themselves. They have not, as is commonly the case, suppressed institutions that played a vital role in traditional life, leaving social chaos and demoralization in their wake. Their economic dealings with the Tapirapé set them apart from most other missionaries, since they have largely entered into traditional Tapirapé patterns of reciprocal exchange rather than involving Indians in wage labor and thereby introducing new and exploitative relations of production foreign to the native system.

The fact that the Sisters are an order of women is worth considering in an attempt to understand their role in Tapirapé life. For one thing, their general attitude of support and self-effacement, while not an invariant feature or automatic consequence of European sex role structuring, is nonetheless more in line with the behavior expected of females than of males. Looking at it from the Tapirapé perspective, and given the relative positions of men and women in Tapirapé society, one might hypothesize that they themselves would have seen a group of male missionaries as being in a more dominant position; the sex of the Sisters thus, in some measure, acts as a counterbalance to the social asymmetry between themselves and the Tapirapé. Finally, the sex of the Sisters has had an influence on the attitudes of local Brazilians to their mission and to Tawaiho more generally. The respect with which the Sisters are viewed by members of the Brazilian population is mingled with feelings of protectiveness that extend to the Tapirapé as well, reinforcing the perception of the Tapirapé as an essentially pacific and gentle people. There is, in effect, a certain similarity in the behavioral styles of the Sisters and the Tapirapé. While it is possible that this reflects an influence of the Sisters on the Tapirapé, it seems more reasonable, considering the way in which the Tapirapé have been characteristically described by outsiders, to see this as a matter of compatibility rather than acculturation.

Another major missionary presence in Tapirapé life, in addition to the Little Sisters of Jesus, has been Father François Jentel, who arrived in the region two years after the Sisters and worked there until his imprisonment by the Brazilian government and expulsion from the country in 1974. During his stay, Father Jentel's parish included not only Tawaiho, but a couple of nearby Brazilian settlements as well; his relationship to the Tapirapé thus did not have the same continuity and intimacy as the Sisters'. At the same time, his impact on Tapirapé life was greater in terms of the changes he initiated and fostered.

The new items of technology that Father Jentel introduced into the village include a tractor that serves to transport produce from the gardens, making it easier for the Tapirapé to cultivate plots located some distance from their village, and a generator that is used in pumping water and in a new technique of manioc processing that is used in addition to the traditional method.[17] Father Jentel was also responsible for adding three modern buildings to the village circle: his own house, a schoolhouse, and a church. The buildings are of whitewashed concrete with tiled roofs; the priest's house and schoolhouse have flush toilets. Given Father Jentel's intermittent pattern of residence at Tawaiho, his house serves for much of the time as a storehouse or a place where guests to the village can spend a few days. The building officially designated as the schoolhouse has, in fact, more often been used as a residence, mostly for those who have served as teachers in the Tapirapé school program.[18] When classes are being taught, they generally meet in the church, which in turn is only infrequently used for religious services.

The school program, which was established for the purpose of teaching the Tapirapé to read and write both in their own language and in Portuguese, has operated off and on, depending upon the availability of qualified teachers. It has been in regular session for the last several years, with separate classes for men, women, and children.[19] While the buildings in which school activities take place were constructed under the supervision of Father Jentel, the Sisters have played an important role in organizing the program and finding teachers.

Though building a church at Tawaiho was one of Father Jentel's projects, he did not engage in active proselytism among the Tapirapé. When he said mass in the village, it was usually in the small chapel of the Sisters' house and was performed for the Sisters themselves. When mass was said in church, a number of Tapirapé turned out for the occasion and many sought to join in the singing. Here, as in the case of the aforementioned interest of the Tapirapé in the Sisters' ritual activities, there is some ambiguity as to what Tapirapé participation meant.

In defining his own mission among the Tapirapé, Father Jentel saw his most pressing and immediate obligation not in terms of conversion, but in terms of helping the Tapirapé to secure rights over the land they occupied and depended on for their livelihood. A representative of the growing radical movement within the Catholic Church,

Father Jentel had come to re-examine the role of the clerical establishment in nations like Brazil and to question whether the Church could minister to the spiritual needs of its members without concerning itself also with their material well-being.

Father Jentel's activist engagement in the social and economic problems of his Indian and Brazilian parishioners was particularly important in view of the political situation that had been developing in the region since the 1950s. At that time, the government of the state of Mato Grosso began selling large tracts of land to development companies; as is commonly the case in such sales, the land was disposed of without concern for the constitutional rights of the Indian populations and Brazilian squatters who happened to be living on it. Land in the area changed hands several times and, by the time of my visit in 1966, 320,000 hectares, including large stretches of Tapirapé territory and the land on which the town of Santa Teresinha is located, had been acquired by the Companhia do Desenvolvimento do Araguaia (Araguaia Development Company). CODEARA, as the company was known, had been attempting to consolidate its position in the region, engaging in land surveys, using strong-arm tactics to displace squatters, and setting up in the vicinity of Santa Teresinha what can only be described as a slave labor camp composed of migrant workers brought in from the northeast.

The company came into direct confrontation with Father Jentel, primarily because of the priest's activities in Santa Teresinha, where he had aided in the establishment of a farmers' cooperative (see Shapiro 1967), but also because he opposed the company's efforts to take over Tapirapé lands and have the Tapirapé population relocated. Father Jentel urged the Tapirapé to survey and demarcate the boundaries of their land, and worked with them at this task. He engaged in negotiations with the Indian Protection Service (and, after 1968, with its successor, the National Indian Foundation), with a view toward helping the Tapirapé acquire clear legal title to their land and having the company relinquish its own claims. He suggested ways that the Tapirapé might discourage company land surveyors from intruding into their territory. One such tactic was for an armed Tapirapé man to appear close to where a surveyor was engaged in his activities, and merely to remain there immobile. The Tapirapé discovered, to their amusement, that this masquerade proved an effective means of intimidation.

The position of the Tapirapé has been a precarious one ever since CODEARA moved into the area. For several years, at the end of the 1960s and beginning of the 70s, the Tapirapé delayed rebuilding their men's house because they were afraid the company would take away their land. For a while, it was rumored that the Tapirapé were to be relocated to the Island of Bananal, which had recently been made into a national park for indigenous groups. Such a move would have been disastrous to Tapirapé, given the unavailability on the island of sufficient land suitable for horticulture. The Tapirapé would have been deprived of what is not only the basis of their economy, but also the focus of their lives more generally, and would be forced to become, like the Karajá, increasingly dependent upon commercial relationships with local Brazilians and welfare aid from the National Indian Foundation.[20] The company presently has ceded only a small portion of the land the Tapirapé currently occupy and cultivate. The Tapirapé are still in de facto possession of the rest, but do not have legal title to it. With the departure of Father Jentel, they have lost an important source of support in their fight to hold on to their territory.

In aiding the Tapirapé in their battle against CODEARA, Father Jentel provided the Tapirapé with vital information about the economic and political factors that were impinging upon their lives from the outside. The political consciousness of the Tapirapé also developed in the context of various company-related events. For example, the arrival in their village of refugees fleeing from the company work camp to hide out with the Tapirapé until they could escape from the region, and the appearance in Tawaiho of military police who arrested Father Jentel and placed the Sisters under armed surveillance (Shapiro 1967) were two such instances.

Because Father Jentel worked both with the Tapirapé and the local Brazilian population, he was able to serve as a bridge between them and, in particular, to create an awareness that they faced a common plight and a common enemy. There has thus come to be a sentiment of solidarity in the attitudes of the Brazilian settlers toward the Tapirapé, an unusual state of affairs for a frontier area. While it cannot be said that the inhabitants of Santa Teresinha and Furo de Pedra are without prejudice against Indians, they nonetheless do not perceive the Tapirapé as a threat, nor do they question their right to exist as a people. It is interesting to note that local Brazilians generally use the term "Tapirapé," the group's own auto-designation, rather than the broader and pejorative term "indio."

The roles that Father Jentel and the Little Sisters of Jesus have played in Tapirapé life have complemented one another: the Sisters, in accommodating themselves to the Tapirapé as a part of their own religious vocation, have supported the preservation of Tapirapé customs and the traditional bases of Tapirapé identity and self-esteem; the priest, for his part, has provided the Tapirapé with certain information and skills that have made them better prepared to deal with the larger society that will ultimately determine their fate. While the relationship with either the Sisters or the priest would alone have provided an unusual case of Indian/missionary contact, the combination of the two has made the Tapirapé experience unique.

The Tapirapé have managed, up to the present, to strike a balance between maintaining their cultural integrity and adapting to a changing set of social circumstances. They continue to dispose of resources sufficient to meet their needs and to enjoy a full and rewarding communal life; their village presents a striking and positive contrast to the Brazilian and Karajá settlements in the region. The crucial question is whether they can hold on to their land, and thus be able to confront Brazilian national society from a position of political strength. Given the general experience of indigenous peoples in lowland South America, it is difficult to be optimistic about the prospects of the Tapirapé. Even if their territory were to be declared a national park, or reservation, their troubles could hardly be considered over; the most famous of Brazil's Indian reservations, the Xingu National Park, created in 1961 and up until recently a symbol of the possibility for an enlightened and humane Indian policy, has been invaded and divided by national highways that form part of the larger Trans-Amazonian project.

In response to the problems they face, the Tapirapé have begun to come together with several other Indian groups in what looks like an incipient pan-Indian movement. This new level of political action has involved meetings among representatives of different tribes and visits to Brasília, with a view to making the national government take action with respect to the rights of tribal groups. In September of 1977, the Tapirapé were themselves hosts to a gathering involving Shavante, Bororo, Paresí, Nambikwara, and Kaingaing delegates, who declared themselves prepared to participate in the efforts of the

Tapirapé to maintain their territory. The Tapirapé, for their part, can, given the history of their relationships both with other Indian groups and with Westerners, be expected to play an important role in such an emerging unified Indian movement in Brazil.

## Notes

1. Bibliographies of Wagley's and Baldus' writings on the Tapirapé can be found in their respective monographs. Galvão's work was done in collaboration with Wagley and resulted in an article on the Tapirapé for the *Handbook of South American Indians* (Wagley and Galvão 1948), as well as a comparative study of Tupian kinship terminology, which incorporated the results of their field research among the Tenetehara (Wagley and Galvão 1946a, 1946b). Cardoso de Oliveira accompanied Wagley to the Tapirapé in 1957 and published a report on their situation at that time (Oliveira 1959). My own visits to the Tapirapé took place in 1966, when I did field research from June to September under the sponsorship of the Ford Foundation's Frontier Research Project, administered through Columbia University's Institute of Latin American Studies, of which Wagley was then director; in August of 1967, when I returned for a month before going on to do doctoral research elsewhere in Brazil; and for two weeks in March 1974. The first two trips resulted in publications on kinship (Shapiro 1968a) and ceremonial activities (1968b), as well as an unpublished report on local political developments that were endangering the welfare of the Tapirapé (Shapiro 1967).

2. See Baldus 1970, ch. 2, for a review and analysis of the earliest documentary evidence concerning the Tapirapé.

3. Wagley (1977:32) reports that two informants mentioned a sixth village, but that others failed to confirm its existence. See Wagley 1977:33 for a map showing the location of the five Tapirapé villages and indicating the date when each was abandoned.

4. One major move to Chechutawa occurred during the early 1940s and was prompted by fear of the whites who were coming to settle in the region in increasing numbers. Most of the Tapirapé returned to Tampiitawa shortly thereafter because of homesickness and in the wake of a dispute that involved the killing of a shaman.

5. The Indian Protection Service was founded in 1910 with the dual purpose of creating safe conditions for the colonization of the interior and protecting the Indian groups that stood in the colonizers' path. Though these were contradictory aims, the service, under the aegis of its founder, General Rondon, took what was for its time an unusually enlightened and altrusitic approach to native peoples. The subsequent record of the service was at best erratic and, at worst, a national scandal. In 1968, publicity concerning the nefarious activities of various of its functionaries brought the service to an end. It was replaced by the National Indian Foundation (FUNAI), which now serves as the government agency in charge of Indian affairs. See Ribeiro 1962 for an account of the founding of the Indian Protection Service and of its activities up until 1960.

6. Of the three French nuns who formed the original group, one, Sister Geneviève-Hélène, has continued to live with the Tapirapé for the greater part of the succeeding years. Sister Mayi-Baptiste, who arrived in 1956, has been in the Tapirapé village almost continuously since that time. The group, in line with the philosophy of their order, has become more international in its composition and has sought to include at least one Brazilian Sister among those resident at any time. During the period of my research in 1966, there were four Sisters in the village whose respective countries of origin were France (Basque region), Brazil, Portugal, and Luxembourg.

7. See Wagley 1940 and also a later study, Wagley 1951, in which a contrast is drawn between the Tapirapé and the Tenetehara in regard to the groups' respective success in adjusting to their post-contact situations.

8. It should be remembered that the nuclear family unit is presently larger than in earlier times, given changes in the birth policy.

9. For further information on these institutions, see Wagley 1977: chs. 4 and 5; Shapiro 1968a and 1968b; and Baldus 1970: chs. 11 and 12. Recruitment to the men's moities is generally by patrifiliation, though exceptions and changes of moiety affiliation also occur. Membership in the feasting societies seems to have been regulated traditionally by parallel filiation, boys joining their fathers' groups and girls their mothers'; patterns of membership were, however, quite fluid at the time I was in Tawaiho. These two sets of groupings bear a clear resemblance to institutions found among the Gê-speaking peoples of the region. Another Gê-related socio-ceremonial institution that existed formerly among the Tapirapé, but now exists only in memory, is a relationship of formalized friendship that involved exchange and an extreme form of respect marked by avoidance (Shapiro 1968b:12–13).

10. See the analysis presented in Murphy's (1958) study of Mundurucú religion.

11. This was a ritual in which shamans battled the spirit of Thunder at the onset of the rainy season. Wagley witnessed it in 1939 and described it in a photographic essay (Wagley 1943).

12. Personal communication from the Little Sisters of Jesus, September 5, 1977.

13. The Karajá term for this dance is *ijaso*. See Tavener 1973 for a discussion of the ritual and how it was being performed among the Karajá in the 1960s. According to William Lipkind, an anthropologist who did earlier research among the Karajá, the Tapirapé learned the dance from the Javaé, a Karajá sub-group, at a time when some Tapirapé were living on the island of Bananal (personal communication from Lipkind to Baldus, cited in Baldus 1970:36).

14. The Tapirapé term for both the mask and the ceremony is *tãwa*, commonly rendered in Portuguese as "cara grande," or "big face."

15. Personal communication from the Little Sisters of Jesus, September 5, 1977. See note 17.

16. "Um modêlo de atuação missionária, altamente meritória é a realizada, hoje, entre os índios Tapirapé, por freiras católicas da irmandade Michel Foucault" (sic; the order was founded by followers of Charles Foucault). Ribeiro 1962:164.

17. The traditional method of processing bitter manioc, which is still the most common at present, is to soak the roots in a submerged canoe for several days, allowing the prussic acid to be leached away, set the roots in the sun to dry, pound them in a mortar, strain them in a sieve, and then roast the flour over a fire, sprinkling water on

it as it is cooking. The end product, called "farinha d'agua," can only be kept for a few days. The generator-powered processor is used in the preparation of a dry flour that can be stored for long periods of time.

18. During my visits in the 1960s, the house was occupied by a couple working as teachers and later by a linguist from the Museu Nacional in Rio de Janeiro, Yonne de Freitas Leite, who has been carrying out linguistic research among the Tapirapé.

19. Personal communication from the Little Sisters of Jesus, December 30, 1975, and September 10, 1977.

20. See Tavener 1973 for a discussion of the Karajá situation.

# FOUR

# The "Chapel" as Symbol: Italian Colonization in Southern Brazil

## Thales de Azevedo

THE OCCUPATION AND peopling of the extreme south of Brazil took place in roughly four stages. From the first half of the sixteenth to the middle of the eighteenth century, the Portuguese explored and gradually occupied the vast eastern plains, overcoming in the process the region's scattered Guarani inhabitants. They then moved west, displacing those Indians who had been brought into *reduções* by the Spanish Jesuits of Paraguay, establishing definitive frontiers through treaties with Spain, and developing large horse and cattle ranches, especially near the Uruguayan and Argentinian frontiers. Even today the rancher and the cowboy are symbols of the area.

The second stage of development centered around Portuguese speaking colonists from the Azores who were brought to southern Brazil beginning in the second half of the eighteenth century. These immigrants established small farms in the central part of the territory and, on the Atlantic coast, wheat agriculture and the jerked beef industry.

Around 1800, the provincial boundaries of São Pedro de Rio Grande do Sul were established, thus formalizing the southernmost

This article was translated from the Portuguese by Linda Hahn Miller and William E. Carter.

politico-administrative unit of Portuguese America. By 1822, when Brazil became independent, most of the province was settled, if not by Azoreans, at least by Brazilians from other regions. The major exception was the northeast, consisting of a low-lying area in the proximity of Porto Alegre, the provincial capital, and a mountainous area farther north, near the border of Santa Catarina.

The year 1824 saw the beginning of the third stage of settlement, with the introduction of close to 80,000 Germans. Most were given parcels of up to 120 hectares each, between the Rio dos Sinos and the Encosta da Serra, in the northeast quadrant of the province. The bulk of German migration occurred before 1835, when a revolution erupted that lasted almost ten years and profoundly disturbed the life and economy of the region. At the termination of hostilities, a few additional German settlers arrived and, like their predecessors, engaged in subsistence agriculture and small cottage industries such as weaving, preserving, tanning, woodworking, and metallurgy. From these humble beginnings was to develop the industrial power that today undergirds Rio Grande do Sul's economy and society.

With the end of the Farroupilha Revolt (1835–45) and the Paraguayan War (1865–70), the provincial government drew up new colonization plans by which it hoped to attract additional Europeans through a variety of incentives and subsidies, the objectives being to complete settlement of the territory and to increase agricultural production. German colonization had produced such worthwhile results that both government and public opinion favored its continuation. However, open competition from the United States, combined with negative feedback from recent German and Swiss colonists to São Paulo Province, led Prussia and other German kingdoms to discourage the recruitment of new emigrants for Brazil.

As a result, European recruiting agents from Rio Grande do Sul turned their attention to the north of Italy and to other European nations in which there was, at the time, a large surplus of labor. Between 1875 and 1914 such efforts generated a total of some 80,000 migrants from Veneto, Lombardy, Piedmont, and the Austro-Italian Tyrol. Most were peasant farmers, although about 10 percent were artisans, factory workers, and other urban types. Their trip to Rio Grande do Sul began usually in groups of 100. Leaving their homes by train, they were taken to a major port and placed on a steamship, where they found themselves surrounded by fellow emigrants from other regions of Italy with a variety of dialects, traditions, antagonisms, and destinations. Some were slated for Argentina, some for Uruguay, and some for other regions of Brazil such as São Paulo, Espírito Santo, Paraná, and Santa Catarina. Until the time they were thrown together in this disrupting manner, they had been little aware of their common conditions as Italian citizens, even though the country had been united in 1860. They knew little of the country to which they were traveling; the engine driving them was the misery that reigned in their place of birth. They were poor, and most were illiterate; all were Catholic. Although a few brought a little capital, most had to depend on the imperial government of Brazil and the provincial administration of Rio Grande do Sul for everything: passage, foodstuffs, land, farming implements, and seed.

Their process of adaptation began, thus, at the port of embarkation—Genoa for most. In the first weeks after leaving their homes, they had their first contact with a large city, with other displaced persons speaking unknown languages and dialects, and with intense and painful changes in schedules and habits. Their immediate, transitory society was a chaotic one, the ship's command often appeared arbitrary, and immigration agents and authorities dictatorial. One of their greatest difficulties was communication. None knew Portuguese and few could understand the many regulations to which they were subject. The individuality enjoyed as peasants in the mountains of northern Italy had little place in the world they were about to enter. Fear of the unknown ocean, the ship's roll, exposure to heat and cold, cramped quarters, storms, strange food served at unaccustomed times, the possibility of losing the few possessions they had brought—all contributed to their anxiety and trauma. Only a lucky few were reunited with others from the same region on reaching their destination. (For descriptions of the trauma experienced by these migrants, cf. Cecchi 1959; Ianni 1972; Hutter 1972. The reader can also consult memoirs, accounts of voyages, and the emigrants' own correspondence [cf. bibliography of Azevedo 1975].)

After disembarking at the ports of Rio de Janeiro or Santos and transferring to other ships, colonists destined for Rio Grande do Sul arrived in Porto Alegre and from there were transported in small river boats to Montenegro and São Sebastião do Caí. They then journeyed by foot or on mules along rustic, arduous roads to Alto Da Serra in the northeastern corner of the province, where they were received and lodged in crude barracks with a capacity of 300 to 400 people each. A few days later they departed for the forest, where they were to choose parcels for settlement. The region was mountainous, temperate or subtropical, and marked by rugged valleys and some partially navigable rivers. It was still totally uninhabited and barely connected with the outside world. Its roads, if they could be called that, were usable only by ox cart and mule train.

Covered by dense stands of pine, the land had been divided into sixteen sections of about one square league each (six sq. km.), which in turn had been subdivided into parcels of 15 to 60 or so hectares in elongated rectangular form, perpendicular to narrow roads called *travessões* or *linhas,* similar to the arrangement that had been followed in the German colonization zone. Because of their geometric form, parcels situated in the valleys tended to be quite steep. Where they bordered on a river, a large number could be irrigated simultaneously. Although all parcels were of the same length, they varied considerably in width, corresponding to presumed differences in soil quality. Each colonist could choose between purchasing an entire parcel or only a fraction of the same. The size of this purchase would depend on the number of workers in his family, the amount of his capital, and his ability to open up roads, clear forest, and provide a dwelling.

Once he had chosen his parcel, the immigrant was transferred from the barracks to a temporary house that the government had placed in a clearing of about 4,800 square meters (1,000 *braças,* an agrarian measure used at that time). These structures were of rough wattle and daub and measured only about 4 by 6 meters. They were barely sufficient to protect the family from the rain, sun, wind, frosts, and snow that sometimes fell in these mountains.

The travessões extended in parallels, one behind the other, at intervals of one to two kilometers. Their regularity came to be one of the chief determinants of subsequent neighborhood development. Each house was several hundred meters distant from its neighbor. Because all faced the aforementioned roads, communication between neighbors and transportation of products were relatively easy. However, correspondence and chronicles of this first period emphasize solitude and isolation. These feelings probably derived in part from the fact that the dwelling was surrounded by dense groves of trees and by animals unfamiliar to Europeans; small monkeys, jaguars, peccaries, rats, foxes, snakes, lizards, and strange insects. The colonists also feared the appearance of Indians, who were said to be living in the immediate environs, but who in reality had already withdrawn to an area some ten kilometers away.

Adaptation to the new environment meant profound changes. The immigrants had to gradually create a type of habitation more satisfying and functional than their initial shelter. This they did by installing a water-powered sawmill and building two separate units, a sleeping house and an eating house, as had been the custom in Italy. The former served as a residence and as a locale for large reunions of family and friends: christenings, weddings, anniversaries, and the ordination of priests. The latter, situated a few meters away, sheltered a large stove and food storage area, around which people would pass a considerable part of the day and evening. This was the place to eat, to converse after returning from work, to bathe, to pray, and to wash clothes. The warmth of the stove was particularly welcome during the autumn and winter months.

There was a separate administrative center for each group of travessões. This contained a colonization office, the barracks in which newly arrived immigrants were housed, the dwellings of workers employed in the demarcation of parcels and the opening of roads, the leading church of the region, some commercial establishments, and workshops for the repair of farm tools. Although most of these buildings were frame, some were of substantial stone and brick, especially those occupied by officials such as the colony director, the agronomist, the physician, and the secretary-accountant. It was these administrative centers that were to become district and municipal capitals when the colonies became state administrative units. With the passing of time, they developed into the largest cities of the region.

European travelers who passed through the region during the first decades of development could not help but comment on how its settlement type differed so fundamentally from that of nucleated peasant villages in Mediterranean Europe. In the Old World the colonists had lived in villages or small cities, going out to their fields by day and returning by night. Their place of residence had constituted a natural center for religious ceremonies, entertainment, trade, receiving visitors, and paying taxes to the State and tribute to the landlord. In their new setting, their houses were dispersed throughout the countryside, albeit along straight and eventually good roads. Each travessão was, in many ways, an autonomous and integrated unit of fifty to sixty households. Occasionally other networks would develop around foot trails and by-paths. But, by and large, the travessão provided the basic design for the neighborhood, just as it had in the areas of German colonization.

Once this neighborhood structure began to solidify, the colonists came together to build small wooden chapels and cemeteries—both important symbols of corporate life as they had known it in Europe. Then came community meeting rooms, community kitchens, warehouses, and schools—all in close proximity to the chapels.

The chapel, then, very early assumed a variety of functions. It symbolized the corporateness of the newly assembled human group; it reminded them of their distant homeland; it served as a place of worship where the parish priest, also an Italian, would lead prayer, processions, funerals, christenings, and weddings. It also functioned as a recreational center with its adjoining *copa* (community kitchen). Colonists could gather there at night, on Sundays and on feast days to converse, to play cards, and to keep alive the Italian games of *mora* and *boccia*, all the while drinking wine that had begun to come from their very own vines. Undergirding these activities was, of course, the chapel society, controlled by the priest, and responsible for planning religious activities, overseeing morality, fostering cooperation, and awarding status in each micro-society delimited by a travessão.

Selecting the site, building and equipping the chapel, developing the cemetery, and establishing the school were all crucial activities through which leadership was winnowed, always, of course, with the priest serving as chief arbiter. Thus the chapel was, from the beginning, a political as well as a religious institution. It united and represented each rural neighborhood in a fashion similar to that described for German settlements in Rio Grande do Sul (Willems 1940, 1946), for the *tifas* in the German colonies of the neighboring Brazilian state of Santa Catarina (Aldersheim 1962; Seyferth 1974), and for the *rangs* of French Canada (Wagley and Harris 1958:173).

Life on the travessões followed a rhythm which was determined by the techno-economic structure of the colonization system. The region had two foci for consolidation: the administrative center, and the chapels. The administrative center drew people in on Sundays and saints' days, for market exchange, to shop for imported merchandise, to pay taxes, to prepare legal documents, to repair farm tools, and occasionally to meet distant relatives. The centers offered a variety of specialized skills. In 1884, for example, the Dante Center of Caxias Colony boasted of almost thirty different professions and services. A similar situation held for Dona Isabel Conde d'Eu, Alfredo Chaves, and Antonio Prado.

On the travessões, work in the first years of colonization was given over to the collection of wild fruits such as the native piñon nut, to the cultivation of annuals such as maize, beans, wheat, and potatoes, and to the raising of chickens and pigs, indispensable to the family's diet. By enlarging the clearing on which the pioneer house was built, the settlers obtained timber for improving their dwelling, firewood for their stove, and extractive materials such as honey and pyrethrum, a product sold regionally as an insecticide. Grape vines, started from cuttings brought by the migrants themselves from Italy, were cultivated first for domestic wine making, and then gradually for a cash market. Oxen and horses were introduced in small numbers for plowing and the transport of cargo, but neither natural environmental conditions nor the settlement pattern favored the development of intensive animal husbandry. Therefore, production in the region and in each establishment was diversified, with neither large, extensive cultivation nor monoculture. Each parcel was subdivided into portions with different uses, in an approximately uniform manner. As a result, the rhythm of activities was virtually identical for all the colonists. Crops were rotated, with well established cycles for both annuals and perennials.

As a dual system of family subsistence and cash cropping became established, an ideal type of individualized parcel, consisting of about twenty-five hectares, also became fixed, with the land functionally subdivided into specialized areas. Subsistence agriculture, with beans, potatoes, wheat, and vegetables, the care of which fell to women and children, occupied about three hectares. Grape vines occupied another two or three. Although periodically renewed by pruning, replanting, substituting old or unproductive cuttings, and protecting from pests by persistent spraying of insecticides and fungicides, the vines were a permanent crop. The *potreiro,* a small enclosed pasture for draft and saddle animals, covered some four hectares. The other fields were set aside for rotation. They were periodically allowed to rest for periods of approximately six years. This area of fallow, approximately sixteen hectares, or half the parcel, furnished wood for domestic necessities and timber for fences, house repairs, and plowing tools. Besides the mulberry tree, the leaves of which were gathered for silkworms, cultivation during the first years of the rotational cycle would include mate (Ilex paraguariensis), the leaves of which were either used by the household or sold in the regional market. Such a variety of production permitted the colonist to earn a satisfactory living without either selling his labor to others or engaging the salaried labor of non-relatives.

The family and its land thus constituted a single unit of production and the essence of the society. But for this complex to endure, limits had to be placed on inheritance rights. To this end, a single pattern was used by all colonies in southern Brazil, a pattern in total accord with that the Italian colonists had inherited from their own tradition. Each family's patrimony was inalienable from its lineage. Ideally it was to persist undivided generation after generation. The heir was preferably a male, although exceptionally a wife, widow, or single woman could also inherit. Usually only one of the sons would remain with the land. If several laid claim to it, it would be held in common. The rest of the offspring would leave, though they would usually be compensated in various ways. The general rule was for the heir to be the youngest capable son or sons. Transfer of rights could occur either during the lifetime of the family head, at a point when he considered himself incapable of continuing, or immediately after his death. As is the case with all rural stem family structures, the purpose of this one was to retain the homestead as an intact and viable economic unit.

Although this arrangement was in full accord with the traditions of the Austrian and Italian Tyrol, and was widespread throughout southern Brazil because it was shared by the German colonists, it was in direct conflict with the Brazilian legal code. Over time it tended to weaken through acculturation. When fully implemented, it could be so only through considerable subterfuge (Azevedo 1975:267).

Summer was the season of greatest activity, especially the period from October through December. But activities were by no means limited to those months. Grapes were harvested from February to March; corn was picked from May to June; wheat was sown in June and July; and potatoes were planted in August and September. The seasons commanded respect. April usually brought one or two frosts; May, an Indian summer. From June to August frosts would reappear, and everything could be covered with ice. Out of season hailstorms and frosts could occur even in the spring period of September to December, and crop damage could be serious.

The most intense activity was that related to grape production and wine making. The vines were pruned from May to August. When the leaves appeared in the early spring, a fungicide (Bordeaux mixture) would be applied and then reapplied every fifteen days. At harvest either the grapes themselves or the juice would be carried to the press, located also alongside the chapel. There the winemaking would begin, with fermentation taking place in large casks, and completion of the process occurring in specialized plants owned by local cooperatives.

During the relative quiet following the grape harvest, the potreiro was cleaned, the vineyard was fertilized with animal manure, and new grafts were set into the vines. Residents moved constantly back and forth, visiting the provincial capital, going up neighboring travessões and linhas, and even traveling to other provinces.

Social and religious activities fit into the interstices of this economic cycle. Weddings peaked two or three times a year, reflecting the availability of adequate financing and the strict canonical prescriptions and proscriptions of the Church. Many marriages occurred in January and February, for the Church forbade the solemnization of unions during Advent and, during the first two months of the year, all crops, including grapes, were maturing but not yet ready to harvest. Lent, during which there was also a proscription against weddings, coincided with an upswing in the agricultural cycle. The vines had to be weeded, the harvest begun, and new wine had to be prepared.

In May, the month of "Indian Summer," the procession and the feast of Our Lady of Caraveggio were held. These attracted tens of thousands of pilgrims from all over the "Italian" region. October was the occasion for celebrating our Lady of the Rosary and for solemnizing another wave of weddings. Most marriages took place, however, in autumn and winter, especially June and July, a period of lowered activity and of abundance from the recently completed harvest.

Weddings were events of intense social interaction, bringing together the relatives and friends of the betrothed both for the religious ceremony in the chapel and for the accompanying banquet and dance either in the bride's parents' home or in the copa. Similar gatherings occurred in relation to christenings, the ordination of a priest, the taking of religious vows by a nun, or funerals. The society was dominated by a sacred concept of the cosmos, a concept that was intimately related to the agricultural cycle. Crops were annually blessed by the priest and he, in turn, was sustained by a portion of the harvest. First fruits were carried to the church either on St. Anton's day (the patron saint of animals), or on one of the Rogation days (i.e., Monday, Tuesday, or Wednesday of Ascension week). The strongest association within each neighborhood was the Society of the Chapel, a kind of brotherhood charged with the organization of worship and care of the unfortunate. Typically the constitutions of these groups specified that in case of serious misfortune the entire neighborhood would help the stricken household by clearing their fields, planting, harvesting, reconstructing their house, or supplying whatever else might be needed. The societies were also charged with deterring blasphemy and intoxication and seeing that everyone in the neighborhood act in a "dignified and Christian" manner during both religious feasts and secular parties. Improper conduct within the neighborhood could, as everyone knew, lead to the priest's refusal to appear when needed. There were times, of course, when the priest simply could not be present. To cover those, the societies had trained laymen.

In spite of their rather chaotic beginnings, the early neighborhoods became, then, communities in the fullest sense. A century or more has now passed since they were established. In that time much disruption has occurred because of industrialization, urbanization, and the simple loss of authority as residents discovered that the religiosity of their Brazilian neighbors of Portuguese origin was much less puritanical and ascetic. But the basic pattern is still discernible. It is a pattern that symbolizes the culture of the "Italian" Brazilian, a pattern as different from that of the *caboclo* as it is from that of the majority of other Brazilians.

# FIVE

# The Negro in Brazilian Society: Twenty-Five Years Later

## Florestan Fernandes

BRANCOS E NEGROS em São Paulo (Whites and Blacks in São Paulo), a book on race relations published in 1951, was the result of an attempt by Roger Bastide and myself to reach an intellectual consensus on some problematic aspects of the Brazilian racial situation. Writing the book forced us to combine our theoretical and empirical techniques, methods of observation, reconstruction and interpretation of the reality we were exploring. Eventually we developed a common working base which we used during the stages of data collection and analysis, as well as during the more complex task of describing and explaining the processes of racial interaction in the city of São Paulo.

In spite of severe resource limitations, the study was an obvious success. It emerged as the first important attempt at assessing race relations in Brazil by working cooperatively[1] and by utilizing systematic, empirical research as a technique for raising "social consciousness." Race relations are one of the historical dilemmas of Brazilian society. Our effort gave rise to other important studies[2] and received ample confirmation from some that were being completed simultaneously. It was based on direct contact with research subjects, many

This article has been translated from the Portuguese and edited by Susan Poats, Maxine Margolis, and William E. Carter.

of whom were blacks and mulattos whose sentiments, attitudes, and behavioral orientations were not well known.

In order to avoid making errors due to an ignorance of the past, we looked at the Negro and mulatto in the full evolutionary context of São Paulo's economy and society from 1640 to the present. The city of São Paulo has always had certain peculiarities. During the colonial period, the city was, for a long time, what today is referred to as an "underdeveloped region," and it remained that way until the coffee boom of the nineteenth century. The fact that São Paulo became the leading urban-commercial and industrial center of Brazil at the same time that it emerged as the major center for foreign immigrants were other factors unique to the city. For these and other reasons, what happened in São Paulo's concentration, growth, and acceleration of the bourgeois revolution often served as a model for other Brazilian cities, especially those along the Rio de Janeiro-São Paulo corridor. In other words, São Paulo experienced a historic process that later diffused throughout Brazil.

We were interested in determining whether this historical diffusion included survivals of the slave period or if the new social, economic, and political structures destroyed the "old regime" in the sphere of race relations. We knew that the Negroes themselves had tried to take command of this process through protest movements and criticism of racial inequities, especially in the 1930s and 1940s.

To adequately study such a process we had to develop careful tools of analysis. We had to explore the anti-racial ideology which was part of the black ethos. The tools we ended up using included interviews, life histories, and the study of written documents, principally Negro newspapers. We suspected that most of what we would describe would hold true for other Brazilian localities. Yet limitations in funds and personnel kept us from doing more than mailing comparative questionaires to a few such selected places. This limitation prevented us from making bold generalizations in spite of the fact that the questionaires which were returned gave us confidence in the general validity of our data. Thus, we hypothesized that, although our study was concerned only with São Paulo, its results were valid for many other regions of Brazil, especially those undergoing a transformation from agrarian slave to urban-industrial economies based on monopolistic capitalism.

We hesitated to use the plethora of descriptive color categories characteristic of Brazilian Portuguese. We preferred rather, simply to use the terms *white, Negro,* and *mulatto,* each with quotation marks to indicate the presence of terminological fluctuations that could not be controlled by the researchers. At the time, only the Negro milieu was explored holistically. We made no attempt to discover what specific role the mulatto would take vis à vis the white and the Negro.

In spite of our intentions, we received criticism, especially from Negro activists who viscerally opposed all distinctions based on degrees of negroid admixture. They equally rejected expressions such as *elemento de côr* (color factor), *pessoa de côr* (person of color), and words like *black, mulatto, dark mulatto, light mulatto,* etc. For them, all people who were not phenotypically white were Negroes; the term *Negro* was looked upon as a symbol of psychological and racial identity.

This inclination seems to have become even stronger in recent years. Negroes and mulattos who are not "racially conscious" have abandoned the old typologies, asserting that they reflect perceptual categories constructed by whites in the past.

Now, twenty-five years after the study, our purpose and accomplishments can be seen in clearer perspective. The recent economic, social, and cultural transformations of the city of São Paulo have radically affected the picture we had observed and attempted to describe. Racial inequality remains an unquestionable fact. Nor could it have been otherwise. Throughout Brazilian history, the failure of the Negro protest movement has derived from the absence of Negroes in the battle for their identity. Had Negro protest movements persisted, history would have been different. There would have been a real movement toward racial democracy; in all probability, pressures on racial inequality would have come from diverse quarters.

In light of this background there are three points which the following discussion will explore: the critical utilization of the original research results by both white and black activitists; why the recent transformations of Brazilian society have not engendered any basic alteration of existing racial inequities; and those aspects of the 1950s race situation in which recent significant changes have taken place.

## The Maturation of the Critical Conscience

Since its inception, sociology has been perceived as a "technician of social conscience," oriented toward a critical description and explanation of the present, as seen within its historical and processual context. This role was obliterated in countries where institutional professionalism disassociated sociological research from important social questions, while isolating sociologists from radical or non-conformist social movements. Such has not been the case in Brazil in spite of the often repressive control over scientific research and anti-democratic behavior on the part of the economic, cultural, and political elites. Intellectual Brazilians who are activists continue to serve as a forum for the great issues of the day and the important historical changes in progress. Over the years, in discussions and through the written word, they have spread a number of nonconformist and radical ideas. Institutional repression itself has helped maintain this role. When social groups or classes lack a means of explaining to themselves the causes of their plight, they often turn to "intellectual critics," and more specifically, to "militant sociologists" in their search for an informative, articulate vision which, in recent history, has tended to derive either from bourgeois radicalism, the counter-culture, or revolutionary socialism.

This is what has happened, to some degree, with regard to our 1951 study of race, despite its censure by conservatives and armchair intellectuals. Although there has never been a truly efficient and practical utilization of the study, it has had an unexpected impact, even among the illiterate sectors of the Negro population. First, in the absence of institutionalized racism, the study has been received very favorably by Negro radicals and activists, who perceive it as an extension of their own efforts, begun in the 1930s and 1940s, to unmask racism. Second, the study has been accepted and incorporated by non-conforming, democratic whites. But, with both Negroes and whites, it has been the openly radical sectors that have most warmly embraced the empirical and theoretical findings of the research. This may be because the acceptance of such findings requires a prior rupture with dominant conservative and traditional ideas, at least in the sphere of racial ideology. Thus the Negro milieu has linked the findings with "revealed or proven truths," whereas conservative whites frequently have been much more moderate and restricted in their appraisal. For example, one conservative white has gone so far as to say that, rather than solving anything, the study has actually introduced the racial problem into Brazil! If the study has done nothing else then, it has unmasked the myth of racial democracy in the country.

The study not only "confirmed" the diagnosis of the Brazilian racial situation; it affirmed the historical dignity of the Negro social movement of the 1930s and 1940s in São Paulo, the only truly populist one in the recent past. This Negro protest failed due to intrinsic weaknesses and because of its lack of impact in a world dominated by whites. But its intellectual and political inheritance (ignored until the 1951 study), became defined and well known. The study deeply penetrated the ambivalence and weakness of Negro protest, as well as racial misery in a society that pretends to be democratic while maintaining racial structures inherited from the colonial and slaveholding past.

Negro protest was condemned to die at the frontiers of the black community, since it could not weaken existing patterns of racial domination and inequality which remained institutionalized in the republican order. The racial structures of Brazilian society will be threatened and destroyed only when the "mass of *homens de côr*" (men of color), i.e., the entire Negro population, can institutionalize conflict under equal conditions with whites without any type of discrimination. This implies equal racial participation in the power structures of the national political community.

It is obvious that the maturation of a critical consciousness in the Negro milieu could not be unilateral progress in one dominant direction. The same motives which explain the relative failure of the protest movements also explain the destruction of critical reaction today. However, they do not explain the continuing differences in socioeconomic, cultural, and political levels between Negroes and whites. The Brazilian pattern of racial domination has engendered unrelenting apathy within the Negro milieu. It is an apathy that cannot be overcome without the elimination of this pattern. As long as Negroes do not relinquish their deceptive visions of racial reality, and refuse to push whites into the center of the inevitable conflict between "race" and "class," they will continue to be the victims of moral confusion, incapable of collectively fighting for positions within the power structure. The protest movements of the 1930s and 1940s support this conclusion: unless the established order is overturned, and unless this break with the status quo reaches down to the foundations of Brazil's racial and social structure, Negroes will end up favoring, in one way or another, the dominant race's ideologies and forms of hegemony.

Because of these "implicit" ideologies it seems equally unrealistic to expect the unmasking and overcoming of Brazil's existing racial situation to come from whites, be they "non-conformists," "radicals," or "revolutionaries." Their class non-conformism, radicalism, or revolutionism can only partially and incompletely counter their heavy historical heritage.

Changes in attitudes that can be seen today among Negroes and whites alike have little to do with the original impact of the 1951 study. Rather, they have been brought about by changes in lifestyles and mentalities springing out of massive industrialization and urbanization. Yet the study has had its place. One can no longer think about a "fight against color prejudice and discrimination" without considering sociological contributions and procuring collaboration with sociologists.

## Innocuous Non-Conformity

At the time we carried out the 1951 study, we were barely familiar with Negro protest, its racial counter-ideology and the ideas which oriented the frustrated struggles of the "Second Abolition." Today, the focus of Negro consciousness is the reverse: innocuous non-conformity. Adhering to this consciousness are a variety of Negroes. Some may be categorized as "traditional" in that they come to terms with white expectations through passive adjustment. Others are often designated by Negroes themselves as "deserters" because they flee the racial problem and consciously or unconsciously suffocate their pride. Still others may be characterized as "new Negroes" because they are disposed to compete and even accept personal conflict with whites in order to "climb socially." Finally, there are those whom whites conceive as "racist Negroes," who want to replace the asymmetrical pattern of racial domination and its corresponding racial ideology and astigmatization with the "black is beautiful" concept. All Negroes, wherever they fall within this typology, exhibit some degree of non-conformity when interacting with whites. This non-conformity operates in various and often contradictory directions.

The crux of the problem is that Brazilian society will not accept these various types of non-conformity, and allow them to be transformed into systematic radicalism. Negro non-conformity must remain suffocated within its own milieu. Brazilian society continues to inhibit these natural impulses; the freedom to use tension and conflict continues to be a privilege of the dominant social strata of the "dominant race."

Despite the many transformations that have occured in Brazilian society, in the racial sphere there is little difference between the present, the recent past, and the remote past. Slavery disappeared but was substituted by strict despotism, which converted class dominance into caste domination. For things to have been otherwise, the bourgeois revolution would have had to have been open to popular, democratic, and national pressures,[3] and, at the same time, the Negro would have had to have established the legitimacy of racial protest—for conservatives the most dangerous type of protest aside from labor conflict. Neither of these happened.

All this means that Negro non-conformity can be a psychological, cultural, and moral reality, but it cannot be transformed into an active social force or a political reality. In a class society that preserves an elitist pattern through mental domination, racial conflict can rarely erupt. In the past, such conflict was expunged legally and was strongly suppressed. At present, it is deliberately confused with class conflict or "communist subversion of the social order," and is solved through the use of police tactics. Only whites can manipulate this kind of tension and, when they do, they represent dominant class interests, and are scarcely concerned with bringing democratic economic, social, and political structures to the lowest echelons of society. When whites monopolize decisions concerning which changes should be implemented, they also select and monopolize which tensions are to be increased.[4] These tensions do not make for a democratic revolution of the established order. Rather, through the consolidation and perpetuation of the present structure, a social order benefiting the elite continues, with merely sops for the working classes and the masses in general.

If the racial question, then, is not a matter of policy, this is because Negroes themselves cannot promote, either materially or politically, serious consideration of the issue. The social structure is capable of repressing any racial pressure which threatens to return democracy to the social order and, implicitly, to the racial order within it. Abolition did not increase the economic, social, cultural, or political participation of the "Negro element." It was a revolution of white against white. It did not touch the asymmetrical patterns of race relations and racial inequality, whether institutionalized or not (see Bastide and Fernandes 1971, and Fernandes 1965). The only attempt by Negroes to alter this situation has been the protest movements of the 1930s and 1940s, and they failed. Thus, the existing social order is not democratic for everyone. It is not at all democratic for the Negro people in general, who are lost within the innermost recesses of the poorest and most marginal populations of the country.

The processes involved in the formation of a "modern Brazil" have changed during the past thirty years. "Developmentalism" has been widespread, but completely conditioned and directed from outside, and this despite sufficient internal potential to develop and direct a capitalist economy with a vast internal market and abundant raw materials and export products. As this new Brazil developed, three major power groups have emerged: the nationalistic bourgeois classes, the international business community, and the Brazilian state. The bourgeois elites, through state pressure, have been forced to adopt autocratic and ultra-conservative forms of economic, sociocultural, and political domination. The movement which generated an open democratic bourgeoisie in certain European countries and in the United States has produced a closed autocratic one in Brazil.

The historic despotism inherent in traditional bourgeois domination has given way to a type of capitalistic accumulation which, in turn, has generated an elitism equipped with all the resources of modernization, including a strong concentration of state political power. Both the old and new elites have found their place within successive phases of the urban and industrial transformation of Brazilian society. The dominant classes have been able to block popular pressures and maintain their concentration of wealth, social prestige, and political power. Since, at the same time, the working masses have experienced a constant increase in numbers, with internal migrations continually increasing their urban segment, wealth and power have remained concentrated among the top 1 to 10 percent of the Brazilian population, i.e., those with the highest income levels and the best potential for institutional participation.

One ameliorating factor has been the fact that those in the next 20 percent bracket, for the most part, have received relatively satisfactory compensation. However, an unfortunate spinoff of this situation is that populism has become diluted. (see Ianni 1968, and Cardoso 1972). No segment of the bourgeoisie has been able to serve as a liaison between the privileged classes and the common people. Of equal importance is the fact that, in order to defend themselves and, at the same time, accrue greater status, the bourgeoisie have needed support from the armed forces and from the nation's technocrats. Thus, even they have been forced to utilize the apparatus of the state to repress the established legal code and restrict civil rights.

In such an atmosphere, even the liberties of the elites and the dominant classes have suffered a drastic curtailment. The masses, containing the majority of the Negro and mulatto populations, have been reduced to silence and inactivity. They have been politically neutralized even though they participate marginally in socioeconomic development and ritually in the "political process."

The significance of these changes must be examined with care. The height of the capitalist revolution has corresponded with the massive marginalization of the bulk of the population, and with their conversion into a silent majority. The so-called bargaining power of the popular masses and the working classes has been reduced to zero. The precarious interchange with the plebian class has disappeared and with it has gone the already reduced political sphere which articulated the "dialogue" between the masses and the conservative despotism of the dominant classes (see Fernandes 1975b, especially chs. 5 and 7).

The Negro's "critical consciousness" emerged, therefore, during a historical vacuum. Contrary to expectations, the protest movements of the 1930s and 1940s—silenced by Vargas' *Estado Novo* (New State)—closed, rather than opened, a historical cycle. They constituted the last gasps in the battle against the vestiges of the "old regime," a regime that had been so injurious to the Negro and to the destitute population in general. As long as the present despotic regime, installed by the bourgeois autocracy, lasts, protest movements will be impossible. As much as the current situation favors the "new Negro" personality type, present political conditions do not favor the simultaneous development of a "Negro bourgeoisie" or a "Negro capitalism", along United States and South African lines.[5]

Brazil's famed "tolerance," found in conjunction with a strong system of racial inequality, has severely restricted the Negro's range of opportunities and regulated his/her upward social and economic mobility. In turning their backs against the interests and values of the dominant social strata and its elites, Negroes have substituted a precocious and deformed elitism which has irremediably isolated the Negro masses and their problems from those of the larger society. The "new Negroes" are trapped with personal, familial, and social success within a closed and elitist world. They are not disposed to overturn the established order, since they run the risk of being stymied in their move up the social ladder.

Open and radical non-conformity is "institutionally" banished from the legal order. "Racist Negroes" see themselves, therefore, condemned to impotence. Like the "traditional Negroes" and the "deserter Negroes," they are compelled to swallow their pride. Racial frustration does not utilize social, institutional or spontaneous channels to reach the surface. Instead, this frustration is repressed inside people and stored within the Negro milieu. Whether or not it will be usable in the future is a question for historical research. For the present, at least, these suppressed and stored racial frustrations are not being converted into productive psychodynamic or sociodynamic forces. They either destroy themselves, or they destroy the personality of the Negro and the equilibrium of the Negro milieu.

Until now, neither accelerated social change nor the bourgeois revolution have helped Brazil break pre-existing patterns of racial inequality or overcome the country's class structure. It is possible that the continued expansion of capitalism will bring with it new means of undermining racial inequality. But, for the present, what has happened during the past thirty years stands as evidence to the contrary, i.e., that archaic patterns and structures are being incorporated into a class society which is in the process of expansion.

Let us return, once more, to the central argument. The simple raising of a "critical consciousness" among Negroes has led nowhere. Rather, it has brought a new form of frustration that has been more corrosive and pernicious than its predecessors. All this convinces the Negro that "enlightenment" and a "new mentality" are useful only on a personal and individual level. Such a conviction leads Negroes away from action.

Changes in the current race-class structure of Brazilian society must be prior to the Negro's translation of a "critical consciousness" into political action. It is only through such changes that Negroes will turn against the residues of the past as expressed in ritual tolerance, asymmetrical patterns of race relations, and their corresponding racial ideology. The Negro must try to construct the bases for realistic new forms of progressive equality between the races. Only in this way can a new pattern of egalitarian race relations and a new order of "race" and "class," with a democratic base, be constructed and perpetuated.

If Negro non-conformity can be thus converted into a constructive social force and incorporated into the web of social structures and institutions, such a social force will produce profound changes in the racial foundations of Brazilian society. Should this occur, even within the framework of capitalism, Negro non-conformity will bring decolonization to the point that should have been reached when slave labor was suppressed and free labor was implemented.

One can concede that such reflections are optimistic; societies seldom are aware of the evolutionary changes that lie ahead. It is very well known that capitalism liberates certain revolutionary forces but represses others. In this case, since the Negro masses are valuable as workers, it is not very probable that class society in Brazil, under a dependent and underdeveloped capitalism, will be able to achieve what capitalism did not achieve even in the United States.

One possibility is that Brazil will maintain the parallels of "race" and "class" as they are found in contemporary society and in the castes under colonial and imperial rule. If this occurs, any pattern of egalitarian race relations and re-ordering of "race" and "class" on a democratic basis simply will not be viable. A greater number of Negroes will be integrated into the higher levels of the existing classes. But this will not break with the racial contradictions inherited from the past and incorporated into the present class regime. It will permit the Negro world to be organized in patterns symmetrical with those of the white world, and, eventually, it will allow for greater communication between different racial groups of the same social level.

An alternative possibility could be one in which the "new Negro" will flourish within dependent and underdeveloped capitalism. A Negro minority would stand out from the Negro masses and would occupy various class positions within the existing social order. If this were to occur, the "poor Negroes" would continue to be left to their own destiny, isolated from the Negro elites and ignored by the rest of society.

Although massive industrialization and the urban explosion are opening more opportunities, it will be difficult for economic and cultural conditions to improve sufficiently to overcome the profound political problems of the Negro masses. In all probability, an upward movement of some sectors of the Negro population will merely lead to new levels of expectation and resentment. Although violence can and will be avoided, nothing can impede the fermentation of racial tensions among the Negro masses that are being ignored today.

## Visible Transformations in São Paulo

The contemporary situation is not as bleak for the Negro as it was during São Paulo's initial economic boom at the end of the nineteenth century and during the crisis of 1929. At those times, the Negro population lived within the city without belonging to it. It was a period of extreme cultural and economic isolation and marginalization. Opportunities went to whites, especially to immigrant families. Progress did not exist for the Negro, who was submerged in the most extreme pauperism. It was a dramatic and bitter time that resurrected the image of the "caged Negro."

In the last twenty-five years, massive industrialization and metropolitan growth have convulsed the national scene. Rivers of internal migration have flowed into the cities and from them have come contingents of both skilled and unskilled laborers. The poorer and dependent sectors of the city have benefited from the economic upswing. Negroes, both migrants and those of local origin, have found a means of social identity through their work, however humble or poorly remunerated it may be. The lack of work or the impermanence of work has become a thing of the past. With a job, the Negro has more easily been able to attain the material base for institutional participation from which he formerly was almost completely excluded.

A large contingent of mixed racial origins has been part of the internal migration to the city. This has increased the mulatto sector of the population and stimulated the search for new racial stereotypes. The term *baiano* (person from the state of Bahia) has tended to be substituted for the term *Negro* in negative stereotypes.

Urban slums, poverty, prostitution, menial labor, and vagrancy have long given the Negro unfavorable visibility. With rapid urban growth, however, this visibility has been diluted as slums have dispersed and have come to be concentrated at the periphery of the city. At the same time, many slums have taken on sizeable contingents of poor whites. There has even been considerable occupational mobility, and occasional upward social movement by Negroes. As a result, the Negro is no longer automatically associated, as was the case in the recent past, with negative stereotypes. Racial stereotypes have not totally disappeared and they still produce devastating effects on the aspirations of the Negro. But they no longer automatically serve to exclude him from certain positions in the labor force.

Many Negroes remain in a marginal condition: young people without work or prospects, unwed mothers, abandoned children, broken families. Yet the total picture is less gloomy than it was in the past. Where jobs, new occupations, and professional mobility incorporate the Negro into the working class or into some sectors of the middle class, there has been some improvement. The past has not been forgotten entirely. It is revived in certain parts of the city, in the islands of social desperation embedded in the shantytowns (*favelas*) or new types of slums (*cortiços*) at the outskirts of the city. But the "successful Negro" appears with greater frequency in social affairs. He may be driving his car, living in his own house in a respectable neighborhood, or showing off his prosperity with an impeccable suit or a high standard of living—a tradition that has not disappeared from the Negro milieu and reveals a strong need for status compensation.

We now have, therefore, two types of visibility: the "bad," which arouses in whites negative memories and stereotypes, and the "good," which obliges whites to reconsider their old attitudes and convinces Negroes that their "luck is changing." Even though it is still too soon to draw conclusions with respect to this dual social visibility, it is evident that it is helping to draw the Negro out of limbo, out of the ignominy of infamous white stereotyping and out of the harm which results from being a scapegoat. Economic, educational, intellectual, and political opportunities are still too few to break the traditional barriers of racial inequality or to make the whites swallow their pride. Still, the Negro is no longer a spectator on the fringes of life and history.

Even if the "good image" does not yet predominate, the "bad image" is losing the demoralizing character that it had for so long. Negroes and their problems are not simply disappearing from society; this would be a gross simplification. Where slums and shantytowns exist—large or small—on the borders of rich neighborhoods, the negative image increases. But what often escapes outsiders is that the Negroes and mulattos living under these sub-standard conditions are not necessarily living a life of misery, family disorganization, systematic unemployment, etc. A new type of slum (cortiço) has emerged particularly in peripheral neighborhoods of the city. It is internally self-policed and, even though extremely impoverished, demands a minimum of institutional participation. This means that, in spite of poverty, there is "some hope." Social solidarity exists, and education for children is both attainable and encouraged. The influx of migrants from rural areas seems to be the principal factor contributing to this change. It has reduced or eliminated the "irresponsibility of the Negro"; and it is strongly reinforced by the opportunities for regular work and occupational stability. Cuisine, music, patterns of self-help—both from family and neighbors—lend an exotic or "northeastern flavor" to the emerging lifestyle of the poor in São Paulo. The Negro has submerged himself in this lifestyle, and it has helped him to achieve a modest launching pad.

All this indicates that it would be worthwhile to undertake a new study on the subject. Little is known about what is happening in the various areas of Greater São Paulo with relations between Negroes and whites and changes in the old patterns of racial accomodation and integration. It is clear that, for the majority of the Negro population, proletarianization and occupational stability—or at least job opportunities—have completely altered their material base. On the other hand, it seems doubtful that these changes have broken down class barriers.

Internal migrations have brought to São Paulo Negroes with the ability to compete professionally with whites of the same social level, in the scramble for good jobs that pay well. Traditionally, the educational system of São Paulo has not favored Negroes of local origin. Here too, the migrants have opened up a new path by seeking "a better education" for their children, and exposing their neighbors to these aspirations and their corresponding social values. All of this means that new patterns of competition for jobs, education, housing, higher standards of living, etc. are being consolidated. As a result, Negroes are making themselves more visible as students, from elementary through university levels, without the intervention of white patrons.

One process of vertical social mobility noted in our 1950 study—individual infiltration and competition—has become more prominent among the Negro population. With the dissolution of the Negro protest movement and the loss of hope for collective Negro ascent, this has become, in fact, the dominant form of social mobility. Attitudes that we noted in the past now appear in a new historical context. Then, as now, the "Negro who wants to climb" repudiates open racial protest and seeks individualistic and egotistic solutions to his problems. He often prefers cooperation with whites to a not always efficient or effective solidarity with his own family. This is not to imply that he is neutral with regard to prejudice and discrimination; he condemns forms of racism which can block his ascent, but he becomes convinced that the correct path for combatting prejudice is gradual and indirect. For this reason, he repels the collective process. As does the conservative white man, he values education, professional competence, character, work, the accumulation of wealth, and family, often taking an exaggeratedly elitist stance vis-à-vis these traits.

This makes for two tendencies in the Negro today. First, he absorbs an elitism mostly from whites who are of the old circles dominated by traditional families. He, therefore, does not value the elitism of the "nouveau riche," but rather an "aristocratic elitism." Second, as an immigrant, he accepts any occupation as an initial apprenticeship, something which is necessary even though undesirable. He seeks the utopias of the old immigrants without access to the material and institutional resources they enjoyed. With the limited resources available to recent immigrants, real economic opportunities are few and difficult of access. Even so, motivation is high, and it is this that makes for institutional participation among Negroes and keeps at least some of them from exclusion and marginalization.

Insecurity is another adverse factor. It leads to a destructive attitude of self-preservation and to social isolation, in the family as well as in the Negro milieu. This isolation is not as great as it was in the past, since the family is more stable, more socially stratified, and embraces a greater number of people. But such stability is accessible only to those Negroes who have moved into the middle and upper classes. Where this sort of isolation occurs it, too, restricts the social universe of the Negro. Racial solidarity becomes impossible and must be substituted by a unity among cliques within the same elitist stratum.

Thus, through this developmental process, the Negro population becomes divided between those "elites" who have been successful and the masses who have not. Successful Negroes set up a type of patron-client relationship within the Negro milieu, in which the non-elites are viewed as a labor force incapable of bringing about the "redemption of the Negro race" or collective protest. This Negro clientism merits further study. It has placed the Negro elites in the same position as the old immigrant elites with their preoccupation with giving social assistance to their fellow countrymen. However, the assistance being offered is nothing compared with the precariousness of the Negro's situation and the terrible exigencies of his racial inequality. It has served more to increase the social value of the "middle and upper classes of color" than to ease the extreme needs of the Negro masses. Thus, Negro elites have launched into the realm of social welfare for social reasons. They know, as did immigrants of the past, the value that traditional families place on such behavior. The only result which benefits the Negro in general is "good visibility." By means of newspapers, television, and radio, the affluent Negro makes free use of a new economic, social, and cultural situation—that of taking care of the "disadvantaged people" of his community.

This effect should not be slighted. Rather than forcing collective racial equality that Brazilian society will not permit, the "new Negroes" try indirectly to revolutionize the cultural horizon of the white. Unlike the North American Negroes of the 1930s, they do not use economic, cultural or political pressure, or psychological coercion. They use subtle, sometimes malicious ways, like maintaining a "high" and "aristocratic" standard of living, being of "unsurpassable competence" and "faultless character," and leading an "organized and responsible" lifestyle. Since Negroes have neither the liberty nor the material base to use conflict, they must be content with "re-educating whites" in their moral appraisal of the Negro. In doing so, they achieve some success in disassociating the Negro image from stereotyped and stigmatized "black failures." The "new Negroes" proceed as if they desire equality purely on a personal level and as if they want to convince whites that "there are Negroes and there are Negroes," just as "there are whites and there are whites." Through their own behavior they try to show that there is no reason to evaluate the Negro by means of a false, stereotyped and unreal image. This tactic glosses over prejudice and systematic discrimination. But Negroes have not created the game, much less its rules.

With ambiguity and reluctance, whites may someday repeat a historical learning process they already confronted with regard to Portuguese, Italians, Lebanese, and other immigrant groups. The stereotypes and stigmas have lessened as these groups have increased in size. But, in the case of the Negro, this kind of acceptance is not yet a reality. As in the past, "Negroes with white souls" continue to serve as the basis for simplistic manipulations since the "protection" of some whites was always used to explain such "miracles." Through this mechanism sweeping generalizations about the Negro are maintained. Where the notion that the "exception proves the rule" continues, the Negro is placed on a dead end street in which social re-evaluation is impossible. As the middle and upper sectors of the Negro population increase, an erosion of the mechanism may occur, but this is not inevitable.

Such potential changes say nothing about the intellectual and moral liberation of Negro youth. The conflicts between egalitarian aspirations and the Brazilian pattern of racial prejudice and discrimination cause these individuals devastating harm. These conflicts lead to what can be termed self-defensive cynicism. Little by little, young people are forced to accept two truths: one which affirms and one which negates racial democracy. This leads to sharp and painful tensions, and an ambivalence of attitudes and alienation, through which evasion becomes a form of psychological and moral self-protection. If a new style of collective racial protest had prevailed instead of elitism and individual social mobility, it is probable that the young Negro would have found means of self-realization that were less tortuous and ambiguous. The propensities towards self pity, sublimation of fantasies, hopelessness, and escapism would have been substituted by more positive approaches.

In a class society, Brazilian Negroes need to initiate a more realistic search for self-affirmation, and leave their "merry-go-round of illusions" that so prematurely destroys their young talent, especially in the middle and upper classes. As things now stand, the affluent young Negro, the individual who should be the strongest link in the rise of a "militant non-conformity" and in the chain of democratic revolution, is neutralizing and converting himself into a contemporary equivalent of the Bohemian of the 1920s and 1930s, but without the same historical justifications. Veterans of the collective protest movements criticize these young people, saying they do not realize that they are alienated and poisoned.

If the same social criticism applied by Negroes to whites in the 1930s and 1940s were applied to these young people, it would become clear how they too have been "victims" of the Brazilian racial situation. Would it not be advisable that they attempt to establish such a bridge between the generations? Perhaps then, and only then, collective racial protest could be recycled and set to sail once again amidst the new economic, social and cultural conditions of the country. Perhaps, in that manner, Brazilian society could become, in truth, both multi-racial and democratic.

**Notes**

1. See the list of principal collaborators in Bastide and Fernandes, 1971, pp. 16–17. The global investigation, of which the study of race relations in São Paulo was merely a part, included a sociological study of race relations in the municipality of Itapetinga in São Paulo state by Dr. Oracy Nogueira, and two psychological analyses by Drs. Virginia Leone Bicudo and Ahiela Meyer Ginsberg (see Bastide and Fernandes 1955).

2. The principal group of contributors includes Bastide and Fernandes, 1971; Fernandes 1965 and 1972; Bastide 1960 and 1970; Azevedo 1953; Costa Pinto 1953; Ribeiro 1956; and Wagley, ed. 1952.

3. For a sociological characterization of the bourgeois revolution in Brazil see Fernandes 1975b, especially chs. 5, 6, and 7.

4. Concerning the conservative political control of social change see Fernandes 1963, 1974, 1975a, and 1975b.

5. A Negro bourgeoisie as described, for example, in Frazier 1957 and Kuper 1965.

# ═══════════════════PART II═══

# Environmental Adaptations

THE DIVERSITY OF the Brazilian landscape has long fascinated observers of the national scene. Early travelers supplied lengthy descriptions of Brazil's exotic flora and fauna (see, for example, Bates orig. 1864), and debated the merits of the country's luxuriant rain forests. Portions of Brazilian territory were variously depicted as "green hells," unfit for "civilized society" (Huntington 1924), or as abundant bread baskets that, if properly developed, could easily meet the nation's, if not the entire world's, nutritional needs (Wallace 1899). In recent years these simplistic generalizations have been supplanted by detailed studies of the nation's natural landscape and the cultural adaptations to which it has given rise.

Yet the debate goes on concerning Brazil's development potential, and it centers around its tropical regions, specifically the Amazon Basin, which constitutes some 43 percent of the country's land area but contains only 5 percent of the nation's population. The major point of contention is whether tropical environments can support highly productive agricultural regimes, and thus sustain denser human populations. Betty Meggers (1974) takes a rather pessimistic view, arguing that contemporary policy makers have failed to recognize the "delicate ecological balance that exists in Amazonia" and are courting danger when exploitative agricultural techniques appropriate to temperate environments are applied to the region. Other anthropologists interested in the recent attempts to develop and populate this vast region have expressed similar concerns.

Since a significant portion of Brazil's surviving aboriginal cultures are concentrated in the humid tropics, anthropologists focusing on these populations also have had to deal with the problem of the

**115**

Amazon Basin's carrying capacity, and, by extension, its potential for cultural evolutionary development. Many have sought to delineate the environmental factors affecting aboriginal subsistence regimes and the size and density of their human population aggregates (see, for example, Meggers 1954, 1971; Carneiro 1960, 1961; Gross 1975).

It has been suggested that a number of Amazonian cultural practices have the effect of maintaining small, dispersed settlements and limiting the overall growth of the human population. The fissioning of villages, the lack of strong political leadership, witchcraft accusations, and postpartum sexual taboos are some of the cultural mechanisms which appear to keep the human population in balance with its food resources. There has also been much recent debate as to whether warfare among tropical forest populations serves a similar demographic function. Here the central question has been: Do raiding and armed conflict have latent ecological functions which prevent the Amazon's population from growing beyond the region's natural resources?

Marvin Harris, in the first contribution to this section, argues persuasively that they do. He focuses his argument on the Yanomamö, a group of some 10,000 Indians living in the Brazil-Venezuela border area, that have been studied extensively by Napoleon Chagnon (1968a, 1968b, 1968c, 1977) and others. Harris criticizes Chagnon's claim that Yanomamö warfare's only function is the purely political one of maintaining the sovereignty of individual Yanamamö villages. Following Gross's (1975) suggestion that protein availability is the limiting factor in the size and density of tropical forest settlements, Harris argues that Yanomamö warfare, by selecting for male warriors, encourages female infanticide. The resulting reduction in the size of the adult female population, in turn, is an extremely effective means of limiting overall population growth.

Discussions concerning the Amazon Basin's potential carrying capacity are by no means limited to those concerned with the region's indigenous population. Quite to the contrary, the entire question has gained new currency in very recent years as plans for the region's development have gotten underway. The Brazilian government has sponsored construction of an ambitious road network (see map, figure 7.1) in an effort to bring the area fully into the national orbit. In addition, the government has granted generous concessions to mining, ranching, and agricultural interests as part of its development program, and has established a planned colonization project along one of the main arteries in a new road network, the Transamazon Highway.

Since the colonization scheme began in 1971, it may seem too early to determine its overall success or failure, or the role that the Amazonian environment will ultimately play in it. Yet despite the relative newness of the project, Emilio Moran reports in his article that it already is possible to discern clear cut patterns of success and failure on the individual level, and he develops a four-fold typology to illustrate the different strategies used by colonists in adapting to their new environment. He singles out what appear to be key variables— prior land ownership and frequency of migration—for predicting how well individual colonists will fare in the development scheme.

Although the newcomers' experience before coming to the Transamazonica colored their perception and utilization of the resources at hand, very few took advantage of the local *caboclo* population's intimate knowledge of the region's plant-soil associations. Many colonists' disappointing agricultural yields, therefore, are more a consequence of uninformed land choice, than of the absence of fertile soils. In stating this, Moran appears more optimistic than some (see Meggers 1974) about the Amazon's inherent potential. He seems to argue that it is the lack of knowledge of environmental resources and the exploitative techniques to best utilize them, rather than poor quality soils or meager resources per se, that are the limiting factors in Amazonian development.

The emphasis thus far on environmental variables and the concept of carrying capacity is not meant to imply that these are the only factors affecting resource utilization. Other, often equally important, forces impinge upon a population's exploitation of its environment. The population's position within the local and national stratification system, its access to capital and credit, as well as the demands of the world market may all deeply influence a group's adaptive stance vis-à-vis its environment.

A case in point is the behavior of cultivators on the coffee frontier in southern Brazil. Maxine Margolis claims that a series of economic and ecological factors have combined to create a particular variety of environmental exploitation that appears within similar contexts on frontiers cross-culturally. She notes the structural parallels between the spread of coffee in southern Brazil and the spread of cotton in the southern United States, and argues that speculative cash crop agriculture has led to resource depletion in both regions. In each case, the availability of inexpensive or free frontier land, the world demand for a valuable cash crop, the ecological effects of clearing virgin land for cultivation, and a dearth of capital and labor created an exploitative mentality among frontier cultivators. This mentality was reflected in their disregard of soil conservation and a footloose posture which led them to abandon their land for greener pastures at the first sign of decreasing yields. She makes the point that these conditions along with the opportunistic attitudes to which they give rise are by no means unique to Brazil; they occur wherever similar circumstances prevail.

A population's world view is directly influenced by its access to environmental and economic resources. This access, in turn, is affected by the population's links to the larger society—its position within the class system, its geographical location vis-à-vis centers of power, and its proximity to markets.

Conrad Kottak analyzes just such variables and how they relate to the world views and attitudes of the populations of two fishing communities in northeastern Brazil. The terms of integration of each community within the wider regional socio-economic system is one of the keys to understanding the differing attitudes and behavioral patterns of each community's residents. Despite the surface similarities between the two villages, there are marked differences in their social structures, and in their inhabitants' outlook including their receptiveness to innovation. Kottak traces these contrasts to dissimilarities in local and regional economic institutions, their different historical experiences, and significant variations in the ecologies of the two coastal environments. Fishing catches are considerably larger and more regular in Arembepe, a small coastal settlement in the state of Bahia, because of its proximity to the continental shelf, than in Coqueiral, a somewhat larger village in the state of Alagoas. This greater abundance of local resources, in combination with the absence of a local elite and individual access to markets, gives rise to the Arembepeiros' "ideology of equality," that has no counterpart in the more highly stratified community of Coqueiral.

Questions such as those raised here underscore the fact that we are just beginning to understand the complex relationships between Brazil's natural resource base and the cultures and social structures of its peoples. Special problems exist, due largely to the fact that most of the country lies fully in the tropics, whereas most ecological theory has grown out of experiences in the north temperate zones of the world. Brazil offers one of our earth's last frontiers. To fully understand the potential impact of human activities on that frontier will require far more knowledge than we presently possess. Indeed the absence of such knowledge constitutes one of the greatest challenges faced by the world today.

# SIX

# The Yanomamö and the Causes of War in Band and Village Societies

## Marvin Harris

THE YANOMAMÖ, AN ethno-linguistic "tribe" of some 10,000 to 20,000 Amerindians who live along the Brazil–Venezuela border near the headwaters of the Orinoco and Rio Negro, are a crucial case for the general theory of conflict and war in pre-state societies. As documented in the dramatic monographs and movies produced by Napoleon Chagnon (1968a, 1973), the Yanomamö exhibit a high level of conflict both within and between villages. At the center of Yanomamö land, allied groups of villages maintain virtually perpetual states of hostility with enemy villages resulting in numerous combat deaths. The Yanomamö are crucial to any theory of "primitive" war, not only because they are one of the best-studied pre-state societies in which warfare is actively being practiced, but because their principal ethnographer, Napoleon Chagnon, has explicitly denied the likelihood that the high level of homicide within and between villages has anything to do with competition for resources or population pressure. According to Chagnon, resources exist in superabundance, even at the two regions at the center of Yanomamö land where the most warlike groups of villages are located:

Enormous tracts of land, most of it cultivable and abounding with game, is found between villages in both regions. Whatever else might be cited as a

**121**

'cause' of warfare between the villages, *competition for resources is not a very convincing one* [Chagnon's italics]. The generally intensive warfare patterns found in aboriginal tropical forest cultures do not correlate well with resource shortages or competition for land or hunting areas. (Chagnon 1973:127).

Again, from the same book:

Recent trends in ethnological theory are tending more and more to crystallize around the notion that warfare among swidden cultivators must always be explainable in terms of population density, scarcity of strategic resources such as territory or 'proteins,' or a combination of both. The Yanomamö are an important society, for their warfare cannot be explained in this way. (194–95)

As a substitute for theories of warfare that focus on demographic pressures, Chagnon proposes to focus on "political" factors. According to Chagnon, the Yanomamö make war because war is the normal political means of regulating relations between sovereign "tribal" groups:

In all tribal groups, local communities are 'sovereign' in that the political behavior of their members is not dictated from above by supra-local institutions. The preservation of this political sovereignty seems to be the universal unstated goal of all tribesmen, the *sine qua non* of tribal culture. The most important single means to achieve this, borrowing a prase from Hobbes via Sahlins, is usually a *political stance* called *Warre*. (1973:77)

Hence for Chagnon, the Yanomamö's use of war to settle disputes scarcely requires an elaborated explanation and should occasion no surprise:

That the relationship between sovereign political groups should also take the form of raid-warfare—is not surprising . . . Warfare is, indeed, the extension of tribal politics in the absence of other means. (*ibid.*)

It should be noted, however, that Chagnon presents no evidence, direct or indirect, that lends support to the assertion that the preservation of political sovereignty is a "universal unstated goal." Indeed to the extent that the Yanomamö are representative of pre-state village communities, they provide vivid evidence that such communities consist of evanescent coalitions of faction-ridden kin-groups which perpetually seek alliances in other villages and which pay so little heed to the alleged universal unstated goal that they are incapable of living together when their populations approach at most 200 to 250 persons (overall, Yanomamö villages contain on the average 40 to 50 persons). If sociocultural systems were to be understood by means of "unstated goals," the rapid fissioning of Yanomamö villages, their perpetually shifting alliances, and their lack of fixed territory would suggest the existence of a "goal" quite opposite to the one Chagnon imputes: namely, never permit a village to become a sovereign political unit. But let us suppose that the "goal" of all the fighting really is to preserve village sovereignty. What does this tell us? Are we not still left with the puzzle of why the Yanomamö persist in pushing towards this end with such bloody determination?

Here the central weakness of Chagnon's theory as a general theory of war reveals itself. By giving everyone the same great unstated goal, it attempts to account for a highly variable phenomenon—war in pre-state societies—by a constant. Pre-state societies differ markedly in the rate, duration, and intensity of intergroup conflict and in the specific weaponry and tactics of armed combat. While some form or degree of intergroup homicide may be universal, it is clear that the Yanomamö pattern involves a higher rate of combat and level of mortality than is usual in many (but not all) village-organized societies. Indeed, this is the reason why Chagnon calls the Yanomamö, "The Fierce People."

Thus Chagnon's theory cannot explain why the Makiritare, close neighbors of the Yanomamö, are relatively peaceful. More importantly, his theory cannot explain the variations in bellicosity among the Yanomamö themselves. For not all the villages in Yanomamö land are inhabited by fierce, warlike people. Chagnon emphasizes the difference between the ferocity of villages located in what he calls the "central" and "peripheral" areas. Among villages at the periphery: "Conflicts with neighbors are less frequent . . . the intensity of warfare is greatly reduced . . . Villages are smaller . . . Displays of aggression and violence are greatly reduced in frequency and limited in form" (Chagnon 1968b:114).

To explain the higher degree of warfare among the central villages, Chagnon (1968c) has introduced the notion of "social circumscription." Social circumscription allegedly exists because it is more difficult for villages at the center to escape attack by moving away. Unlike villages at the periphery, they must pass through hostile territory. Hence, they have no alternative but to grow big and stand

and fight. But this explanation is undermined by the fact that groups at the center are perfectly capable of removing themselves from the zones of most intense conflict. Returning to the Shamatari in 1972, Chagnon (1973:181) was disappointed to find that two of the villages he had intended to visit, Mömariböwei-teri and Reyaboböwei-teri, had "migrated far away," the former over 150 miles to the Casiquiare Canal and the latter to a distance that "would have required walking for at least a week in one direction."

In his theory of the origin of the state, Robert Carneiro (1970) holds that Chagnon's "social circumscription is capable of producing the kinds of demographic pressures that sharp environmental circumscription and resource concentration produce." However, Carneiro's interpretation of social circumscription depends upon a covert and implicit demographic-environmental cost-benefit analysis—the analysis explicitly rejected by Chagnon. For Carneiro, social circumscription leads to a reduction in the size of the territory of each village. Then, as population pressure became more severe, warfare over land would ensue. Yet Chagnon (1973:129) states that "the relationship between warfare intensity and population density is not a simple one." He claims that his data "leads to a conclusion that will, no doubt, perplex some of my colleagues: the Shamatari have more warfare and a *lower* population density than the Nemowei-teri—and their villages are more widely scattered." Thus, by referring to "population pressure," Carneiro covertly and implicitly reintroduces the theory that the Yanomamö are in the final analysis fighting over resources, a theory that Chagnon overtly and explicitly rejects.

Despite Chagnon's denial of a link between intensity of warfare and population pressure, his own data indicates that, for the Yanomamö as a whole, warfare is most intense where village size and density is greatest. Carneiro is thus correct in emphasizing the correlation between warfare intensity and population density but his theory of the origin of the state leads to the unlikely conclusion that warfare is the cause of the higher population density at the center of Yanomamöland. This conclusion is contradicted by the three most important demographic facts about the Yanomamö: villages fission when they reach a maximum of 200 to 250 persons; even in the central areas population remains below one person per square mile; and the central villages are spaced on the average more than twenty miles apart. If warfare under conditions of social circumscription (or environmental circumscription or resource concentration) leads to larger villages closer together, why have the Yanomamö villages remained so small and far apart as compared with villages at the proto-state level? It cannot be said that not enough time has elapsed for the effect of warfare to become manifest because, as will be seen below, the population of the central groups has increased tenfold during the past 100 years.

Chagnon (1975) attributes the fissioning of Yanomamö villages to the absence of political mechanisms (i.e., strong chieftainship) capable of preserving intra-village solidarity. The larger the village, the greater the frequency of inter-personal disputes and the lower the density of close kinship bonds. However, this hypothesis fails to state the nomothetic conditions under which such political mechanisms can be expected to arise or not to arise. Thus, what is lacking in the social circumscription theory, both in Chagnon's and Carneiro's versions, is the means of explaining why the Yanomamö villages fission at the observed level of population density and village size.

Another feature of Yanomamö warfare for which Chagnon's general theory cannot account is the practice of female infanticide. The supreme paradox of the Yanomamö is that the central war-intensive villages have a distinctive sex ratio in the age group 14 and under. Eleven Yanomamö villages located in the intensive war zone averaged 148 boys to 100 girls whereas in twelve villages that were peripherally located the ratio was 118:100 (Chagnon 1973:135). In the two villages studied by Jacques Lizot (1971), one more warlike than the other, the juvenile sex ratios were 260:100 and 77:100 respectively. There is no doubt that among the warlike villages departures from the expected ratio of about 105:100 are produced by the practice of female infanticide, and the benign and malign neglect of female infants and young girls (Chagnon 1968b:139; Neel and Weiss 1975:36; Divale and Harris 1976). According to Chagnon, the shortage of females, exacerbated by the prevalence of polygyny, is a prime source of disunity and strife.

The shortage of women, indirectly a consequence of an attitude that admires masculinity, ultimately leads to keen competition and thus reinforces the entire *waiteri complex* (male fierceness complex) by resulting in more fighting and aggression. In practical terms, nearly every village fissioning I investigated resulted from chronic internal feuding over women, and in many cases the groups ultimately entered into hostilities after they separated. (Chagnon 1968b:141)

Elsewhere Chagnon makes it clear that, as far as the Yanomamö themselves are concerned, all Yanomamö wars, not merely those which are the aftermath of a fission event, are due to feuding over women: "The Yanomamö themselves regard fights over women as the primary causes of their wars" (1968a:123).

Does Chagnon's political sovereignty theory account for the prominence of feuding over women both as an observed (etic) and stated (emic) precondition of hostilities? I cannot see how. If the Yanomamö go to war because of a "shortage of women," why don't they end that shortage by rearing as many girls as boys? It cannot be said that warfare prevents this. There is nothing logically incompatible between practicing warfare and rearing as many females as males. If warfare places a premium on the rearing of males for combat, the quickest way to rear more males is to rear more women. *Only if rapid population growth is systematically undesirable does it make sense not to rear as many females as males.*

To sum up: Chagnon's universal quest for village sovereignty theory fails to account for the loss of sovereignty due to the need to have war allies; the regular breakdown of sovereignty as village populations approach a maximum of 200–250; the relative peacefulness of many tropical forest peoples, including close neighbors of the Yanomamö; the greater intensity of warfare at the center than at the periphery of Yanomamöland; female infanticide and the neglect and abuse of young girls despite the need for more women due to the practice of polygyny.

A general theory of band and village warfare which accounts for all these facts has been proposed by Divale and Harris (1976) and Harris (1977). This theory views warfare as part of a widespread system of population regulation. Warfare regulates village-level populations not by combat deaths but by selecting populations which rear more males than females. By rearing more males than females, maximum combat efficiency is achieved while restoring or maintaining optimum average band or village densities with respect to given modes of production. That is, warfare regulates both total population and its dispersion with respect to resources. The theory predicts that a rapid increase in population density caused by a shift to a new mode of production will be followed by an increase in warfare (and not the reverse, as in Carneiro's theory). Concomitantly the theory predicts that an increase in warfare will be accompanied by an increase in the imbalance of the ratio of junior age males to junior age females. The theory holds that female infanticide and the benign or malign neglect of pre-adolescent girls is the least costly of a series of costly alternatives for slowing population growth rates that threaten to deplete resources vital to band and village modes of production. In contrast, pre-scientific abortions kill adult females as well as fetuses; abstinence is unreliable, prolonged lactation is useless with high calorie/low protein diets and at best cannot achieve a growth rate lower than .5% per annum (Van Ginneken 1974; Frisch and MacArthur 1974; Kolata 1974; Dickeman 1975a, 1975b) and natural controls through infant diseases are ineffectual in well-nourished, low-density band and village isolates (Black 1975). Moreover, the loss of adult males in combat is less disruptive than the death of women by abortion because it shifts the blame to external agents and makes the group's enemies responsible for the entire system of population control.

It must be emphasized that this theory involves the assumption that band and village populations normally fluctuate narrowly above or below essentially stationary levels (Polgar 1975; White 1976; Dumond 1975; Coale 1974) and that band and village warfare is normally less intense than that characteristic of the central Yanomamö villages. Because of the wastage of female infants, any innovation in the techno-environmental equation which leads to higher densities without a concomitant loss of techno-environmental efficiency or lowering of per capita protein and calorie intake will tend to be adopted. Population will then tend to rise to a new stationary level defined by the density beyond which previously established levels of techno-environmental efficiency and metabolic and other standards of well-being begin to erode. It is predicted that the period shortly before and after the new density level is reached will be characterized by a peak intensity of warfare and female infanticide. The intensification of warfare at such periods is a manifestation of the pressure to maintain adult living standards by exploiting larger or more productive areas in competition with neighboring villages, while the intensification of female infanticide is a manifestation of the pressure to cut back on population growth and to increase combat efficiency. An important deviation amplification effect may be expected at this point in relation to any shift in diet away from high protein intakes. Such shifts may render spacing through lactation ineffectual and thus step up the demands placed on infanticide and infant mortality as regulating mechanisms.

The Yanomamö case appears to conform well with many aspects of this theory. One hundred years ago the Yanomamö were typical "foot-Indians" living in the intra-fluvial highlands of the Orinoco and Rio Negro headwaters (Chagnon et al. 1970:340; Wilbert 1972:33). According to Lizot:

The indigenous settlements were traditionally established far from navigable rivers and one had to walk several days through dense unexplored forest to find them. . . . It is only recently, following their remarkable expansion into unoccupied areas—an expansion due as much to fissioning, war, and conflict as to an astonishing demographic increase—that some groups established themselves, around 1950, on the Orinoco River and its tributaries. (1971:34–35)

Neel and Weiss (1975:34) believe that the total number of Yanomamö villages has more than doubled in the last hundred years and estimate that the overall rate of population growth during the same period has been between 0.5 and 1 percent per year. However, the rate of growth at the center of Yanomamöland where warfare is most intense appears to have been much greater. Starting from a single village one hundred years ago, there are now 2,000 people in twelve Shamatari villages. If the original village fissioned when it attained a size of 200 people, the rate of growth for the Shamatari would be over 3 percent per year. But since to this day the average Shamatari village fissions when it reaches 166 people and seldom reaches 200, there is reason to suspect that the rate of growth has been still higher at the center. Indeed, since the average Yanomamö village in the peripheral zones where warfare is less intense contains only 40 to 60 persons per group (Zerries 1968; Lizot 1970), the actual rate of growth at the center may have been quite astronomical.

What caused the population explosion at the center of Yanomamöland? The general theory predicts that it was a change in the mode of production and there is some evidence that such a change did indeed take place. The principal crops planted at the center of Yano-mamöland are bananas and plantains. These crops are not native to the New World. Although they may have been used by the Yanoma-mö long before the population explosion began, it seems likely that only in the last hundred years or so, have the central Yanomamö villages devoted the major share of their gardening effort to these crops. The intensification of banana and plantain production may have been triggered by the introduction of steel axes and machetes which were first traded into the area through the Makiritare (Chagnon et al. 1970:343). Barandiarán (1967:29) reports that before the introduction of steel axes "several days were needed to fell a single tree." Another factor promoting the intensification of banana and plantain gardens may have been the pacification or extinction of the Arawak and Carib groups who previously dominated all the navigable rivers in Yanomamöland. Large gardens planted in perennials such as plantains and bananas would have constituted an inviting target for the more numerous and better organized river-dwelling Indians such as the Makiritare who to this day intimidate the Yanomamö through their control over trade goods (Chagnon et al. 1970:343). The process of pacification and extinction of the riverine Caribs and Arawaks may have reached its final phase about one hundred years ago when Brazilian rubber traders and Venezuelan gold prospectors converged along the Venezuelan–Brazil border following the Rio Negro and the Orinoco to their sources.

The theory predicts that, in general, the adoption of a new mode of production leads to population growth which leads in turn to pressure against resources at a higher level of population density. There is no doubt that the population density in the region now occupied by the Yanamamö has increased greatly during the last century. Most importantly, there is the disparity between the 140–166 average size of Yanomamö villages at the center compared with 40–60 average size at the periphery. The question remains, however, whether these densities and nucleations have in some sense led to pressures against resources which are causally related to the high frequency of warfare and the 140:100 junior age sex ratio.

General agreement now exists that the limiting factor in Amerindian tropical forest populations is not a declining margin of caloric efficiency or a drop in calorie rations as mediated through the availability of forests suitable for swiddens (Carneiro 1961). Attention has shifted accordingly to the role of protein capture (Ross 1978; Morren 1974; Gross 1975). These inquiries suggest that tropical forest habitats are characterized by low over-all animal biomass productivity. Tropical forests are especially unproductive habitats for large herbivores. Since the Yanomamö have only recently occupied sites close to the navigable rivers and still lack the technology for exploiting fish in the major streams, it seems likely that availability of animal biomass is the principal limiting factor on the size to which Yanomamö villages can grow without fissioning. The research necessary to measure rates of animal capture in relation to stages of village expansion should have preceded the declaration that Yanomamö warfare "cannot be explained in this way."

To explain Yanomamö warfare in conformity with the general theory of warfare under consideration, it is not necessary to show that there is an absolute shortage of protein manifesting itself in clinically detectable symptoms. Nor is it necessary to show that the average per capita consumption of animal protein is lower than recommended minimum requirements set by FAO and WHO (Harris 1979a, 1979b). All that is necessary is to show that, as Yanomamö village size increases, there is a progressive deterioration in the cost/benefit ratio of protein capture as manifested in the need to walk longer distances, an increasing reliance on insects and grubs, and the substitution of plant protein for animal protein.

The empirical test of the adequacy of the general theory of warfare applied to the Yanomamö is the extent to which the increase of a village from about 40–50 persons to 200–250 persons is accompanied by a declining energetic efficiency of animal protein capture and a rising percentage of plant and small animal protein in the daily ration on the one hand, matched against the recovery of protein capture efficiency and protein quality after fission, on the other. The theory assumes that any human population will initiate some kind of compensatory activity if it experiences a sharp erosion of its levels of material comfort and well-being, well before the erosion proves fatal to the population or its ecosystem.

The question to be solved therefore by Chagnon and others who are continuing the field research into the causes of Yanomanö warfare, is whether the growth of a village from 40 to 200 or more persons leads to a decline in the standards of protein consumption and the cost-benefits of protein capture severe enough to cause the observed levels of fissioning and dispersion. That this question is worth pursuing can easily be demonstrated by modeling the effects of village growth based on reasonable estimates of tropical forest animal biomass productivity and moderate levels of per capita animal protein consumption. One can use the following formula for estimating $D$ (the average distance between villages) as a function of $C$ (daily per capita biomass consumption), $P$ (village population), and $H$ (productivity of harvestable animal biomass per hectare).

$$D = 2\sqrt{\frac{365CP}{\pi H}}$$

NOTE: $D$, hectares, must be converted to linear miles by being divided by 16.09.

The average size of a Shamatari village is 166 persons. If $C$ (per capita biomass consumption per day) is set at 300 gms. (equal to a modest 39 gms. of animal protein per day) and if each hectare produces 200 gms. of medium to large ungulates, rodents, primates, and birds which can be harvested annually without degradation or migration of the prey species, the average distance between Shamatari villages should be 21.1 miles (cf. Martin 1973; Fittkau and Klinge 1973). This corresponds to a density of .47 persons per square mile as compared with Chagnon's (1973:127) estimate of .42 persons per square mile for the Shamatari. (Chagnon [1973:129] estimates that the average distance between Shamatari villages is 50 miles, but this figure may in fact be in error.)

Assume that only 200 gms. of animal biomass (equal to 26 gm. animal protein) are consumed per capita per day, while the harvestable medium to large biomass productivity is stepped up to 300 gms. per hectare. Distance still increases rapidly as a function of village size. Cutting animal protein rations by half, say from 400 gms. per day biomass (a modest 52 gms. protein) to 200 gms. biomass (a low 26 gms. protein), results in reducing the distance between villages by only one third (22 miles to 15 miles). In other words, very severe cuts in animal biomass consumption are required in order to achieve modest gains in the efficiency of hunting as measured by the distances which must be traversed by hunters living in villages close to the maximum Yanomamö fissioning point.

Mechanisms by which pressure against the animal biomass is translated into increased levels of warfare and fissioning as villages approach 200 in size should also be identified, although they are not integral to the verification of the general theory. Chagnon stresses the fact that fissioning is preceded by a crescendo of fights over women. From the account of Helena Valero (Biocca 1970), a Brazilian woman who was captured by the Yanomamö, it is clear that women make a point of taunting their husbands when the supply of game falters, a practice which Yanomamö women probably share with many other tropical forest groups (cf. Siskind 1973:96). Hunting failure probably makes the men more touchy with respect to real or imagined insubordination on the part of wives and junior males at the same time that it emboldens wives and junior males to probe the weaknesses of their husbands, seniors, and headmen. Adultery and witchcraft increase in fact and fancy. Factions solidify and tensions mount, for fission cannot take place peacefully. Those who leave suffer great penalties. They must transport heavy banana and plantain cuttings to new gardens, seek refuge among allies and pay for food and protection with gifts of women, while waiting for new gardens to mature. Many raids between villages represent the prolongation of the disputes which led up to the fissioning event. Raids between unrelated villages would also increase as tensions mounted within villages. As hunting expeditions ranged over greater distances in pursuit of dwindling game resources, incursions into buffer zones between villages and even into enemy gardens would become more frequent. Tensions over women would lead to more frequent raiding for women as an alternative to adultery and as validation of threatened headman statuses. No doubt there are other emic mechanisms that serve as well to transmit the threat of animal biomass depletion, and to mobilize the etically compensatory behavior of fission and dispersion. The validation of the existence of such mechanism, however, is not crucial to the proof or disproof of the predicted etic relationship between population density, animal biomass, village size, intensity of warfare, female infanticide, junior sex ratios, and rate of population growth.

# SEVEN

# The Trans-Amazonica: Coping with a New Environment

## Emilio F. Moran

RAPID POPULATION GROWTH, plus efforts to improve living standards, has led a number of nations to exploit heretofore undeveloped areas of their national territories. Brazil is among those nations. Both its population and its economic activities have been concentrated along the Atlantic coast for most of the nation's history.[1] Only in the 1950s, beginning with the construction of Brasilia, did the western states begin to develop. It was not until the 1970s that the federal government initiated a vigorous program of economic development in its largest and most tropical region—the Amazon Basin (Smith 1972; Wagley 1971, 1974).

The area affected by the Amazon development scheme was not wholly unpopulated. There was already present a sparse population well adapted to life in the tropical rain forest (Lathrap 1968; Moran 1974).[2] Government efforts to develop the Amazon and to bring farmers to the land encouraged a second, and more heterogeneous, population to migrate from all other cultural areas of Brazil.

Both population groups have colonized the lands transected by the Transamazon Highway (see figure 7.1),[3] and the presence of both makes this an exceptional area in which to study cultural adaptation in the tropics.

133

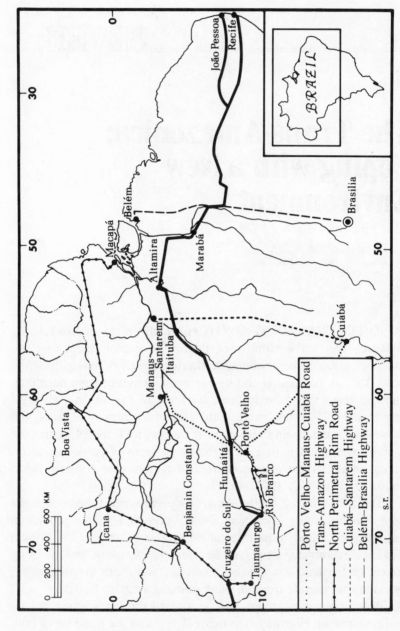

**Figure 7.1.** Brazilian Amazon Highway System (Wagley 1974:292).

The Transamazon colonization project, begun in 1971, was planned and financed by the Brazilian Federal Government.[4] By 1974 some 6,000 landless farmers from all parts of Brazil had been given 100 hectares (250 acres) of virgin land,[5] credit assistance, and other supportive services as colonists. Some had succeeded as farmers in this new physical, social, and institutional setting, while many others had not.

Unlike traditional homogeneous populations such as those studied by Nietschmann (1973), Rappaport (1967), and Waddell (1972), those of the Transamazon do not yet have a singular or universally accepted cultural response to the physical environment.[6] The immigrants have brought a stripped-down version of the cultural blueprint that once fitted their respective regions of origin.[7]

While all Brazilians share in a national culture to one degree or other, regional subcultures also exist and are made up of specific responses to the physical and social features of various geographical regions (Wagley 1948:457-64). One such subculture has developed as a particular response to the tropical forest-riverine environment now crossed by the Transamazon Highway. This is the culture held by the Amazonian caboclo (Wagley 1952; Moran 1974).[8] It is a response both to the physical environment of the tropics and to the traditional social isolation of a region with precarious transportation facilities.

Among the colonists, whether of migrant or caboclo extraction, adaptation to the physical environment of a rain forest, the social environment of planned villages,[9] and to the institutional environment created by the colonization agencies has led to a variety of coping strategies. To best deal with these various behaviors, a typology will be used to group similar strategies. This typology is derived both from the various backgrounds of the colonists and from their current performance in the Trans-Amazon. While every aspect of a farmer's background is not indicative of his farming potential, certain elements of his employment history have visibly affected his farm management strategies and, consequently, his success or failure as a farmer. Of these, previous ownership of land and frequency of migration will be shown to be particularly useful in predicting cultural adaptiveness and farming success.

Transamazon farmers can first be divided into two major groupings: brokers and clients. This two-fold division describes the most basic social and economic relationships present in the area. Brokers consist of those homesteaders who, through their managerial skills, can generate their own capital, and re-invest a major portion of this capital back into their enterprises. The clients are those who depend on the brokers or on outside institutions to provide them with a steady cash income in order to survive. Clients employ most of their capital resources for consumption items rather than farm investment.

Brokers tend to be more stable geographically than clients. Brokers at one time or other have owned land or durable goods such as trucks and machinery. Their managerial expertise has come from learning to exploit the physical and financial resources of an area, and investing heavily in their use. The clients, on the other hand, are basically a labor force; they go where there is a demand for their labor, and their constant mobility keeps them from acquiring the managerial acumen necessary to run their own commercial or agricultural enterprises. Within each of these two broad categories, two subtypes may additionally be defined. Clients can be subdivided into laborer-farmers and artisan farmers, and brokers into entrepreneurs and independent farmers.[10]

Laborer-farmers come from largely rural, sharecropping or migrant labor backgrounds, and are characterized by a high degree of mobility and possession of few durable goods. Figure 7.2 compares previous migrations among the various types of farmers. The high level of migration of laborer-farmers would suggest that these are persons who customarily work for others. They have many years in low-skill agricultural work but little experience in farm management, and have repeatedly failed to do well economically. They are traditionally tied to the landowner-patrons by symbiotic bonds which provide them with security, yet effectively keep them in their low economic position (Johnson 1971). Patrons deal with them paternalistically and, in bad times, may provide a minimum subsistence. The patron gains by this arrangement by paying low wages, expecting hard work, and charging high prices in the fazenda-run store where credit is available to laborers. Since laborers tend to repay their patron in farm produce and deal with the local store on a debit-credit basis, they have gained little experience in managing cash resources.

Nelson (1973:288) points out that this type of farmer is found less frequently in areas of spontaneous colonization than in government-directed schemes. This situation probably explains in part the

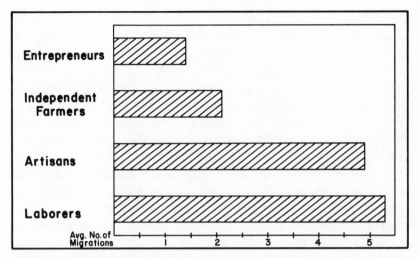

**Figure 7.2.** Number of Previous Migrations among the Four Types of Colonists (Moran 1975).

lack of personal initiative of those accustomed to the dependency-breeding fazenda environment (Diégues Júnior 1973). Many laborer-farmers are attracted to the Transamazon Project due to the numerous services and opportunities promised by the federal government. They expect the colonization agency to be a far more benevolent patron than those they had heretofore known.

The second client group, the artisan-farmers, are also character-ized by a high degree of mobility (see figure 7.2). A major difference between this group and the laborer-farmers is the former's urban ex-perience which has led them to acquire craft skills or more education. In turn, this qualifies them for better-paying jobs. While their various skills might be considered second-rate in most urban areas, and would not merit substantial remuneration, such skills are in great demand in rural areas undergoing rapid development. Thus, in the Transamazon, artisans have sought and found well-paying jobs with the government agencies as carpenters, stone-masons, construction foremen, and professional chauffeurs. Since the artisans have come to depend on these jobs for their livelihood, rather than on their farm production or their managerial talents, they are classified as clients rather than brokers.

In the broker category, the independent farmers are a group of largely rural persons who previously have been the owners of small landholdings or managers on landed estates. Unlike clients, they have lived in the same place for most of their lives (see figure 7.2). Independent farmers of the Transamazon are, in a way, like the European mixed farmer in that both emphasize self-sufficiency.[11] They plant a wide variety of crops for both home use and market sale. Cattle raising is commonly practiced, but only the few colonists of German descent employ draft oxen and use cattle manure as fertilizer. In general, all independent farmers who own cattle process milk into curds (*coalhada*) and home-made cheese (*requeijão*), some of which is sold. Canning and preserving are not practiced in the Amazon, but other cottage industries more adapted to the tropical environment are utilized. Broadly speaking, the strategies of the Transamazon independent farmers and the European mixed farmer are similar, although their specific practices may differ. The differences in their strategies result from their adaptation to particular environmental demands. Most of their day-to-day needs are met through diversified production, and the cash profits from their agricultural production are returned to the farm in the form of livestock, payment for new clearings, replacement of farm equipment, and a few consumer goods. The independent farmers and their families supply most of their own labor needs in farming and in cottage industries. Therefore, with relatively few farm expenditures and constant re-investment of farm profits, independent farmers show ever greater agricultural production.

The second category of brokers, the entrepreneurs, is one of limited membership. The Altamira region, where colonization began,[12] abounds with adventurous entrepreneurs but most of these are engaged in the town's commercial sector, rather than in the farm sector; any new area needs such a group to organize people and resources into a profitable flow of goods, services, and capital. Active entrepreneurs in the area, like the independent farmers, are characterized by previous land ownership or farm administration experience, and by a low degree of previous migration. They differ from the independent farmers, however, in having more urban experience and higher capital assets on arrival in the Amazon. While the majority of farmers indicated that they had very little money when they arrived, entrepreneurs came with an average of US $500. This small, but nevertheless significant, amount of capital allowed them to proceed quickly with land preparation and other capital-generating activities without having to depend on the release of government-subsidized loans. Local dry goods stores and vehicles were often acquired with this capital and now generate a substantial income for this small group.

Besides general stores and motor vehicles, the entrepreneurs' main interest has been to invest their profits in pasture development and cattle. Their previous management experience and exposure to urban financial institutions have given them a facility in dealing with banks, bureaucracies, and clients. They may serve even as middlemen between the government and the other colonists in both economic and social transactions.[13]

Each of the aforementioned categories includes persons native to the Amazon region. Transamazon caboclo colonists largely come from a riverine environment where they planted small intercropped fields, and fished or hunted for their protein. Some of them have spent time panning for gold in the Tapajós River region, or tapping rubber in Acre or Xingú River areas. In the 1950s the county of Altamira made some municipal lands available and attracted prospectors, rubber gatherers, and subsistence farmers to the area. In these pre-highway years their activities differed little from those of caboclos elsewhere. Some of the caboclos' parents or grandparents had come during the Rubber Era (1880–1920) and had stayed on after it was over. Rubber collecting continued along the nearby Iriri River, for instance, until 1967. With the coming of the highways, this local population sought guaranteed land titles and close proximity to the main highway artery. Caboclo independent farmers were among the first to occupy the Altamira Project lands.

This presence needs to be explicitly mentioned since the colonization scheme neglected to take the local people into consideration or to employ their knowledge of the region. Many colonization officials assumed caboclos to be uneducated and uninterested in modern farming techniques. The caboclo population, however, became an important informal source of information to newcomers, particularly in exploiting the forest resources.

## Traditional Uses of Amazonian Resources

In terms of long-term survival, not only must resources be recognized, but adequate strategies must be developed to insure their preservation as they are exploited. Traditional populations, whose lives have not been seriously disrupted by modernization, show a remarkable balance between their exploitation and conservation of local resources. Rappaport (1967), for example, has described the elaborate homeostatic regulatory mechanism built into the culture of the Tsembaga Maring which indicates the proper times to go to war and to engage in conspicuous consumption of taro-yams and pigs. Reichel-Dolmatoff (1971) found an elaborate cosmology among the Tukano Indians of the Northwest Amazon which links the reproductive energies of people and animals to such an extent that cultural restrictions limit both the size of families and the intensity of hunting and fishing. As a result, the population remains stable and has an adequate and easily obtainable supply of protein. The Hanunóo, studied by Conklin (1957), possess what he has called an "integral approach" to shifting agriculture. This is a complex system which gives ample fallow time, provides good soil cover through the use of intercropping, and utilizes hundreds of cultigens and wild plants which diversify the food resources of the population.

Like these traditional groups, the Amazonian caboclo population is familiar with its tropical environment. The various resources of the forest are utilized in ways which closely replicate aboriginal adaptations. Hunting and gathering activities provide protein, vitamin, and mineral-rich food sources, while a fail-safe horticulture, based on manioc, provides the bulk of needed calories. Their crops are planted in small horticultural patches prepared by slash-and-burn methods. The relative isolation of the Amazon area led to a self-sufficient lifestyle which has been linked to an extractive economy based on the collection of rubber, wood, or pelts. It is this historical antecedent that largely explains the caboclos' presumed neglect of horticulture. Rubber, Brazilnuts, and timber bring good prices, while surplus agricultural production yields comparatively lower cash profits and is much harder to market (Wagley 1953; Moran 1974).

With the coming of the highway, government funds poured into the Amazon in the form of minimum salaries, credit, jobs, and larger potential markets for agricultural produce. The caboclos did not wholly change their subsistence mode but adapted it to these changing conditions. They first began by choosing fertile areas marked by thin-trunked liana forest growth (*paus finos*). Soils associated with such forest growth have good organic content, low exchangeable aluminum levels, adequate potassium and phosphorus, and a pH of 6.0 or better.[14] Many of the newcomers are confused by the lush vegetation and simply assume that the maxim they use in their home areas also applies in the tropical rain forest. As so many of us are likely to do, they equate larger trees with farming potential. In the Transamazon, however, such criteria leads to a choice of infertile land, with very little potential for intensive agriculture.

Few, if any, of the newcomers utilized the full range of the caboclos' knowledge of plant-soil associations, since caboclos were reputed to be more interested in hunting than in agriculture. Ironically enough, it was during their hunting and rubber collecting that caboclos came to recognize those species of vegetation which are indicative of both agriculturally productive and infertile soils. Table 7.1 lists the vegetational criteria used by caboclos to judge soil potential in the Altamira region. Vegetation indicators are, most likely, different in other Amazon micro-environments. Soil samples taken in the Altamira region confirm the accuracy of these folk agronomic in-

**Table 7.1** Plant-soil Associations

| Good Agricultural Land (cover term: paus finos) | |
| --- | --- |
| Local Term | Scientific Name |
| Açaí | Euterpe oleracea Mart. |
| Babaçú | Orbignya martiana |
| Faveira | Piptadenia spp. |
| Maxarimbé | Emmotum spp. |
| Mororó | Bauhinia spp. |
| Purple pau d'arco | Tabebuia vilaceae Hub. |
| Yellow pau d'arco | Tabebuia serratifolia D. |
| Pinheiro Preto | unidentified |
| Poor Agricultural Soils (cover term: paus grossos) | |
| Acapú | Vouacapoua americana Aubl. |
| Cajú-Açú | Anacardium giganteum Engl. |
| Jarana | Holopyxidium jarana Ducke |
| Massaranduba | Manikara huberi or Mimusops h. |
| Melancieira | Alexa grandiflora Ducke |
| Piquí | Caryocar spp. |
| Sapucaia | Lecythis paraensis Linn. |
| Sumaúma | Ceiba pentandra Gaertn. |

dicators. Elsewhere I have noted (Moran, 1975:82, 85, and 176–93) that fertile soils are present in many areas of the Amazon, and that poor agricultural production is more often a result of uninformed choice of farm land than of the absence of fertile soils per se in the region.

The land along the Transamazon highway is parceled out in rectangular 100 hectare holdings, as illustrated in figure 7.3. Colonists either live on the land, or in nucleated village settlements (*agrovilas*). Caboclos prefer to live on their own land, and show a marked preference for lots facing the main highway. This is probably a logical response to their long-experienced isolation and a recognition of the serious constraints presented by poor access to local trade centers. Newcomers often opt for residence in the nucleated villages which provide educational and health services. By living in villages, however, their farms may be situated 3 to 20 kilometers away. In figure 7.3 the lots of farmers residing in one village, marked in the map as Vila Roxa, are indicated. This great distance differential is repeated in other villages as well. Most lots face sideroads which transect the main highway. Farmers soon find, however, that sideroads are not given high priority for construction or maintenance, and that the rainy season makes them practically impassable. Farmers located at more than 10 kilometers from their village residence engage in a less intense approach to farming than they might otherwise. Technical assistants and buyers are, therefore, unable to reach farmers located in sideroads too deep to be easily maintained by construction crews. In short, many newcomers are limited by both distances from the main highway and by uninformed selection of infertile soils.

In addition to felicitous land choice, caboclos adapted to the new conditions by enlarging their previously small subsistence plots to meet the expanded local market for basic foodstuffs. But, unlike newcomers, they plant a wide variety of plants rather than highly seasonal cash crops (rice, corn, and beans) encouraged by the government. While other farmers await their income to be derived from the sale of these three crops, caboclos have a steady year-round production of manioc flour to supply their own needs as well as local market demands. Manioc, the Amazon's traditional staple, grows abundantly and has relatively few natural enemies. It is also well-adapted to poorer and depleted soils and provides a solution to problems of storage in the tropics by its capacity to stay in the ground for

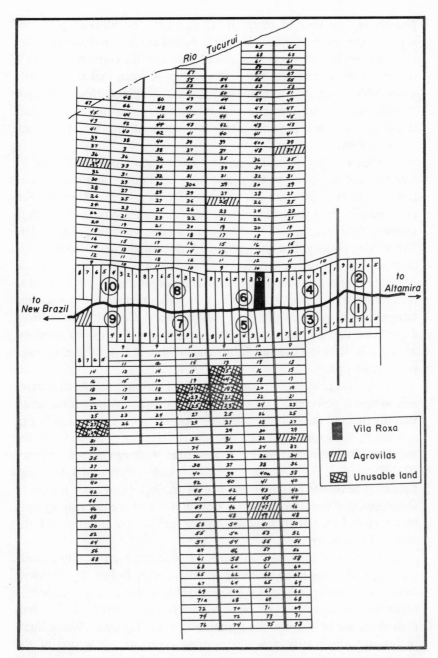

**Figure 7.3.** Distribution of Land in one Transamazonian planned village. (Moran 1975).

periods of one year or more. It is, therefore, an ideal crop for the small farmer in the tropics. Unlike seasonal cereals, manioc provides a steady source of food year-round and can be converted, with a minimum of technology, into a dry, storable form that is eminently marketable since it is a traditional staple throughout Brazil. Manioc production does not compete with other activities of the farmer since it can be harvested anytime after six months of growth (cf. Moran, 1976a, 1976b).

Other sources of ready cash that have traditionally been used by caboclos include poultry, pigs, and tobacco. Poultry and pigs require little attention as they are left to forage for themselves. Manioc peelings, surplus fruit, and food scraps are sometimes provided—both to increase their weight and to keep the house surroundings clean. Unlike cattle, poultry and pigs require little initial capital and do not demand the expensive development of pastures. Yet, they provide eggs, lard, and meat for family consumption and are well-adapted to pioneering conditions. Tobacco is also well-suited to the tropics and brings a good price at the local marketplaces. Caboclos know from experience that a combination of agricultural and livestock products are easy to raise on a small farm, and minimize risk of loss through pests or disease.

Caboclos also exploit the environment through fishing and hunting, whereas newcomers do so only infrequently. Although the small streams that cut through the caboclos' lots do not carry the larger fish species of Amazon rivers (cf. Honda, 1972; Veríssimo, 1970), the use of a simple hook-and-line is rewarded with catches of "traíra" (*Hoplias malabaricus* Block), some of which weigh four kilograms. Caboclos have not forgotten the use of fishing spears, nor a type of aboriginal fish trap, the cacuri.[15] Fish in the area are not usually sold by colonists but, rather, used mainly for family consumption and distribution among friends.

Much more important in terms of securing high-quality protein on a regular basis is the hunting of wild game. Before the highway came, wild game was much more prevalent in the area. Caboclos recall killing large tapirs (*Tapirus terrestris* Linn.) a few meters from their secluded huts. Now the situation is quite different. While hunting is not universally practiced among colonists, their use of the forest for agriculture has driven the game further back into untouched areas. Tapir and other large game, such as capybaras, jaguars, and giant armadillos, are hard to come by. Among the larger species, the hunting of white-lipped and white-collared peccary (*Tayassu pecari* Link, and *Tayassu tacaju* Linn. respectively) is still rewarding but requires time-consuming pursuit and several hunters.

After three years of intensive settlement, the region near Altamira yields mainly small game: *paca* (*Agouti paca* Linn.), agouti or *cutia* (*Dasyprocta prymnolopha* Wagler), armadillos (esp. *Dasypus novemcinctus* Linn.), deer (*Mazama americana* Erx.), land turtles (*Testudo* spp.), and monkeys of various species.[16] Only caboclos unhesitatingly eat monkey meat, although some newcomers have been known to eat it in time of need. There are numerous other forest animals, but they are not culturally acceptable as food.[17] For example, thin-spined porcupine (*Chaetomys subspinosus* Oefer), anteaters (*Myrmecophaga tridactyla* Linn.) and *Tamandua tetradactyla* Linn.), rabbits (*Sylvilagus brasiliensis*) and sloths (*Bradypus infuscatus marmoratus* and *Choloepus didactylus* Linn.) are rarely hunted.

Caboclos are conservation minded when it comes to hunting. The belief in "lucky days"[18] and social[19] and legal[20] proscriptions diminishes the amount of hunting which takes place. Game is hunted not for profit by Transamazon caboclos but rather for their own consumption or sharing with neighbors. By contrast, newcomers hunt any day, do not believe in "bad luck" (*panema*), and in some cases, sell game meat to supplement their incomes.

In the area studied, most hunting goes on during the late evening and at night. The only exception to this rule is the hunting of the diurnally-active peccary. Since these travel in bands of twenty or more, the prospect of an exciting and high-yielding chase engages a number of men on a single hunt. Otherwise, hunters generally leave their agricultural pursuits in the late afternoon and walk to a "waiting point" (*espera*) by the time dusk has fallen. This is usually a spot near a flowering or fruit-bearing plant which is known to be attractive to game animals. Table 7.2 lists the species of trees most commonly mentioned by hunters who relied on the espera method. Hunters tie their hammocks about three meters above the ground and wait for the arrival of the game. Conversation is practically absent. All wait to hear the distinct footsteps of various nocturnal animals. When an animal is nearly under a man's hammock and begins to eat the flowers or fruit, it is blinded by a flashlight and shot. On occasion, a hunter will pass up a chance to kill say, a "paca," because his wife

**Table 7.2** Trees Used in Waiting for Game in Night Hunting

| Local name | Scientific name |
|---|---|
| Açaí | *Euterpe oleraceae* Mart. |
| Babaçú * | *Orbignya martiana* |
| Bacaba | *Oenocarpus bacaba* Mart. |
| Castanha do Pará † | *Bertholetia excelsis* |
| Cupuaçú ‡ | *Theobroma grandiflorum* Spring |
| Frutão | *Lucuma* spp. and *Pouteria* spp. |
| Jaracatiá | Unidentified |
| Jarana | *Eschweilera jarana* Ducke |
| Matamatá | *Eschweilera* spp. |
| Ninharé | Unidentified |
| Piquizeiro | *Caryocar* spp. |
| Sapucaia § | *Lecythis paraensis* Hub. |
| Tamburí | *Enterolobium maximum* Ducke |
| Toarí | *Couratari* spp. |

NOTE: The above list is a composite list with all trees mentioned by hunters interviewed. None of them included all of the above, but all regular hunters had a minimum of ten trees they used to seek a point of waiting. It is important to move each night, especially if a hunter has killed an animal at a given spot.

\* Only deer and pacas eat the fruit after agoutis open the hard shell.

† Only agoutis eat the fruit of the brazilnut.

‡ Only deer, paca, and tapir eat the fruit.

§ Flower and fruit consumed by most species except armadillos and birds.

has asked him to bring home a deer. Shooting the first available animal scares others from coming to the spot. Yet, such requests are rare; usually hunters kill whatever they can on nightly hunts.

While conservation beliefs and practices are not held by the newcomers, it is well worth noting that food preferences act to restrain the impact of human occupation on the forest game species. Furthermore, in cases of illness and during pregnancy, the postpartum period, and lactation, game meats are not consumed because they are considered too dangerous (*remoso*). Indirectly, food taboos act to lessen hunting intensity and make game available for a longer period as a protein source.

The use of wild plants also differs between caboclos and the new settlers. The latter use only the fruit of the "cupuaçú" (*Theobroma grandiflorum* Spring), wild cocoa (*Theobroma* spp.), and brazilnut (*Bertholletia excelsis*), and even the use of these is rare. Wild plants are viewed as more dangerous and unknown than game. Fruits in general tend to be considered "acid" and are especially avoided during periods of disease and physical weakness. Caboclos follow the same food proscriptions during illness and crisis periods, but more commonly they use a wide variety of seasonally available forest fruits. Caboclos use the fruits and edible cores of various palms, such as *açaí* (*Euterpe oleracea*), *bacaba* (*Oenocarpus bacaba* Mart.), and *babaçú* (*Orbignya martiana*). The fruits of *piquí* (*Caryocar* spp.), *sapucaia* (*Lecythis* spp.), *cupuaçú, taperebá* or *cajá* (*Spondias lutea*), cocoa (*Theobroma* spp.), and passion fruit (*Passiflora edulis* Sims.).[21]

More often than not, use of these wild fruits demands a certain degree of processing. Their pulp is commonly mashed and mixed with water and sugar to make a juice (*vinho*). Children can rarely wait for juice to be made, and most frequently consume fruits in their natural state.

Some of the exotic fruits are unusually rich sources of vitamins. The nuts of babaçú, sapucaia, and brazilnut are rich sources of oil. Though few tropical fruits have been adequately analyzed for nutritional content, those which have would combat vitamin and other dietary deficiencies. For example, taperebá provides a great deal of vitamin C; the brazilnut is rich in the amino acid methionine,[22] açaí is rich in vitamin A and fats (Castro 1967:51–52;[23] Pechnick and Chaves 1945); and "pupunha" (Guilielma speciosa Mart.), "burití" (*Mauritia vinifera*), and "tucuma" are richer in vitamin A than are carrots.[24]

Unlike other colonists, the caboclo does not view the forest as an enemy that must be beaten back. He sees it, rather, as providing a great variety of animal and plant foods, as well as being a source of raw materials for household needs: vine for rope, bark for basket-weaving, palm leaves for roof thatch, vine sap for potable water when away from streams, dried straw for brooms, raw materials for medicine,[25] and many other materials of daily use. Such knowledge is being acquired by newcomers at different rates. These differences in the rate of adoption can be explained by the general characteristics and needs of each group of farmers.

## Strategies of Newcomers

The pioneers who came to farm the Transamazon at first recognized neither the resources of the forest nor the alternative ways of exploiting them. Their first impulse was to clear the forest and push it as far back as possible. This is especially evident around the house, where not a blade of grass or natural vegetation is allowed to grow. The few vegetable gardens which are started by some are planted at least three meters away from the dwelling. Some fear having even domesticated plants near their houses. They envision snakes, scorpions, spiders, and other disagreeable forest dwellers lurking among the plants. Newcomers do not distinguish between the types of forest vegetation, and forest fruits and animals are not prized as food sources, except for deer meat.

Independent farmers were the first colonists to overcome fear of the natural milieu. In their aim for self-sufficiency they were relatively quick to ask caboclos about the location of fertile land, the climatic conditions of the area, and crops which are amenable to local conditions. Manioc is certainly foremost among the diverse number of crops grown by independent farmers. Tobacco, cowpeas (*Vigna sinensis*), corn, and local varieties of pigs and poultry are also raised for home and market use.

In addition to these diverse local products, independent farmers also plant small vegetable gardens, utilize an increasing variety of wild plant and game resources, grow the government subsidized crops, and invest in a few head of cattle. They are involved in "cottage industries" such as the making of manioc flour and curing of tobacco, both of which involve the participation of children and adults.[26] Wives and children of independent farmers work at producing farm surplus for sale, rather than leaving home to earn wages. Newcomers have often adopted the Amazonian method of soaking bitter manioc to remove its prussic acid. This process demands less labor and results in a yellower, coarser meal known as farinha puba. Such manioc flour sells well on the local market and is produced year-round to supplement farmers' cash income. Independent farmers have become suppliers of many staple goods for both the marketplace and for retailing to neighbors. Diverse utilization of resources, both domestic and wild, is a strategy that is paying off (Moran 1975:145–154).

Independent farmers began with a relatively low amount of capital (see table 7.3), but set up profitable production units through judicious use of bank loans, family labor, and farm diversification. Their accumulated liquid assets, in the form of animals and farm

**Table 7.3** Economic Performance

|  | Brokers (40%) | | Clients (60%) | |
| --- | --- | --- | --- | --- |
| Owners or managers previously | yes | | no | |
| Frequent previous migrations | no | | yes | |
|  | Entrepreneurs (8%) | Independent Farmers (32%) | Artisan-Farmers (24%) | Laborer-Farmers (36%) |
| No. of prev. migrations | 1.5 | 2.1 | 4.8 | 5.3 |
| Beginning capital in Transamazon* | 4,000 | 678 | 1,700 | 140 |
| Yield/ha. (1973–74) in kgs./ha. | pasture | 804.7 | 503.3 | 283.3 |
| Salaried income/yr.* | 48,000 | 5,603 | 18,269 | 4,500 |
| Farm income per yr.* | 5,000 | 8,798 | 3,752 | 2,666 |
| Gross income per yr.* | 53,000† | 14,401 | 22,021‡ | 7,166 |
| Net income per yr.* | 29,000 | 6,301 | 12,831 | −902§ |
| Debt to bank and INCRA* | 37,740 | 12,498 | 6,462 | 5,247 |
| Liquid Assets after 3 yrs.* | 50,500 | 8,000 | 370 | 440 |

*Figures are averages in 1974 cruzeiros (1 cruzeiro = U.S. $0.18) based on a 50 percent sample of a planned village made up of 50 families.
†Largely a function of store and livestock profits.
‡Largely a function of wages from skilled jobs.
§A negative net income suggests that laborers are using credit obtained from bank and individuals to supply the balance. It also indicates inability to keep consumption within the limits of their capacity to earn. Net income is figured by subtracting expenses from gross income.

equipment, is particularly notable, as is their high yield per hectare. Bank credit is used to acquire those assets that are likely to increase farm income, such as griddles for toasting manioc flour, cattle, horses, and powersaws. Such investments reflect both a commitment to the farm as a main generator of income, and the farm's successful management.

Entrepreneurs in the Transamazon utilize a combination of farm production, cattle raising, general stores, and transportation services. Their strategy is seldom based on agriculture alone. Their main goal in the first few years is to plant the government-subsidized cash crops in order to pay back outstanding bank loans. Then they buy cattle or fencing to get a cattle ranch underway. In the meantime, while most of the agricultural work is done by hired laborers, entrepreneurs are busy providing transportation for people and produce and operating stores in local villages and along the highway. One harsh reality of the physical environment is the general lack of navigable streams in the colonization area that can be used to transport produce to nearby markets. Some entrepreneurs exploit the situation by investing in trucks to haul farm produce and people to marketplaces. They also establish general stores near concentrations of farmers. The trucks are fully utilized as they leave the villages for town, loaded with farmers' produce, and return with supplies for the truck owner's store.

Entrepreneurs vary in managerial capacity, but most show sensitivity to seasonal fluctuations in demand. For example, they are busy during the weeks preceding the harvest, attempting to convince the farmers to sell their whole harvest at a fairly low price. This is often successful, as the farmers tend to be low in cash just preceding the harvest. This is especially true among the laborer-farmers. The entrepreneur is able, then, to resell the produce at a better price in town or hold on to it for a few months until the market is less flooded and the prices are higher.[27]

The artisans have also used the colonization project to their own advantage and have overcome the problem of their deficient farming experience by hiring others to work for them. This is a highly effective adaptation, particularly for those urban persons coming into a tropical forest region. By working for high wages, artisans simply pay others to prepare their land. Whenever the artisans are free, they take time to learn about farming techniques from their workers. Over time they gain experience and may opt to become competent independent farmers. In the meantime, a minimal amount of their income is invested in farm equipment and livestock (see table 7.3). Their urban tastes have created a demand for various foods, clothing, and household items which are expensive in the markets of the Transamazon frontier.

The entrepreneur and the artisan-farmer alike are essentially skilled businessmen who are using the opportunity of a pioneer zone to expand their holdings. Both spend relatively little time actually farming on their own land, and hire others to do this work for them. Thus they are relatively unfamiliar with their physical surroundings. Their non-farm pursuits leave them little time for hunting and gathering, and their emphasis on cash earnings rather than self-sufficiency leads them to purchase both staples and luxury goods in the marketplace. Both, on the other hand, are keenly aware of the social and economic situation of the area and its inhabitants. The artisans are particularly sensitive to the labor market, and the entrepreneurs to the produce market and to the various farm surplus producers. However, one is not likely to see any creative strategies for exploiting the physical environment coming from these two groups, except perhaps in the development of pastures and use of various cattle breeds among the entrepreneurs.

Finally, a sizable proportion of pioneers belong to the laborer-farmer category. Accustomed to sharecropping or wage labor arrangements, the ownership of a 100 hectare farmstead has brought them landowner status, but not the necessary financial expertise to run it. Laborer-farmers seek credit from the bank to carry out ambitious cash cropping schemes for rice, corn, and beans—all of which present agronomic and storage problems in a humid tropical environment. Such schemes often are beyond their managerial capacity, as well as that of local transportation facilities. For example, the areas cleared by laborer-farmers are often too large for their capital resources, which generally consist solely of what the bank can provide in loans (US $55/hectare). Since such credit seldom is provided "on time," and since laborer-farmers lack personal savings, they are unable to carry out the operations of underclearing, tree felling, and burning in accordance with the schedule set by tropical weather conditions (cf. Moran 1975:105–25). Many augment their cash income by doing odd jobs. However, as they do not have artisan skills, they take on low-paying manual labor (see table 7.3). They have come to depend on the brokers and on government agencies for such employment. To help out, their wives also perform low skill jobs such as washing clothes for neighbors, gardening, and selling eggs.[28]

The laborer-farmers' emphasis on cash crops leads to neglect of basic subsistence crops and of forest resources. Household gardens are not planted in their planned village homes, because they are never quite sure when they will move again (see figure 7.2). Low initial capital and mismanagement of bank credit and farm operations leads to debt and loss of bank solvency (see table 7.3). As the vicious circle of indebtedness closes in, some begin to sell their land as a way of paying off the debts, while others become full-time wage earners in the area. As a further requirement of subsistence, laborer-farmers turn to hunting to provide needed protein for their families, and in some cases as a source of ready cash. Laborer-farmers are slow to learn from others, but hunting information is one type of knowledge that they have gleaned from their caboclo neighbors.

Their consumption of 22 kilograms of game meat per month is second only to the 36 kilograms utilized by independent farmers, and greatly exceeds the 11 and 0 kilograms, respectively, consumed by artisans and entrepreneurs.

The four types of farmers vary greatly in their farm management strategies. The independent farmers produce most of their needed foodstuffs. This gives them the highest total yield per hectare (see table 7.3). They raise or hunt their protein, and make their own household tools and items of prime necessity. Entrepreneurs provide transportation services, operate stores with basic inventories, run small cattle concerns, and serve as spokesmen for others with government officials.[29] Their agricultural goals aim at quick returns on cash cropping and subsequent pasture development. Artisan-farmers and laborer-farmers spend a considerable amount of time earning wages outside their farms, and thus their agricultural yields tend to be much lower than those who invest both time and effort in farm management. Figure 7.4 illustrates how farmers who spent a minimum amount of time earning salaries also reached the highest yields per hectare (1,000 and up).

Laborer-farmers try to carry out the government directions as they understand them. They plant relatively large areas in cash crops, and neglect subsistence activities. Meanwhile, they rely on bank loans to pay for the day to day needs of their large families. Artisans would be in the same predicament had they lacked the skills which have allowed them to obtain well-paying jobs. Both the independent farmers and the entrepreneurs serve as brokers to the other two groups in our typology. Entrepreneurs provide credit and services of various kinds.[30] Independent farmers serve as a source of basic food items, information about the land, and wages when seasonal labor is required. The survival of the clients is dependent on the success of these brokers who provide a market for both skilled and unskilled work.

## Conclusions

The physical environment, whether the natural forest or cultivated fields, offers a wide variety of economic possibilities. Newcomers to

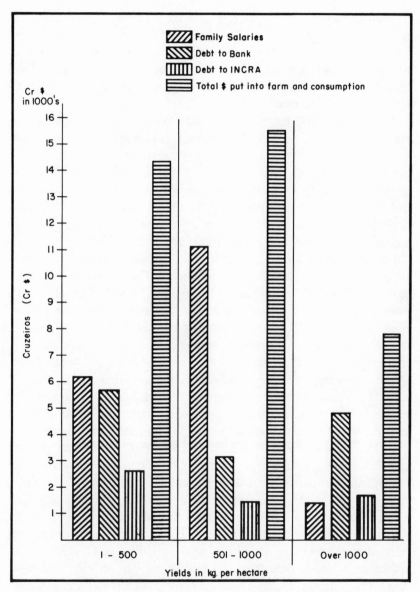

**Figure 7.4.** Relationship Between Non-Farm Sources of Income and Farm Productivity (Moran 1975).

a tropical rain forest are dazzled and confused by the lushness and mystery of the environment. The decisions they make in the early adjustment period are often crucial to their economic and physical well-being. However, without information inputs from experienced local inhabitants, the immigrants' choice of land, crops, and farming strategies may be erroneous.

Sahlins (1968) has noted that adaptation to one's physical surroundings is never perfect. Adaptation is a process subject to modification from both physical and social requirements. In the case study presented here, both the "adapted" caboclos, and the incoming migrants have made adjustments to the complex physical, economic, and institutional setting presented by the Transamazon colonization project. Ideally, one might envision a group of immigrants who could forget all their past experiences and habits and readily accept a tropical lifestyle from the local people. But adaptation is always a compromise between past cultural experience and the requirements to adjust to changing situations. All migrants bring their "cultural baggage" to a new area. This past experience colors their perceptions, use of, and thus their adaptation to, their new environment.

From a variety of cultural experiences emerged a multiplicity of individual economic strategies in the first few years of tropical settlement. The adaptive strategy chosen by the colonists in the Amazon reflects the past managerial experience of each individual farmer. The nature of this expertise, in turn, determines the nature and quantity of environmental information that is sought from the local population.

The most successful colonists, in terms of agricultural production and financial stability, are those who combine previous farm management experience, residential stability, and use of the caboclos' knowledge about the environment. These are the colonists classified as brokers, and they have taken full advantage of the opportunities offered in the Amazon frontier. By virtue of their management backgrounds, they recognize the need for site-specific information, information which only the local inhabitants can provide. They ask about soil, climate, location, and crops so that their farming and business efforts may succeed. They, therefore, create the conditions for making greater adjustments in their strategies and coping with the tropical environment. But in making such adjustments, the basic goals of self-sufficiency for the independent farmer, and of commercial activity for the entrepreneur, continue to be met.

The least successful colonists are the clients, especially those of migratory sharecropping backgrounds. They have never manipulated production factors as farm operators and are not attuned to the need for a broad range of information about the local environment. Accustomed to doing wage labor and following orders, clients were not sufficiently aware of their unfamiliarity with local resources and their need to consult caboclos about them. The single area of cultural exchange was hunting, an alternative chosen out of a necessity to feed their families following their poor results in farming. In time, many clients may be forced through indebtedness to give up their landholdings and will become a wage labor force in the area.

To conclude, then, neither past strategies nor present trial-and-error alone makes for rapid or successful adaptation to a new environment. For both short and long-term success, immigrants with broker backgrounds have two important advantages: they have past experience in mixing production factors, and are attuned to asking for information from knowledgeable inhabitants. While the Amazonian caboclo may not be familiar with modern agricultural techniques, his familiarity with the region's resources provides the baseline information needed in any effort to settle and utilize the Amazon rain forest. Out of the multiplicity of strategies based on such information, new adaptive solutions to life in the Neotropics are likely to emerge. Such solutions are crucial both to Brazil and to the many countries with large humid tropical territories.

## Notes

1. Two brief boom-and-bust cycles took place west of the Atlantic Coast. The first was the mining boom (1702–60) in Minas Gerais and Goiás states; the second was the Rubber Era (1880–1920) in the Amazon. Neither boom was long-lived, nor did much remain of those eras except for impressive architecture to remind the inhabitants of a golden period (Simonsen 1969:247–301).

2. This population includes both Armerindians and rural Brazilians. This paper deals only with the Brazilians as they were the only ones present in the area studied. However, what is said about them applies in all its essentials to aboriginal groups.

3. The Transamazon Highway links the Northeastern cities of João Pessôa and Recife to the Amazonian towns of Marabá, Altamira and Itaituba, and is expected to reach the Peruvian border in 1976. The above mentioned Amazonian towns served as nuclei for colonization project administrators and roadbuilders until new communities

were created along the highway. For a discussion of these planned communities see Kleinpenning (1975) and Moran (1975). The shaded area in figure 7.1, between the cities of Altamira and Itaituba, was the main focus of colonization efforts (1971–74).

4. The research on which this paper is based was made possible by funds from the Social Science Research Council and the National Institute of Mental Health. However, the conclusions, opinions, and other statements in this publication are those of the author and do not necessarily reflect those of the funding agencies. Field research was carried out between 1973 and 1974 in the Altamira region of the Brazilian Amazon (see figure 7.1 and note 3). This region was selected over others because it was selected by the Brazilian government to demonstrate the development model to be applied elsewhere in the Amazonian lowlands.

5. While these areas have the appearance of virgin lands, indigenous populations are known to have lived in this area, clearing small gardens by slash and burn methods. Species associated with secondary succession (esp. *Cecropia* spp.) were observed in the fields still unoccupied by the colonists.

6. Although it is true that a great deal of individual variability is present in all cultures (cf. Pelto and Pelto 1975), traditional cultures tend to be far less pluralistic than modern societies (White 1949).

7. Billington has suggested in his studies of the American frontier situation that this simplification of a pioneer's "cultural baggage" is a process that often occurs in migration (1967:16).

8. The term *caboclo* is widely used in Brazil for persons living in the backlands, or for anyone in a lower social position than the person speaking. *Caboclo* can indicate different racial mixtures in different areas of Brazil. For instance, while the southern caboclo studied by Willems (1952) is largely non-Indian, the Amazonian caboclo shows a predominance of the aboriginal element (Wagley 1952). However, the term *caboclo* as used in this paper will refer to a cultural type rather than to the degree of racial mixture.

9. Part of the government development plan was to provide health and educational services. To facilitate this process nucleated villages were built and farmers were encouraged to live in these planned communities rather than on their land. Besides the nucleated villages (agrovilas), the plan also included planned towns (agrópolis) of about 300 persons and planned cities (ruropolis) of 1,000 families or more (cf. Kleinpenning 1975; Moran 1975 for details).

10. We have added the hyphenated "-farmers" to make clear the fact that, despite their chosen strategies, these persons came with the primary intention of farming the land and turned to other interests when their efforts were not adequately rewarded. The hyphenated -farmer was not added to the entrepreneurs because it was awkward. Peons are also present in the area. These are commonly single men who have not expressed interest in having a title to the area's lands but who work for wages for various farmers. Unlike the farmers, who tend to be reasonably abstemious, the peons are rowdy during their weekend trips into town where they go for drinking and "having a good time."

11. The group bears some similarity to the European-type mixed farmers, but are by no means identical (Wagley 1968:126). The European independent farmer operates a self-sufficient agricultural enterprise that integrates the use of cattle and crops. Alfalfa and oats are planted to feed the cattle, the manure is collected and used to fertil-

ize the crops, and butter and cheese are made from the milk. Other crops are planted to supply household needs and an efficient cottage industry, including canning and preserving, stores away supplies after the harvest. Such a system was not transplanted to Brazil except among a relatively small southern population of German and Dutch descent. Sioli (1973:330–34) had indicated that just such a system has worked well in the Brazilian Amazon, in an area colonized by some Germans in Pará State's Zona Bragantina.

12. The Altamira area seems to have been chosen as the center for Transamazon colonization efforts because of the presence of good soils in the vicinity of the town. Before the arrival of the road construction crews, the county had an average population of 0 to 10 persons per square kilometer. The county seat, also named Altamira, is served by the Xingú River, one of the larger Amazon affluents. Average temperature is 26 degrees centigrade, and rainfall approaches 1700 mm. per year. It has two marked seasons: a dry period (June–October), and a wet period (November–May). The area through which the road cuts is in the upland region, or *terra firme*, and has tropical moist forest characteristics.

13. This is a role similar to that of the "cultural broker" who, in Wolf's terms, are "individuals who are able to operate both in terms of community-orientation and national oriented expectations," (Wolf 1956:1072). It is different in that many of these entrepreneurs, though not all, are newcomers operating in an area without strong traditional patrons and which are strongly influenced by national economic development plans.

14. Caboclo soils were of remarkable quality: the pH was 1.6 higher on the average than those of other colonists; phosphorus content was even more dramatic—15.8 ppm on the average vs. 2.4 ppm for newcomers; Potassium, carbon, and nitrogen were not significantly different. Caboclo soils tend to be of 10 YR hue (brown or brownish black) while those of newcomers were of 7.5 YR hue (brown and dark brown). For full soil analyses see Moran (1975).

15. No caboclo colonist was, however, reported to use these methods. Nor do they use *timbó*, a general name given to a wide variety of poisonous vines which can stupefy fish in a dammed up stream.

16. Large bands of forty or more howler monkeys (*Alouatta* spp.) roam the area. Capuchins (especially *Cebus appella* Linn.) are the most often killed for food. Also found in the area are *sauim* or squirrel monkeys (*Saimiri sciureus* Linn.), *macaco barrigudo* (*Lagothrix* spp.), *zogue-zogue* (*Callicebus* spp.), owl monkeys (*Aotus trivirgatus* Humb.), and other unidentified species with local names such as *mão de ouro, cara branca, quatro olhos,* and *cuambá*.

17. For a thorough discussion of local food tabus and how they related to the people's conceptualization of health and disease, see Fleming-Moran (1975).

18. Caboclos in the area said that there were days for the hunter (*dias do caçador*) and days for the game (*dias da caça*). Tuesday, Friday, and Saturday were lucky days for the hunter, while Sunday and Monday were lucky days for the animals. On the latter days, hunting was not rewarding and was generally avoided. Wednesday and Thursday were neutral and ambiguous. Even on days when luck was on his side, the hunter could come home empty-handed. On such occasions he became concerned and began to investigate the possibility that he was *empanemado* (having bad luck) and began to seek the source so as to begin an effective cultural cure (Wagley 1953:79–80; Galvão 1951).

19. *Panema* is a sort of bad luck in hunting (Galvão 1951). Panema can be caught by the touch of a menstruating woman on a hunter's or fisherman's articles; through not sharing game catches with needy neighbors or relatives (*desconfiança*); through mutilation or abandonment of the carcass of hunted game; and through permitting a pregnant non-relative to eat his game. Fear for the loss of protein sources, namely game and fish, seems to reside at the root of caboclo beliefs in *panema* (Wagley 1953:81; Moran 1974:148).

20. The Brazilian Institute of Forestry Development (IBDF) will prosecute a man who sells animal pelts and see that he and his family are expelled from the colonization area for such violations. Game hunting is allowed only for consumption purposes. Of course, it is extremely difficult to police the forest and its inhabitants.

21. The Altamira region is relatively poor in forest fruits. Among the notable absences are: *aracá* (*Psidium araca* Raddi); *buriti* (*Mauritia vinifera*); *bacurí* (*Platonia insignis* Mart.); *biribá* (*Rollinia orthopetala*); *ingá* (*Inga* spp.), *jenipapo* (*Genipa americana* L.); *muricí* (*Byrsonima crassifolia*); *mirití* (*Mauritia flexuosa*), and *pupunha* (*Guilielma speciosa* M.).

22. This is the amino acid sorely lacking in the make up of manioc protein. This lack has been used to condemn manioc as a low-quality food. In a recent article Gross (1975:534) suggests that methionine may well be the ultimate factor limiting the size of aboriginal settlements in the Amazon. Gross admits that symptoms of protein deficiency have never been noted among relatively unacculturated tribal peoples in the Amazon region (1975:534–35) but he does not make the further step of asking or suggesting why. Consumption of brazilnuts and manioc provides a balanced amino acid and carbohydrate diet. Sweet potatoes are also rich sources of methionine and are an important item in the tuberous diets of tropical forest peoples.

23. Fat intake among rural Brazilians is usually considered as too low (Castro, 1967). Açaí is consumed in enormous quantities whenever it is available. It is Pará state's favorite fruit as indicated by their saying: "quem para em Pará para, se toma açaí fica" (who comes to Pará stops, if he drinks açaí, he stays). Newcomers to the Amazon are initiated into the pleasures of açaí drinking immediately and their reactions carefully observed.

24. Pupunha is comparable to carrots (8,900 micrograms per 100 g.) while buriti and tucumã are many times richer (30,000 and 31,000 micrograms per 100 g. respectively). Pupunha is also rich in fats (Chavez et al. 1949).

25. For a discussion of medicinal plants in the area consult Fleming-Moran (1975). Instrumental in the diffusion of such information among the farmer groups are the children. Being less restricted by cultural preferences and far more gregarious, they learn about the local foods and experiment with them. This method of diffusion also applies to medicinal plants, game meats, and methods of obtaining wild food sources. Since children act as family messengers and carriers, they gain exposure to people's habits and resource use.

26. Children are gradually taught the skills needed to carry on these small-scale industries, first in the form of play and assuming increasingly larger shares of the labor. By age fifteen most children are able to perform all tasks except perhaps for the most strenuous.

27. For example, while beans sold for Cr $100 per sack at harvest time, the price skyrocketed to CR $200 per sack within four or five months. Some who could store

their purchased supply of beans were able to sell them and buy as much as 30 head of cattle from the profits earned in the transaction. The main limitation to more of these sorts of operations by local entrepreneurs is their lack of adequate storage space.

28. While none of these jobs are very lucrative, nevertheless, client wives tend to make a bigger contribution to the total household cash income than do the other wives in the community.

29. The rise of a patrão class has been more fully explained in a recent paper dealing with the emergence of social class in the Transamazon (cf. Fleming-Moran and Moran 1975).

30. Other farmers often asked the entrepreneurs for informal credit. Although the latter tried to discourage borrowing, it is provided informally and is an effective ally in the entrepreneurs' control over local agricultural production. If a farmer owes a certain amount at a local store, it is common practice for the entrepreneur to drive out to the debtor's land and buy off his harvest at the lowest price or carry off some of the farmer's poultry or swine as payments for the debt. The debtor is usually thankful that his debt has been cleared by the forceful creditor. However, in strictly economic terms, he has suffered a net capital loss. His only consolation is that he has personalized credit available whenever he is unable to pay for needed goods and services, because of a lack of cash resources.

## EIGHT

# Seduced and Abandoned: Agricultural Frontiers in Brazil and the United States

Maxine Margolis

Frontiers, like those who come to sudden
wealth, are inclined to be spendthrifts
Avery Craven (1925)

MANY ECOLOGISTS AND economists have decried the constant advance of exploitative agricultural systems into the world's last remaining unsettled lands. The current occupation of Brazil's Amazon Valley immediately comes to mind. The settlement of fertile frontier lands for the purpose of cultivating cash crops is hardly a recent development; indeed, it has had a very long history. Much of the North and South American continents, to cite just one world area, was colonized by planters and farmers lured onward by the promise of cheap virgin land on which lucrative cash crops could be grown. The imaginations of residents in the older, more settled regions of the New World always were captured by the idea that "out there" fortunes were to be made.

The impact that the frontier has had on many phases of American life has received a great deal of attention from historians and political scientists; debates concerning the nature of "frontier democ-

A briefer version of this paper was presented at the 71st annual meeting of the American Anthropological Association in Toronto, Canada in 1972.

racy'' and social institutions have been nearly endless (see especially, Turner 1920 and Hofstadter and Lipset 1968). While some have focused on the destructive effects that the settlers' headlong rush to "get rich quick" have had on the seemingly limitless resources of the frontier (Leeds 1957), few have looked into the specific ecologic and economic settings in which the settlers found themselves. Yet this seems essential for an understanding of the behavior of frontiersmen, so often dismissed as simply reckless, materialistic and "now oriented." How are we to explain their "restless response to the invitation of the land" (Bowman 1931:38)? It is the thesis of this paper that the availability of fertile frontier land, along with a market for a valuable cash crop, gives rise to a particular variety of agricultural exploitation, along with a mentality that complements it. Agriculture, under these circumstances, tends to be destructive of natural resources, since the cultivators pay little attention to the long-term effects of their often crude farming practices. But why should this shortsightedness be so characteristic of frontier cultivators? Why should frontier farmers be imbued with an immediatist mentality? The answers to these questions will be sought in the etic conditions of frontier existence.

In order to demonstrate that broadly similar economic and ecological conditions exist on many of the world's agricultural frontiers and produce similar reactions on the part of their inhabitants, this paper will describe the settlement of two such areas, the coffee region of southern Brazil and the cotton region of the southern and southwestern United States. A review of the strikingly parallel careers of those areas' attendant cash crops will provide insight into the nature of frontier agriculture.


## The Advance of Coffee in Southern Brazil

The westward march of coffee in Brazil may
be likened to the pseudopodic motion of the
amoeba in search of sustenance: the initial
thrust of part of its mass (or 'feet'),
followed later by the filling in of the new
region, and the transformation of the former
nucleus into a fringe area. The process is

renewed each time as the food supply (soil
fertility) becomes inadequate to sustain
plant activity at a desirable level.

Frederick Gifun (1972)

The spread of coffee cultivation in Brazil comprises three distinct historical and geographical phases. Coffee was introduced into Brazil around 1723 from French Guiana. At first it was grown in scattered patches along the coast from the port of Santos northward to the mouth of the Amazon. Coffee became a commercial crop as a result of its increasing popularity in the United States and Europe in the early 1800s. At about this time, coffee spread from the hillsides around Rio de Janeiro, where it had been grown as an exotic decorative plant, to the Paraíba Valley just north of the city. Coffee cultivation became concentrated in the valley because of its well drained land and fertile soil. Settlement of the area was very rapid with a large portion of the population coming from the mining regions of the state of Minas Gerais. With the expanding demand for coffee abroad, there was a related demand in the Paraíba Valley for more land and more slaves. This land hunger absorbed most small and medium-sized holdings, and the few farmers who managed to survive the encroachments of the plantation earned their livelihood by supplying its masters and slaves with food crops. Both land and labor on the plantations were too valuable to "waste" growing subsistence crops.

The decade 1850–1860 marked the "Golden Age of Coffee" in the Paraíba Valley. Even then, however, the signs of decline already were apparent to the careful observer. The trees were aging and gave indications of producing lower yields. Soil erosion and insect pests (sauva ants) plagued many plantations and heavy rains hastened the process of decay. Another warning signal was the sharply reduced supply of virgin land for new coffee plantings.

At the start of the economic squeeze, around 1860, some planters began to question their methods of cultivation and processing. While some invested in costly milling equipment to clean and hull the coffee beans, few used fertilizer or irrigation. Profits were still high and expensive technological innovations did not seem necessary. Instead, virgin forests gave way to new plantings in an effort to keep production high. The large coffee yields of the 1860s and the continued availability of some virgin land held off the impending crisis for at least a decade. By 1870, however, most planters realized that their once lucrative plantations were doomed. They blamed their hard times on the inefficiency and scarcity of slave labor, the lack of modern coffee processing equipment, and the near absence of cheap agricultural credit; few attributed the decline to sapped soils and weakened trees (Stein 1957:214).

By the 1880s the crisis had worsened. A considerable portion of the planters' capital was wiped out with the abolition of slavery in 1888, while owing to its scarcity, prices for virgin land continued to spiral, reaching a peak in the mid 1880s. The most serious blow, however, was the sharp fall in production: where 1,000 trees had once produced up to 4,500 kilos of coffee, they now only produced 750 kilos (Stein 1957:219). The death knell of coffee cultivation in the Paraíba Valley had sounded. Planters were forced into bankruptcy when they could not pay off long-standing debts. Ranchers from Minas Gerais moved in and established huge cattle ranches on the worn out coffee lands. Unemployment became a problem and hundreds of workers and owners left the region as cattle raising came to dominate the scene. The entire character of the Paraíba Valley changed, leaving depopulation and temporary destruction of the once fertile soil as the legacy of the coffee boom.

The interior of the State of São Paulo was the site of the second phase of coffee's advance. The gradual westward expansion of coffee into the state gained momentum in the 1860s and within 30 years São Paulo's production surpassed that of Rio de Janeiro. The rich virgin soils surrounding Ribeirão Preto, an early locus of coffee cultivation in São Paulo, produced yields four to five times greater than those of the sapped lands of the Paraíba Valley (Gifun 1972:8).

At first, coffee cultivation in São Paulo was limited to areas of rich *terra roxa,* a deep red porous soil particularly well-suited to that crop. But, as coffee continued its westward advance, it was planted in regions of less fertile, sandier soil. These soils, however, were not unprofitable for coffee production. They gave very high yields when the land was first cleared, although production declined as the same lands were continually cultivated (James 1959:486). No attempt was made to intensify the methods of production or to conserve the initial fertility of the soil; such practices were very costly and there was still an abundance of cheap virgin frontier land on which to settle should yields on one's present land begin to decline.

In a discussion of the founding of coffee *fazendas* (plantations) in the Ribeirão Preto region, Gifun notes "the influence of the still heavy forest cover on climate and soil seemingly made unnecessary any concern about soil exhaustion or the climatic consequences of the wholesale destruction of woodland" (Gifun 1972:88). A similar lack of attention to soil erosion and leaching occurred on the early coffee fazendas in the Araraquara region of the state (Little 1960:4). The consequences of such unconcern—depletion of resources and reduced yields—were several decades away.

The rapid march westward of coffee in São Paulo brought hundreds of thousands of acres under cultivation. In a mere two decades, between 1880 and 1900, more than 420 million coffee trees were planted in the state and production skyrocketed from 3.7 million bags [1] to 10.2 million bags during the same period (Gifun 1972:109). Further, by the 1890s Brazil accounted for 75 percent of the world's total coffee production (Pan American Coffee Bureau 1964:15). There seem to be four factors which account for this "boom": land was both abundant and cheap; prices for coffee were high; transportation for the crop was no problem since the railroads followed the advance of the frontier (Moore 1962:128); and, in the words of one commentator on the period, "profits were fabulous" (James 1959:488).

As coffee cultivation continued its westward spread in São Paulo, some of the state's older regions of settlement became subject to a fate similar to that of the Paraíba Valley. In the northern and central zones yields declined, many of the groves were abandoned or turned into pasture, and a partial depopulation of the area ensued. In Ribeirão Preto, for example, yields which had averaged 1,275 kilos of coffee per 1,000 trees between 1900 and 1916 fell to an average of 850 kilos per 1,000 trees during the decade of the 1920s. The killing frost of 1918 which severely damaged half of the state's coffee trees, affecting 90 percent of them in some areas, was a major factor in declining yields (Gifun 1972:161). But the aging of the trees, erosion, and leaching also took a serious toll on production.

Whenever signs of soil exhaustion were detected, there was at least some justification for the planter's abandonment of his current holding in order to invest in rich frontier land farther west. The reserve of virgin forest seemed inexhaustible which accounts for land-owners' unwillingness to spend vast sums on "rational agriculture"—mechanization, seed selection, reforestation, fertilizer, and erosion control—when, for far less, they could purchase a frontier plot which was guaranteed to produce high yields for at least a few years. In the words of one commentator: "The whole structure of the coffee industry has been founded on an advance into new land" (Little 1960:339). This lack of concern for natural resources, while deplorable from a long-range perspective, "is justifiable from the viewpoint of the private entrepreneur, whose goal is to obtain the maximum profit from his capital. Soil conservation becomes a major concern . . . only when it has an economic basis" (Furtado 1965a:179).

The very high prices paid for coffee just prior to the 1929 crisis spurred the settlement of other regions of São Paulo still farther west. Many settlers in these areas had migrated from the older coffee zones of the state, seeking to recapture the fabulous profits that can be made when prices are high and coffee is grown on virgin soil. During the crest of the green wave in the extreme west, *cidades cogumelos* (mushroom cities), as the new towns on the frontier were called, sprung up overnight, providing a striking contrast to the dying towns of the older coffee regions of the state. But, here again, a similar pattern developed and within two decades prices fell, farmers lacked the money to fertilize or even to do common pruning tasks, and yields declined. Coffee was no longer the sole topic of conversation: "Travelers . . . who used to bring back stories of the green oceans of new coffee trees stretching beyond the horizon now talked of brown plains of land plowed for cotton stretching away in the distance" (Little 1960:186).

By 1935, most of the older "coffee counties" in São Paulo were no longer devoted to monocrop cultivation. In many, cattle and cotton had become the principle products. The changeover was prompted by a reduction in coffee yields and great fluctuations in price (Monbeig 1952:ch. 3). Today, many areas of the Paulista plateau resemble the desolate region of the Paraíba Valley after coffee's demise. Coffee has left in its wake exhausted fields, unused drying terraces, empty barns, and vacated colonists' houses (Little 1960:339).

At this point, two ecological factors which are linked to the decline of coffee yields in São Paulo and elsewhere in Brazil should be mentioned. The warm climate and relatively warm soils in the regions of coffee cultivation produce a very rapid oxidation rate of organic materials once the forest cover is removed. The leaching of nutrients becomes a problem and soils must be fertilized if yields are to be maintained. In addition, the benefits of fertilizer are short-term so that it must be frequently re-applied (Moore 1962:227,433). Rainfall also is a critical factor in coffee yields. While an average annual rainfall of 60 inches is necessary for optimal production, and this average was usually surpassed during the early decades of cultivation, between 1936 and 1943 an average annual rainfall of only 51 inches was recorded for some coffee zones in São Paulo, and increasing dryness, particularly during the winter months, cut the size of harvests (Little 1960:199–200). This decrease in rainfall, in turn, was clearly related to the massive destruction of virgin forest which preceded the advancing tide of "green gold." [2]

The westward march of coffee in the state of Paraná, which is still in progress today, marks the latest phase of Brazil's boom crop. Coffee was introduced into northern Paraná during the final decade of the nineteenth century. The impetus for settlement of the region did not come from within the state itself, but from across the border in São Paulo. By 1900 coffee cropping and the railroad simultaneously penetrated the western plateau region of northern Paraná. Settlement of the area initially was slow, but rising coffee prices after World War I greatly stimulated new plantings. Many of the colonizers during this period had owned tracts of land in contiguous areas of São Paulo, but were prohibited from planting new coffee trees as part of the government's program to limit production. The ban did not extend to Paraná, however, and its rich untouched *terra roxa* beckoned the planters onward (Margolis 1973: 19–21).

In the mid-1940s, following an interval of relative inactivity during the Great Depression, coffee prices once again soared, profits from the sale of the crop were enormous, and the settlement of frontier lands in extreme western Paraná continued rapidly. In recent years, Brazilian entrepreneurs have crossed the international boundary and have begun planting coffee in the fertile soil of Paraguay, earning for themselves the title of "imperialists of South America" (Galeano 1968:20).

With the advance of the Paraná frontier, lush sub-tropical forests gave way to millions of rows of coffee trees, rural hamlets, and dirt roads as settlers from Brazil's Northeast, Minas Gerais, and São

Paulo carved farms out of the dense undergrowth. Towns and cities sprung up overnight as marketing and processing centers for coffee. Maringá, for example, now a city of over 200,000 inhabitants, the third or fourth largest in the state, was founded in 1945. During its first years it was a dusty frontier town with a "wild west" atmosphere and unpaved streets which became impassible muddy streams after a heavy rainfall. Today, it is a modern bustling city with "skyscrapers" (of five stories) and paved roads linking it to the ports of Paranaguá and Santos.

The early and mid-1950s marked the peak of the coffee boom in northern Paraná when the newly planted trees began producing their rich harvests and prices soared to a high of $15 a bag for unprocessed coffee (Margolis 1972:10). Between 1949 and 1959 the area planted in coffee in the state increased fivefold (Moore 1962:408). This was an era of prosperity in the region; small general stores were stocked with luxury goods and many landowners abandoned their traditional *cachaça,* a cheap alcoholic drink distilled from sugar cane, preferring to toast their bountiful harvests with French champagne. The atmosphere was suffused with adventure and hope; euphoric residents believing that this was a place in which fortunes could be made.

But the boom was not to last and again we find a pattern similar to that of Brazil's older coffee regions; profits were large at first since both prices and yields were high. No attempt, however, was made to insure the trees' continued productivity. In one Paraná "coffee county," for example, yields declined from a high of just over 35 million kilograms of coffee during the 1957–58 harvest to slightly under 8 million kilograms in the 1968–69 harvest (Margolis 1972:9). Fertilizers were used only after an alarming decline in the size of harvests, but by that time, prices had fallen to a low of $5 per bag of unprocessed coffee, making planters loath to cut into their already meager profits by investing in expensive conservation techniques. Then, too, there was the threat of frosts; mild frosts which might halve the harvests, or severe ones, as occurred in 1955, 1963, and 1975 which destroyed the coffee trees altogether.

As a result of these factors, today in many parts of Paraná the amount of land devoted to coffee cultivation has been greatly reduced, and cattle ranching is becoming an increasingly important enterprise.[3] Since the labor requirements of a cattle economy are far smaller than those of coffee, these same areas have suffered large-scale unemployment and partial depopulation. Schools and farm houses have been abandoned as small landholdings have been consolidated into large cattle ranches. Day laborers and sharecroppers are leaving the region in droves; unable to find work locally, they hope for employment in the newly opened coffee lands of extreme western Paraná or in Paraguay (Margolis 1973:ch. 3). Thus, like the Paraíba Valley and the interior of São Paulo state in earlier years, much of northern Paraná has witnessed the destructive effects of frontier agriculture.

Any number of historians and social scientists have commented on the rapid spread of coffee cultivation in Brazil, while decrying the despoilment of natural resources it left in its wake. "Immediatism" and "improvidence," it was said "rode along with the frontier" and the "bonanza spirit" and an "exploitative psychology" were blamed for declining yields, a result of the failure to employ conservation techniques (Little 1960:260,399; Moore 1962:465). The lack of a future orientation and a "blind faith in continuing prosperity" are held accountable for the planters' failure to develop a "sentimental attachment" to their holdings which led to the constant advance into new lands (Stein 1957:38; James 1959:482). As we shall see shortly, amazingly similar "explanations" were offered for the expansion of cotton cultivation during the nineteenth century in the southern United States. In neither case, however, is there any attempt to *account for* the appearance of these values in conjunction with frontier agriculture by examining the economic and ecologic milieu in which they arose.

## The Cotton Frontier in the Southern United States

Our small farmers, after taking the cream
off their lands, unable to restore them by
rest, manures or otherwise, are going
farther west and south, in search of other
virgin lands which they may and will despoil
and impoverish in like manner.

> Senator Clement C. Clay of Alabama
> Quoted in Clement Eaton (1961)

Cotton culture in the United States also had a number of distinct historical and geographical phases. From the coastal plain, cotton spread to the Piedmont area of the Atlantic seaboard, and then on to the bottom lands of the Gulf states, and finally, to southwest Arkansas and northeast Texas. The rise of "King Cotton" in the American south dates from 1793 with the invention of the cotton gin, a major technological breakthrough, which made the commercial exploitation of short-staple or upland cotton possible for the first time. Prior to this invention, it took an entire day for a slave to gin one pound of lint by hand, but using a gin, 350 pounds of cotton could be cleaned in the same period (Eaton 1949:228).

At the end of the seventeenth century the inventions of spinning and weaving machinery in England created a major market for cotton fiber and the southern United States was an ideal site for filling the demand. Its warm climate was well suited to cotton cultivation. The requirements of at least 200 frost-free days and a minimum annual rainfall of 23 inches were met throughout most of the region. Short-staple cotton could be grown on a variety of soils: on alluvial bottom lands, on the red clay hills of the Piedmont, on the black prairies of Alabama, and on the loess soil of southwest Mississippi. Of the cash crops, only tobacco could be grown as widely, but tobacco planting was a less profitable enterprise (Sydnor 1948:13–14).

The South offered still another advantage: cotton cultivation could be performed satisfactorily by slave labor organized in large forces. The plant was low enough so that as they worked in rows plowing, hoeing, and picking the crop, the slaves were not obscured from the eyes of the overseer. The spread of cotton, in fact, is often blamed for breathing new life into the nearly moribund institution of slavery. In addition, unlike tobacco, rice, and sugar cane, upland cotton grown on fertile soil does not require delicate cultivation procedures to insure abundant yields. While most of the tasks associated with cotton demand a fairly constant labor force, none of them require great skill (Gates 1960:136).

The northern limits of cotton were defined by trial and error. By 1825, the crop was planted in southeastern Virginia and the Piedmont of North Carolina, but early frosts combined with falling prices wrecked the enterprise in those areas (Phillips 1929:99–100). Production fell drastically; the combined product of both states was 104,000 bales in 1828–29, but only 22,500 bales in 1842–1843 (Gray 1933:889). Local planters moved south and west in search of better climes for their crop, leading legislators in Virginia and North Carolina to decry the loss of population in their states. A number of contemporary travelers in the region were dismayed by its desolation and decay; old plantation houses were abandoned and in disrepair, land prices had declined tremendously, and towns were deserted by their inhabitants.

The Georgia–South Carolina Piedmont was an early center of cotton cultivation, and in 1821 those two states produced 190,000 bales, slightly more than half of the national crop (Sydnor 1948:14). The typical planter in this region owned few slaves and not a great deal of land. But cotton could be grown successfully by the farmer with a small holding and a few simple tools, as well as by the planter with huge acreages and hundreds of slaves under his command. The crop, therefore, offered economic opportunity to people with little capital. Profits made from cotton grown on virgin soil at first were extremely high. In 1801, for example, when cultivators were receiving 44 cents per pound, one planter's yield from 600 acres of frontier land was valued at $90,000 (Eaton 1949:231).

Cotton prices, however, were not always high; indeed, they fluctuated greatly during the first half of the nineteenth century. Between 1800 and 1807 the price fell from 44 to 20 cents per pound due to over-production, a result of the headlong rush to plant cotton spurred by its original high return. The War of 1812 made for a further decline in price, but by 1815 the market had recovered rather spectacularly and planters could sell their crop for 30 cents per pound (Phillips 1929:99). Although great over-production broke the price from time to time—in 1819, 1825, and 1837–1845—the expansion of cotton continued until 1861.

The reign of "King Cotton" in the Georgia–South Carolina Piedmont never reached full flower since the region had two distinct disadvantages for cotton culture: its soil was less fertile than that of other areas to which cotton eventually migrated, particularly the Black Belt and river bottoms of Alabama, and it was without adequate transportation facilities, being cut off from the coast by pine barrens and lacking navigable rivers (Abernethy 1922:99). While the Piedmont was the site of prosperity and rapid development for the first three decades after the introduction of cotton culture, by 1825 its lands were gullied, its soils depleted, and its cotton yields low. Farmers and planters from the area began migrating to the newly opened frontier lands of the Southwest, making one contemporary critic deplore the "Alabama fever" which was carrying off local citizens and threatening to depopulate the region (Eaton 1961:31).

The flood of humanity into Alabama and Mississippi between 1820 and 1830 came almost entirely from the older southern states. This drain of population is well illustrated by the fact that in the decade 1830–1840 the population of North Carolina remained stationary, despite one of the highest birth rates in the nation, while that of Alabama increased 76 percent and that of Mississippi increased 154 percent. As early as 1830 the Gulf states surpassed those on the Atlantic seaboard in cotton production, and by the outbreak of the Civil War, they produced three-fourths of the cotton grown in the South (Eaton 1961:44–45). In order to appreciate the importance of the crop, not only for the Gulf states, but for the nation as a whole, it should be stressed that it accounted for 60 percent of the total value of United States exports on the eve of the Civil War, and employed three-quarters of all slaves engaged in agriculture (Phillips 1929:100).

Once the rush was underway in the Southwest, land prices skyrocketed; in Alabama, land that had sold for $8 to $10 an acre went for $20 to $30, while superior cotton land on the river bottoms commanded $50 to $70 an acre (Abernethy 1961:473). During times of high prices, planters and farmers threw caution to the wind and sowed their entire holdings in cotton, forcing them to buy corn and other staples in the market. In 1825, when there was a sudden upsurge in the price of cotton, corn actually was plowed up to make way for the more valuable cash crop. Planters simply refused to "waste" labor on growing food crops when it could be more profitably used producing cotton. As a result, the states of the lower South became increasingly dependent on other regions for the necessities of life.

Fluctuations in the price of cotton constantly buffeted its cultivators, but they were helpless to do anything about it since the impersonal forces of the world market were beyond their control. Nor was crop diversification a solution; cotton cultivation requires a long growing season and a good deal of labor, so that there were rarely surplus hands available to plant and harvest other crops. But even when prices were fairly low, as they were in the 1850s, the large plantations could grow cotton for 5 cents a pound and sell it on the market for 11 cents, turning a neat profit after all expenses were paid (Cohn 1956:51-52). Then, too, during times of high prices and favorable weather conditions, it was possible to lay the groundwork for amassing great fortunes.

The settlement of the Gulf states occurred with great speed. The richness of the soil and the thousands of acres of good cotton land within easy reach of navigable rivers beckoned with the promise of seemingly limitless riches. Within 30 years the great forests had vanished and been replaced by cultivated fields, plantations, and roads. Hardly had a plot been cleared and planted in cotton, when the slaves were set to work felling trees and preparing additional land for eventual planting—with the expectation that the newly planted clearing soon would be abandoned. The rude log cabins of the first years of settlement quickly gave way to the southern "mansion house," with its sweeping veranda and imposing white columns. The large profits of the "good" years often made for personal extravagance among the planters who demanded luxury items of all kinds. This stimulated the Mississippi River trade which flourished during these years, as steamboats carried passengers, cotton, and other goods up and down the river. Indeed, these were often "flush times in Alabama and Mississippi," as a book written during the period was titled.

In the midst of this prosperity signs of decay slowly became evident. As early as 1840, in many parts of Alabama, the decline in cotton yields and lower land prices indicated that soil exhaustion was setting in. In one county, where the best farming land had sold for $30 to $60 per acre, it had fallen to $10 to $15 an acre,[4] and yields of seed cotton per acre had declined from 1,000 to 500 pounds (Davis 1939:170). In another Alabama county, a contemporary traveler reported abandoned, gullied fields covered by broom sedge. One observer of the period remarked that Mississippi farmers were eroding their land by "skinning" the soil, only scratching the surface with their plows (Eaton 1961:41). As a result, in the 1840s and 1850s, farmers and planters began to leave these states in droves, seeking fresher cotton lands in Texas and Arkansas.[5] Again, the story is the same: deserted fields, desolate towns, and abandoned "Gone to Texas" farms (Weaver 1945:106).

Cotton culture made a relatively late arrival in Texas; it had poor marketing facilities and its slave status was uncertain until after the Texas Revolution. As late as 1835, this vast territory produced only 3,000 to 4,000 bales of cotton a year. But by 1853, production had risen to 120,000 bales annually, and by the end of the decade, east Texas alone accounted for over 430,000 bales (Gray 1933:906). The fertility of the state's virgin black soil far surpassed that of the older cotton producing regions, a fact that explains much of the attractiveness of this hinterland. In newly settled areas of Texas during the 1850s yields of three bales of cotton per acre were not unusual, while at the same time the badly depleted lands of the upper south were producing only one bale per acre (Eaton 1961:45). Also during the decade preceding the Civil War, cotton prices rose to 11 or 12 cents per pound, once again assuring at least reasonable profits for its cultivators.

"Texas fever" swept the South between 1850 and 1860. Newspapers gave glowing accounts of the state's fertile soils, ideal climate, and the fortunes to be made from cotton culture. Farmers and planters from throughout the older cotton growing regions sold their land and moved west, hoping to cash in on the opportunities afforded by this newest American frontier. Emigration to Texas was so rapid during the decade that its population nearly tripled. Still, what eventually became the most important cotton producing region of the state awaited the introduction of the railroad, and therefore, was not settled until after the Civil War. The expansion of cotton culture in Texas continued for decades, and with the advent of irrigation, thousands of additional acres were brought under the plow. Still today, Texas is the largest cotton producer in the nation.

The westward trek of cotton in the United States is a well documented fact of our history. Equally well known are the destructive effects this advance had on much of the region's natural resources. Many contemporary observers complained of the cotton planters' and farmers' exhaustive cultivation methods, of their seeming indifference to the future of the land, of their overwhelming desire for huge profits which engendered a restless spirit and a constant search for fresher, more fertile soil in which to plant their crops. They also decried the conditions that this movement left in its wake; the abandoned farms and desolate towns, the decaying mansion houses, the lifeless gullied countryside covered with broom sedge and foxtail, and the social and political consequences of mass emigration from exhausted lands that could support no one. Different critics offered different explanations for the "evil" they saw. Abolitionists cited the destructive effects of slave labor; politicians orated against the cultivators' acquisitiveness and lack of attachment to the land; agronomists blamed the nature of cotton cultivation itself, which required a large amount of tillage, a constant turning and loosening of the earth which exposed the soil to destructive washing, particularly during heavy rains. Planters' journals criticized cotton cultivators for their opposition to innovation and their unwillingness to modify debilitating land-use practices. Specifically, they rallied against over-cropping with insufficient labor which led to careless cultivation. They lamented the failure to use selected seeds and condemned negligent ginning techniques which injured the cotton bolls (Gates 1960:139).

There is no doubt that most methods of cotton cultivation in the South were destructive of the land. The slopes were plowed and planted with cotton year after year without using clover or peas to plow under and restore the soil's humus. Humus also was destroyed by the practice of clean planting in rows which reduced the capacity of the soil to absorb moisture. Tiny drainage channels became clogged with soil so that heavy spring and summer rains ran down the slopes carrying off the topsoil with them. Although sheet erosion was not apparent at first, gullies began to appear and then deepen, ultimately making cultivation impossible and the abandonment of land inevitable (Gates 1960:142).

There were pleas for crop rotation and diversification, for manuring of worn-out fields, for using better seed, for planting less cotton and more food crops, for building drainage ditches, and for deep plowing (Weaver 1945:88). A few of these were heeded, but most were ignored. In the early period of cotton's expansion, planters and farmers alike readily adopted better strains of cotton imported from Mexico which increased per capita production. The plow was more widely used for cotton than for staple crops, and some wealthy planters began buying greatly improved cotton gins and presses. But as for soil conservation and crop diversification, little or nothing was done. The same exploitative techniques used in the Piedmont were carried to the Gulf states and points west. Planters and farmers tilled the soil without apparent concern for tomorrow, treating the land as merely a current expense, to be used and if need be, destroyed, in the endless quest for profit. In the southern United States, as in southern

Brazil, the heritage of frontier agriculture was largely one of despoilment and desolution.

## Discussion and Conclusion

The fact that resource users do not behave
as they "should" from the standpoint of some
observers is so easily "explained" by
ignorance.
                    S. V. Ciriacy-Wantrup (1963)

The parallels between the advance of the coffee frontier in Brazil and the cotton frontier in the United States are striking. But now we must answer some pertinent questions: Why is frontier agriculture destructive of natural resources? Why, in both cases, were millions of acres ravaged by the advance of cultivation? Why were measures not taken to preserve the fertility of the soil? The answers are neither simple nor obvious, but rather reside in economic and ecologic factors common to many frontier regions.

However much we may deplore the "wastefulness" of Brazilian and North American cultivators, it is a fact that intensive land usage is never employed by a people when extensive usage proves to be more profitable. One of the salient characteristics of frontier regions is the scarcity of both labor and capital and the abundance of cheap tillable land. Given these conditions, the practice of "lightly skinning the soil" and failing to restore it is, in the words of one agricultural historian, "almost inevitable" (Gates 1960:3). In frontier regions there will be no incentive to develop more intensive and costly methods of production until land becomes scarce.

There is no question that most cultivators in Brazil and the United States lacked the heavy labor and capital inputs necessary for establishing long-term conservation measures. For example, São Paulo's coffee lands badly needed "scientific restoration and fertilization which few fazendeiros could afford" (Little 1960:184). And in Alabama, "Generally speaking, soil conservation was a luxury far beyond the planters' means" (Davis 1939:173). It is not surprising that there is evidence of a strong relationship between capital availability and the acceptance of capital intensive soil conservation techniques (Blaut et al. 1959).

Under conditions of scarce labor and capital, and ample land, the aim of the cultivator is maximum production per hand and per unit of capital rather than per acre. Land is no more than an object to be used and abandoned once its original fertility is depleted. Cultivators with access to vast expanses of unsettled frontier land soon come to believe that "there's always more where that came from." Given this situation, even a small decrease in crop yields is an excuse for leaving the old and seeking the new; land is something to be worn out, not improved.

Market conditions also contribute to the exploitative nature of frontier agriculture and its long-range depletion of natural resources. The prices received for coffee and cotton varied widely from year to year, a circumstance which the cultivator was helpless to effect. During periods of high prices farmers and planters were stimulated to produce more; to take profit through quantity, not quality, to increase yields not through more intensive methods of production but through expansion—there was plenty of cheap land for that purpose.

The agricultural economist Ciriacy-Wantrup has noted another side effect of high prices: the speculative expansion of cultivation "into areas which, under more conservative price expectations, would not be suited climatically or topographically. Such speculative expansion of crop acreage has frequently led to serious soil depletion" (1963:120). This was certainly the case during periods of high prices in both Brazil and the United States. In São Paulo and Paraná, for example, coffee advanced into regions of sandy soil not ideally suited to it, once all available terra roxa land was under cultivation. In addition, coffee was planted in areas subject to periodic frosts, with often devastating results (Margolis 1973:215–16). Cotton also was planted in hilly, topographically unsuited areas of the Piedmont as well as in the sandy loams of central and west Florida (Phillips 1929:273).

Conditions of uncertainty in market price are perhaps even greater contributors to resource depletion in frontier zones than are periods of high prices which lead to speculative expansion of cash crops. Agricultural economists have noted a greater reluctance on the part of cultivators to invest in conservation methods during times of price fluctuations. "Even expenditures of costs sunk for shorter periods, e.g., fertilizer, will be reduced if there is an increase in uncertainty" (Ciriacy-Wantrup 1963:118–19). Presumably, this tendency would be magnified in frontier situations characterized by cheap, abundant land. Since uncertainty in market price marked the careers of cotton in the United States and coffee in Brazil, it becomes clear why cultivators were unwilling to invest heavily in soil conservation techniques, to say nothing of the more expensive and slow process of land restoration.

At this point, the question of the cultivators' seemingly blind devotion to one crop might well be raised. Why, given the uncertain market situation for cotton and coffee, did North American and Brazilian farmers not diversify their holdings and plant crops with more stable price structures, or for that matter, plant subsistence crops? The answer is that in both cases the principal cash crops were the only ones of high value in the areas in which they were cultivated. Cotton in the southern United States always was marketable, and it not only provided cash, but also credit to buy slaves, to enlarge plantings, and to acquire more land (Gates 1960:142). Similarly, coffee was the most profitable cash crop in southern Brazil. In the words of one cultivator, "with coffee trees you can get credit in the bank; they are as good as cash" (quoted in Margolis 1973:84–85). In a very real sense, then, these crops were the primary, if not the only, medium of exchange in the regions in which they were grown.

There is another cause for the destructive effects of frontier agriculture. Virgin soil covered with its natural vegetation changes very slowly in composition. When it is cleared and planted, however, when the soil covering is broken, change is far more rapid. A number of processes are involved in soil modification and depletion: the loss of nutrients through the growth and harvesting of crops; erosion and leaching caused by rainfall on land no longer protected by a forest cover; and the introduction of harmful toxins, fungi, and diseases into the soil (Craven 1925:9). The point is that cultivation on virgin land, cultivation of whatever sort, opens the way for deterioration. These processes are further enhanced because of the nature of the crops in question—cotton and coffee are "demanding crops" which deplete soil rather rapidly. As Gifun remarks about coffee cultivation "the question . . . is not whether there will be soil depletion, but the degree of, and the speed with which it occurs" (Gifun 1972:103). Much the same is true of cotton.

The uncertainty of natural conditions is the final factor which contributed to the exploitative mode of agriculture on the Brazilian and North American frontiers. While frosts, droughts, and insect pests are hardly unique to frontier areas, they did constitute serious cultivation hazards in the regions under consideration, amplifying the uncertainty brought on by price fluctuations. In Brazil, frosts were the principal natural phenomenon affecting yields; they could and did periodically eliminate harvests and kill the coffee trees. As we have seen, speculative expansion of cultivation into frost-prone areas was related to the high price paid for coffeee, but at the same time, this expansion significantly increased conditions of uncertainty because of the greater risk of frosts. Then, too, droughts and insect pests, particularly *broca* (*Hypothenemus hampei* Ferrari), often cut the size of harvests and reduced the quality of the coffee beans.

The major natural scourges of cotton cultivators in the southern United States were droughts, excessive rainfall, and the infamous boll weevil. Too much rain often delayed harvesting while it damaged the crop; it fostered noxious plant life, and encouraged the growth of insect pests. On the other hand, droughts during critical phases of the growing cycle influenced both the quality and the quantity of the yields. Finally, the boll weevil, which multiplied in enormous numbers in the rainy climate of the south, had to be controlled or it destroyed the crop (Cohn 1956:175). Natural conditions, then, played a vital, but unpredictable role in southern cotton cultivation.

Uncertain natural conditions and price fluctuations, along with scarce labor and capital, combined to influence the cultivators' decisions in regard to conservation measures (Margolis 1977). With the ever-present threats of lower prices and adverse weather conditions, farmers and planters alike were very reluctant to invest the relatively large sums required to maintain their soil's fertility; a single frost or drought or a sharp fall in price might wipe out their investment, or even leave them in debt. Given these circumstances, along with the presence of untapped frontier land to which they could easily migrate, cultivators would have been imprudent to expend their limited capital on their current holdings, particularly if the depleting effects of cultivating recently cleared land already had set in. Thus, despite its long-term costs to natural resources, the failure to employ conservation techniques must be seen as a rational choice within the economic and ecological contexts of frontier agriculture.

We now come to the final question: What of the "get-rich-quick," "no thought for tomorrow" attitudes said to characterize frontier cultivators? It is certainly true that farmers and planters in both Brazil and the United States failed to heed the dire warnings of their critics. But was this apparent blindness to the long-term consequences of their actions due to their lack of concern for the land? Did their values override consideration of the destructive effects of their behavior? I would argue strongly that they did not; their actions can be fully accounted for by the material conditions which prevailed on the two frontiers. Their "now oriented" attitudes, in fact, should be viewed as adaptive, given the unstable circumstances under which they lived. Thus, while an excellent case can be made that an exploitative mentality was an outgrowth of frontier conditions, this mentality was a result, not a cause of the nature of frontier agriculture.

## Notes

1. One bag contains 60 kilograms of coffee.

2. The phrase "green gold" (*ouro verde*) was a synonym for coffee during periods of high prices.

3. Since the mid-1970s soybeans and wheat have been planted in many former coffee lands, but since both crops are highly mechanized in northern Paraná, they demand relatively little labor. As a result, the depopulation of the region has continued. (Margolis 1978)

4. There is no contradiction in the fact that while land prices *rose* in the Paraíba Valley as coffee yields declined, land prices *declined* in Alabama and other cotton states as yields declined. In the first instance, prices rose for *virgin frontier land*, while the Alabama figures cited are for lands already sapped of much of their original fertility by cotton cultivation.

5. Despite a great deal of evidence to the contrary, Fogel and Engerman (1974) claim that soil depletion was not the cause of the southwestward advance of cotton. Rather, they argue that the impetus for the movement was the fact that the soils of the southwest, particularly those of the Mississippi flood plain, were better suited to cotton cultivation then those of the east. However, the abandonment of lands in Alabama and Mississippi, due to soil exhaustion disproves their argument.

# NINE

# Ecology, Behavior, and the Spirit of Fishermen

## Conrad P. Kottak

AREMBEPE, BAHIA, IS a Brazilian coastal fishing community about forty miles north of Salvador—now a metropolis of more than one million people and capital of the state of Bahia. With the completion of a paved road from Salvador in the 1970s, Arembepe has become a popular beach resort for Bahians. While Arembepe is now fully recognizable as a suburb of Salvador, its residents, who market their fish and coconuts in the capital, have been linked economically to the city throughout Arembepe's relatively brief history.

As a fishing village, Arembepe presents something of a paradox. It has been simultaneously *more of* a fishing community than others that have been described (Cf. Comitas 1962), but also a *less typical* fishing community. The variety of factors—local ecology, marketing patterns, and class structure—that produce this paradox are analyzed in this paper. To demonstrate the variable effects of these factors on behavioral strategies, personality, social structure, and life styles, Arembepe may be compared with Coqueiral, a raft fishing community in Alagoas studied by Shepard Forman (1970).

A number of granting agencies have contributed to my research in Arembepe and analysis of data gathered there in 1962, 1964, 1965, and 1973. I gratefully acknowledge here my debt to the Columbia-Cornell-Harvard-Illinois Summer Field Studies Program in Anthropology, Columbia University, The National Institutes of Health, The Foreign Area Fellowship Program, and the Horace H. Rackham School of Graduate Studies of the University of Michigan. I thank Shepard Forman for his thoughtful comments.

**180**

By examining interrelationships between ecology, economy, social structure, and behavior in Arembepe, differential success among Arembepe's fishermen can be explained in terms of certain differences in individual behavioral strategies or patterns. Etic interpretation of the determinants of fishing success can also be contrasted with a variety of explanations that Arembepeiros themselves offer. Certain emic explanations can be seen as mystifications that function to obscure the perception of contradictions which, if openly recognized, would threaten community social structure.

## Variation Among Arembepe Fishermen

In order to understand the significance of behavioral variation within Arembepe, one must first recognize that fishing plays a more prominent role in Arembepe than in other "fishing communities" that anthropologists have studied. Comitas's (1962) generalization that, given several occupations to choose among, people prefer agriculture and wage work to fishing, describes Forman's Coqueiral much more accurately than Arembepe, where agriculture was the primary occupation of only four men, or 2.2 percent of working adult males, compared to 38, or 19.6 percent of the working male labor force in Coqueiral. In Coqueiral, only 97 out of 193, barely 50 percent of the working or retired males, were or had been fishermen; 71.2 percent or 128 out of 180 working males were fishermen in Arembepe.

Reflecting the local marine environment and exchange relationships with outsiders, fishing is a more lucrative profession for Arembepeiros than for residents of other fishing communities. Because of the proximity of the continental slope only seven miles offshore in Arembepe, as compared to twenty miles in Coqueiral and a world average of thirty miles, Arembepeiros, more easily than other fishermen, can take regular advantage of runs of migratory fish species, particularly the horse-eyed bonito, whose annual run occurs during the Lenten season. The slope's nearness enables some Arembepeiros to risk the rough seas and sudden storms of the winter rainy season to fish over the slope. Arembepe's marketing situation is also considerably more favored than Coqueiral's. Salvador, a growing metropolis and tourist center, is less than 40 miles away. Travel between Arembepe and Salvador has become progressively easier over the last decade or so. Even in 1962, vehicles with four-wheel-drive could usually make it to Arembepe during the winter rainy season when, because of rougher seas, fishing is most irregular. By 1973 a paved road ran from Salvador to a point about two and a half miles from Arembepe, overlying an improved clay route constructed during the mid-1960s. During the entire span of my fieldwork (North American summers of 1962, 1964, 1965, and 1973), Arembepeiros had ready access to several fish buyers from the city.[1] Compared to Coqueiral, where marketing is controlled by the mayor of the municipality that includes it and by an autocratically run local fishing guild, Arembepeiros have been able to obtain good prices for their fish.

In 1964 Arembepe was a community of 159 inhabited houses and 750 people, most of whom made their living directly or indirectly from the fishing industry. The settlement is fringed on the east by the Atlantic Ocean and on the west by a series of freshwater lagoons that sometimes dry up during the summer (the dry season between November and March). Legal title to the non-tidal portions of the land on which Arembepe is located belonged, during my fieldwork there between 1962 and 1965, to a condominium jointly held by the heirs of a former landowner. Until the 1960s the landowners, all residing elsewhere, took little active interest in Arembepe, other than in their coconut groves in and around the village.[2]

As noted, Arembepe is primarily a fishing community.[3] Of the 180 male wage-earners in Arembepe in 1964, 128, or 71.1 percent, were full-time fishermen, and 7.8 percent fished as a secondary occupation. Seven times more men engaged in fishing than in business, the second most common occupation. Of the secondary occupations, agriculture was the most important: 10.6 percent of adult males farmed small plots on agricultural estates to the west as an additional source of food and cash. While few professions were open to women, most supplemented their husband's income or supported their children through a variety of small-scale activities: preparing food and straw hats for sale, working as domestics for tourists, running small stores alone or with their husbands. Coconut trees provided additional cash to 67, or 42.2 percent of Arembepe's households. Twelve small stores were distributed throughout the village. Of 9 artisans in Arembepe in 1964, only 1, a boat carpenter, was a skilled professional. Opportunities for work outside the community were available through

**Table 9.1** Annual Budgets of Households in Arembepe According to Occupation of Household Head and Areas of Expenditure*

| Occupational Group (household heads) | Mean Annual Expenditure in U.S. Dollars | | | % Spent on Food |
|---|---|---|---|---|
| | Food | Other | Total | |
| Ordinary fisherman | 153.33 | 100.00 | 253.33 | 60.5 |
| Captain, non-owner | 196.00 | 78.67 | 274.67 | 71.4 |
| Captain, half-owner | 179.33 | 125.33 | 304.67 | 58.9 |
| Captain, half- or full-owner with additional occupation | 210.67 | 197.33 | 408.00 | 51.6 |
| Businessman, boat owner | 301.33 | 164.67 | 466.00 | 64.7 |
| Minor artisan | 130.00 | 28.00 | 158.00 | 82.3 |
| Storekeeper only | 277.33 | 32.00 | 309.33 | 89.7 |
| Outside employment | 277.33 | 185.33 | 462.67 | 60.0 |
| Matrifocal and supported | 81.33 | 40.00 | 121.33 | 67.0 |
| All Households | 182.67 | 132.00 | 293.33 | 62.5 |

*U.S. equivalency based on exchange rate of Cr 1,500 per U.S. $1.00 July 1964.

the national oil monopoly (Petrobras) and in commercial fishing in Rio de Janeiro, Salvador, and other major ports.

Although income varies with occupation, a single specification of annual cash income is an inaccurate measure of placement within Arembepe's socioeconomic hierarchy, since some occupations provide subsistence, while others do not. In table 9.1, one sees that as the number of different food-producing niches that individuals and households exploit increases, annual food expenses constitute a smaller percentage of the household's annual budget. While fishermen normally earn smaller cash incomes than storeowners, they derive subsistence directly from their occupation. Unless they are also boatowners or small plot farmers, storekeepers have to spend larger amounts on food, especially on meat, even though they receive food at cheaper prices than other Arembepeiros as supplies for their stores.

As is true, for various reasons (Kottak 1966, 1967), for the community generally, no sharp cleavages of socioeconomic stratification distinguish between those who own Arembepe's 31 active hull sailboats and those who do not. The sailboat, fully equipped, is the largest capital resource within the Arembepe fishing industry.[4] The owner of any boat receives approximately 25 percent as his share of the total catch. The annual marketed catch of the average boat was approximately Cr 2.1 million, or US $1,400, in 1964–1965. The owner's share was therefore approximatley Cr 500,000 or US $350, thus allowing him, even after annual maintenance expenses of Cr. 100,000, or US $65, had been deducted, to recoup more than his original capital outlay (about Cr 300,000 or US $200–250, in 1965) in less than a year. If a boat is purchased new, an average of seven years elapses before major repairs are required. In each sailboat there are two potential shares. This is a convenient extrapolation from the existence of co-ownership in nineteen boats. There are never more than two owners of a given boat. In 1965 no one owned more than four sailboat shares. At that time, I determined that the specific limitations to the control of the fishing industry by non-fishermen was a result of a scarcity of willing captains and a general shortage of fishing personnel in Arembepe. The non-fishing owner derives little from investment in a sailboat if he is not associated with a reliable and competent captain. However, the most ambitious and industrious young captains earn enough and prefer to buy their own boats rather than to enter into a partnership with a non-fisherman. Those captains who are attracted into association with non-fishermen tend to be less ambitious and to produce smaller catches.

A shortage of labor means that very few fishermen in Arembepe lack regular positions in crews. In 1964 there were 128 fishermen for thirty-one active boats. This is 27 men less than the number required to staff all thirty-one boats with crews of 5. It is also 20 less than would be needed to fill the thirty-seven active and inactive boats in Arembepe with 4-man crews.[5] The scarcity of fishing personnel also limits the further expansion of the fleet, which seems to have stabilized at thirty-one boats in 1959. It allows ordinary fishermen to choose carefully among the crews with which they affiliate and ensures a great deal of shifting around among different crews.

Captains may be grouped according to their differential ownership, owning all, half, or no share of the boat in which they fish. As a crew member, each captain receives the same share as an ordinary fisherman. In addition, he receives part of the owner's share. If he is sole owner, he receives 25 percent of the catch in addition to his share as a crew member (15 percent in a 5-man crew, 18.75 percent in a 4-man crew). As half-owner, the captain gets 12.5 percent of the catch plus his share as crew member. If he does not own the boat, the captain receives a commission of 25 percent of the owner's share.

Thus, in a 5-man crew the captain gets 40 percent, 27.5 percent, or 20 percent of the boat's annual cash income, as he owns all, half or no part of the launch. Comparable figures for captains of 4-man crews are 43.25 percent, 30.75 percent, and 23.25 percent.

Working from the record book of the local fishermen's society, to which owners were supposed to contribute 10 percent of their annual cash proceeds, but actually gave, on the average, about 2 percent, I was able to rank boats in order of their success in fishing. Their contributions to the society are assumed to indicate only their *relative* success, since it is generally the owners of the least successful boats who cheat most. These figures, along with my own monitoring of daily catches and consultation of marketing records, indicate that certain launches recurrently catch more fish than others. Some captains therefore receive cash incomes that are lower than those of some ordinary crew members. For example, the crew members who each receive 15 percent of the annual marketed catch of the five most successful boats have higher cash incomes and more adequate living standards than captains who own no shares in the least successful group of boats.

Thus, any ranking of fishing personnel either according to annual cash income or consumption patterns does not invariably place owners or captains above ordinary fishermen. The largest household budget for an ordinary fisherman (Cr 608,000 = US $405) exceeded the smallest budget for a non-fishing businessman who also owned a boat share (Cr 490,000 = US $325) and was almost three times the lowest budget of a non-owning captain (Cr 184,000 = US $125). Thus, there is only a tendency for captains to obtain greater wealth from the fishing industry than ordinary fishermen.

It is usually relatively early within their fishing careers that captains and ordinary fishermen are distinguished. This differentiation may emerge either in Arembepe or when a young fisherman leaves the village and receives greater income from a period of commercial fishing out of Rio de Janeiro or Salvador. In 1964, 9 of the 31 captains had fished commercially, while only 7 of the 97 ordinary fishermen had similar histories. Income earned from such outside employment was often invested in a sailboat when the man returned to Arembepe.

While the mean age at which all fishermen had begun to fish was 17 years, the youngest captains in Arembepe in 1964 were 20 and 21 years old. The group of current captains is about five years younger than the average age of ordinary crew members. Likewise, the oldest captain is about thirty years younger than the oldest ordinary fisherman. The youth of captains also reflects the fact that men who served as captains during the prime years of their lives, between ages 25 and 50, retire from the captain's role when physical debilities of advancing age begin to limit the effort they can expend in fishing. Those captains who were formerly successful can usually afford to relinquish the more strenuous obligations of captaincy because they were receiving incomes from coconut trees and other alternative sources of wealth which they have built up during their active years. Furthermore, their retirement as captain does not mean the end of their fishing careers, since they can join other crews.

The crew is a working unit in which bonds between crew members and captains are closer than between either and the non-fishing owner. The basic unit of production, that is, the sailboat crew, provides a context in which behavior of captains and crew members may be examined. Captains are expected to manage fishing operations. They are responsible for crew mobilization, the decision to fish on a given day, where to fish, and navigation. If the captain is also co-owner of the boat, his functions are expanded. He generally keeps records of the catches, delivers his boat's contribution to the local fisherman's society, decides when the boat needs repairs, and arranges to have them made. When the captain owns no share, but fishes on a commission basis, these responsibilities devolve on the non-fishing owner.

Yet the captain is also a worker. On arrival at a fishing spot, after the anchor has been lowered, the captain begins to fish like all the others. He sits in the sun and rain and equally shares the dangers of rough seas. The special skills required to be captain end when fishing begins. They resume only when the captain gives the order to draw anchor and set sail, and they end again when all fish have been unloaded, and resume only on the next fishing day. If his share of the catch is larger, his risks are also greater. He remains in the boat longer than the other fishermen and organizes its beaching if a storm comes up. As owner or co-owner, a captain faces the possibility of losing his investment through accidents and wrecks, and he assumes financial responsibility for all repairs. The competent captain has unquestioned authority in the boat and the power to force crew members to seek positions elsewhere. While other positions in the crew are named, the only real functional distinction is between the captain and the rest of the crew.

**Cognitive Variance.** Within a socioeconomically homogeneous community like Arembepe, where, for several reasons, transgenerational perpetuation is far less significant than individual achievement in determining the distribution of wealth, ideological mechanisms must exist for justifying differential success. Arembepeiros recurrently mention three factors: luck, knowledge of fishing spots through a landmark system, and hard work. Evaluation of the attributes of a successful captain varies with the reference group of the evaluator. Four such reference groups are relevant: successful captains, generally men from their twenties to their mid- or late-forties; older captains who once belonged to the first group; the least successful captains, spanning several ages, who fish more irregularly, primarily because of alcoholism; and ordinary fishermen (including retired captains and captains-to-be). Opinions associated with certain of these groups powerfully mystify Arembepeiros' understanding of the factors that actually determine differential success of captains, and therefore their crews.

Ordinary fishermen and unsuccessful captains, composing the majority of Arembepe's fishing personnel, usually say that captains catch more or less fish depending on their luck. Some captains, they contend, seem to "walk in luck" (*andar na sorte*), so that wherever they choose to drop anchor, they will catch fish. Unsuccessful captains and even ordinary fishermen deny that some captains are more successful than others, although differential success is readily apparent in catches, life styles, and contributions to the fishermen's society. The less successful say that, although some captains are sometimes luckier than others, all are really equal. The attribution of success to luck, and the unwillingness to recognize differential success, may be viewed as ideological devices which counter a very different emphasis, among the successful, on individual achievement, success, and the rewards of hard work and austerity. For most Arembepeiros, however, there is no need to try harder, since success is viewed as reflecting luck, which is beyond human control.

On the other hand, the successful captains, when asked what determines success in the fishing industry, uniformly cite attributes reminiscent of Weber's (1958) "Protestant ethic." They readily admit, though they do not boast, that some captains are "better" than others. One told me that the boats that catch and sell the most fish are simply those that fish more regularly, stay out longer, and on which crew members generally work harder. He divided captains into three classes, paralleling my first three reference groups, but even his discussion of criteria of success shows another theme that contributes to the mystification of skills associated with the local fishing industry. "First-class captains" included the young, hardworking captains who generally contributed most to the fishermen's society. His mystification relates to the "second-class captains": those with "failing vision." In this category he included formerly successful captains who are said no longer to be able to see the landmarks of fishing spots. These tend to be respected older or middle-aged men who belonged to the first class fifteen to twenty years ago. Their contributions to the fishermen's society are, in fact, generally less than those of members of the first class.

Finally, in the "third class" the informant placed captains of all ages who never have been and never will be successful, primarily because of excessive consumption of crude Brazilian rum (*cachaça*). These are the men who own no shares in their sailboats, who frequently shift from one launch to another, who command weak allegiance from crew members, and who sometimes serve as ordinary fishermen in other boats. They frequently miss fishing days because of drunkenness, and their small crews usually consist of people whose only basis for union is a mutual dependence on rum.

Other than the mystification introduced by assertion of a relationship between the landmark system and differential success, this captain's classification of his colleagues accords in many respects with my own. Differential success is manifest within the Arembepe fishing industry. The primary contributor to the fishermen's society in 1965 gave more than twice as much as the average boat owner. An objective evaluation of differential success would, of course, find some truth in both accounts. Luck is certainly a factor, given equal fishing time over short spans. However, chance applies to all boats equally, assuming they spend the same amount of time fishing.

Objective analysis gives greatest credence to the belief of the successful captains. In fact, on the basis of my own observations, the following partially characterize the behavioral patterns and life styles of successful captains:

1. Because they are generally in their twenties and early thirties, they enjoy good health, which permits their boats to go out regularly. They attract hard-working crew members because they are dependable. They are also able to remain at sea for longer hours and to tolerate more work and weather conditions that are often unpleasant.

2. Like Weber's Protestant capitalists they take calculated risks. They stray from the dominant fishing pattern within any fishing season. During the winter, they occasionally go to the continental slope where certain species are concentrated in an area geographically smaller than would exist had the shelf extended further out (Cf. Eldredge 1963:2, 3, 8). They also sometimes travel farther to the north to fish in grounds that Arembepeiros do not normally use. In some cases their risks pay off in larger catches.

3. Although to a lesser degree than Weber's ascetic Protestant, they value sobriety. Successful captains drink less; they prefer beer to *cachaça,* and they drink only on festive occasions. Because it is more expensive in relation to alcohol content, beer is a status symbol. It is also less intoxicating than rum. Thus, successful captains can drink more without getting drunk; they miss no days from fishing because of insobriety.

4. Like Weber's Protestant entrepreneur, who had to be able to command the absolute confidence of customers and workers, successful captains command greater crew allegiance and attract better crew members, people willing to work harder and work longer hours.

5. Successful captains have better homes, diets, more material possessions, and generally a better life style than less successful villagers. In a sense this partially violates aspects of two "world views" which have been attributed to people who in many ways are like Arembepeiros. Weber (1958), for example, tells us that Protestants, when successful in the context of developing capitalism, continued to value the simplicity and asceticism of the middle-class home. In a well-known and controversial article, Foster (1965) has identified a peasant tendency to avoid ostentation which, he argues, reflects a widespread worldview: "the image of limited good." Since, according to Foster, peasants view wealth, health, success, and all other good things as finite, they regard life-style differences as

evidence that one member of the community is profiting at the expense of others, and respond with a series of leveling mechanisms.

Arembepeiros are neither peasants nor members of the middle class. Mild differences in life style are tolerated, especially when successful individuals are careful to satisfy certain moral obligations that villagers generally associate with relative good fortune. Successful Arembepeiros are expected to act in accordance with the overarching ideology of equality that characterizes the community, to avoid boasting and behavior that seems even slightly arrogant. More than others, the successful are expected to share with kin, in-laws, godparents, co-parents, and godchildren[6] and, in the presence of extreme distress, with unrelated villagers. Obeying these common injunctions, successful captains are generally respected within the community. They are elected officers of the fishermen's society, the main arena of local politics. Other fishermen are aware of their success and are eager to gain admission to their crews.

**The Paradox of the Spots.** All of these behavioral patterns are far more important in determining success than the one attribute that most Arembepeiros cite to explain two aspects of role differentiation within the fishing industry: why some people are captains and others not; and why, aside from luck, some captains are more successful than others. This attribute—differential ability to locate and remember discrete fishing spots through a visual triangulation system of landmarking—has been analyzed quite differently by Forman (1967, 1970) in a discussion of Coqueiral.

Consider now the significance of landmarking within the two communities. Arembepeiros recognize and name both broad ecological zones of the ocean floor and smaller spots. Both are called *pesqueiros*. A total of nine named zones, covering a very gradual change in depth from 8 to 32 fathoms in about seven and a half miles, intervene between shore and the continental slope. After this, as the slope begins, there are more radical changes between 32 and 200 fathoms, the limit of sailboat fishing in Arembepe, as in Forman's Coqueiral. Most winter fishing is done within two miles of shore in four named zones of rock and sand bottoms from 8 to 20 fathoms deep. Between February and June, most fishing is done in one of three 60-fathom zones at the beginning of the continental slope, where horse-eyed bonito is sought. Each of these Lenten season-fall zones is large enough to allow boats to line up and fish within sight of one another. Most summer (September to January) fishing proceeds in two named zones with depths of 35 and 60–70 fathoms respectively. Informants did not agree on which of the three seasons was most lucrative. All concurred, however, that the winter season was the worst.[7]

The shelf off Coqueiral is divided into named zones, each running perpendicular to the shoreline. Zone subdivisions are made on the basis of depth and bottom composition and, as in Arembepe, these major zones are separated by areas of sandy bottom. Particular fishing spots are located within zones. As in Arembepe, spots may be jutting rocks, stretches of identifiable reefs, or submerged rocky areas that are frequented by fishermen because they have yielded good catches in the past (Forman 1967:418). Forman reports that, as in Arembepe, fishing spots are marked and remembered by individual fishermen using a visual system of triangulation that uses a series of landmarks visible on clear days from most of the community's fishing grounds. In contrast to Arembepe, where spots predominate in shallow areas of winter fishing, the system of demarcated fishing spots in Coqueiral concerns itself only with first-quality species inhabiting the fishing zones seaward of the 50 meter mark and in the northern and central parts of Coqueiral's 200-square-mile fishing territory.

Forman reports that fishing spots are regarded as secrets and that attempts at infringement constantly cause contention in Coqueiral (Forman 1967:422). Such secrecy, Forman argues, functions as an ecologically adaptive mechanism with regard to certain areas of the total fishing operation. Suggesting that the number of good spots for catching first quality fish within the Coqueiral fishing territory is sharply curtailed, he speculates that an increase in fishing intensity could lead to a decrease in yield per individual raft once the optimal level of production has been reached (Forman 1967:423). According to Forman, maintenance of independent production at least at a steady state follows from the *spacing* based on named fishing grounds and landmarks. "Secrecy of fishing spots within these grounds serves to minimize competition by affording temporary property rights to individual fishermen" (Forman 1967:424). "By spacing rafts within the area, the daily productive efficiency of individual units is kept high, while overall production for the village is maintained" (Forman 1967:424).

It may be that the need for systems of spacing increases with the number of fishing craft, rather than with the number of fishermen. If so, this could partially explain the greater importance of the landmarking system in Coqueiral than in Arembepe. Nevertheless, I doubt that the intensity of fishing in either Arembepe or Coqueiral, given the rudimentary technologies in use, could seriously threaten the ecological balance of locally available marine fauna. Indeed, Forman (1967:424) admits the unlikeliness of overfishing. Since neither Forman nor I have precise information on the number and carrying capacity of fishing banks in either community, any argument based on the danger, or lack of it, of overfishing, must remain speculation.

The use of systems of landmarking through visual triangulation among coastal fishermen throughout the world suggests, however, that Forman is correct in citing their utilitarian functions. I question neither the existence nor utility of landmarking systems in Arembepe; I argue, rather, that *Arembepeiros' exaggerated belief* in the precision, scale, and significance of their landmarking system mystifies their understanding of the actual determinants of relative success within the local fishing industry. However, the mystification is fully compatible with, and indeed expectable in, a relatively egalitarian community which, like Fried's "egalitarian society" (1960), conceives differential success as resulting from no individual attributes other than age, sex, and ephemeral personal characteristics capable of distinguishing one individual from another in the performance of specific activities. Making luck (which is impersonal and beyond human control) and acuity of vision (a personal physical characteristic over which an individual also lacks control), the criteria for success resolves the contradiction to egalitarian structure and ethos posed by the fact that individuals, through hard work, can raise the level of production. In Arembepe, the captain is culturally endowed with certain special skills that justify his receipt of a larger share of the catch. Ability to locate and remember fishing spots becomes the primary mechanism used to differentiate captains from other fishermen. By claiming eyesight too poor to permit them to see or line up landmarks, ordinary fishermen have a ready excuse for not being captains.

As in Coqueiral, Arembepeiros expect to find in a given spot an abundance of fish of a particular species. When returning to a spot that has been previously marked, the boat sails until the captain lines up one set of the markers, then on line with the first set until the second set comes into line. Before lowering anchor and dropping sail, the captain or another crewman commonly plumbs the bottom. Sometimes plumbing continues for more than half an hour; when many plumbings are required, the markings may be forgotten, and positioning done solely on the basis of plumbline results.

An exaggerated impression of the precision of the location system originates in the reference group of older captains, some of whom, for example, claimed to know how to find quite small spots the size of a boat. Since younger captains denied that fishing spots could be so small, I suspected that the older men's statement was an exaggeration that they maintain, that younger men ponder, and that is best understood as a means of gracing impending or actual retirement as captain. A commercial fishing boat owner and navigational expert whom I consulted in Salvador sided with the younger captains, suggesting that landmarking techniques used by Brazilian coastal fishermen could differentiate no spots smaller than 625 square feet.

Failing vision is a convenient excuse for an older captain's waning productivity, the cause of which actually lies in increasing frequency of a variety of maladies and a general loss of vitality which the community's emphasis on machismo (Cf. Kottak 1966:54–55) makes it necessary to mask. The physical infirmities of age, which limit exertion and regular egress, may actually include, but are certainly not limited to, failing vision. In fact, a number of older men have obtained prescription glasses, but have not resumed the role of captain. By citing failing vision as the reason for their retirement, older captains maintain the respect of younger Arembepeiros for a physical attribute that supposedly gave them large catches in the past. By insisting that failing vision is the inevitable outcome of a life on the sea, older captains hold out the prospect of a similar unavoidable fate to their younger colleagues.

The older captains' mystification concerns not just the system's precision, but also its scale. When asked how many different fishing spots they had marked and memorized, captains claimed between 5 and 200. The number of spots named varied systematically with the age of the respondent. One 55-year-old retired captain claimed to remember about 100 different spots, but considered this knowledge insignificant compared to captains who, he asserted, knew from 200 to 300. Two of the most successful captains in Arembepe, both younger men, claimed to know about 20 spots; considering 20 the average number, they found it hard to believe that any Arembepeiro had memorized even 100 spots, viewing 50 as a remarkable achievement.

If the spots are fewer, less precise, and generally of less significance than Arembepeiros believe, what is their utilitarian function? Eldredge (1963:27) has reasonably argued that spots are marked and maintained in memory, usually not because they produce so many more fish than the next rocky area 200 yards away, but because use of a definite marking system eliminates a great deal of time-consuming plumbing activity. This utilitarian reason, combined with the function of locating *general* areas of the ocean floor, may be sufficient to explain the widespread use of landmarking through visual triangulation among coastal fishermen throughout the world.

Although secrecy attaches to certain fishing spots used by Arembepeiros, jealousy over spots appears to be less intense than Forman found in Coqueiral, for reasons to be discussed below. The local lore of jealous behavior related to spots contains only a few incidents. Arembepeiros did tell me that captains were so possessive of certain spots that, should a crew fishing in such a spot see another boat approaching, the captain might draw anchor and sail away rather than risk having the spot marked by another. I never observed such an incident during my days of fieldwork in *saveiros*. I was, however, told about one case in which a lifelong enmity had supposedly been engendered by one captain's discovery of another boat fishing at one of his favorite spots.

While Forman argues that secrecy about the spots functions as a spacing mechanism and allocates temporary property rights, it is important to realize that these rights are temporary and cannot be exclusive. Spots are not privileged property that can be inherited or exchanged, but merely locations where people have had successful fishing experiences. Certain areas of the sea probably yield more fish than others, either because the general area in which the spot is located is not fished much or because environmental factors are particularly propitious, or a combination of the two. In a field report based on research in Arembepe in 1963, Eldredge (1963:28) reached essentially the same conclusion about differential productivity of fishing spots, pointing out that the relatively few closely guarded spots used by Arembepe's fishermen seemed to produce little or nothing when fishing was generally bad, and no more than most others on days of good fishing. The fishermen have no blind faith in their spots. They realize that within a given zone almost any rocky area is as good as any other. They readily admit that spots are regularly lost and discovered. Such discoveries are never planned, but occur as the boat moves from spot to spot. When one or more fisherman has a line out, and three or four fish are caught within a fairly small area within a fairly short time, the boat will stop and the crew members will plumb. If they are over rock, the captain will mark the spot and is likely to return there for future fishing.

Add to the spots' questionable differential value the fact that there is nothing to stop any enterprising fisherman from marking spots himself. Merely by looking at the land, captains and most ordinary fishermen can indicate the depth of the water that the boat is traversing. In the same way, most fishermen can state when the launch arrives in a given fishing zone. Even if the captain tried to keep the discovery of new spots secret from others, fishermen reveal spots as they pass from crew to crew. The crew may contain a young man who has ambitions to become a captain. If he has good eyesight, an adequate memory, and a knowledge of simple navigational procedures, he may mark the spot and return to it later, when he is captain of a boat. Most current captains reported having learned their first spots in this way. Others have been taught to mark by kinsmen and unrelated captains.

Finally, a major contrast between Arembepe and Coqueiral reflects the fact that most of the fishing done in Arembepe does not depend on marking small spots at all. The zones that are most regularly and frequently exploited in summer and fall, when there are more frequent fish migrations and when bonito fishing is in full swing, do not have spots in the limited sense. Only the zones that are commonly fished in winter and that are nearest shore have landmarks. In the summer fishing zones, plumbing rather than landmarks is used to determine rocky bottoms. Likewise, during the fall run of the bonito, boats from Arembepe and neighboring communities line up in sight of one another and fish in one of three rectangular zones. While these more distant areas do have landmarks, Arembepeiros report that even captains have a hard time sighting them. For this reason, plumbing is always done.

It should be remembered that even the valued attributes of the captain are defined by technological and economic limitations that constrain Arembepe's fishermen. As one ordinary fisherman told me, if he had sufficient money to buy a motor and a small launch, he could travel daily to the farther zones that are normally fished in summer and fall and catch more fish than captains who are confined by an exclusive reliance on windpower to the closer zones. He insisted that he could in this way be as successful as any captain in Arembepe even though he had "bad eyes for landmarks" and a "poor memory," which, he said, always had prevented his marking fishing spots. Insofar as individual characteristics explain differential success in Arembepe's fishing industry, therefore, those reminiscent of Weber's Protestant capitalist type are far more important than the ones usually stressed by Arembepeiros themselves.

## The Material Conditions of Variation

Arembepe and Coqueiral present an ideal case in controlled comparison. Most of the people of Coqueiral and all Arembepeiros belong to the national lower class in a relatively impoverished area of Brazil. The communities are located in adjacent states and lie less than 250 miles apart on the Atlantic Coast. While Arembepe traditionally has been more of a fishing community than Coqueiral, marine hook and line fishing extending to the continental slope is a common feature of their economies. Furthermore, Forman and I worked in the two settlements at approximately the same time, so that many of the national economic and political forces percolating into the two communities can be held relatively constant. Somewhat masked, however, by their many similarities are important differences, including Arembepe's urban versus Coqueiral's rural dependence.

Detailed consideration of similarities and differences between Arembepe and Coqueiral should enable us to understand the extent to which local and regional economic factors contribute to social structure, personality and behavior, including reaction to conditions of change. Arguing correctly that analysis on an individual psychological level does not satisfactorily explain innovation and change, Forman (1970:119) observes that acceptance or rejection of innovations can be understood only through the social structure that impinges on the local peasantry. Peasant decision-making and subsequent behavior, Forman (1970:127) argues, are conditioned by the complex interplay of ecological, social structural, and organizational factors that comprise the totality of the system known as the peasant economy. If so, to understand contrasts between Arembepe and Coqueiral, one must consider both historical and contemporary aspects of their local productive systems and of their exchange relationships with outsiders. An apparently narrower range of personality variation in Coqueiral and a greater subservience in demeanor (Forman: personal communication) on the part of the people of Coqueiral are functions of a very real contrast in objective, material advantages available to Arembepeiros as opposed to the people of Coqueiral. Local and regional factors combine to favor Arembepe over Coqueiral.

**The Local Economy.** Obvious differences in the local fishing economies of Arembepe and Coqueiral involve technology and the marine environment. Use of hull sailboats as fishing vessels, in combination with the closer proximity of the continental slope, enable Arembepeiros to catch more fish in a considerably smaller fishing territory (63 square miles versus 400 square miles) than the raft fishermen of Coqueiral. Forman (1970:97) observes that, given hook and line fishing, the possibility of catching fish increases in proportion to crew size. Arembepe crews typically consist of 4 or 5 men, while the rafts of Coqueiral accommodate crews of 1, 2, and only rarely 3. I estimate that the average fishing boat in Arembepe caught approximately 3,500 kilograms of fish annually between 1962 and 1965. Forman reports for Coqueiral a monthly average of 100 pounds, which, on a yearly basis, is approximately one-seventh the catch of the average boat in Arembepe. The thirty-one sailboats in Arembepe in 1965, therefore, were catching approximately 108,000 metric tons of fish each year, while the maximum actual catch of the hundred rafts in Coqueiral did not exceed 55,000 metric tons, assuming an average annual catch of 1,200 pounds or 545 kilograms for each raft. Forman (personal communication) considers that these figures more likely underestimate than overestimate differential productivity of the two communities.

Arembepe is favored not only in total production but in amount of fish caught per fisherman and per inhabitant per year. Coqueiral's 85 active fishermen each caught an average of about 650 kilograms of fish annually, while Arembepe's 128 active fishermen each produced an average of about 850 kilograms. With populations of 852 and 750 respectively, if all fish were consumed locally, 64 kilograms would be available per capita in Coqueiral, compared with 149 kilograms in Arembepe.

The critical local environmental factor explaining greater productivity of the Arembepe fishing industry is the proximity of the continental slope, which lies only seven miles offshore, as compared to twenty miles in Coqueiral. The proximity of the slope, with its greater concentration of fish species, means that seasonality is a less important determinant of production in Arembepe than in Coqueiral. Apparent similarities mask differences: the same three fishing seasons—winter, summer, and the fall or Lenten season—are recognized in both fishing economies; in both winter is the time of least productive fishing.

A nearer slope and safer vessels accommodate enterprising Arembepeiros who are willing to assume calculated risks even during the winter. Arembepeiros simply have more time to fish over the slope's rocky areas. In Coqueiral, slope fishing is confined to the summer and the Lenten period, when there is a demand for first-quality fish; it requires a twelve-hour trip, as compared to six or seven hours in Arembepe, and Coqueiral's fishermen must spend the night at sea (Forman 1970:61–62). Only the largest rafts journey to the slope. As Forman observes, a vessel's catch is limited by its storage capacity; the dimensions of the basket used by raft fishermen limit the size of the catch and the duration of fishing, as does the necessity for the raft to dry after a day at sea (Forman 1970:74). Capacity of Arembepe's launches is considerably larger, and they are beached only when a winter storm approaches, or for repairs.

**Regional Factors.** Local technological and environmental variables within a cash-oriented adaptation function within larger-scale systems. To understand differences between Arembepe and Coqueiral, it is even more essential to examine the external factors that affect significantly local technology and that provide incentives to produce. In particular, marketing relationships that favor Arembepe over Coqueiral must be examined. Since at least 1950, Arembepeiros have had ready access to an open marketing system in which a number of buyers from Salvador have come to Arembepe offering relatively high prices for all qualities of fish. Arembepe's situation, therefore, presents a significant exception to Forman's (1970:13) observation that Coqueiral's raft fishermen have limited access to marketing conditions and limited control over the prices they receive for their fish.

The considerably less advantageous marketing conditions encountered by Coqueiral's raft fishermen are a direct result of their degraded position within what Forman (1975:73) describes as a community hierarchy of relationships based on access to outside sources of power. In contrast to the gradual and continuous socioeconomic hierarchy I have described for Arembepe, Forman (1970:37) indicates historical and contemporary reasons for "incipient stratification" in Coqueiral. Of direct relevance to the marketing system is the fact that artificial ceilings have been imposed on the price paid to fishermen for first-class fish by the mayor of the municipality that includes Coqueiral and the president of the community fishermen's guild, the area's chapter of the Brazilian National Fishermen's Guild. Forman describes the autocratic and nepotistic manner in which the incumbent guild president reaps innumerable benefits from his official position. In contrast to Arembepe where, during the mid-1960s, officers of the less formally organized local fishermen's society were almost invariably fishermen, not one of the officers of Coqueiral's guild was a fisherman. While, in contrast to Arembepe where there are no pensions, the Coqueiral guild administers monthly pensions of $15 to 12 retired fishermen, much of the guild's capital, derived from fishermen's contributions, is either drained off for taxes or used for nonfishing endeavors (Forman 1970:45).

As a result of price ceilings on their produce, raft fishermen's incomes were not keeping pace with rampant national inflation—a situation in marked contrast to contemporaneous Arembepe, where, because of increasing demand from Salvador, the price of fish was actually outpacing the national inflation rate and the costs of their hull sailboats. Arembepeiros have been able to profit from Salvador's seemingly inexhaustible demand for fish. Contrast this with the limited market for Coqueiral's first-quality fish (Forman 1970:83). It is mainly during the Lenten season, when demand for first-quality fish surpasses supply, that the raft fishermen make the overnight trip to the continental slope. Ordinarily, because of the very slight difference in margin of profit between first and second quality fish, the harder work and longer time required to bring in first-quality fish are hardly worthwhile (Forman 1970:64). Market forces impinge directly on the type of fishing done, but also on fishing technology. Forman (1970:104) reports a decline in the number of larger rafts capable of fishing at the edge of the shelf. A general size decrease in, and increasing cost of, available logs have also reduced investment in larger craft and slope fishing. Raft fishing in Coqueiral is also limited by a chronic shortage of bait (Forman 1970:105).

In addition to establishing price ceilings, the municipal mayor's office and local fishermen's guild prohibit local fishermen from assuming the role of middlemen, thus closing off another avenue of potential profit, which brought 26 Arembepeiros a combined income of Cr 5.65 million, or almost US $4,000.00 in 1965. Neither fishermen nor fish hawkers are permitted to surpass an established margin of profit in Coqueiral (Forman 1970:87). The large number of middlemen in Coqueiral explains why, in contrast to Arembepe, local entrepreneurs have not risen through fish-marketing activities (Forman 1970:92).

The present impediments to profitable production and distribution of fish in Coqueiral represent merely the latest local manifestation of a historical pattern of county-wide socioeconomic stratification, in which Coqueiral's fishermen have stood at the bottom. At the time of Arembepe's first settlement around 1900, Coqueiral was a thriving port community of three hundred buildings. Cargo vessels transported sugar from a mill in a nearby valley, salt mined before the 1930s in local salt flats, and other county products. In the 1960s the stratified hierarchy was still headed by large-scale sugar planters and the owners of the mill; immediately below them were certain residents of the municipal seat: smaller landowners and lesser bureaucrats, professional people and tradespeople. Below these levels, and linked to them through debt relationships, were such people as Coqueiral's local bigwigs. The raft fishermen belonged to the lowest stratum. I have elsewhere (Kottak 1966: ch. 4) described in detail a bifurcation between political ties (to the municipality of Camaçari) and economic ties (to the city of Salvador) that has significantly shielded Arembepeiros from dependence on and exploitation by members of both county and urban elites.

Access by Coqueiral's local bigwigs to landowning and commercial elites provided a context of power and privilege that Forman (1975:73) found highly evident in Coqueiral. Correspondingly, For-

man reports that mayor, guild president, and other local bigwigs
sought to maintain the county elite's supply of inexpensive fish with
the intent of retaining the favor of the sugar planters from whom they
derived their power in municipal politics (Forman 1970:122). Contrast the marketing opportunities available to Arembepeiros. In 1965,
when Coqueiral's raft fishermen were receiving between Cr. 400 and
500 per kilogram of first-quality fish, Arembepeiros were receiving
between Cr. 700 and 750, 62 percent more. Since Arembepe's annual
catch is also at least twice that of Coqueiral, if all fish caught were
first quality and if none were extracted for subsistence, Arembepe's
sailboat industry would have produced about Cr 79 million compared
to Cr 25 million in Coqueiral in 1965, over three times as much. Differential benefits of fishing therefore reflect, as Forman (1970:16) observes, complex interrelationships in complex settings.

Local and regional differences also help explain why Arembepe
contradicts Comitas's (1962) generalization that, given several occupations to choose from, people prefer agriculture and wage work to
fishing. More profitable fishing is merely the major feature of a generally more favorable economic situation in Arembepe. Reflecting the
paucity of local job opportunities, migration from Coqueiral has removed the equivalent of 78 percent of the adult male population and
35 percent of the adult female population, producing a skewed adult
sex ratio of 43 percent male to 57 percent female. Despite the short
distance to Salvador, Arembepe's adult sex ratio, 47.5 percent male
to 52.5 percent females, is more evenly balanced. Compared to
Coqueiral, Arembepe's economy also offers males greater opportunities for secondary cash pursuits and investment. Sale of the yield of
more than 10,000 mature coconut trees brought into the community
approximately Cr 7.5 million in 1965 and about Cr 3 million more in
profits to 6 local coconut marketers. While only 35 residents of
Coqueiral had coconut crops of any commercial value (Forman
1970:24), 77 adult Arembepeiros supplemented their income through
coconut sales. The largest grove owner in Coqueiral derived an income four times that of the owner of the community's largest raft.
Tree ownership is more evenly distributed in Arembepe.

The lives and life styles of people in the two communities must
be  viewed  against  their  economic  horizons.  Forman  found
Coqueiral's raft fishermen generally earning far below the region's
minimum income (US $20 per month) for wage workers. Mean and

median annual household expenditures in Arembepe in 1964 stood at approximately US $300. Demographics and economics ramify throughout daily life and social organization. Forman notes that the continued low earnings of the raft fishermen necessitate the participation of all members of the extended family in the economic life of the village (1970:105). While, as in Arembepe, most households are composed of nuclear families, Forman found that the functioning economic unit often included several nuclear family households. The pooling function of interhousehold cooperation stands in sharp contrast to the greater household and individual autonomy I found in Arembepe. In Coqueiral "If it were not for the cooperation of all members of an extended family and the neighbors who sometimes assume the obligations of kinsmen, it would be impossible to maintain a minimum livelihood" (Forman 1970:105).

Pooling and cooperation in the face of scarce resources involve the labor and kin links of females to a greater extent than in Arembepe. While 46 percent of Arembepe's women lack occupations other than housewife, women produce relatively more cash in Coqueiral. Forman found that manufacture and sale of straw products by 214 women of Coqueiral accounted for a large part of Coqueiral's income, especially during the winter fishing off-season, when monthly income from basketry reached nearly Cr 1 million or US $500. Only 107 women worked for cash in Arembepe.

**Manifestations: Structure.** Not only the fishing industry, but Arembepe's total economy provides a context in which other attributes of Weber's Protestant ethic can be perceived. According to Weber, early Protestantism saw individuals, rather than families or households, as the objects of salvation, and promoted severance of extended kinship ties. Although I found no evidence for interhousehold cooperation in Arembepe paralleling Forman's observations in Coqueiral, Arembepeiros, probably because their economic situation is only *relatively* more favorable than Coqueiral's, do not confine kinship ties and obligations as severely as Weber's Protestants, or twentieth-century North Americans. Successful Arembepeiros must perform a delicate balancing act, weighing ambitions for the advancement of themselves and their children against the social obligation to share with relatives, in-laws, and fictive kin.

Elsewhere (Kottak 1967), I have demonstrated several ways in which customary social obligations, framed in an egalitarian ethos, limit Arembepeiros' chances of escaping the national lower class. Men who, through hard work in fishing or commercial activity, have become successful within the community are expected to share their wealth with an increasingly large number of people. If not, they inevitably fall prey to leveling mechanisms, including gossip, social ostracism, witchcraft accusations, and crew desertion. One's primary obligations are to close kin. Since a successful man provides his family with a better diet, more of his children survive than in poorer households. Furthermore, other relatives are likely to move in, or at least to ask for doles. Obligations associated with marriage also drain wealth from the enterprising Arembepeiro. While poor couples are generally involved in common-law unions, ambitious young men add to their prestige by being married in civil and religious ceremonies. A legal marriage brings obligations to affinals that do not exist with a common-law union. Finally, as wealth increases, a man will accumulate more and more fictive kin, godchildren, and co-parents, to whom obligations of assistance are extended. Thus, the harder a man works, the more successful he becomes within Arembepe, the greater the number of dependents he must support. If he foresees any possibility that he or his children will spend their lives within Arembepe, he must fulfill his obligations to others in socially prescribed ways.

Again Arembepe poses an exception to Forman's generalization that peasant societies (including Coqueiral) operate so near to the bare margin of existence that the security of the individual becomes one with the security of the group. Although Arembepeiros do share, they make every effort to limit their sharing by narrowing their kindreds to parents, siblings, children, nieces and nephews, and first cousins. However, they eschew the common Brazilian term for first cousin, *primo irmão*, "brother cousin." For Arembepeiros, therefore, no more distant cousins are included within the kindred, and first cousins are emphatically not siblings. Although Arembepeiros cooperate in crews and in beaching their sailboats before a winter storm, they, or hired masons, construct their own houses, rather than employing the *mutirão* or cooperative housebuilding party that Forman found so common in Coqueiral.

In the context of cooperation and competition, I turn again to fishing spots. Forman relates competition and secrecy over fishing spots to the context of general economic cooperation in Coqueiral.

He argues that economic competition between individual productive units is actually *minimized* by the maintenance of secrecy about fishing spots. If this is so, one would expect, and we do find, that secrecy and the general significance of the landmarking system diminish in the less cooperative context of Arembepe. Arembepe and Coqueiral can now be seen as inverting a number of scaled oppositions: the greater individualism of a raft's small crew vs. the greater cooperation of a sailboat crew; greater secrecy and competition at sea; greater cooperation on the land (Coqueiral) vs. a less significant landmarking system, minimal secrecy, and competition at sea; and greater individualism and less cooperation on land (Arembepe).

These oppositions and inversions, like the behavioral differences found in the two communities, are, however, embedded in a material context. Forman's observation of a high degree of inter-household cooperation and sharing in Coqueiral may be a corollary of a widespread correlation noted by Jorgensen (1972) and others between extreme poverty and pooling among kin of their minimal resources. Although insufficient to raise them out of the national lower class, the economic opportunities available to Arembepeiros did reward individual initiative, the ensuing fragmentation of interhousehold groups, and severance of all but the closest ties based on kinship and marriage.

The behavior related to, and the variable significance of, the landmarking systems in the two communities should be considered again in this context. While the raft fishermen use the landmarking system only during the most profitable fishing period, Arembepeiros rely on spots mainly during the winter, the least productive season. Incidents expressing tension over fishing spots, therefore, are concentrated, and perhaps limited to, winter, when catches and incomes are at their lowest. Contention related to violation of fishing spots may perhaps now be seen as a function of the absolutely lower productivity of the Coqueiral fishing industry. It seems reasonable to suppose that when opportunities are limited, as they are in Coqueiral perpetually and in Arembepe most notably during the winter, tension would occur among producers seeking to obtain and market the same scarce resources.

Forman's interpretation of maintenance of a fishing spot system in Coqueiral is that it is a spacing, and therefore, it seems to me, a randomizing, balancing, or leveling mechanism. Yet the absence in his reports of other leveling mechanisms, such as gossip, ostracism, and witchcraft accusations in Coqueiral, may reflect the fact that marked life-style variance is rendered impossible by objective conditions of extreme poverty. Other than the local bigwigs, whose privileged positions are protected by external benefactors, who is there to level?

The contrast between Arembepe's graded and continuous socioeconomic hierarchy and Coqueiral's incipient stratification, expressed in a sharper distinction between the relatively affluent guild managers, large scale coconut lords, and municipal bigwigs, on the one hand, and the impoverished majority on the other, is manifest in ideology and social behavior. In contrast to Arembepeiros, the people of Coqueiral must view differential distribution of wealth and power as an attribute of groups rather than of individuals. Even Arembepeiros' relations with wealthier outsiders are permeated by the community's prevalent ideology of equality (Kottak 1966: ch. 5), are organized on an individual basis, and demonstrate little, if any, class consciousness. More than Arembepeiros, the raft fishermen of Coqueiral can be

. . . . . well aware of the nature of the bonds which tie them to the dominant segments of society and which clearly limit their mobility. They think in terms of 'we and they' and 'everything for them, nothing for us.' They contrast themselves to the rich and the powerful and fear that they themselves are 'nothing in this world.' When queried as to why they do not try to improve their situation, they correctly cite lack of opportunity: 'Não tem possibilidades' (Forman 1970:137–38).

Confronted daily with the contrast between their own wealth and lifestyles and that of the local and municipal elites, Forman's raft fishermen can develop a class consciousness.

That the local economy, for whatever perceived reason, offers differential rewards has impeded the emergence of class or even group consciousness in Arembepe. Yet Arembepeiros, though favored, are ultimately mystified. Viewing differential success and upward mobility only in local terms, Arembepeiros ignore both local social structural leveling mechanisms and the larger-scale obstacles that block upward mobility within the national class structure.

**Manifestations: Personality.** Forman (personal communication), who is also familiar with Arembepe, having done fieldwork there in summer 1964, has mentioned his admittedly subjective impressions of differences in the personalities and demeanor of people in the two communities. Forman found the people of Coqueiral more subservient than Arembepeiros, whom he found to be friendlier, more open, and generally less obsequious. Again, the contrast reflects the distinction between incipient stratification and a graded socioeconomic hierarchy. It seems that perception of objective material contrasts and limitations constrains, compresses, and depresses the personalities of the majority of the people of Coqueiral. Indeed, Forman (1970:36) asserts that the raft fishermen's ties with local bigwigs are built upon and maintained through fear. In Arembepe, on the other hand, different personality traits may find expression in differential participation in the local economy, community political activity, and throughout social life. An overarching ideology of equality, an insistence that, despite apperances, "everyone is really equal here," reflects larger-scale impediments to upward mobility while protecting and allowing individual freedom of expression in the context of relatively egalitarian local social structure. Material limitations emanating primarily from the nature of Coqueiral's political and economic links to outsiders lessen the value and constrain the expression of individual differences, producing a sameness in perception, cognition and behavior. The apparent lack in Coqueiral of Arembepe's entrepreneurial types reflects an environment in which conscious attitudes and values, skills, knowledge, preferences and tastes, and other attributes of personality are flattened against the overarching fact of poverty. Forman's observations about the determinants of variation and change can be extended to the contrast of Arembepe and Coqueiral. In the final instance, acceptance or rejection of innovation reflects not variance in individual motivation but complex interrelationships in complex settings (Forman 1970:16). The conditions of variation and change are not so much psychological-cognitive as they are economic and social (Forman 1970:16). Not in Arembepe, but in Coqueiral, where there is almost no capital available for fishermen's experimentation with new techniques, there is no objective context for the entrepreneurial type. Not in Arembepe, but in Coqueiral, where the most important factor of production, the fishing vessel, is within the means of most fishermen, the distinction between captain-owner and ordinary fishermen is less significant, and a major reward for the achievement-oriented, Protestant-capitalist type is removed. Not in Arembepe, but in Coqueiral, where history and prior structure dictate that local and regional elites directly define peasants' local activities and regional opportunities, fishermen cannot be expected to initiate change. In Coqueiral change must begin with bigwigs and may spread down. In Arembepe, achievement oriented locals—fishermen, marketers, and others—have negotiated their own access to new technology and new marketing possibilities including, during the eleven years spanned by my field work, the introduction and spread of trammel nets (and through them the development of a lobster fishery), motors, larger boats permitting longer distance fishing, and even restaurants, lodging, and food preparation and sales catering—after the opening of a paved road—to a thriving tourist industry. The raft fisherman of Coqueiral, cut off from the suburbanization of a major metropolis, is aware that there can be no greater accumulation of wealth for him, given fishing techniques available, no matter how hard he works. Innovation occurs only when the risk is low (Forman 1970:135), when rewards are manifest, and when material conditions permit.

## The Atypicality of Fortune

Arembepe poses exceptions to a number of generalizations that have been made about fishermen in other parts of the world. Arembepeiros have usually managed to escape significant exploitation by outsiders throughout their relatively short history; they have enjoyed relatively open access to fish and coconut marketing systems; the separation of their economic orientation to Salvador from their political inclusion in Camaçari has protected them from the Coqueiral situation in which political and economic roles are merged and thus reinforce control by the same external individuals and their agents. Local and regional benefits have combined to create an economic framework that attracts more fishermen and offers them greater rewards than most fishing economies. While, in the final instance, larger-scale material determinants operate, the observed variation in behavior among Arembepeiros, summarized in my earlier delineation of reference groups, has, I believe, provided important raw material that has facilitated rapid changes in Arembepe since 1962.

In its exceptions to other fishing communities studied by anthropologists, Arembepe presents a paradox. Arembepe is more of a fishing community than Coqueiral and most others (Cf. Comitas 1962), yet it is a less typical fishing community. More people are attracted to fishing in Arembepe because fishing offers greater and more immediate profits than among other populations that fish. This, as has been shown, reflects not only favorable features of the local marine environment but, more significantly, an advantageous marketing system. Finally, Arembepe must be considered unusual not only among fishing communities, but among Brazilian rural communities generally. In 1973, I was somewhat surprised to find that the material conditions of Arembepeiros, through the growth of Salvador, had actually improved rather than worsened. There is no reason to believe (Cf. Gross and Underwood 1971), however, that regional and national forces that have impinged on most rural communities of lower class Brazilians during the past decades have had such fortunate results.

## Notes

1. Their access to Salvador had steadily improved since the 1930s (Cf. Kottak 1966).

2. During the 1960s, however, one of the landowners, Jorge, a young man with the family's first university degree, gained influential employment with the State Department of Highways and Roads, a position that enabled him to promote the development of Arembepe as a tourist resort. In 1965 Jorge was in the process of legally surveying the estate in order to sell lots of different sizes to residents and outsiders. Formerly, all Arembepeiros had paid nominal rents for the land on which their houses were located. Their houses ranged in quality of construction from huts with wattle and daub walls and palm frond roofs to brick homes with tiled roofs and indoor toilets. At the time of my last fieldwork there in 1973, Arembepe had changed from a relatively quiet fishing village into a thriving tourist resort. In the 1960s the village proper had been divided into three parts, a lower or southern road, a central square, and a northern rectangular area. Throughout the settlement, the eastern row of houses had exposure to the beach in back. Beachfront land is more valuable in the central and northern portions of the village proper than to the south, where there is an abrupt fall to the harbor. Jorge gave residents of the valuable beach strip two alternatives: buying their lots or leaving their houses to live on lots and in newly constructed houses which Jorge gave them on the western side of Arembepe, near the freshwater lagoon. Most people with brick houses paid for their lots and remained in their original dwellings, though a few moved, and Jorge sold their houses and lots to middle-class outsiders. Not just Arembepe proper, however, but the entire estate

north and south of it had been divided by 1973. Several wealthy Salvadorians, including a former governor of Bahia, had constructed sumptuous summer houses about a mile south of the settlement. Arembepe had changed in eight years from a relatively isolated fishing community to a thriving tourist center for Salvadorians of all classes.

3. The ethnographic present is used throughout to refer to statistical data gathered in Arembepe in 1964 and 1965. Where reference is to a later time or involves the numerous changes in community life since 1965, the text so indicates.

4. This is even more true now that the fleet is motorized. Government sponsored loans have enabled most captains to obtain their own motors.

5. The local labor pool is depleted as many young men leave Arembepe to seek outside employment, which they hope will be more lucrative than ordinary fishing.

6. I specifically examine the leveling effects of these obligations elsewhere (Kottak 1967).

7. The introduction of motors has increased considerably the range of the zones that Arembepeiros exploit.

# Social Structure

THE TERRITORY OF Brazil encompasses most of South America's tropical lowlands, and accounts for most of those tribes classified by Steward (1948) as representing the tropical forest level of sociocultural integration. Much of the work among these tribes has focused on kinship. Yet, unlike Africa, South America has not provided great breakthroughs in the field of kinship studies. This may be due in part to the fact that most kinship structures discovered there are bilateral in nature and that, until the past two decades, bilateralism was comparatively neglected, with most theory deriving from detailed analyses of unlineal groupings. On taking a general look at lowland South America, Robert Murphy argues that, if one defines lineage as a conceptual grouping of at least three generations of adults, living and dead, the area would have very few true lineage systems. Rather, what he finds are "Clusters of co-resident kin who are not bound by careful reckoning of common descent nor unified by a unilineal ideology." Residence appears to be the principal binding principle; at the most descent is putative, not demonstrated.

Murphy is aware of the considerable literature regarding sibs and moieties in one or another lowland South American tribe. However, he argues that even where such structures exist, there seems to be no pressure toward tight closure of access, no rigid determination of group membership. In Goldman's (1963) classic study of the Cubeo, for example, it is explicitly stated that, although the sibs control sections of river, these sibs are not lineages. Individuals participate in the grouping not because of strict ancestral ties, but rather to bind themselves together in the management and enjoyment of an estate, and to exclude others from such privileges.

**211**

This principle of reciprocal aid and its corollary, exclusion, per-
meates, as we shall see, all levels of Brazilian society. Its ubiqui-
tousness would seem due more to the independent development of
functional equivalencies and actual structural parallels than to diffusion. At the tribal level, hunting and fishing rights usually fall
under the proprietorship of local groups rather than kin groups, and
the usual form of corporate kin-group holdings is agricultural lands.
In Murphy's words, among lowland Brazilian tribes, one finds a
"virtual universality of lands as general community property, entailed to neither individual nor kin group and falling only under
usufruct rights which result from the expenditure of labor in clearing
the terrain."

Murphy concludes that, if unilineality exists, it tends to be of the
undifferentiated type that goes with moiety and clan organization. In
general, both lineage systems and segmentary process are virtually
absent, and descent is either bilateral or of the vague kind that incorporates timelessness and unspecificity.

Immediately following Murphy's general discussion of unilineality comes an analysis, by William Crocker, of the problem as exemplified by a single tribe: the Ramkókamekra-Canela of the state of
Maranhão. The experience of the R-Canela indicates how even the
more isolated tribes of the area have been deeply affected by acculturation. The R-Canela have retained their tribal identity, but this has
been at the cost of a long struggle and repeated losses. As early as
1814, they sought the protection of the Brazilian government.
Yet not even this protection has prevented their regularly losing
land to local Brazilians. This constant loss of land has brought both
food scarcity and depopulation.

Crocker suggests that the R-Canela's prolonged, disastrous contact with representatives from Brazilian national society has shattered
a fuller matrilineality of earlier times. What he finds today is a bilateral kindred, plus moieties based on age-class rather than on ma-
trineality.

One of the reasons Crocker posits a historically greater emphasis
on matrilineality is the fact that, today, matrilines have permanent
locations on village circles until the village is moved or the matriline
dies out. Yet, he admits that the matrilines are weak organizations,
and that seldom are the dead remembered for more than two or three
generations. The R-Canela today reckon kin from ego out. All of this

corresponds, of course, with Murphy's view that most lowland South American groups are basically bilateral.

One valuable insight from Crocker's work is that lineality may be stronger in one societal institution than in another. With the R-Canela, the societies of the Fish Festival are the most lineal, while the two initiation festivals have almost no ceremonial lineages. The remaining festivals fall somewhere in between.

On the basis of these facts, Crocker hypothesizes that the R-Canela migrated from an earlier location, and that with migration has come a transition from a more matrilineal to a more generally bilateral system. He suggests that the occasional ritual lineages and ceremonial sibs of the current festivals could in their origin have been named, daily functioning lineages and descent groups in the period when the tribe was riverine. Today they survive only in certain festival contexts.

The theory to which Crocker turns in his attempt to explain inconsistencies between a largely Crow terminological kinship system and the present reliance on the bilateral kindred is that of cultural lag. His careful exploration of varying degrees of bilaterality and unilineality in a single society and his attempt to relate these to historical processes demonstrate the qualifications needed for generalities such as Murphy's. Nothing in his treatment of the R-Canela, however, refutes the basic principles on which, according to Murphy's argument, lowland tribes are organized today.

In the third of this group of discussions, "Secrets, Exclusion, and the Dramatization of Men's Roles," Gregor gives us an important clue as to the function of both kinship units and secret societies, i.e., that they draw their primary significance not from whom they include but from whom they exclude. His insights have universal applicability. The principle of exclusivity is as relevant for extended kindreds and secret societies among Brazil's highly urbanized elite as for analogous groupings among the nation's relatively few surviving tribal groupings.

A remarkable example of this secret society tradition at the level of the modern Brazilian nation-state is Umbanda. Diana Brown argues that Umbanda is far more than a class phenomenon; it is, she states, the only truly national Brazilian religion. For some leaders Umbanda symbolizes Brazil's potential world power; they project it as a future world religion. Umbanda, in Brown's terms, "provides symbols of Brazilian identity which transcend class differences," and which have "potential appeal to both middle and upper classes, although they may be experienced differently by these two groups."

In terms of class, Brown discovers that the occupational sectors most often represented among Umbandistas are those of middle management, small commerce and civil service among the middle class, and self employment and employment in small shops among the lower classes. These are the very people to whom patron-client relationships remain important, and Brown argues that it is no accident that Umbanda is essentially a patron-client religion. It is a tradition, at the national level, that parallels in many ways processes already observed in traditional Brazilian tribal society. Individuals affiliate with a given social grouping for the convenience of access to economic resources, for the carrying out of religious rituals, and for the maintenance of distinctiveness from the rest of society.

How individuals in Brazil's cities determine who shall and who shall not be part of their active, cooperating, in-group is explored in the next contribution to this section. In a discussion of *parentelas* (large extended kin groupings) among the middle class of urban Minas Gerais, Charlotte Miller argues that the traditional concepts of community neighborhood and other territorially defined units are of questionable relevance in the urban setting. She discovers that Brazilian urban parentelas can be quite large; in her case studies they range in size from 125 to 263 members, excluding dormant kin of whom her respondents knew nothing. Miller finds that interaction within this group is frequent. Responses to her questionnaire indicated that 80 percent of the upper middle class and 69 percent of the middle class have weekly contact with family members outside the nuclear family.

These contacts are usually in the areas of business arrangements, professional consultations, shared home life, patronage of services, exchange of information and gossip by telephone or by personal visits, family gatherings, and regular babysitting services. The existence of this active cooperating kindred gives even the elderly a useful role. Miller finds that the old are regularly and dutifully visited by their children and grandchildren, nephews and nieces, and many other kinds of relatives who ask them for advice and help.

While these bilateral parentelas do not derive historically from the extended kindreds and secret societies of Brazilian tribal societies, they do offer functional equivalencies to the individual. As do the tribal secret societies, they gain their importance as much from those they exclude as from those that they include. And as do the bilateral kindreds of tribal societies, they give their members access to important sources of power and economic well-being.

Miller explores how such kin groupings can make even the recalcitrant Brazilian bureaucracy work for their purposes. While it is true, she admits, that these networks create barriers to the mobility of members of lower strata, in that their access is limited by intra-class endogamy, for parentela members they work because of kin-based contacts within administrative structures. Seen in this light, Brazilian middle-class networks function as mutual aid associations.

Certain themes, then, cut across all of Brazilian society, whether Amerindian, Luso-rural, or Luso-urban. Tightly sealed unilineal groupings, if they ever existed, have long since become things of the past. The essential kinship units are bilateral, and are often manipulated so as to respond best to an individual's interests and needs. Non-kinship based social units also exist, and are reinforced by commonly held secret lore. These may be sex based, as with the men's houses among tribal society and male and female clubs among Brazil's urban groups. Or they may be based on a series of patron-client relationships, offering an identity that eclipses kinship, as with the Umbanda cult.

Race and class still sharply divide Brazil, as witnessed in the discussion on race by Florestan Fernandes, presented in the first section of this book. However, the country is far from being static. Fluidity of social affiliation exists, and apparently has existed for many centuries. Historical continuities linking tribal with modern Brazilian society may be few. Functional equivalencies and structural parallels, however, abound.

# TEN

# Lineage and Lineality in Lowland South America

Robert F. Murphy

SOME TWENTY-ODD years ago, in the course of field work among the Mundurucú Indians of the Tapajós River, Brazil, I found the co-existence of a system of patrilineal descent and an essentially uxorilocal residence preference. The discovery hardly rates with Watson's and Crick's development of the spiral helix model of DNA, but it was of some ethnological interest because such redoubtable figures as Alfred Kroeber, Claude Lévi-Strauss, and G. P. Murdock were dubious that the arrangement was even possible. Similar systems have been found since that time, some in South America and others in Africa, and we now know that it is merely improbable, something we can say, for that matter, of all of social life.

In my analysis of Mundurucú social structure, certain facts emerged clearly from the discontinuity of descent and residence. Clanship is indeed patrilineal, but the dispersion of male clan members through uxorilocality, and matrilocality, prevented the development of local nucleii of agnatic kin. This, and the virtual absence of genealogical reckoning, effectively blocked the formation of patrilineages. The residence preference—and I shy away from the hard term "rule"—did, however, produce localized, household clusters of kinswomen, related in the female line. Despite the subsequent characterization of these household units as "small matrilineal lineage(s)" (Steward and Faron 1959:338), it was clear that they were

217

anything but lineages. They were delineated by neither ideology nor genealogy and remained just as I described them: women related through women who shared a house (Murphy 1956:425).

This raises a basic question. Does any group of unilineally related kinfolk who interact with each other in certain contexts and for certain purposes constitute a lineage? Are we correct in imputing lineages to people who do not define themselves in terms that are consistent with the concept of a lineage? This is actually an old argument, though it usually revolves around section systems, or sometimes moieties, rather than lineages. The question is very simply whether there are unarticulated and unstated lineages existing in behavioral reality, or whether such groups may really have their locus only in the conceptual system of the anthropological observer. My own position is clear on the matter: a lineage exists in the realm of social action, to be sure, but it is articulated at the level of social thought. Without the latter component—the ideology of the lineage— one can find lineages wherever one finds kinship.

The issue of what is a lineage is not a matter of semantics and definition, for it has affected our understanding of tropical South American social systems. I first commented on some of these misunderstandings during a symposium on South American marriage systems in 1971, when I pointed to the marked weakness, or absence, of lineage depth and delineation in the lowland area. In a recent, and excellent, review of the present status of lowland ethnography, Jean Jackson has presented several instances in which the presumed unilineality, and presence of lineages, in societies of the region must be called into question (Jackson 1975:320–21). Dr. Jackson argues that many of the so-called unilineal systems are essentially cognatic, and descent and existence of lineages have been inferred from kin groups constituted by a unilocal mode of residence, as in Mundurucú. She suggests that the term ''lineage'' would be better restricted to ''genealogically reckoned unilineal descent groups'' (ibid:320).

The usual definition of lineage is congruent with Dr. Jackson's own formulation. This sees the lineage as a group constituted by a unilineal ideology in which descent is traced from a common ancestor through demonstrated genealogies, and which includes at least three generations of adults, living and dead, in its calculations. From this perspective, there are very few true lineage systems in lowland South America. Rather, what is usually found are clusters of co-resident kin who are not bound by careful reckoning of common descent nor unified by a unilineal ideology. If a rule exists, it is one of residence, and the resultant groups are ad hoc in nature rather than jural. At the other extreme, where true unilineality does exist, it is of the clanship variety. That is, descent groups are based upon a myth of common origin, quite commonly from a totemic ancestor in the timeless past, and genealogies are either absent or highly incomplete; at best, descent is putative, not demonstrated.

One of the more striking aspects of lowland social systems is their lack of genealogical depth of any kind. I spent two months trying to extract genealogies from recalcitrant, discomfited and resentful Mundurucú before one old man finally broke down and told me that they do not bandy the names of their dead around the way we white men do. One could assume, of course, that this is esoteric knowledge—covert but known and accessible through ethnographic doggedness—but this would miss the whole point of the name taboo. Its function is not to keep such information out of the notebooks of nosy anthropologists, but to keep it from *being* information. That is, the informants knew a bit more about their ancestry than I did, but not much more. And that is a social fact in the true sense of the word, albeit a negative fact. The results of my investigations were genealogies that interconnected people by cognatic and affinal links; I started off my charts lengthwise on the pages but soon had to turn the papers sideways. The absence of genealogies had another result, and one that went beyond the failure of the Mundurucú to live up to the definition of the lineage—that relations within clans were not internally segmented. Beyond the close circle of demonstrably related kin—a bilateral circle at that—relations within clans were diffusely recognized and distributed, uninvaded by considerations of relative closeness of ancestry. Indeed, this very diffuseness extended throughout the moiety. In short, there are very important structural characteristics that flow from lineage organization as opposed to clanship and these are largely absent in lowland South America.

Space does not permit a group-by-group survey of lineality in the forest area, and I will turn attention to but two of the better known reports of lineage organization, the Yanomamö and the Shavante. Jackson notes that the Yanomamö do not have names for their lineages—these were bestowed by the ethnographer—and characterizes them as "convenient analytic terms," following Needham's des-

ignation of Sirionó matrilineages (*ibid:* 320). If the Yanomamö can be
said to have lineages, then their nature is typologically unique. First
of all, the Yanomamö do not maintain genealogies, and Chagnon
himself tells of the considerable difficulties he experienced in collecting this information (Chagnon 1968a:10–13). According to the ethnographer, however, the Yanomamö really did know the names of
their ancestors and used the linkages in ordering social relationships.
Genealogy does not, apparently, defeat strategy among the Yanomamö, for they reorder their kin ties to suit marital convenience
(*ibid:*65). These manipulations go even beyond the usual genealogical ploys occurring within the context of Iroquois kinship and the
redefinition of relatives to place them in the opposed, marriageable
category. Such structural flexibility has been reported by Thomas
Gregor (1969) for the Mehinaku of the Upper Xingu area, where
basically Iroquois systems are also found but in thoroughly bilateral
societies. With regard to Yanomamö kinship terms, Chagnon states
that the Iroquois system segregates out one's own lineage mates from
affines, but if the system is consistently applied, the non-marriage-
able category should extend well beyond one's own lineage. In any
event, the manipulation of kin ties to maximize marriage choices
within the context of a two line system is a characteristic of bilateral
groups and would be rather unusual in a lineage organization.

The nature of the groups and their internal relations also raise interesting questions. Chagnon writes that local descent groups "rarely
include more than two generations of males" (1968a:68), but that
these must nevertheless be understood as corporate groups (*ibid:*69).
Their corporateness does not lie, however, in scarce resources but in
control over the marriages of their women. I cannot accept women as
an "estate" any more than I can view them, in Lévi-Strauss' terms,
as inert counters in an exchange system. Aside from the usefulness of
the concept, one can question it in practice. It would seem that what
really governs marriage among the Yanomamö is brother-sister
equivalence, and adult brothers govern the disposition of their sisters
(*ibid:*69). This, and competition over available women are responsible for the fact that the closest ties of solidarity are with brothers-in-
law and not with brothers. In summary, lacking genealogical depth,
residential continuity, self designation and internal solidarity, I would
question the utility of reifying patrifiliation among the Yanamamö

into lineages, a conclusion borne out by Judith Shapiro's research among the Brazilian Makiritare (1971).

The Akwe Shavante present an interesting parallel with the Mundurucú in that both combine patrilineality with uxorilocality. Lineages having local nucleii are possible in the former group, however, because marriage is usually endogamic to the local community. The lineages are, nonetheless, of a quite different order from the common African models. Genealogies are shallow and rarely include more than three generations, including children (Maybury-Lewis 1974:342 ff.). The lineages are not named after ancestors but after qualities of the group; the same lineage can have several names, and different lineages can have the same name (ibid: 170). Membership is not fixed by genealogy despite the ascription implied in the term "lineage." One can switch lineages when moving from one group to another, and such moves are apparently frequent. The lineages are, however, said by Maybury-Lewis to be corporate groups, though their only discernible corporate function is to stick together in factional disputes. Even here, one finds only a general overlap between faction and lineage, for most factions are eclectically composed, with one or another lineage as the core of the faction. Given these circumstances, one may consider Maybury-Lewis' statement that "Shavante consider people of their own faction to be fellow clansmen rather than to assume that they consider fellow clansmen to be members of their own faction" (ibid: 168) and ask whether this is also true of the dynamics of lineage recruitment.

It has been well known since Evans-Pritchard's Nuer research that on the ground social relations often differ from cultural models and that all sorts of shifts and strategies are possible within the framework of a lineage structure. These shifts and strategies, however, occur within the context of culturally articulated lineage units, and the anthropologist is not entitled to parse lineages out of the strategies and then declare their vagueness and fluidity as primary properties. Let us turn now to the notion of the corporation, which, following Morton Fried (1957), is characterized by "continuity of possession to an estate which consists of things, persons, or both" (ibid:23). Given the evanescent and shifting nature of lineages among both the Shavante and Yanomamö, one may question whether they possess the requisite continuity. Moreover, the corporateness of both consists exclusively of an estate in persons, in one for marriage purposes, in the other for solidarity in feuding. I would question the usefulness of either as a criterion of corporateness, for, to the extent that a group has any cohesion or internal authority at all, it may be said to exert rights over people and therefore be corporate. In short, it is close to tautology.

It would be much more useful for our purposes to consider instead the corporate rights of lineages in scarce resources, for here we find useful comparative data. In 1956, Peter Worsley published a reanalysis of Fortes' Tallensi data and concluded that the strength of the lineage principle and degree of corporateness within Tallensi society were contingent on pressure on agricultural land, this being the principal item in lineal estates (Worsley 1956). This theme was later developed by Mervyn Meggitt in his analysis of the Mae Enga of New Guinea, in which he showed that agnation and lineages become firmer in areas of land scarcity (Meggitt 1965). Meggitt poses the basic question of why a people disposed to patrifiliation do or do not use this principle as a mechanism to determine, bound, and delineate ascriptive groupings with clear-cut memberships. The answer is very simply to keep other people away from access to a scarce resource, for any principle of membership is also a rule of exclusion. The formalization of the lineage sets clear boundaries around its personnel and, thereby, sure barriers around its estate.

South American lineality has certain resemblances to descent in New Guinea, whose students many years ago realized that they were being misled by African lineage models. John Barnes describes Highland New Guinea descent systems as often being genealogically shallow with gaps between founders and remembered ancestors, as failing to extend genealogies outward to include ancestral siblings—the major point of fission in lineage systems—and as being characterized by a lack of lineage activity, qua lineage (Barnes 1962:6). Each of these characteristics is equally applicable, and to a greater extent, to Lowland South America descent. And the reasons, in both cases, involve the relative plenty or shortage of productive natural resources.

New Guinea differs from the area of our own interest in greater population pressure on land and a fuller development of lineage organizations. Not all Highland New Guinea societies have lineages, but most are patrilineal. On the other hand, unilineality has a quite spotty distribution in South America, and true lineage systems are rare. The reasons for this lie in the tropical forest productive system, based as it is on slash and burn horticulture and a mixed economy of hunting, fishing and collecting. With the exception of such anomalies as the individual hunting trails of the Cashinahua, hunting areas throughout the region are open to all members of communities within their reach, and it is difficult in most cases to determine from ethnographic reports whether there are even village hunting territories. Fishing rights are similarly held by local groups, if indeed they are held at all, but even where the local unit is conceived of as a descent group there seems no pressure toward tight closure of access through rigid determination of group membership, that is, through the lineage mechanism. Thus, the Cubeo sibs control sections of river, but Goldman specifically states that the sibs are not lineages (Goldman 1963:99).

It may be generally conceded that hunting and fishing rights usually fall under the proprietorship of local groups rather than kin groups, and that the usual form of corporate kin group estate is in agricultural lands. In this connection, it is important to note that the results of ethnographic research in the region show the virtual universality of lands as general community property, entailed to neither individual nor kin group and falling only under usufruct rights which result from the expenditure of labor in clearing the terrain. One can venture only guesses as to what the situation may have been in times past, when population density was greater, for our evidence comes only from the recent period. Moreover, it is not necessary to speak of land scarcity today in terms of finite carrying capacities and other such considerations, for the lack of pressure on land is amply bespoken by the lack of social closures upon access to it. That land is a relatively free resource may also account for the egalitarianism of lowland South American society, an egalitarianism that fits well with diffuse ties of clanship rather than with the incipient stratification tendencies inherent within lineage systems, based as they are on a calculus of distance from one's ancestors and one's fellows. This is a theme that has, of course, been richly developed by Paul Kirchoff (1955), Morton Fried (1957) and by Irving Goldman with specific reference to the forest area (1963:99).

For the first time in the history of South American studies, we are in a position to make quite definitive generalizations about the social systems of the region. Not only have large and growing inventories of societies been studied, but they have been the subject of fine ethnography, the richness of which allows us to do ethnography within the ethnography, to make reinterpretations from one angle of what has been perceived from another. In making these reinterpretations, I would urge that we not become trapped in the metaphors of other areas, but to see in South America contrastive phenomena as well. In the case of descent, the contrast is clear. Lineage systems and segmentary process are virtually absent and descent is either bilateral or of the undifferentiated type of unilineality that goes with clan and moiety organization, a kind of descent that incorporates within itself qualities of timelessness.

# ELEVEN

# Canela Kinship and the Question of Matrilineality

## William H. Crocker

WHEN BRAZILIANS SPEAK of the Canela, they refer to two tribes of Gê-speaking Indians, the Apânyekra and the Ramkókamekra, living about thirty miles apart and about fifty miles south and southwest of Barra do Corda in the center of the state of Maranhão (see figure 11.1). Kinship among the latter, the Ramkókamekra-Canela, will be the major focus here. The monograph *The Eastern Timbira* by Curt Nimuendajú (1946), translated and edited by Robert Lowie, is largely devoted to this group, as are also at least two reconstructive kinship analyses.[1]

The Canela are of particular interest because of the great number of field studies being done among Gê-speaking tribes by scholars of the Harvard-Central Brazil Research Project as well as by some other active teams. These tribes include the Shavante and Sherente among the Central Gê (Maybury-Lewis 1974), and the Kayapó (T. Turner 1966 and J. Turner 1967), Apinayé (Da Matta 1973), Gaviões (Laráia and Da Matta 1967), Krikati (Lave 1967), Pukóbye (Newton 1971) and Krahó (Melatti 1970) among the Northern Gê. All of these except the Kayapó are known as the "Timbira," with the Tocantins River dividing the group into an eastern and western branch. The Canela belong to the eastern branch and the Apinayé to the western.

Special thanks go to Darrell Miller, graduate student at the University of Florida, for a number of ideas incorporated in this chapter.

225

GÊ INDIANS OF CENTRAL BRAZIL

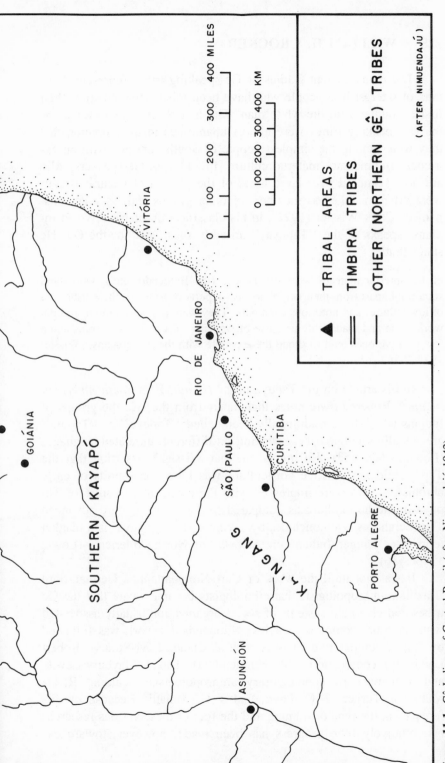

**Figure 11.1.** Gê Indians of Central Brazil (after Nimuendajú 1942).

The many current studies of Gê-speaking tribes represent a climax of interest in a people who have been misunderstood since their first encounter with the white man. The first chroniclers to report on the Gê-speaking tribes were almost unanimous in their opinion that they were among the simplest people of South America with an extremely rudimentary material culture. In addition, Gê-speakers, who are now scattered over large areas of the plateau of Central Brazil, were often mistaken as members of other groups and, as such, misnamed. Clark Wissler (1922), in his classification of New World Indians, speaks of the "Tapuya," an early misnomer for the Gê. He states that:

on the interior plateaus were the Tapuya (the Botocudo, etc.), who stand somewhat apart from their neighbors. All reports considered, these tribes are of low culture, and notorious cannibals. They were non-agricultural, did not work stone and made little pretense of weaving. These negative traits and a few positive ones tend to group these people with the Patagonians. (Wissler 1922:255).

In his article on the Tapuya in the *Handbook of South American Indians,* Robert Lowie notes that, apart from the Gê, the groups of Indians which have traditionally been called "Tapuya" or "Tapuia" are actually separate tribes speaking six different, unrelated languages (Lowie 1946c:553). He points out that Wissler's assertion that the Tapuya did not practice horticulture was based on reports of early chroniclers who were impressed with the rudimentary nature of Tapuya or Gê horticulture as compared to that of their more advanced Tupi neighbors. He concludes by saying that " 'Tapuya' is a blanket term like 'Digger Indian' or 'Siwash' in North America" (Lowie 1946c:556).

It was not until the work of Curt Nimuendajú, a German-born Brazilian anthropologist, that ethnologists became aware that the Gê tribes had elaborate systems of social organization usually associated with far more complex societies. Nimuendajú's work was followed by that of comparative analysts such as Claude Lévi-Strauss, Robert Lowie (in conjunction with Nimuendajú), David Maybury-Lewis, and a number of contemporary anthropologists including R. Da Matta, T. Turner, J. C. Lave, and J. C. Melatti. Because of differences in the type of training and the foci of these various researchers, relatively little progress has been made, however, toward ex-

plaining the great disparity between the simple material culture of the
Gê-speakers and their complex social organization. (See Gross article
in this volume.)

Steward (1946) classified the Canela as "Marginals" because
they depend largely on hunting, fishing, gathering, and simple slash-
and-burn horticulture. However, historical documents indicate that,
since 1814 when the Ramkókamekra-Canela first sought the protection of the Brazilian government, they have continually lost land to
local Brazilians, except for two recent periods. This has caused a
scarcity of food and brought about depopulation of an earlier rather
large Canela population (estimated in documents at over 1,000).
"This consistent lack of foodstuffs from year to year has been a factor in the development of the begging trip pattern that has become so
prevalent, as well as in increasing the general dependency upon the
*sertanejos* (hinterlanders) and the Service" (Indian Protection Service, Crocker 1961:72).

Consistent with their pronounced intratribal focus, the Canela
manifest a high level of group solidarity and social cohesion.
"Various ties bind the individual to his family, such as obligatory
food exchanges, mutual economic responsibilities, and food and sex
taboos when another member is sick or in a crisis situation. On the
ideological level, 'giving to please others' and 'compromising to satisfy another' are stressed values so that many conflicts are avoided or
fail to continue for long" (Crocker 1961:75).

Because of their relatively early surrender to the government,
and consequent familiarity with the hinterland settlers, the Ramkókamekra may have been ready earlier for adaptive acculturation and
population maintenance than many other Timbira tribes. If so, this
may be a factor in explaining why they have been able to sustain their
complex social organization as a functioning unit to such a significant
extent. Another very important factor contributing to their survival as
a sizeable community is the relatively undesirable territory in the Brazilian hinterland in which they live—having no Brazil nuts, poor agricultural riverine forests, and barely marginal cattle grazing savannas. Moreover, the Canela, located near the headwaters of small
streams instead of along navigable rivers, have been relatively isolated from outside influences. Feeder roads to the famous Trans-
amazônica highway bypass the Canela by at least forty miles to the
north and fifty miles to the south. Access to the northern highway is

by an ungraded dirt road, passable for jeeps and trucks with official permission, while movement to the south is possible only by horses and mules.

## History

Nimuendajú states that the Portuguese probably did not come into close contact with any Timbira tribes until well after 1624 (Nimuendajú 1946:2). In that year Bento Maciel Parente established a fort near the coast and began to afflict the tribes of the interior with slave raids, but whether these conflicts included any Timbira tribes remains uncertain. Nevertheless, it is clear that the Timbira and the Portuguese had a one-sided relationship over the next three centuries, the Timbira being the losers of territory and population as encroachments by Europeans and Brazilians increased.

Several chroniclers and explorers have dealt with the Timbira, the earliest of whom is Francisco de Paul Ribeiro, an officer in the army who fought against tribes in the area between 1800 and 1823 (Nimuendajú 1946:6). The second was Dr. Carl Martius (around 1819) whose legacy is the identification of the Gê language family (Nimuendajú 1946:8). Further study of the Gê languages was undertaken by Dr. Karl von den Steinen in 1886. He grouped the Gê together with the Botocudo and Goytaca to form the Tapuya family. Paul Ehrenreich conducted further research and elaborated on Von den Steinen's classification. Both Von den Steinen's and Ehrenreich's work helped to establish a solid basis for further distinctions, using principally linguistic materials (Nimuendajú 1946:8–9).

In 1925, the anthropologist Paul Rivet published a new classification of the Gê tribes with special emphasis on the Timbira. Nimuendajú characterized his system as "retrogressive" because it classifies a number of tribes for which there was little or no ethnographic or linguistic information (Nimuendajú 1946:9). Rivet's work was followed by that of Wilhelm Schmidt and Heinrich Snethlage. Schmidt corrected Rivet's errors and put the Timbira tribes back into their proper classifications. Because of the different interpretations given by these various authors, however, there is general confusion concerning the correct name for various tribes. As Nimuendajú observed, "The same tribe under three synonyms occasionally figures as three separate tribes, even in the same publication" (1946:13).

In this book *The Eastern Timbira,* Nimuendajú gave the history of various Timbira tribes and attempted to clear up the confusion. He also set down some of the main characteristics of the Timbira tribes. His approximately fourteen months of fieldwork between 1929 and 1936 served as the basis for his volume.

The Timbira know that they are the several tribes of a major ethnic unit, which they define above all—apart from the greater or lesser linguistic homogeneity—by the presence of the hair furrow, earplugs, circular form of settlement, and log racing. Whenever I told them about some strange people they invariably questioned me as to the occurrence of these traits in order to determine whether I was speaking of congeners or aliens. (Nimuendajú 1946:12)

The three tribes known traditionally as the Canela were the two already mentioned, the Apânyekra and the Ramkókamekra, plus the Kenkateye. How these Indians obtained the name Canela is not clear. Nimuendajú speculates on the meanings of the Portuguese word "canela," or "canella." It signifies both "shin bone" and "cinnamon." He finds little to support the reference to "shin bone" since it has no valid significance to any Canela trait. On the other hand, there is some evidence that the meaning "cinnamon" is relevant: . . . "in northern Brazil there are several trees whose bark emits a cinnamon-like odor and which are for that reason quite generally called canella. Conceivably—but only conceivably—the Serra da Canella (fina) got its name from a (slender) cinnamon tree, and the Indians in turn were called after the mountain in their country" (Nimuendajú 1946:30).

The Kenkateye (Gê: hill people, or sierra enemies) Canela, no longer exist. They were dispersed among the Apânyekra and Krahó after a massacre in 1913 by a local rancher and his followers. The second group, the Apânyekra (derived from the Gê word *apän,* referring to the flesh-eating fish, the piranha), are located near the headwaters of the Rio Corda. Originally, these two tribes were often at war with the third Canela tribe, the Ramkókamekra, but since 1814 relations have been less hostile. In 1929 the Apânyekra-Canela numbered about 130 (Nimuendajú 1946:31) and by 1975 their population had grown to 225. The size of the Ramkókamekra-Canela (in Gê, *räm-kô-kām-me-'kra:* almeceiga-tree grove in pluralizer children-of: people of the almeceiga grove) was placed at about 300 in 1936 (Nimuendajú 1946:33). By 1975, their numbers had grown to 514.

## Ecological Setting and Economic Base

The Northern Gê are essentially Brazilian "closed savanna" (*cerrado*) adapted peoples relying for subsistence on hunting and gathering, and to varying degrees on horiculture. The Northern Kayapó groups who inhabited an area of comparatively heavy rainfall (60–80 inches per year) (T. Turner 1966) and larger gallery forests aboriginally practiced slash-and-burn horticulture to a greater extent (cf. T. Turner 1966 and Frikel 1968) than did the Canela who lived in regions of lower rainfall (35–45 inches per year) and smaller gallery forests. Even the Krikati who live just some 100 miles to the west of the Canela apparently do not suffer from the crop insufficiencies (Lave 1967:31) which, at least since the 1930s, have been a major Canela problem. This economic uncertainty has forced both Canela tribes to work frequently for local Brazilian hinterland families to obtain food and supplies. In addition, the Ramkókamekra make and sell Indian artifacts in the cities. Since the early 1960s this has been a growing source of income.

Most of the Timbira groups had surrendered to Brazilian military detachments or local communities in the first half of the last century. Since that time, the Timbira have undergone so much deculturation and acculturation that their social and cultural forms must be studied as vestiges of earlier structures. Among the Timbira, the Ramkókamekra-Canela constitute something of an exception, in that their culture is still fairly well preserved. This can be explained in part by the fact that their over 160 years of culture contact has been mild and relatively non-exploitative (see Crocker 1964:342), and in part by the larger population of the Ramkókamekra village.[2] A fundamental ecological difference between the two tribes of the Canela is that, while both live in the savanna, the Apânyekra are situated near the Corda River on the edge of uninhabited dry forests. They have suffered considerably less from lack of protein because the area is abundant in fish and wild game. The Ramkókamekra have had to make the best of the lesser savanna game and the fish of small streams, living as they do away from the dry forests on the Santo Estevão. In spite of these drawbacks, they have been able to maintain many of their traditions.

Nimuendajú reports that the Canela tribes practiced horticulture, and he lists fifteen plants which he believes were cultivated aboriginally (Nimuendajú 1946:58). These include maize, manioc, sweet potatoes, yams, peanuts, and cotton, among other products. He recounts the failure of the manioc supply among the Brazilians of the small city of Barra do Corda in 1930 when "the Ramkókamekra suddenly appeared with several horseloads of manioc flour and saved the townsmen since by an odd chance they alone had saved their yield" (Nimuendajú 1946:61).

Nimuendajú reports that aboriginally the Ramkókamekra had no domestic animals, but by the early 1930s there were at least two dogs per household. In the last century, the Ramkókamekra adopted the use of chickens and pigs, along with most of the material culture of the neighboring hinterlanders. Whereas horses, mules, and donkeys were sometimes utilized, cattle could scarcely be raised because calves were eaten before they could mature.

All Northern Gê and Timbira villages are traditionally circular. Paths run from each house on a circular street to a round plaza in the middle. This village plan reflects the uxorilocal residence pattern whereby women who are sisters or parallel cousins through female kinship links live in adjacent houses, while their husbands come from houses "on the other side of the village circle," as Canelas say. Villages are periodically moved to keep them near the farm plots because a new clearing has to be cut from the stream-edge jungles each year since the soil cannot support the principal crops for a second year. Land encroachments by the local Brazilians since the middle of the nineteenth century have limited such movements, leading to a decrease in crop yields. Because of these earlier encroachments and the later fixed location of the Indian service posts, the Ramkókamekra village has remained in the same general area for thirty-eight years except for a brief period from 1963 to 1968 when it was forcibly removed to a forest region thirty miles away (Crocker 1972a).

In short, there are three significant changes among the Ramkókamekra-Canela since the middle of the last century which have affected their adaptation to the environment. First, land encroachments by local farmers and cattle ranchers have decreased the size of land holdings which in turn has caused a decline in harvests and available game. Second, the relative stability brought about by protection through the government Indian service (SPI and FUNAI) since 1938 has resulted in a population increase from about 300 to over 500. Third, because of the necessity of working for local farmers and living in close contact with government agents, there has been an increasing adaptation to local Brazilian customs, mostly material but some social.

## Social Organization

The social organization of the Gê tribes is complex. For the Ramkókamekra, Nimuendajú isolated nine separate social units to which the individual may belong. They include: 1) the individual family; 2) the matrilineal extended family; 3) matrilineal exogamous moieties; 4) non-exogamous rainy season moieties; 5) the plaza groups; 6) the plaza moieties; 7) the age classes; 8) the age-class moieties; and 9) six men's societies (Nimuendajú 1946:77). There were also formalized friendships, informal friendships, and ceremonial rankings (hämren).

Nimuendajú described the groups as follows:

Of these, the first four embrace both sexes, the remainder only men except that most of the primarily masculine organizations each have two girl associates. Membership in the matrilineal extended family and the exogamous moieties is hereditary; in the rainy season moieties, the plaza groups, and the plaza moieties, it is hereditary in the sense that it hinges on the bearing of certain names transmitted from an older kinsman. An age class is constituted by joint initiation into adult status. Admission into the Clown society depends upon one's talent for buffoonery; into other societies a male enters by virtue of his names, which determines affiliation of an individual with two of the five organizations. (Nimuendajú 1946:77)

It must be pointed out, however, that the Ramkókamekra-Canela extended family is a bilateral kindred and not matrilineal; there are no matrilineal exogamous moieties, and most probably never were (see Crocker 1973);[3] and the principal active units are the age class moieties. The non-exogamous rainy season moieties are all but non-functioning and, besides the six men's societies, there are others, some of which are entered, instead of by talent for buffoonery and by virtue of name-relatedness, through "ritual matrilineal" inheritance, that is, largely by membership in a ceremonial house or segment of houses (*haakat*) along the village circle. Membership in no Ramkóka-mekra-Canela social unit "hinges on the bearing of certain names;" name-related memberships are transmitted from a name-giver (an older kinsman) to a name-receiver (that kinsman's sister's son or his classificatory sister's son). Thus it is the transmission relationship and not the name that matters (Crocker 1972b).[4]

The Ramkókamekra kinship terminology reported by Nimuen-dajú and Robert Lowie (1937:573–576), has several similarities with both the North American Crow and Omaha bifurcate merging type terminologies.[5] The Crow similarities include using the same term for father's sister's daughter and paternal aunt, despite the fact that they belong to different generations. In addition, the father's brother and the father are classed together, as are a man's brother's children and his own children, and a woman's sister's children and her own children.

Since the time of Nimuendajú's study, there have been two important shifts in the Canela social order (Crocker 1961). The first of these involves the breakdown of the forces of political and social authority. In Nimuendajú's time, the chiefs were still relatively powerful. A chief would assign tasks to individuals and to each of the age classes. At the end of the day, he would verbally shame wrongdoers and slackers in front of the evening council meeting.

In 1951, the Indian Protection Service appointed a much younger man who could speak good Portuguese as chief after the death of the old chief. The replacement of the traditional leader in this manner reinforced an already developed attitude that the service was the highest line of authority, even higher than that of their own Canela chiefs. This fundamental change caused a certain amount of unrest. In 1955 personal rivalries between the young chief and the older age class leaders were factors in dividing the tribe into two separate villages.

A second change involved the shift in the disciplining of a boy from his mother's brother to his father. The partitioning of the tribe, which weakened the social structure, often made uncle and nephew roles difficult to carry out. Nimuendajú reports that these maternal uncles played a major role in the socialization of their nephews. They accomplished this through a process similar to fraternity hazing whereby they would shame their nephews in public if they did something they should not have done. With the arrival of the Indian Protection Service and their families, and increased contact with local Brazilian families, this practice disappeared. A man began to spend less time in the home of his mother and sisters and more time with his wife. This change in emphasis reflected both the mother's brother's weakened authoritarian role and the example set by the hinterland Brazilians.[6] The trend continues. Not only is the prestige and influence of a boy's mother's brother in the socialization process shifting to his father, but the control of a man over his daughter's husband, his son-in-law, is also significantly decreasing (Crocker 1973). These are two of the most obvious examples of the relative loss of traditional authority between older and younger people—a generation gap (Crocker 1974:192–94).

Although the weakening of traditional practices and role relationships have brought about some societal disorder, social cohesion has been maintained relatively well. This is a reflection of the fact that most social institutions have not been abandoned entirely, but rather have continued to operate with slight changes and adjustments. It is nevertheless obvious that the Ramkókamekra-Canela adaptation to the environment is no longer in its aboriginal state of ever-changing relative balance. No warfare, very reduced postpartum taboos, and little social or ritual control over fertility has resulted in over a 4 percent per annum population explosion since 1969.

In fieldwork done from 1966 to 1971, a large collection was made of both real and ideal terminological responses between ego and most of the possible consanguinal and affinal alters. The ideal responses were necessary, partly because the real data were so inconsistent and contradictory due to the existence and interplay of the numerous terminological systems and subsystems. Ideal materials followed a regular pattern and contained only a few variations. They indicated the existence of a fully extended Crow-like terminological system. They also showed that the Canela divide their world into those persons who are terminologically "first-linked" (biological parents, siblings, and children) (see Crocker 1971:338), or who are structurally equated as such ("parents," "siblings," and "children"), and those who are "further-linked" (mehüükyê)—a dualism.

The biologically first-linked individuals only, however, not the structurally equated ones, are held together by the belief that they share very similar blood so that when one such "close blood" person breaks a taboo, this adversely affects any weakened biologically first-linked member in the blood system, such as a sick person or a newborn baby.

Ego's first-linked relatives—biological *and* structural—are usually treated somewhat differently from further-linked relatives, so that social roles and terms of address at this general level can be held to be somewhat consistent.[7] The general distinction contrasting these two terminological spheres is that the first linkers, who may be called "nurturers,"[8] are supportive and serious, whereas the second-linkers, "the jokester-counselors" (my expression), mix counseling attitudes with joking. The former type of relatives play important roles in matters dealing with birth, physical and psychological nurturance, and economic support. The latter are important in societal and ceremonial affairs. They have the right to discipline and counsel ego in matters of food and sex taboos, marital and extramarital problems, juridical rights in the Council of Elders, and the transference of names, ceremonial rites, and privileges (Crocker 1971). This Canela first-link/further-link terminological dichotomy could be congruent with either a Crow or an Omaha type of terminological pattern. (See Da Matta 1976:193 and Crocker 1977:263–64.)

## Matrilineality

Particularly because of Nimuendajú's earlier claim (1946:77) that the Canela were matrilineal, it is important to carefully consider the possibility that they were once more fully matrilineal than they are now. Did they have the following usual characteristics of lineality not found among them today such as deep, daily functioning lineages with traditional special names, and were these groupings thought of as being ancestor-oriented and corporate through time? We know early sources raise the possibility that similar Timbira tribes numbered over a thousand, so a current residential kin structure such as the "longhouse" (a series of non-ceremonial houses, adjacent along the village circle and connected by all female kin links) might have been more extensive, exhibiting more completely the traditional characteristics of lineality. (The haakat, mentioned earlier, is always ceremonial and contained within the limits of a longhouse [ikre-lïï: house-long].)

It is now clear that Ramkókamekra informant kinship specialists can reckon their kin system more extensively in general depth (in one longhouse, seven generations) and in the number of matrilines included in a kin unit (in the largest longhouse, between twenty and thirty lines) than has been recognized by current anthropological Gê specialists.[9] The Ramkókamekra informant kinship specialists even have a word with which to distinguish what would be a person's "lineage" (kwë: a part of any whole)—or his/her father's, mother's father's, or father's father's "lineage"—which groups together the proper cross-generational kinship terms and persons almost exactly as they can be found in certain classical matrilineages (see Eggan 1950:23–24). This expression, kwë, however, is general in its usage in many part-to-whole distinctions applied throughout the society instead of being specific to such lineages. Moreover, there are no special traditional names for any particular lineage of this sort these days, and the principal Canela kin groupings are usually thought of by the Canela as being ego- rather than ancestor-oriented (Scheffler 1973:756)[10] and bilateral rather than unilineal. For instance, it is ego's kindred (mehūūkyê), not just matrilateral kin, who assemble for the frequent life-cycle rites.

On the other hand, matrilateral kinsmen do unite or are emphasized over patrilateral ones in certain limited situations. A man's terminological sisters related through all female links (uterine sisters and parallel cousins) make an effort to support him in jural matters. In addition, it is more likely to be the matrilateral uncles who become male and female ego's strong counselors and discipliners (see note 6). Moreover, the observer of Canela life cannot help but be overwhelmed by the pervasiveness of their matrilocality: Canelas say husbands are "bought," sisters living in the same house help each other extensively, and a matriline has a permanent sun-oriented location on present and future village circles until the line dies out.[11]

Since the Ramkókamekra-Canela rely to a greater extent on genealogical blood links for defining their longhouses and kin groups than other Timbira tribes appear to do in the literature, their membership distinctions in these matrilateral units are more precise and permanent, approaching corporateness. Membership in these units can be defined precisely by Ramkókamekra kinship specialists, but for most Canela such delineations are vague so that what could be commonly recognized as longhouse membership corporateness when seen through time, is actually scarcely thought about and even often violated by individuals, especially today. Consequently, these units are not fully matrilineal in the classical sense because their membership is not sufficiently precise through time (i.e., corporate); they have no special, distinctive names; they do not act together in daily life as specific units; and they come together only infrequently and when they do, they usually meet with patrilateral kin, as they always do in the case of life cycle rites.

Turning to a different but specific Canela kin unit with more aspects of matrilineality than can be found in the longhouse, a particular longhouse—or part of a longhouse—may possess a specific, named, festival rite (not a life cycle rite) which is held by a matriline or certain matrilines within the longhouse until this matriline or these matrilines die out. In performing this festival rite, the longhouse members handle the activities completely matrilaterally without any assistance or participation from the patrilateral kin in sharp contrast with the attendance at life cycle rites. While some festival rites are transmitted strictly within the prescribed matriline or matrilines (i.e., in correct matrilineal practice), others are passed on in connection with name transmission (again, not in connection with a particular name) so that they do not necessarily remain within certain traditional matrilines or even a specific longhouse but rather go to some distant "sister's" son in some other longhouse.[12] Keeping the rite within the longhouse may be brought about where this is traditionally necessary either through deliberately close name transmission or simply by passing the rite to any suitable younger member in the festival longhouse regardless of name transmission relationships. Sometimes all male and female members of a longhouse perform in a certain rite, but usually the ceremony is owned by a particular older woman of a matriline who holds the rite for the performers—maybe for her brother, son, daughter, or for others.

When a rite must remain within a longhouse, a set of matrilines, or a single matriline within this longhouse, depending on the particular rite's tradition, is restricted to the haakat of that rite.[13] A haakat always has a special name, not just a general one, namely, the name

of the rite. The number of matrilines of the longhouse included in the
haakat usually depends on direct descent from an alive ancestor. This
kind of rite transmission is referred to as being haakat-kôt (its-vine-
origin following) in contrast to being "name-following" (haprë-
'kôt), that is, name transmission following. In this institution, the
haakat, the Canela have named, corporate, ceremonial descent groups
or ceremonial lineages. The only aspects in which these ceremonial
groupings of persons are not fully matrilineal in the traditional sense
are: first, that the haakat is only occasional in activation; this varies
from twice a year to once in about every five years; second, a number
of longhouses do not possess haakat rites at all so that the haakat is
not a universal characteristic of even the occasional festival structure;
third, the haakat is not, in most cases, dead ancestor-oriented, as
should be the case of traditional matrilineality; the rite tends to be
passed on to descendants of alive persons so that the festival haakat
comes to pertain to a narrower range of descendant matrilines within
its longhouse as older people in the direct line of ascendency pass
away. This general, but not unexceptional, limitation to the descendants of alive rite holders may be the practice because the dead are
seldom remembered for more than one or two generations, except by
certain Ramkókamekra informant genealogical specialists. The ordinary Canela explain longhouse genealogical relationships, at least
these days, reckoning from ego "up" and "across" through alive or
recently dead "sisters" (i.e., parallel cousins) not "up" to and
"down" from a common great-ancestor, link by link, as do certain of
the Ramkókamekra informant kinship specialists. Keeping these considerations in mind, a haakat may be said to be "alive ancestor-
oriented."

## Recruitment to Ceremonial Groups and Ecology

Considering some kinds of memberships in the various ceremonial
groups, the Canela practice the following ways of recruiting: by
female ceremonial lineage or ceremonial descent group membership;
by male ceremonial lineage or ceremonial descent group membership;
by male name transmission relatedness within a ceremonial lineage or
ceremonial descent group; by male name transmission relatedness

outside of a ceremonial lineage or ceremonial descent group; by both male (Crow) and female (Omaha) name transmission relatedness not in a ceremonial lineage or ceremonial descent group; by the age of individuals for age class membership. (For brevity, the expression "ceremonial lineage" will be understood to pertain to "ceremonial descent group" as well.)

A careful study of the Ramkókamekra festivals reveals that some kinds of recruitment to ceremonial group membership are more characteristic of certain festivals while other kinds are more typical of other festivals. An associated observation to be taken up later is that the kind of recruitment to a ceremonial group may be related to a festival's relative antiquity as well as to the ecology of the location where the festival might have evolved.

Quite conspicuously, "female ceremonial lineage . . . membership" appears only in two of the Fish Festival societies. In one of them, the right to perform the Cô-yamprô (water-foam) role is held in one ceremonial lineage and passes ideally from a woman to her daughter. Name transmission relatedness is not a question.

The other festival society where the membership follows female matrilineality is the Crab Society (Pay) of the Fish Festival. Here all of the female members of two related longhouses and the older males born into the same longhouses carry out the rite. Again, membership is not name transmission related. This is also true for the one male role in the Cūmtūm (*capivara:* a large water rodent) Rite of the Fish Festival. It is important, nevertheless, to note that whenever male ceremonial lineage transmission is found without being accompanied by female ceremonial lineage transmission, membership through name transmission relatedness within the ceremonial lineage is sometimes (not always) a convenient alternative to Canela lineal rite transmission.

Although some festival lineage recruiting for male roles is completely lineal, and other such recruiting is more often lineal than not, still other festival society recruiting is entirely by name transmission relatedness. What may have been a hermetic separateness between these two systems of rite transmission has most certainly broken down; the result is that if the Canela find it difficult to transmit a rite one way, they will do it the other way. Consequently, distinctions by either ceremonial lineage or by name transmission recruitment have become arbitrary for the Canela and therefore cannot be used as diagnostic factors to determine which rites were once held in ceremonial lineages and which rites were passed on in ceremonial societies through name transmission relatedness. Only the Fish Festival can be quantitatively set apart from other festivals as being more fully characterized by ceremonial lineal (non-name) transmission.

In a continuum of festival groups ranging from high ceremonial lineage to low ceremonial lineage frequency of elements, the societies of the Fish Festival are the most highly lineal, while the societies of the two initiation festivals (Kêêtúwayê and Pepyê) have almost no ceremonial lineage elements. The remaining festivals fall somewhere in between, all having festival lineage elements in varying numbers, or relying to different degrees on name transmission relatedness, according to their respective places on the ceremonial lineage element frequency continuum.

Another special characteristic of the Fish Festival is that a number of its societies are named after fish and animals typically found along a large river with lakes and swamps and not in and around the small headwater streams of the present Canela savanna location.[14] In contrast, the names of the initiation male societies (plaza groups) and the names of the creatures in the origin myths of the initiation festivals are more associated with a savanna than a riverine environment.[15] These details, on the one hand associating festival lineages with a riverine ecology, and on the other hand associating festival name transmission related recruitment with a savanna environment, allow the researcher to start thinking about a social structure transformation from a near matrilineal to a more generally bilateral system, as well as about an hypothetical migration from an earlier geographical location to a later one.[16]

Turning to the incidence of festival recruitment by name transmission relatedness, this kind of membership in festival societies can be found in the plaza groups and in the men's societies of every summer season festival. Moreover, the winter season moieties, which lack festival lineages entirely, are characterized by both male (Crow) and female (Omaha) name transmission relatedness. Consequently, some kind of name transmission relatedness, whether within the festival lineage or independent of it, male only or by both sexes, can be found in every major festival, whether summer or winter season oriented.

This broader reliance on name transmission relatedness for festival group recruitment together with the extent to which name transmission is a pan-Gê phenomenon suggests the hypothesis that this principle is more ancient than the festival lineage principle which is found less widely spread among the festivals. Such a reconstruction includes three festival recruitment structures possibly related to different ecologies. Whereas the association of male and female name transmission relatedness to the earliest period must be held very tentatively, the later festival lineage (haakat) association with river ecology and the still later age class association with a savanna environment (and warfare) [17] seem to be more tenable hypotheses. (For pertinent evolutionary approaches, see Service 1962 and Dole 1972.)

Expanding this line of thinking, the following hypothetical scenario is suggested. Winter season moiety membership follows the pattern of name transmission which currently exists in daily living—Crow for men and Omaha for women, and this principle is the same for all the Northern Gê tribes, whether they are Crow-like (Canela) or Omaha-like (Kayapó) in terminological orientation (see Bamberger 1974). Together with uxorilocality, this parallel, nepotal (both sexes) type of name transmission seems to be a pan-Northern Gê basic social structure, and therefore, could be held to be characteristic of a pre-"lineage" development era. (Full lineages with all the classical matrilineal aspects probably never evolved.) During this hypothesized near full lineal period, developed under affluent and stable riverine influences, Omaha female name transmission recruitment, being inconsistent with matrilineality, could have been replaced by mother-to-daughter succession within the "matrilineage", while male name transmission recruitment could have been retained and/or new lineal transmission could have been developed, depending on the particular "matrilineage." (These "river era" "matrilineages" could have still evolved ancestor-focus, a specific term for "lineage," a terminological differentiation between "uncles" and "grandfathers," etc., and the elimination of certain Omaha elements from the terminology before encompassing all classical Crow matrilineal aspects.) Then, when the near-lineal river era had terminated, due to pre-contact and post-contact pioneer front influences, the named daily operating lineages could have lost their bases in economic and kinship reality, being retained later only as named ceremonially activated lineages in a festival context. The principal "summer" festival structures left after such a transformation, would have been male (only) name transmission relatedness within a ceremonial lineage and male (only) name transmission relatedness outside of any lineal structure together with some near-lineal remnants—the case with the present-day Canela (Ramkókamekra and Apânyekra) festival systems. It is quite pertinent to this hypothesized scenario that in the Fish Festival, the Fish Otters, though a plaza group, are said—as an exception to plaza group recruitment practices—to come from two particular longhouses.

An alternative explanation of the Ramkókamekra-Canela festival diversity may be that the different sorts of festival entities (ceremonial lineages, plaza groups, men's societies, winter moieties, and age class moieties) may actually have come from various tribes that merged with the Ramkókamekra-Canela during the pre-contact or early contact times of conflict and tribal movements.[18]

From the above materials and their obvious uncertainties, the most recommendable hypothesis for early testing is that the Ramkókamekra-Canela, or a closely related Timbira tribe, once lived for a considerable length of time near a large river basin with marshes and lakes, and that during this river era, their tribal population was probably considerably larger and more stable so that it could support a society with more of the traditional aspects of matrilineality.

## Summary

After a survey of historical and ecological data from Nimuendajú's monograph on the Ramkókamekra-Canela (1946) and a review of a number of concepts found in this author's earlier publications dealing with the same tribe, the question of early fuller matrilineality for the Ramkókamekra-Canela, and by implication for other Timbira tribes, was raised. In comparison with other Timbira tribes, the social structure and festival system of the Ramkókamekra-Canela appear to be better preserved, due possibly to their more protected location and to their greater numbers.

Today, a relatively extensive Crow-like terminological system can be identified, with cross-generational terms up to three and four generations in depth, and theoretically even more. The Canela have a term for the concept "lineage" (kwë) which they can use to identify what is essentially ego's lineage ("people") as well as his/her father's, mother's father's, and father's father's "people." These "lineages" are not named, and in daily life are ego- rather than ancestor-focused. The consanguineal terminological system as a whole can be divided into terms that are first-linked to ego—parents, siblings, and children—and into further-linked terms (mehūūkyê)—the rest. This dualism corresponds to a certain extent with actual behavior.

Marriage these days takes place between distant relatives and nonrelatives. For any one person (including same-sex siblings), the village universe may be divided differently into three categories of people—consanguines, affines, and individuals not related in any way.

Socialization, life crisis rites, and matters of justice are handled for any person by both the matrilateral and patrilateral relatives—his/her kindred, but the matrilateral relatives carry out at least three-quarters of these duties.

Rights to perform roles in rituals and festivals are given to the younger generation mostly either because of their membership in festival lineages, because of name transmission, or because of their membership in age classes. It happens that festival lineages (haakat) are far more highly developed in the Fish Festival than in any other festivals, all of which have ritual lineages to a lesser extent except for the initiation festivals which almost have none at all and are characterized by age classes that do not even exist in the Fish Festival. Another contrast is that the names of the ceremonial groups in the Fish Festival—fish otter, swamp deer, great turtle, etc.—suggest the environment of a large river basin with swamps and lakes, whereas the names of creatures found in ceremonial activities of the initiation festivals (Kêêtúwayê and Pepyê)—armadillo, roadrunner, field rat, etc.—suggest "closed" savanna (cerrado) living or the adjacent dry forests more than river living.

Quite characteristic of cultural lag in general, the consanguinal terminological system has remained largely Crow-like but is currently disintegrating in "lineage" depth, extensiveness, and maintenance of the father's sister's son as "father." There is a tendency for every term beyond the biologically first-linked ones to become further-linked ("uncle/nephew" and "aunt/niece"), with the reciprocal choice of "senior/junior" address being determined by relative age as is already largely the case between Apânyekra-Canela cousins. Most probably, this trend toward the utilization of relative age as a kinship principle reflects the great influence of hinterland Brazilians on the Canela.

The hypothesis is then offered that the Canela once lived with more nearly corporate, daily activated, named matrilineages near a large river, but because of contact pressures with pioneer fronts, migrated into their present, small stream savanna lands, turning more to their war-related age class system to defend themselves from the intertribal turmoil caused by the advancing pioneer fronts. In the course of this migration, it is hypothesized that named matrilineages were abandoned in daily living, but retained as occasionally activated ceremonial lineages, especially in the Fish Festival. During the same period of transition, responsibilities with respect to ego's socialization and village rights may have shifted into a more bilateral pattern.

## Notes

1. Roger M. Keesing and Carol Steffens Schilling have written manuscripts which have been of considerable help. Drs. Priscilla Reining, Floyd Lounsbury, Gordon Gibson, and Gertrude Dole have also been of great assistance in discussing certain conceptual problems.

2. Apinayé in 1962 (Lave 1967:20):150 and 80; Krahó in 1963 (Melatti 1972:4):169, 49, 109, 50, and 130; Gaviões in 1962 (Laráia and Da Matta 1967:138):23, and 17, Krĩkati and Pukóbye in 1964 (Lave 1967:19):152, 58, 90, 30, and 25; Apânyekra in 1959 about 170; Ramkókamekra in 1960 (Crocker 1972a:240):269 and 143, but in very close contact and recent in separation (1956). Around 1930 (Nimuendajú 1946:13–36) it appears that the Ramkókamekra numbered just under 300, and that all other Timbira villages were well under 200.

3. The current Canela belief is that each man married "across the village" (90 to 270 degrees) from his natal house, wherever that was, and not that the tribe was divided into exogamous halves. In 1970, of 117 Ramkókamekra-Canela men, 70 had married in the "other half" of the village, 27 on their own side, 17 into a neighboring "longhouse," and 3 into their own "longhouse" (formerly forbidden), though several houses away. (For "longhouse," see 9.)

4. A man passes a set of names to some "sister's" son, seldom to his full sister's son, and may give a rite with these names or with the transmission of some other set of names which he also possesses. He may even convey a newly created name to a "sister's" son, transferring a rite to him. Rites may have once been transmitted, attached to specific names but not during this century, because I have traced most rite ownerships back several generations. The more deculturated and acculturation altered Krĩkati rely almost entirely on name transmission for defining relationships, with the

genealogical kinship applying only to ego's nearest relatives—not the cousin terms (see Lave 1967:217).

5. Crow terminology tends to be matrilineal with the mother's brother being the most important individual in relation to the speaker. The children of the father's sister are called by the same terms as paternal uncle and aunt while mother's brother's children are classed with fraternal nephews and nieces. Omaha terminology often is patrilineal and as such represents the mirror image of Crow. The father's sister is most important. Her children are classed with sororal nephews and nieces and the mother's brother's children with maternal uncles and aunts (Murdock 1960:102). Old Ramkókamekra-Canela informants maintain that a person's father's sister's daughter's daughter, and even this latter woman's daughter, are classed with father's sister (*tïy:* "aunt" or even better, "grandmother"). Likewise, these women's brothers are classed with a person's father. Actually, the recently collected Canela data support the distinction that these people are not Crow/Omaha-type (see Lounsbury 1964) in kinship classification but rather are characterized by the "parallel transmission" patterns of Scheffler and Lounsbury (1971). (See Crocker 1977:272.) Further information on kinship will appear in a monograph soon to be published by the author.

6. A person's "senior," male mehũūkyê include his/her mother's brother, mother's father, father's father, and certain other relatives, all classed as "uncles." More correctly, the expression, "grandfathers" should be utilized, but the Canela prefer *tio* (uncle) to *avô* (grandfather) in most cases. Any of these "uncles" may discipline a "nephew" (who may really be a grandson). The expression, *menquêt-yê* means "uncles," "grandfathers" or "ancestors"; and *tämtswë* signifies opposite-sex "sibling's" children, "grandchildren," or "descendants" (including children and "children" in the latter context).

7. Male and female ego's mother's brother, their principal further-linked male counselor, and their name-giver (these three separate roles may or may not coincide in the same person) counsel and discipline but do not joke. All other further-linked relatives of male and female ego such as their grandparents and also their father's sister's, their mother's, father's sister's and their father's father's sister's uterine descendants—with the exception of these "father's sisters' " brothers, who are called "father" (therefore, structurally first-linked)—counsel and joke a great deal.

8. Lave (1970:69), Da Matta (1971:356), and Melatti (1971:347–53) emphasize that whereas the primary Timbira family procreates the child, nourishes it, and raises it physically (i.e., the "nurturers"), the name transmitter forms it socially and ceremonially; but I find that a principal Canela counselor or a mother's brother, who may be some person other than the name transmitter, usually carries out a more significant role in the *social* formation of the child than the name transmitter.

9. Among the fourteen Ramkókamekra-Canela "longhouse" residential units, out of a total of 58 houses (in 1975), five longhouses exist as single houses with one mature woman in each; a sixth consists of 2 small houses and two senior women. The largest longhouse is comprised of 14 houses, whose women are all direct descendants of the longhouse's oldest living woman's great-great-grandmother, Amyi-yakôp, who was born an Apânyekra-Canela and whose direct female line descendant's names are all known. Consequently, all these women are, most correctly, Apânyekra-Canela in ethno-tribal affiliation, according to Canela reckoning. The tradition is that men are affiliated with the tribe of origin of their father and women with the tribe of their mother.

10. The concept of "ancestor-focus" may not be necessary to the definition of a "lineage" in lowland South America as it has been in Africa and the United States because "lineage" depth of more than two or three generations and memory of ancestors beyond grandparents were generally not characteristic of the area except in the northwest Amazon (see Murphy article this volume).

11. When asked about the location of their *kä-tsä* (breast-place: the place of their mother's breast), certain men pointed to a position between two houses on the village circle saying, "there is the place of my mother's ashes"—all that was left of their matriline and probably their natal longhouse.

12. Canelas say that rites which are transmitted by name transmission relatedness (membership in plaza groups, men's societies, etc.) "circle around the village." This is because while such rites may be given to a matrilateral "sister's" son within the same longhouse, they may also be given to a patrilateral "sister's" son across the village plaza, such as the son of a father's sister's son's daughter, who may be a Crow "sister."

13. A festival lineage (haakat) comes to an end for a longhouse when they have insufficient personnel to carry out their rite or fail to have the appropriate person or persons in age or sex to perform their particular ritual. Then, the Elders transfer the haakat to another longhouse which does have the appropriate personnel who are willing to accept the responsibility. A haakat can, however, be shifted to another matriline, or other matrilines, within the longhouse simply by agreement between key persons in the longhouse.

14. The swamp deer (*suçuapara: Blastocervo dichotomus* Illiger), the fish otter (*ariranha: Pteronura brasiliensis* Zimmerman and Gmelin), the heron (*garça*), the large anaconda and large turtle, and other creatures that inhabit sizeable rivers and the adjacent areas do not exist in the present Ramkókamekra lands, though they are featured significantly in the Ramkókamekra Fish Festival.

15. Some of the names of the creatures found in origin myths, festival activities and ceremonial societies of the initiation festivals are the following: armadillo, emu (South American ostrich), roadrunner, bat, falcon, wild boar, hummingbird, field rat, jaguar, parrot, great falcon, etc.—of both the savannas and their adjacent "gallery forests."

16. The obvious large river area from which the Canela, or similar tribes, could have come is the Tocantins-Araguáia basin. This region is linguistically central to the Northern Gê, but pioneer fronts of Maranhão generally forced tribes westward not eastward. The São Francisco must not be left out as a possibility, however, and neither must the lower Parnaíba around the town of Porto, the lower Itapicuru near Coroatá, nor the Mearím below Bacabal. The São Francisco and Parnaíba seem too far, while the Itapicuru and Mearím seem too small, but at least the latter two would be consistent with the known pioneer front movements and be in earlier Timbira territory. Hopefully, more precise ecological studies will eliminate four of these five areas in the years to come.

17. The term "Pep-," as found in Pepyê and Pepcahäc, is said by Nimuendajú to mean "warrior," though the Canela cannot explain this today. Nevertheless, the performances of the "troops" in these festivals leave little doubt that these groups had something to do with warfare.

18. A recent study by the author of Canela (both tribes) war stories suggests (see Crocker 1978) that, during the late pre-pacification period, warfare was very devastating with the result that some tribes were greatly diminished in size and military strength, and it became necessary for the purposes of security to join forces with other reduced tribes in order to facilitate the survival of both groups. Apparently, because of this warlike orientation, it was extremely difficult and dangerous to attempt intertribal visits. There are stories of individuals caught in another tribe's area being killed on sight and of visiting groups being temporarily taken in but slaughtered later. Unlike the Kayapó and the Shavante, for whom inter-village movement for certain purposes was traditional, Canela-like tribes appear to have mixed with each other principally through the merging of already weak tribes. These "mergers" have been institutionally preserved in the *Täm-häc* (King Vulture) Rite of the Pepcahäc Festival where six remnant groups of formerly independent tribes identify themselves (see Nimuendajú 1946:223). In contrast, Melatti (1975:336–37) offers a less war-oriented, more intervillage related early picture for the Krahó.

# TWELVE

# Secrets, Exclusion, and the Dramatization of Men's Roles

## Thomas Gregor

MOST SOCIAL GROUPS draw their significance from the functions they perform for their members. Families socialize children and provide an outlet for sexuality and reproduction, while lineages define territorial or economic rights and politically organize those who belong to them. Groups such as these are best studied in terms of the substantive things they do for their members, their structure, and the rule of recruitment that maintains them.

There is another, though smaller set of groups, however, which are quite different. These groups draw their primary significance not from whom they include, but from whom they exclude. Their main functions are not usually to provide substantive services for their members (though they may do so), but rather to patrol the group boundaries and dramatize the difference between members and outsiders. The analysis of such groups requires a methodology sensitive not only to patterns of communication, inclusion and interaction, but also the secrecy and exclusion which give these groups their special character. A case in point is men's secret societies, and specifically a men's cult among the Mehinaku Indians of the Northern Mato Grosso in Brazil's tropical forest.

## Men's Cults

The striking similarity of men's societies in historically and geographically separate areas of the world is an old anthropological puzzle. Nearly everywhere women are rigidly excluded from participation in the cult, often on pain of gang rape or even death (Murphy 1959). The cult is commonly associated with secret initiations or paraphernalia such as bull-roarers, masks, flutes, or trumpets, all of which are used to intimidate the women and terrorize the uninitiated. An origin myth frequently forms the charter of the cult, asserting that in ancient times the women controlled the ritual objects and acted out masculine roles until a revolution by the men reordered social relationships as they are today.

A surprisingly large number of men's cults seem to lack manifest, substantive functions within the communities in which they appear. Although they are almost invariably socially important, they are usually not organized around explicit economic or political tasks; indeed, much of their attendant ritual and social activities seem self-generated. As Rivers aptly remarked in a discussion of some Melanesian men's societies, they "exist for the sake of existing." Similarly, Wedgwood, in a classification of men's societies by the functions they performed, was forced to provide a category of men's secret societies which had "no ostensible functions" (1930:130).

Although men's cults show considerably more variation than this sketch indicates, the similarities outlined above and the dramatic conduct associated with the cults have stimulated a large anthropological literature. Diffusionists (Lowie 1920; Loeb 1929) have argued that the common traits exhibited by men's societies spread from an ancient common source. Evolutionists have regarded men's cults as having grown out of the development of puberty initiations (Webster 1932) or even the cooperation of hunters in early periods of human evolution (Tiger 1969). Investigators influenced by Freudian psychology have focused primarily on the cults' initiation rituals and myths which are often redolent with obvious sexual imagery. Reik (1975) attributed some of the features of cult initiations to Oedipal rivalry, and Bettelheim (1954) examined the same material as a manifestation of male envy of female genitalia and sexuality. Whiting, Kluckhohn, and Anthony (1958) have taken a social-psychological perspective, and argued that initiation rituals are a method of severing the bonds between mother and son that develop during a prolonged period of childhood intimacy.

A more structural approach is exemplified by Murphy (1959) and Allen (1967). Murphy argues that, although many features of men's cults may reflect the tension inherent in a universal dilemma, the Oedipus conflict, why, then, do not all societies have men's secret cults and their associated rituals? "Why . . . are we not all swinging bull-roarers or playing sacred flutes?" (1959:96). The answer, according to Murphy, is that the themes of sex antagonism and the rituals that seem to reflect the basic psychological conflicts become institutionalized primarily in technologically simple societies which encourage the cooperation of persons of the same sex in the performance of their work. Allen (1967) is in agreement with Murphy, and attempts to show that in Melanesia the men's cult is most prominent where kinship and residence encourage the solidarity of groups exclusively composed of men or women.

The structural and psychological perspective taken by Murphy and Allen seems to me to be substantially accurate. My own approach is somewhat different in that it does not seek to explain the presence or absence of men's cults, but instead explores a facet of the institution that has been given only passing theoretical attention: namely the secrecy of the cults and the patterns of concealment and exclusion which guard it.

The element of secrecy and the pattern of exclusion should receive direct attention because it is a central feature of the institution. Many of the focal activities of the cults seem designed to conceal ritual knowledge and exclude outsiders. Important ceremonies are carefully screened from public view, ritual performers are commonly masked when they appear before the uninitiated, novices are sternly enjoined against revealing cult secrets, and female intruders may be gang raped or even put to death if they trespass in forbidden regions. So significant is secrecy to some of the men's cults that it appears they are otherwise empty of content.

## The Mehinaku Men's Cult

The Mehinaku Indians are one of a number of culturally similar tropical forest tribes located along the affluents of the upper Xingu River in Brazil's Parque Nacional do Xingu. All subsist on a combination of manioc horticulture and fishing. Each group is firmly tied to its neighbors through intertribal marriages, ceremonies, and the barter of specialized trade goods.

The ground plan of the Mehinaku village, like the other Xingu villages, is roughly circular, the large extended family residences forming the perimeter around the central plaza. Facing the east towards the rising sun, near the center of the village circle, is a small men's house that functions as a temple and a social club. Here the men assemble to engage in idle conversation while they work on arrow baskets and other crafts. Here too they play the sacred flutes representing a spirit called *Kowka*. Unless the men play the flutes and drink manioc porridge in the name of the spirit, *Kowka* will become angry and "take away" some of the villagers' "souls" (lit. shadows, *īyeweku*). The representation of other spirits, in the form of masks, bull-roarers, and costumes, are slung from the rafters of the men's house.

The rule of recruitment to the Mehinaku men's organization is simply that "all men belong." There are no formal initiation rituals. The rule of recruitment, however, is sociologically trivial next to the rule of exclusion; for uppermost in the villagers' minds is not that "all men belong," but that "all women are forbidden."

## Policing the Boundaries: The Politics of Exclusion

The men's house in the center of the Mehinaku village is heavily defended against female intrusion and surveillance. Despite its prominent position, the building itself has been designed to minimize exposure. The doorways are smaller than those of any other house, and they are often partly blocked with grass skirts or old clothes. The sacred flutes hang suspended from the framework of the house, usually wrapped in a tattered blanket to protect them from feminine gaze.

A double edged sanction protects the men's house from female intrusion. The women explain their exclusion in terms of fear of the men:

"No, we never enter the men's house or see the sacred flutes. We die without ever having seen the inside of the men's house. If we were to enter the men's house the men would rape us!"

The men, however, are inclined to offer what is from their perspective a more frightening explanation:

"The women can't come in here! The spirit Kowka would kill us if a woman came in here. The women must not see the spirit's flute; women's eyes are disgusting to the spirits."

Admittedly, not all the men are so theologically minded. Some explain the custom of gang rape simply by pointing out that it has always been done:

"That's the way it is with us Mehinaku."

A woman who enters the men's house commits an offense against ancient traditions, and may even jeopardize the life of a husband, a brother, or a son. The only way to prevent such a death is for the men to gang rape the woman in the name of the spirit.

The threat of gang rape is a real one. Women are fearful of approaching too close to the men's house and avert their eyes when they pass by. During certain rituals, when the flutes are played on the plaza, they sequester themselves in the houses and make no effort to peer through the thatch walls. On such occasions the women call through the walls, begging the spirit to go away:

"There is no manioc drink or fish here. Our gardens are empty and my husband did not go fishing!" Kowka, the spirit of the flutes, unlike many other Mehinaku spirits, evokes great respect and seriousness.

Under these circumstances it is not surprising to learn that the women never actually enter the men's house or intentionally see the sacred flutes. On rare occasions, however, a woman will accidentally come upon the men while they are playing the flutes. The last time this misfortune occurred, the flutes were outside the men's house. Normally, all of the women would have been warned in advance, but in this case one unmarried girl was not told. She blundered into the village and to her horror saw the trio of musicians and their flutes. Although thirty years have passed since this incident took place, the Mehinaku chief recalls the course of events in lurid detail:

At night one of the girl's lovers lured her outside where we were hiding. We dragged her off to a distant spot in the forest where the rest of the men were waiting. She screamed and cried, but we held her firmly. The men began to rape her. I decided not to do it because her legs were befouled with semen. All the while the flutes played for the spirit Kowka.

Unlike what occurs in some tribes in South America and Oceania (Murphy 1959), a woman who enters the men's house is not put to death as part of her punishment. The woman in the preceeding case was taken back to the village and bathed in the river by a kinswoman. For a short time she was ashamed of what had occurred and participated only minimally in public village activities. Subsequently she became pregnant and gave birth to an oversized child that was "too big because it had too many fathers." Like all unusual births, this child was put to death.

The sanction of gang rape and the respect owed to the spirit of the flutes is the most dramatic but not the only device that separates the activities of men from women. This separation is also enforced by notions of cleanliness and personal hygiene, ridicule and joking, supernatural sanctions, and even beatings. Let us now take a close look at the mysteries and secrets these sanctions conceal.

## The Sacred Flutes and Their Musicians

The most closely guarded secret is the appearance of the flutes and the identity of the musicians. The flutes themselves are made by a specialist in the village who knows how to select and carve the wood. There are very few individuals in the Upper Xingu who can do this properly, and they are invariably older men. The flutes are expensive, and they must be paid for only with "true wealth," a class of valued things including the finest ceramic pots, headdresses, shell belts, collars, or rifles. The flutes are carved only in the men's house, well out of the women's view.

Each flute has four stops toward the far end, so that the musician must extend his arms at full length to play them. As the flutes are played the musicians take two steps forward, turn and then two steps back. Long chains of dried pods wrapped around the ankle of the center musician enables him to set the rhythm to each of the songs as he stamps the beat. This musician is called the "master of the songs" (*apaiyekehe*). The remaining two are referred to as "those on the sides." As is typical of other Mehinaku rituals the participants are also identified as husband and wife; the central musician is the "man" and those on the sides are his "wives."

When a song master wishes to organize a concert he secretly asks two other musicians to meet him in the men's house. These arrangements must be clandestine, since the men's identity of the musicians must be kept from the women. The song master provides *urucu* (*Bixa orellana,* a pigment), and all three musicians oil and ornament their bodies and adjust their flutes. The master of the songs rehearses his accompanists in the tunes that will be played, for each has his own slightly different repertory of songs. The songs are titled and played in a set order. Iyepe, for example, one of the most proficient Mehinaku musicians, plays "Worthless Fishtrap," "Angry Woman Spirit," "Lizard," and "Sadness." All the songs have a hauntingly beautiful quality which is enhanced by the deep bassoon-like tone of the flutes.

Taking frequent breaks between numbers, the musicians adjust their flutes and whisper together. They are anxious to play well, since the entire community is listening. They will have played several hours before the sponsor of the flutes brings them large tubs of manioc porridge which they will distribute to all the village men. This is the spirits' food, and although the men consume it, Kowka, the spirit of the flutes, has eaten.

The concerts of the sacred flutes are one of the few formal activities in which the men make a deliberate effort to mystify the women. As we shall see, the more casual events in the men's house are usually performed so that the women are often aware of the identity of the men, and ideally, impressed by their behavior.

## Why Secrecy?

The Mehinaku cult seems to resemble many men's secret orders in that there seems to be no objective basis for withholding secrets from the women at all. Indeed, a village girl who managed to slip unseen into the men's house would certainly be disappointed. As Valentine (1961:481) remarks of the Lukalai of New Britain:

All the supplementary mystification which surrounds the masks and the performances not only contributes to masculine pride, but heightens the atmosphere of secrecy and the sense of the uncanny as well. . . . Yet virtually the only real secrets beneath all this elaborate cultural camouflage are the details of the internal structures of the masks and the procedures surrounding their construction.

And, closer to home, Noel Gist (1940), in a comprehensive survey of American fraternal orders, reports that candidates are often disappointed to discover that the only thing secret about the organization is its ritual of initiation. In short, the biggest secret about many secret societies is that there is nothing of great importance to conceal. Why, then, the secrecy? Precisely what is it that the men have that must be so carefully guarded from the women? A myth gives us a look at the Mehinaku answer:

"In ancient times the women occupied the men's house and played the sacred flutes. We took care of the children, processed manioc flour, and spent our time in the residences, just as the women do today. In those days the children even nursed at our breasts. A man who dared enter the women's house would be gang raped by all the women in the village!

"One day the chief got us all together, and showed us how to make bull-roarers to frighten the women. As soon as the women heard the terrible noise they dropped the sacred flutes and ran into the houses to hide. We grabbed the flutes and took over the men's house. Today, if a woman comes in here and sees our flutes, *we* rape her; today the women nurse babies, process manioc flour, and hang around the houses. . . ."

The myth suggests that the men's house and the sacred flute are the throne and scepter of male power within the Mehinaku society, and that being a man or a woman is dependent on access to the secrets and admission to the cult. But why is the definition of sex roles associated with secrecy and exclusion? Here Georg Simmel's theoretical work is useful to us. Simmel (1950) argued that all social relationships are characterizable by the extent of knowledge that the participants have of each other. In order to get along, social actors must know who they are with respect to one another. But this knowledge must be circumscribed and limited if relationships are to be differentiated from each other. To know someone in a specified relationship—that of colleague, for example—is to know him from a certain point of view, a point of view quite different from that of kinsman or spouse. Of course, persons may simultaneously be kinsmen, spouses, and colleagues, but only at the cost of leveling the differences between these kinds of relationships.

Simmel's position is supported by some experimental data. The psychologist Sidney Jourard (1971) constructed a questionnaire in which respondents were asked to indicate whether they concealed, misrepresented, lied or gave inaccurate information concerning their finances, personality, attitudes, body, and work. The degree of disclosure, Jourard discovered, varied in a predictable way according to the relationship in question. Spouses, parents, friends, kin, and members of particular class, ethnic and religious groups produced their own characteristic pattern of secrecy and disclosure. Further, the balance of information and concealment was a reliable index to the mental health of his respondents. These results, Jourard argued, suggest that boundaries to communication are part of the maintenance of self-identity, the organization of important relationships, and the definition of social groups.

Although there are many ways of establishing boundaries to communication, secrecy, perhaps because of its inherent fascination, is an especially effective device for differentiating social relationships. Georg Simmel wrote: "whether there is secrecy between two individuals or groups . . . is a question that characterizes every relation between them" (1950:330). It may well be that the psychological origins of this fascination is in the similarity between that which is secret and that which is sacred. Hence Arnold Simmel notes that both the secret and the sacred are "set apart, isolated, untouchable except by special people with special dispensations." (1968:482).

Whatever the source of our fascination, we know that those who have access to secrets are united by bonds of trust and mutual confidence; those who are kept in the dark will be differentiated from those who are in the know.

What then, of the secrets of the Mehinaku men's house? Clearly, they serve to separate and dramatize the differences between the sexes. The fact that the Mehinaku men conceal neither strategic nor dark secrets is therefore less important than the fact that they have *something* to conceal, something which they and the women regard as important. And a word with the Mehinaku is sufficient to establish that these secrets are important. Not only are the men at pains to conceal them from the women, but the women are undeniably fascinated and even intimidated by the men's activities. The women's gossip frequently has it that one of them has seen the flutes, and the men are planning to take retribution in the name of the spirit. Rich in their secrets and mysteries, the men thereby participate in a world hidden from the women; a world apart from the everyday round of village activities, a world about which the women can only speculate.

Exclusion and secrecy have effects which go beyond the definition of social relationships. They not only draw a psychologically meaningful line between the sexes, but provide the men with a stage for dramatizing their position within the society.

## The Dramatization of Men's Roles

In small-scale societies such as the Mehinaku the same limited set of actors must perform a number of separate parts. That is, the same two persons may be simultaneously kinsmen by blood and by marriage, work partners, members of the same ritual team, and of the opposite sex. Segregating these relationships can be a problem. Max Gluckman, in his well-known article "Les Rites des Passages," (1962) suggests that the rituals and etiquette which are so common in such societies serve to differentiate relationships even though they are performed by the same small cast. I am essentially in agreement with Gluckman, but I believe his position can be carried a bit further. A ritual, or an observance of etiquette, is a kind of communication designed to tell actors who they are with respect to one another, and to define an interactional situation. In a small society, however, an unambiguous communication may sometimes have to go further. Not only should it identify the part that is being played, but it should also eliminate portions of the message that suggest some other part. A mask, for example, not only identifies a man as a ritual performer, but partly effaces his identity as a kinsman, a comrade, and an ordinary citizen. In short, the actor in the small-scale society must not only communicate who he is, but often conceal who he is not. The most effective devices for handling this dramaturgical problem are those that limit communication. Masks, veils, avoidance taboos, and even joking relationships are some of the more ethnographically familiar of these methods. I would suggest that the seclusion of the men's house provides a forum for precisely the same kind of communication; a communication that dramatizes the message while concealing many others. A line of evidence supporting this conclusion is the location of men's houses in primitive communities.

## The Location of Men's Houses and Meeting Grounds and the Content of Interaction

One of the interesting facts of men's secret societies is that the existence of the society is seldom in itself a secret. On the contrary, many men's houses are located in the most prominent part of a community, and when they are located outside of it they are seldom very far from the village. Even the secret meetings of the highly secret men's societies of the Banks Islands are near enough to the village so that the agonized shouts of the initiates and the whirl of the bullroarers is audible to women and children.

Sometimes the location of the men's activities is a matter of deliberate stage management. Bateson writes of the Iatmul:

Even such purely male affairs as initiation are so staged that parts of the ceremony are visible to the women who form an audience and who can hear issuing from the ceremonial house mysterious and beautiful sounds made by the various secret musical instruments—flutes, gongs; bull-roarers, etc. . . . the men who are producing these sounds are exceedingly conscious of that unseen audience of women (1958:128).

Among the Yahgan of Tierra del Fuego the stage management of the men's activities is even more deliberate. Far from hiding the initiation hunt or *kina*, the men move the family dwellings to the hilly place where it has been auspiciously located (Gusinde 1961:1323). Although the women are kept at a distance of about 55 meters, it is apparent that it is they who are the intended audience for the men's ritual performance.

These facts suggest an unexpected puzzle. Men's societies deliberately isolate themselves from their surrounding communities with Draconian sanctions, but they then turn around and deliberately expose some of their activities to the public. This problem is understandable if we regard the men's house as a theater for the dramatization of men's roles, but a theater in which the members of the audience are kept in distant seats. They can follow only the loudest and most raucous interaction, and only those scenes which the men choose to put on for their benefit.

The notion that the men's house is a kind of theater is not a new one. Bateson makes this point with reference to the Iatmul ceremonial house:

. . . we see the men . . . managing to work together to produce a spectacle which the women shall admire and marvel at. Almost without exception the ceremonies of the men are of this nature and the ceremonial house serves as a Green Room for the preparation of the show. The men put on their masks and ornaments in its privacy and thence sally forth to dance and perform before the women who are assembled on the banks at the sides of the dancing ground. (1958:128)

The message of the drama produced by the men is surprisingly uniform from culture to culture. Indeed, as I read the literature, I am continually impressed by the reports of the loudness of conversation and banter and the bold style of quarrels within the men's house. Where in ordinary life based on domesticity and kinship, relations are low-keyed and civil, in the men's house they are loud and even boisterous. Writing of the Brazilian Carajá, for example, William Lipkind notes that the men "behave with a shy and deferential modesty resembling but exceeding that of the Victorian maiden . . . only in the men's house or on fishing or hunting trips is the behavior of men relaxed enough to permit horseplay and casual joking (1948:187).

If interaction outside the men's house encourages bragging and forcefulness, within the men's house it is even more exaggerated. Thus, among the Bororo Indians we learn that the hub of their existence is the men's house, and, compared with the incredibly noisy life that goes on there day and night, the family huts are scarcely more than an abode for women and children (Steinen 1966). And, once again, Bateson is quite explicit about the contrast between Iatmul domestic activities and the men's house:

. . . the men are occupied with the spectacular, dramatic, and violent activities which have their center in the ceremonial house while the women are occupied with the useful and necessary routines of food-getting, cooking, and rearing children—activities which center about the dwelling house and the gardens. The contrast between the ceremonial house and the dwelling house is fundamental for the culture. (1958:123)

Finally, we note that among the Gê-speaking tribes, Maybury-Lewis (1974) suggests that the men's house inculcates bellicosity among its members, and may be responsible for the factionalism and aggresiveness in some Gê societies.

Surely the "spectacular" and "violent" activities associated with many men's houses are not the only events that occur there. Men interact as kinsmen as well as comrades or rivals in the men's house setting, but this interaction is normally of a quiet sort, based on codes of respect and deference, and unlikely to reach the women. Interaction between men as men, however, is often boisterous and therefore more audible.

The extreme conduct characteristic of men's houses, whether bragging, joking or involvement in initiations, may in itself be a product of the rules protecting the men's house from the women's intrusion. A wide range of data from social psychology supports the proposition that conformity to social norms is partly a function of observability. Out of the women's sight, the men are freed from some of the rules of kinship and domestic obligations that constrain them outside the men's house. Their resulting ribald, bellicose, or raucous conduct becomes one way in which they dramatize their masculinity, and differentiate themselves from the women. The characteristics of the setting are thereby a determinant of what constitutes "masculinity." Perhaps for this very reason men's house behavior is cross-culturally very similar.

## The Mehinaku Men's House: The Dramatization of Sex Roles

Stage center on the village plaza, the Mehinaku men's house is ideally located for the kind of performances we have described. Since it is approximately twenty yards from the nearest house, quiet conversations are not easily overheard. Shouted comments, obscene remarks, and whoops of laughter, however, resonate through the entire village. Whenever several men are together, such boisterous interaction is the rule. In the men's house the villagers seem to temporarily forget the constraints of kinship and age differences, and behave as if they were all comrades. Outside the men's house the good citizen is generally quiet, circumspect, and soft-spoken. A man who regularly behaves like this within the men's house, however, may be regarded as sullen, and derisively referred to as a "trashyard man."

The boisterousness and raucousness of the men's house is closely related to the number of men present. A few men in pairs quietly discuss what is appropriate to their personal relationship. As the men's house becomes crowded, however, the topic of conversation, the conversational style, and the noise level all change noticeably. A comment by one man is picked up and amplified by someone for whom the remarks were unintended. The original speaker may respond with a joke, and then all the men punctuate the exchange with a tremendous whoop.

A frequent topic of conversation among groups of men is sex and sexual joking. The crudest sexual jokes are usually aimed at more marginal individuals within the community who are considered fair game for teasing. On one occasion, for example, Kama had just walked into the men's house when one of the men called attention to his pubic hair: "Hey, look at that forest," shouted one of the men. "Are there monkeys there? Where does the jaguar live?" Soon several of the men were speculating about the fauna in poor Kama's forest, while the others roared with laughter.

Much of this boisterous masculine behavior is audible to the women as they sit in the doorways of the houses. When a number of men are joking it is sometimes difficult to say exactly who said what; both the distance and the walls of the men's house provide the men with a degree of anonymity. Nevertheless, the meaning comes through, and the women are aware that some of the jokes are intended for them. The men often make derisive comments about female sexuality and offensively describe the size, odor, and color of womens' genitalia. From time to time one of the men will shout in a high falsetto whoop "Grab clay!" meaning go have sexual relations. The result of this boisterousness is that the women, especially the sexually active women, are visibly intimidated near the men's house; while walking around the plaza they pass by as quickly as possible and avert their eyes.

## Wrestling

In the late afternoon of almost every fine day, the men participate in wrestling matches. This pattern is a pan-Xingu culture trait (Galvão 1953), known in the literature as *huka-huka* (a Kamaiura word) and in Mehinaku as *kapī*. Wrestling ability is both the measure and expression of strength. Powerful culture heroes and mythical human-like animals are all described as great wrestlers who were able to throw all their opponents. Great chiefs, important men, and the villagers' ancestors are all spoken of in the same terms. Champion wrestlers are considered *kowkapapai*, i.e., being worthy of fear and respect. The women especially admire powerful men and champions, and seek them as their lovers.

Each village has a number of informally ranked master wrestlers *kapī wekeke*, who are called upon to wrestle at inter-tribal events. Curiously these champions are not always the best in the village. Kuyaparei, for example, is at present the most powerfully built and skillful wrestler in the Mehinaku community. He is considered a wrestling master, however, because he is *hirikya*, aged, having fathered four children. Being a wrestling champion, then, involves social as well as physical attributes. A champion must not only wrestle well but he must be at a stage of life when men are thought to be most vigorous, youthful, and sexually potent. A villager who is not a champion must also participate in wrestling. To fail to do so would be to mark himself off as a weakling, asocial, or aged.

The late afternoon, after the baking midday sun is lower in the sky, is known as "wrestling time" in the Mehinaku language. At this time the men gradually assemble in the men's house and in front of the log bench outside it. They rub their bodies with oil so that their bones will not be brittle, and smear their faces and torso with ashes. The first to wrestle are the adolescent boys. Wrestling is an activity essential to their growth, and even when they are not wrestling and are in seclusion, they are instructed by their fathers to imagine that they are. After the adolescents have wrestled, the mature men and champions begin. There is no set order. When a man wants to wrestle he simply invites one of the others to join him. Although there are no limitations on who can wrestle whom other than sanctions against matches between young men and their fathers-in-law, observations of many pairs of wrestling partners show that they tend to be of one's own generation, friends, and brothers-in-law.

Once partners have been chosen they step in front of the men's house, stamp the ground, and circle about counter-clockwise rhythmically grunting: "huh-huh-huh-huh." They sink to their knees and approach each other on all fours, generally making first contact with their right hands. The object of the wrestling is to "throw" (*awaintya*) the opponent, or to force him onto his back. Wrestling with fellow Mehinaku, however, is quite different from wrestling members of other villages. Within the village the daily matches are regarded as practice for intertribal bouts. Consequently, throwing the opponent or pinning him heavily is not sporting. It is enough to gain a hold that would enable a wrestler to throw his partner if he wished. An example of such a hold is to get a grip on the opponent's legs, or to encircle him from above.

Although the wrestling is always vigorous it is very seldom that anyone is badly hurt. Punching, jabbing, biting, and pulling hair are simply not fair play. A bout will stop immediately if a wrestler is thrown, and he will always be helped to his feet by his opponent. The men who are spectators to the matches tend to insure that the rules are followed. A man's reputation as a good citizen is worth far more than what he might gain with a few ingenious but illicit holds.

I have argued that wrestling is associated with being a man, and that it is a presentation of physical strength, youthful vigor, sexual potency, and masculine power. The women are an important audience to this presentation. As soon as they notice that the men are preparing to wrestle they bring their work to the doorways of the houses and sit on their benches to watch. They make critical comments about the men who are poor wrestlers, and they are visibly impressed by the stamping, the grunting, the shouts of pain, and the skill of the champions. A good wrestler is *awitsiri*, beautiful. A poor one, however, is laughable. The men are aware of these judgments, and their strenuous efforts are intended to impress the women as well as their opponents.

Much of the other interaction that occurs within and in front of the men's house also is oriented towards the women. They are kept at a distance, so that the men can present themselves to the women as men, and not simply as kinsmen. The reasons for secrecy and exclusion now begin to be a little clearer. The cult of the flutes and the mysteries that surround them are among the least important information concealed by the men's house. Instead the cult and the sanctions against female intrusion guarantee the men a setting in which they can behave as men do in Mehinaku society. In this back region they are free of the expectations that the women may have toward them as sisters, daughters, and wives. In the shelter of the men's house, the men create a life apart from the domesticity of the daily round, a life of comradeliness, ribaldry, and roughhousing. But, as I have shown, this life is never wholly isolated from the women. They are always present as an unacknowledged audience to be impressed by the men's physical prowess and intimidated by their boisterousness. I therefore interpret the men's house as a theatrical setting designed to conspicuously highlight the differences between the sexes. The secrecy, the sanctions against female intrusion, and the sacred flutes, are the stage rules and props that make the performance work.

## Male Identity and Evidence of Insecurity

Men who do not play the sacred flutes, wrestle regularly, and engage in the ribald comradeliness of the men's house may be derisively labeled as "women." Being a man among the Mehinaku means participating in the cult and guarding its secrets. Why should sexual identity and group activity be so closely linked? A full answer to this question takes us well beyond the scope of this article, but a number of investigators suggest that the origins of men's institutions may be in the ecological circumstances of many of the tropical societies where they usually are found. Whiting, Kluckholn, and Anthony (1958) argue that among many of these people protein capture is a serious problem. The response is prolonged infant nursing, and often exclusive mother-child sleeping arrangements. Boys grow up strongly identified with their mothers, and require the crutch of severe initiations and men's cults before they can regard themselves as men.

In some important respects the Mehinaku fit this model. Mothers and their children sleep in the same hammock, and are virtually inseparable until the birth of a younger child—an event which may not occur until well into the child's fourth year. According to Whiting, Kluckholn, and Anthony, the male personality type created by this pattern of development is relatively insecure. Among the Mehinaku, the cultural evidence tends to support this hypothesis. The myth of the origin of the men's house is a case in point; according to this myth men and women are not "naturally" or irrevocably different; in fact their differences are explained simply by the men's current possession of the flutes and the occupation of the men's house. This mutability of sexuality is also evident in other myths, transvestite rituals and an important earpiercing ritual in which the men "menstruate." Ambivalence toward the opposite sex and insecurity in the male role is also suggested by fear of excessive contact with women, fear of menstrual pollution, informal hostility toward women, and numerous rituals incorporating elements of sexual antagonism.

Whether or not Whiting, Kluckhohn, and Anthony are correct in associating this pattern with exclusive mother-son sleeping arrangements, we may reasonably conclude that there is some pressure on the definition of men's roles among the Mehinaku and other peoples with a similar pattern. The men's house with its attendant mysteries may therefore be regarded as an artificial device for conspicuously dramatizing the differences between the sexes in a cultural setting that tends to submerge them. Interestingly from a cross-cultural perspective, secrecy and exclusion seem to be widely used for this purpose; for other than clandestine radical political groups, most secret societies, no matter what their avowed purpose, exclude members of the opposite sex (MacKenzie 1967:15). Needless to say other devices than the men's house with its attendant codes of secrecy and exclusion might also have done the job of status dramatization. Frank Young (1965), for example, demonstrates the importance of initiation rituals in dramatizing male status. The possibility of this and other functional alternatives does not allow us to conclude that secrecy and exclusion have their origin in the men's incomplete identification with the masculine role. The intention here, however, has been to examine the functions rather than the sources of the secrets and sanctions that guard the men's cult.

## Secrecy, Exclusion, and Group Identity

The fact that secrecy and exclusion in male cults seem to accomplish little beyond differentiating men from women should not come as a surprise. Secret organizations of all kinds appear to be prone to becoming ever more occupied with patrolling their boundaries and maintaining themselves as distinct from their social environment rather than serving some other definite business. In fact, the requirements of security may sabotage any other kind of activity. Hence Ritchie Lowry, a former employee of the Army's Special Operations Research Office (SORO), the think-tank that spawned the notorious Project Camelot, reports that secrecy in governmental organizations becomes an end in itself: "Secrecy systems take on latent functions leading to the protection of relatively useless and unreliable knowledge. The producers of such knowledge thereby maintain job security, and security systems become increasingly involved in matters of sensitivity" (1972:437).

Needless to say, SORO is a very different kind of enterprise than men's organizations in simple communities. Nevertheless, there is a parallel here that we should not ignore. Organizations and events such as men's houses, college fraternities, SORO, and even first nights at the opera are all institutions that differentiate those who participate in them from those who are excluded. Obviously they do other things as well; certainly *some* of those who attend the first night at the opera are there primarily because they like music. Similarly, some men's institutions (particularly the West African examples as described by Little (1949)) are clearly organized around important economic and political activities. In many cases, however, men's institutions and other similar organizations require a sociological description that is somewhat different than the traditional approach to groups and social action. This description should be sensitive to the rule of exclusion: the blackball, the secret, and the sanctions that give the group shape and differentiate it from the wider community.

A second area of inquiry should be how the exclusive society dramatizes the identity of its members. In the case of men's cults we have seen that their main line of business is the conspicuous celebration of masculinity. As such, those activities in which the women participate as an audience take on a special significance. The sanctions against intrusion screen out the men as brothers, husbands, and fathers, and present them as anonymous members of the opposite sex. A key to the study of the men's cult, then, is its appearance from the outside. The ethnographer must be sensitive not only to the internal activities of the men's organization from the point of view of the insider, but must also record the sounds and look of the cult from the perspective of the women, for it is their expectations that stimulate much of the men's behavior.

The paradox of the men's cult is that apparently it is an organization which faces inward. Preoccupied with secrecy and patrolling its boundaries against intruders, we could easily believe that it must carry on weighty business. And yet a good part of this business turns out to be confirming the identity of its members and differentiating them from those who are refused admission. In short, the fact of who are excluded and how they are kept out is at least as important as who are members and how they are brought in.

# THIRTEEN

# Umbanda and Class Relations in Brazil

## Diana Brown

I HAD DINNER one evening recently at a small country inn owned by friends. Its atmosphere is informal, but rather cosmopolitan—many of the diners are academics from a local college or professional people visiting from New York City. As we were leaving, the owner, seated at another table, called us over to introduce us to her guests, one of whom was a Brazilian man. The Brazilian seemed very surprised to find in this rural area an American who greeted him in Portuguese. He urged us to sit down and he and I began to chat. He was an expatriate businessman originally from Rio, and showed polite interest at discovering that I was an anthropologist and had recently done research in Rio. Their dinner arrived and we were just about to leave when he inquired casually about the topic of my research. I hesitated. Umbanda, the religion which I had studied, is a controversial subject for Brazilians, and often leads to lengthy and heated discussions which at that point in the evening did not seem desirable. I replied briefly that my research had been on Umbanda,

This paper is based on research conducted in Brazil on Umbanda during 1966 and 1968–69, and the ethnographic present which is used throughout refers primarily to the period 1960–70. The research was supported by the Metropolitan Summer Field Training Program of the Ford Foundation, a Fulbright-Hays Doctoral Research Grant, and the Institute for Latin American Studies at Columbia University. I wish particularly to thank Dr. Mario Bick for his extremely helpful contributions and criticisms in the paper's preparation.

gathered my pocketbook and started to get up, hoping to head off any further discussion.

But even I was unprepared for the extent of his reaction. He put down his knife and fork and stared at me, and his face—his whole body—took on a quality of extraordinary intensity. As if there were no one else present, he began a most probing and intensive effort to learn my reasons for this research—my state of spiritual preparedness for such a study, my understanding of the forces which had impelled me to undertake it, and the extent of my awareness of the many spiritual dangers which it presented for a foreigner, particularly an American woman such as myself. Then, hardly pausing for my responses, he went on to describe his own deep involvement with Umbanda and with other forms of Spiritualism and theosophy in Brazil, and his encounters with various spiritual entities and forces. He then described his more recent involvement in the United States with the works of Edgar Cayce, and various other American and English exponents of Spiritualism. He could not be shaken from his topic, which he pursued throughout the main course. His food remained untouched as he talked, and he grew increasingly agitated as he stared fixedly at me. He was now speaking in English, at the request of his other dinner partners, and they were astonished by the conversation. None of them had had any notion of his spiritualist interests, and they appeared both uncomfortable and rather embarrassed by them, and tried, unsuccessfully, to divert him from his topic. Finally, as the plates, including his full meal, were cleared away, he seemed to recollect himself and abruptly stopped speaking. The conversation shifted to other matters and we soon left.

Reflecting upon this incident I was struck by how incongruous this sudden and passionate revelation of Spiritualist convictions had seemed to all of us, coming so unexpectedly from an educated and worldly middle-class man in these strongly rational and familiar bourgeois surroundings. For me, his behavior recreated vividly the series of emotional responses which I had experienced many times during the early period of my fieldwork in Brazil. Invited to a purely social gathering, a cocktail party celebrating the publication of someone's book, a women's afternoon tea given by my landlady, a university student party, a dinner at the home of a prosperous lawyer, politician, or businessman, I would introduce Umbanda into the conversation and immediately someone, often many of those present, would react in a manner similar to the Brazilian guest at the inn, and launch into a discussion of their spiritualist convictions with the same intensity and passion which he showed. My sense of ease and familiarity with the social setting and with the ideas and attitudes of my companions would be shattered, and would leave me confronting an underlying stratum of alien beliefs, beliefs which violated my image of the Brazilian "middle class."

As my research progressed, the shock which accompanied these encounters diminished. I worked a great deal with Umbandistas who were members of the professions, successful businessmen, and high-ranking military officers, and grew accustomed to the participation by these well to do, well-educated men and women in Umbanda, and to their interest in discussing various mystical and theosophical traditions and in recounting their experiences with spirit communication, spirit possession, and spiritual healing. These experiences, in addition to other data I was gathering, made it clear that many members of the "middle class" were involved in Umbanda and in other forms of Spiritualism and occultism as well.

Yet their participation in these phenomena was little evidenced in the general picture of religious stratification presented in the social science literature on Brazil. This literature, at the time (1968–69) implied a clear distinction between the "orthodox" religions or churches found within the middle and upper classes and the "unorthodox" cults and sects found within the lower classes. The middle classes, with the exception of immigrant minorities, were portrayed as following the Catholic orientation of the upper classes, and while an extensive degree of nominalism was acknowledged to occur among these sectors, almost no one had taken seriously the existence of either alternative or simultaneous participation in other religions.[1]

Since the time of my original research there has been a growing awareness of the social complexity of participation in Spiritualist religions. For example, the revised edition (1971) of Wagley's widely read *Introduction to Brazil* incorporates both earlier indications of middle-class involvement in these religions and the preliminary results of my own research on the middle class in Umbanda.

Nevertheless, most discussions and interpretations of Umbanda still place it within the context of "lower-class" religions (Willems 1966, 1969; Bastide 1960; Camargo 1961a, 1961b; DeKadt 1967), along with "folk" or "popular" Catholicism (Bastide 1951b; Azevedo 1963), pentecostal forms of Protestantism (Willems 1966, 1967, 1969), Afro-Brazilian cults (Bastide 1960), and Spiritism (Willems 1966, 1969), a form of Spiritualism derived from France and known as *Espiritismo* or *Kardecismo*. Discussions of these religions often stress their unorthodox, exotic features: spirit possession, talking in tongues, the use of and belief in the efficacy of various magical rituals, miraculous cures, and in general their high degree of emphasis on ritualism and emotionalism.

Perhaps because of this emphasis on the common features of these religions—Umbanda, Pentecostalism, and Spiritism—as new urban movements (Willems 1966, 1969) there has been a tendency to consider them as new urban mass movements. Umbanda is thus regarded as an urban variant of folk Catholicism (DeKadt 1967), or because of the African elements in its rituals and pantheon, as a more acculturative, capitalistic form of older, lower class Afro-Brazilian religions (Bastide 1960). These comparisons in turn have led scholars personally unfamiliar with Umbanda to treat it as another example of the religions of the oppressed masses (Lanternari 1963) or as a typical form of salvationist sectarian response found among "the less educated and less emotionally controlled sectors of the population" (Wilson 1973:104). While it is certainly true that Umbanda has an extensive lower-class following, my concern in this discussion is to demonstrate that its classification as a lower-class religion does not conform either to its real social composition or to its place in Brazilian society.

This tendency to view Umbanda as lower class has not been unique to social scientists; it has been shared as well by the Brazilian public. Catholic Church leaders, responding to the increasing encroachment of Afro-Brazilian religions, Spiritism, Umbanda, and Pentecostalism on their once undisputed religious hegemony, have made active attempts to denigrate them collectively. This campaign has been marked by general allegations that these religions represent ignorance and social inferiority and, in the case of Afro-Brazilian religions and Umbanda, by implicitly racist references as well (see, for example, Kloppenburg 1961a, 1961b). And until the mid-1960s the same type of denigration characterized almost exclusively the treatment of Umbanda in the Brazilian press and popular magazines.

Thus it is not surprising that its practitioners as well as its detractors have often been influenced by this negative stereotype. The great majority of adherents who are not lower class have as far as possible concealed their participation from public view, which has, in turn, contributed to Umbanda's lower-class image. In the past few years, as Umbanda has begun to gain a degree of social legitimacy, middle-class practitioners have been increasingly open in their adherence as reflected, for example, in their willingness to give interviews for newspaper and magazine articles. The news media increasingly treat Umbanda seriously, whereas in the past it was written about in a condemnatory and condescending manner. Nevertheless, the general visibility of its many middle-class, and possibly as well upper-class practitioners remains low,[2] and its image for most Brazilians and foreigners remains that of a lower-class religion.

Why this contradiction between Umbanda's public image and the social composition of its membership has not received more attention from social scientists is an interesting question. It would appear that many scholars writing on Brazilian religion have simply accepted too readily the pervasive negative labeling of Umbanda as lower class by the Brazilian general public. However, since contradictions between public statements and actual behavior are considered standard features of all societies, social scientists might have been expected to view these statements more critically. What seems to have happened in the case of Umbanda, and often with Spiritism as well, is that the Brazilian view of religious stratification has gone largely unquestioned. It fulfills the expectations of a model of religious stratification widely accepted in the social sciences in which a distinct universe of lower-class religions and religious behavior, emphasizing emotionalism, spontaneity, and magical manipulationism, is opposed to and contrasted with a universe of middle-class religions and religious behavior which emphasizes control, rationality, ethical concerns, and an instrumental orientation. The major elements in this model derive from the work of Weber, yet while he himself cautioned against viewing these particular forms of religious manifestation as limited to particular social classes or occupational sectors, particularly within middle- and lower-class urban environments (see Weber 1964), sociologists of religion have not always exercised equal caution (see, for example, Lanternari 1963; Wilson 1973).

This model of religious stratification derives from a model of society based on studies of the industrialized nations of Western Europe and the United States which delineates three social classes, each with relatively clear class boundaries and distinct life styles. The middle class, in particular, is viewed as relatively large, stable, and autonomous, and a middle-class universe of behavior and values is distinguished from and opposed to a lower-class universe, with a clear break implied between the two. Differences in the form of religious expression, then, appear to be both natural and predictable results of different class memberships. In fact, this model of religious stratification has come to be used almost reflexively by students of religion without reference to the particularities of social structure in the societies under study.

In terms of this model Umbanda presents an anomaly. Religious beliefs and practices which the model would classify as lower class and which would lead to the assumption that they are practiced only within the lower class are, in Umbanda, as I will show, practiced without distinction by both the lower and the middle classes.

I am not principally concerned here with using Umbanda to challenge the validity of the model. Its inadequacies are evident even in industrialized countries such as the United States, where the recent growth of charismatic movements within institutional churches has introduced significant elements of so-called lower-class religious practice within the middle classes. However, its applicability is certainly more questionable in industrializing nations, where patterns of social stratification differ in important respects from those of industrial nations. In Brazil, for example, many scholars working outside the area of religion have argued in the 1960s that, while Brazil possesses the aspects of a three-class occupational and status system, its "middle class" differs substantially from that of industrial nations in its relatively smaller size, its lack of social and ideological cohesion, and its political behavior. They have come to favor the term "middle sectors," or the use of an essentially bi-modal model of Brazilian social structure for analyses of socioeconomic and political behavior.

Yet the applicability of an essentially three-class model of religious expression has not been similarly challenged, nor has there been any attempt to explore the utility of a bi-modal model for the analysis of religious phenomena. It is this which I propose to do here through a discussion of Umbanda. Whereas Umbanda represents an anomaly within the three-class model, I will argue that it can be better, more adequately understood and interpreted within the framework of a bi-modal model, and will then discuss the validity of this model for analyses of Brazilian social structure as a whole.

I will begin by discussing Umbanda within the framework of the three-class model of religious stratification, and will present material on Umbanda ritual and ideology and on its class composition to indicate the areas in which it diverges from this model. During this discussion I will retain the use of the terms "middle" and "lower" class to refer broadly to occupational and status sectors. "Middle class" refers to members of the professions, career military officers, those at managerial levels in firms and industry, middle-level businessmen and small shop owners, bureaucratic employees in the government and civil service, office workers, and clerks. "Lower class" refers to industrial workers and other manual laborers who range from skilled and semi-skilled to unskilled laborers and underemployed and unemployed marginal laborers. I will then discuss the bimodal model of Brazilian social structure and aspects of patronage and will present a reinterpretation of Umbanda on the basis of this latter model.

## Background of Umbanda

Far from being a minor sect, Umbanda is a major contemporary religion conservatively estimated to now have between five and ten million followers, that is, between one-tenth and one-twentieth of the Brazilian population. Since 1965 it has been given a separate category in the official yearly religious census.[3] It is found in virtually all cities from Porto Alegre to Belém, though its popularity appears to be greatest in the large industrial cities of the south. Its adherents include both men and women, the great majority of whom are urban born (see Brown 1974), and a significant number of whom can be classified as members of the middle class. Rio de Janeiro, where Umbanda began around 1930 and where the research on which this chapter is based was principally conducted, has upwards of 20,000 Umbanda cult centers (known as *centros espíritos* or *terreiros*) and over two million practitioners, as well as some ten or more Umbanda federations. These are umbrella organizations which affiliate many but not all individual centros, offering legal protection to members and publicizing Umbanda. In addition, a number of Umbanda politicians and other officials have represented Umbanda interests in the state government since at least the mid-1950s.

To further illustrate the significance of Umbanda in contemporary Brazil, it is interesting to look at the Yemanjá festival held in Santos (the port city for São Paulo) in 1975. Both newspaper and Umbanda sources estimated that at least 300,000 people participated in this ceremony, and some 3,500 buses were used to transport the various centros from greater São Paulo to the beach to make their offerings to Yemanjá, the reigning goddess of salt water. This phenomenon is not limited to São Paulo. For many years, equivalent and even larger numbers have attended similar ceremonies in Rio and Porto Alegre. And it is generally recognized that attendance at these ceremonies does not include anywhere near a majority of the participants in Umbanda.

Additional evidence for the pervasiveness of Umbanda in Brazil is provided by the astounding numbers of Umbanda stores selling the books and articles used in its rituals, the Umbanda periodicals sold openly at newsstands, government sponsorship of and publicity for Umbanda ceremonies and rituals, and the high visibility of Umbanda religious offerings made at points of national ceremonial interest, including Catholic holidays and Brazilian national soccer championships. Given its size, the extent of its popularity in the most urban and industrial areas of Brazil, and the social class composition of its adherents, Umbanda cannot be seen as a minor sect, but instead gives every indication of moving in the direction of competition with the Catholic Church as the national religion of Brazil.

Umbanda is a syncretic, popular religion, and not surprisingly, the beliefs and practices found among its centros show considerable variation, tending toward a greater resemblance to one or the other of the poles formed by its two main parent traditions. One of these, Spiritism, came to Brazil from France in the mid-nineteenth century and became extremely popular among the urban middle class (see Renshaw 1969; Warren 1968b; Brown 1974). The other, which has often gone under the generic (and now pejorative) term "Macumba," includes diverse Afro-Brazilian religious practices which spread throughout the lower classes in Rio de Janeiro at the end of the nineteenth century. Due to Umbanda's ongoing syncretic tendencies, the Afro-Brazilian elements found within it vary somewhat in the several regions of Brazil, reflecting different regional traditions. Umbanda has also become extremely eclectic. In addition to being significantly influenced by Catholicism, it has absorbed elements from the great religious traditions of Asia, European, and Jewish mysticism, and other occult and mystico-historical sources of the past two centuries.

## Umbanda Ritual

Like both of its parent traditions, Umbanda is a religion of spirit possession. Its major rituals are the religious "sessions" (*sessões*) held in the evenings two or three times a week at Umbanda centros. These may be located in a room in the leader's home, in a rented house, or in a building specially designed for the purpose. During the sessions, which are almost always open to the public, benevolent spirits of the Umbanda pantheon are called down from their astral abodes to take possession of the bodies of specially trained initiates and, acting through them, to offer individual consultations to individuals in the congregation who have come in search of cures for their illnesses and solutions to their personal problems.

Participants in these rituals may be divided into two groups. One, which I will refer to as the ritual corps, is composed of the individuals who dress in ritual uniforms and regularly carry out specified ritual roles during the sessions. They occupy the ritual area, which contains the altar, and which is separated from the benches of the congregation, often by a low fence with a gate. The ritual corps includes the leader or *chefe*, the mediums,[4] who are ranked according to their degree of spiritual preparation and ability to enact possession roles, and other individuals who are not mediums but have specific ritual duties. All of these individuals participate collectively in prayers and the singing of hymns to the spirits and in addition they have specific roles during the major part of the ritual when spiritual consultations (*consultas*) are offered to those in the congregation. The size of the ritual corps varies considerably from centro to centro, averaging somewhere between thirty and sixty individuals.

The other group of participants, referred to here as the clients, attends Umbanda sessions in order to obtain spiritual aid in the solution of problems. The clients sit on the benches until the time comes for consultas, when they leave their seats, remove their shoes, and line up to enter the ritual area for individual consultations with the spirit of their choice. The numbers of the clients also vary considerably among various centros, averaging somewhere between fifty and a hundred clients per session. These clients range from regular participants, who may even be members of the centro, contributing small sums monthly to its support, to those who attend infrequently, according to necessity, or who are participating for the first time.

Rather than describe Umbanda rituals in detail (see Brown 1974, ch. 5; also bibliography), I will confine my discussion here to two of its central and defining features, spirit possession and spirit consultations. Spirit possession is the most crucial aspect of Umbanda, since it provides visual evidence of the existence of spirits: benevolent spirits who dramatize their willingness and availability to help mankind by offering their services as curers and advisors, and malevolent or ignorant spirits who are revealed to be at work in the daily lives of ordinary men and women.

Possession is common among clients as well as members of the ritual corps. Within this latter group chefes and high-ranking mediums are possessed by the spirit benefactors, while other mediums help to remove, and in the process are often possessed by, the negative spirits discovered to be plaguing and persecuting the clients. Possession is also induced among clients by spirit consultants during consultas as part of the diagnosis and treatment of spirit persecution, and may even occur spontaneously while clients are seated in the congregation. In contrast to the extremely controlled possession states achieved by experienced mediums, possession among those inexperienced in controlling it is often violent, and such individuals must be protected from injury to themselves and to others.

It is worth noting here that those overcome by spontaneous possession include non-believers who may be attending an Umbanda session for the first time, and that such individuals appear to be just as liable to possession as seasoned participants. In fact, many of my Umbandista informants emphasized to me their shock and fright at becoming possessed during their first visit to a centro. This suggests that belief in, or familiarity with, Umbanda is not a necessary condition for possession. However, among clients, possession often serves as an inducement to enter the ritual corps, since it is often taken as a sign of *mediunidade* (inherent potential mediumship), and clients are warned that unless they develop this potential further, harm may come to themselves or their families.

The other crucial feature of Umbanda rituals is the consultas, which dramatize Umbanda's acknowledged raison d'être—the providing of spiritual aid to the needy, or *caridade* (charity). While members of the ritual corps are concerned with the presentation of consultas, members of the congregation are concerned with obtaining help from them. They may be suffering from illness, family troubles, unemployment, financial difficulties, or any number of bureaucratic problems, and they often seek Umbanda as a last resort after all available secular channels of aid have failed to resolve a persistent problem.[5] They come first to a consulta on the recommendation of a family member, a friend or a neighbor. When their turn comes they enter the ritual area for a consulta with a *Caboclo* (the spirit of an unacculturated Brazilian Indian) or a *Preto Velho* ("Old Black," the spirit of an African enslaved in Brazil).[6] Caboclos stand, wearing stern expressions, puffing on large cigars and often uttering loud piercing cries, while Pretos Velhos, elderly and humble, give consultas while seated on low stools, smoking their pipes. The client receives a ritual hug, a *passe* (a ritual cleansing in which the negative fluids are drawn from his body into the medium's own hands and shaken off with a snapping sound), and is anointed with large puffs of smoke. Then the spirit consultant may ask, "Now, my child, what is your problem?" and the consulta begins.

Clients, depending on their problem, may receive spiritual cleansings, blessings, exorcisms, herbal remedies, ritual obligations to perform, or practical advice. The successful solution of the clients' personal difficulties and their feelings of being helped by consultas generates or strengthens belief in Umbanda's spiritual powers and forms the basis for continued interest and participation. As is commonly said, "O Umbandista entra pela porta do sofrimento" ("Umbandistas come to Umbanda through the door of suffering").

The aid offered during consultas may be supplemented by other, non-ritual activities within the centro. Chefes may provide for or arrange individual favors for members, such as employment, loans, or access to urban services, thus acting as redistributive agents. Some of the wealthier centros even provide medical and dental care, psychiatric aid, legal services, and also distribute food and clothing. These resources derive from members or sympathizers and are made available free or at minimal charge.

This description of the principal features of Umbanda ritual and practice would be interpreted by most social scientists, mistakenly in this case, as a manifestation of a lower-class religion. Differences in the ritual setting in which these activities are carried out, and consequently in what might be called their ritual tone, might suggest the presence of internal class differences within this religion. At one extreme may be found the immaculate, well-lighted centro where mediums of both sexes, dressed in white nurses' uniforms, white socks, and tennis sneakers, line up in neat formations to begin the service punctually at the appointed hour, while attendants distribute tokens to the clients with the name of the requested spirit consultant and the order of the consulta marked upon them. The singing of Umbanda hymns (pontos) which precedes and accompanies spirit possession is a capella or accompanied by hand-clapping, while mediums stand or sway gently in their places. In these centros the prevailing tone is one of solemnity, restraint, and order.

At the other extreme, participants dress in a variety of extravagant outfits, women in long, white, lace-trimmed or highly colored skirts, men in white pants and colored satin shirts. Mediums when possessed by the spirit consultants may wear elaborate paraphernalia. Caboclos, for example, don enormous feather headdresses. The singing of the hymns is accompanied by drums and dancing of a samba step. Members of both the ritual corps and the congregation engage in bantering conversations during the ceremonies, and prospective clients leave their seats well in advance of the consulta period and surge toward the entrance to the ritual area, jockeying for an advantage among the throngs awaiting consultas.

It is true that these differences in ritual setting do have a historical basis in class differences. However, as will be shown, there is no longer a high degree of correlation between ritual setting and social class.

## The Umbanda Belief System

While Umbanda ritual suggests a lower-class religion, its ideology presents a far more complex problem. It is not fully integrated, but is rather responsive to the various interests of its adherents. Thus, as with all religions, it works on a number of levels. Obtaining treatment in an Umbanda centro does not necessitate, although it may lead to, conversion to the beliefs of Umbanda. Many utilize Umbanda with no thought of converting to it, and even among those who join the ritual corps and profess the articles of Umbanda faith, many retain their former religious beliefs and affiliations. The great majority of these are Catholic-Umbandistas, and there is a small minority of Jewish-Umbandistas as well, though no examples were found of dual religious affiliation among Protestants. Umbanda leaders concern themselves very little with conversion or with exclusive adherence on the part of participants. However, considerable numbers of Umbandistas do become "converts," defining themselves exclusively as Umbandistas and drawing a strong distinction between Umbanda and other religions, particularly Catholicism.

The most basic ideological differences, however, relate less to the degree of commitment to Umbanda than to the degree to which the rituals are interpreted within a framework of Catholic belief. Those who utilize this Catholic framework include not only the majority of those who occasionally attend Umbanda centros for instrumental purposes, but many chefes and mediums as well. The inclusion of chefes here is important, since they provide the general ideological orientation for other members of the centro including the members of the ritual corps.

Catholic, or Catholic-Umbandista, participants in Umbanda can find much in Umbanda rituals with which to identify, including Catholic prayers and ritual practices. But the most important Catholic element in Umbanda is the presence of the chief figures of the Catholic religious constellation, including God, the Holy Family, and many important Catholic saints. These sacred Catholic figures always have a dual African identity as Orixás (African dieties drawn from the Yoruba pantheon, these figures are found in Brazil in diverse Afro-Brazilian religions). Thus, for example, St. George is also Ogum, the Yoruban Warrior God, while Yemanjá, the Yoruba goddess of the sea and salt waters, whose festival was mentioned earlier, is identified with the Virgin Mary. One or the other of these aspects, the Catholic or the African, tends to be more emphasized in the various centros.

These divinities are considered too powerful to descend to earth, sending instead their emissaries, foremost among whom are the Caboclos and Pretos Velhos. However, they are considered important protectors and patrons of mankind, and are almost invariably represented, in either their Catholic or their African forms, on the altars of Umbanda centros. They are worshiped in hymns, prayed to for aid and protection, and are frequent recipients of ritual offerings.

As patrons and objects of petitions for spiritual aid, they bear a strong resemblance to, and are clearly influenced by, the folk Catholic tradition, with its emphasis on the Cult of the Saints (see Azevedo 1963; Gross 1971; see also Foster 1963). As in folk Catholicism, these figures are also regarded as capable of working miracles. Thus, general familiarity with the beliefs of folk Catholicism undoubtedly facilitates the acceptance of the roles and activities in Umbanda of these Afro-Catholic divinities and of the Caboclos and Pretos Velhos as well. This familiarity also facilitates belief in the claims of Umbandistas that spiritual aid can be obtained and problems solved through their offices.

These same folk Catholic beliefs undoubtedly help as well to explain the frequency with which Catholic-Umbandista participants in Umbanda tend to perceive Catholicism and Umbanda as parts of a single religious system (see Brown 1974). The fact that middle-class as well as lower-class informants expressed beliefs often considered to form part of "folk" rather than "orthodox" Catholicism (see Bastide 1951b; Azevedo 1963), suggests that folk Catholicism may also require reconsideration as a multi-class rather than a lower-class phenomenon.

Just as the benevolence of the Caboclos and Pretos Velhos may be interpreted within the framework of folk Catholicism, negative spirits may be interpreted more generally as agents of the Christian underworld. Exús, spirits which are believed to work for either benevolent or malignant ends, according to their inclinations and the financial resources of their clients, along with their female counterparts, Pomba Giras, are often portrayed as Devil figures. Still other less clearly identified wandering spirits believed to plague and persecute humans may find their counterparts in similar spirit beliefs which survive from medieval Portuguese Catholicism (see Warren 1968a).

Umbanda rituals may also be interpreted within other ideological frameworks, including those of the Kabbala, Rosecrucianism, and other European occult and theosophical traditions which flourish in Brazil. Of these, the most important is Spiritist, or Kardecist ideology. This form of Spiritism, which was heavily influenced by the social philosophy of Auguste Comte, introduces into Umbanda an emphasis on evolutionism (interpreted as inevitable progress), rationalism, and scientism, to which are added the concepts of reincarnation and the Law of Karma, or Divine Fate. Evolution refers to the transformation of the individual spirit from a state of ignorance and darkness to one of enlightenment, a process which spirits begin with a series of earthly incarnations, through which they move slowly and inevitably away from the impurities of earthly life toward a state of spiritual perfection and a permanent abode in the astral spaces. However, according to the Law of Karma, this process may be retarded, for a wasteful or immoral life, lacking in inner self-improvement and charity, will necessitate expiation and bring reincarnation as a sufferer from the very ills which were previously visited on others.

According to this philosophical scheme, the realms of Heaven and Hell are reinterpreted in terms of enlightenment and ignorance. The benevolent spirit helpers, Caboclos and Pretos Velhos, and the dual Afro-Catholic divinities, thus become highly "evolved" spirits, while the Exús and other harmful spirits are defined as ignorant or "backward," in need of, and susceptible to, moral training. Illness and suffering are due not to original sin, as in Catholic belief, but are generally attributed to the activities of ignorant spirits, to the low level of an individual's own spiritual development, which lowers physical resistance and increases vulnerability to such external influences, or to the Law of Karma. Problems may also be attributed to mankind's generally low level of spiritual development, which breeds much general suffering—organic illnesses, poverty, and other practical difficulties not directly caused by particular spirits. The resolution of these difficulties can be found through the guidance and help obtainable at Umbanda centros from the more evolved spirit benefactors.

This ideological system, and variations upon it, are extremely common among the many Umbandistas who are former Spiritists or who have had some contact with Spiritist doctrine,[7] but may be taught as well by Umbanda chefes and are available in the dozens of popular books on Umbanda, although many of these books present different orientations. Although this ideological position is explicitly rejected in centros of the most Afro-Catholic type, there are evidences of its increasing acceptance within Umbanda centros.

A final area of ideological interest among Umbandistas deserves mention here, for although it is far more restricted in its appeal, it is found precisely among the more educated, more intellectually oriented middle-class Umbandistas who are of particular interest in this discussion. These individuals are concerned with understanding Umbanda as a metaphysical science. The points of departure for such interests are the phenomena of possession and of spiritual healing and aid, which are taken as providing tangible evidence of the existence of paranormal phenomena. Those who seek a deeper understanding of these phenomena and an explanation of the mechanics of spiritual causation turn to the answers provided by other belief systems—to the already mentioned writings of Allan Kardec, to the numerology of the Kabbala, to Far Eastern philosophies, to Theosophy, Magnetism, Mesmerism and, often, to modern science.

The "normal" scientific viewpoint, of course, defines individuals who communicate with or become possessed by spirits as deviant, mentally unstable, or deranged. Thus, Umbandistas turn to the peripheral areas of parapsychology and studies of extrasensory perception which embrace paranormal phenomena. From these diverse studies Umbandistas seek explanations of fluidic emanations, vibrations, and energy transmission which they, in turn, utilize as empirical, scientific evidence of the existence of spirits. They place Umbanda in the forefront of the new age of "psychic science" which will supersede the paradigm of "postivistic science," and thus resolving the conflict between religion and science, declare their religion as a revelation of the science of the future.

It is interesting to note that the three Umbanda ideologies just mentioned, the Umbanda-Catholic, the Spiritist, and the "scientific," closely resemble hierarchical distinctions which Bastide described within Brazilian Spiritualism and which he classified respectively as lower class, lower middle class, and professional middle class (1951b:353–54). However, while he linked Umbanda primarily to the first and lowest level of this hierarchy, the Afro-Catholic, it is in fact practiced in conjunction with all of these ideologies and, as will be shortly seen, at all of these social levels.

One final dimension of Umbanda ideology concerns the nationalist emphasis which has been given to this religion by Umbanda intellectuals and leaders. These leaders portray Caboclos and Pretos Velhos as symbols of Brazil's indigenous populations, and together with the Catholic divinities see them, sometimes with explicit reference to the writings of Gilberto Freyre, as symbolizing the blending of three traditions, the Indian, the African, and the Iberian, which represents Brazil's unique racial and cultural heritage. Umbanda is thus described as the only truly national Brazilian religion. Some leaders go even beyond this and relate Umbanda to Brazil's potential as a world power, thus projecting it as the new world religion.

While this position is held consciously by only a minority of Umbandistas and is probably discounted by non-Umbandistas, it is the only such nationalist manifestation among the non-Catholic religions in Brazil, and provides an interesting comparison to the Catholic Church's efforts to maintain itself as a source of national cultural identity for Brazilians. The potential nationalist appeal of Umbanda makes it a formidable competitor of Catholicism, since its symbols touch the middle classes, who are familiar with their use in Brazilian Romantic Nationalist literature. For the lower classes, the Caboclos and Pretos Velhos may serve as valorizations of Brazil's oppressed minority groups.

## Umbandas and Social Class

While in ritual and practice Umbanda resembles religions generally regarded as lower class, I have tried to indicate that its ideology is far more ambiguous and complicated in its class ascription. Turning now to examine the actual class composition of this religion we find that its divergence from strictly lower-class religions becomes clearer.

The multi-class composition of Umbanda can best be illustrated by examining briefly the membership of a range of centros found in Rio de Janeiro. Data for this section are based on participant observations and interviews in over 200 centros in Rio over a period of three years, and on a questionnaire applied in fourteen centros chosen to represent the widest possible variations.

As in the area of ritual and ideology, striking differences may be found in the social class of the participants and in the physical settings of the centros. At one extreme are the centros located in *favelas* (hillside slums) where narrow paths, also serving as open sewers, lead to *barracos* (wooden shacks) with dirt floors—small, precariously lit, and crowded with people. Here both members of the ritual corps and the general clientele are likely to be extremely poor, and often predominantly black.[8] One such centro, which I visited several times, was run by a woman who made her living by washing clothes. Other members of the ritual corps included eight domestic servants, a dishwasher, a worker in a dry cleaning establishment, and three unskilled laborers, one retired. Of these people, all but three were black. This centro closely approximated the most prevalent image of Umbanda, and it was this stereotype which originally led me to choose to live in a favela to conduct fieldwork on this religion. Even in this setting, however, it was quite normal for a couple dressed in tailored clothing and wearing expensive jewlry to arrive from *fora* (outside the favela) to attend the session and await a consulta. One such couple, somewhat embarrassed at my finding them there, explained that they had heard of the *força* (power) of the spirits there and, desperate for help, had decided to come for a consulta. Explanations for the presence of such middle-class people in favelas and other lower-class neighborhoods where they normally would not care, or dare, to venture were generally based on the centros' reputations for unusually effective spiritual powers.

The other fourteen centros located in this extremely large favela of some 35,000 to 50,000 people generally resembled the centro just described, though some were located in more accessible, better constructed buildings. What was most interesting, however, was that the great majority of Umbanda participants residing in the favela did not attend these centros, but preferred to go to others outside the favela, some similar to those within it, and others which were far wealthier, constituting the other extreme of this socioeconomic continuum.

In these other centros, the same basic rituals take place in far more sumptuous settings. Since centros of this type have received less attention and are especially germane to my discussion, I will describe them in somewhat greater detail. It should be noted that they are not entirely middle class, but rather tend to be run by persons of the middle class; their clientele come from various sectors of the middle and lower classes.

One such centro was located in a large house rented and redecorated for the purpose in one of the most expensive residential suburbs of Rio. Here, the majority of the ritual corps were middle class. Its chefe was a wealthy and well-placed financial consultant. Other mediums included the head of purchasing for one of the largest Brazilian department store chains, the head of financing for a large local industry, and the wife of a dental surgeon. Still others belonged to the less affluent middle class, as, for example, an accountant, a retired teacher of physical education, the daughter of a tax collector, the wives of small businessmen and civil servants, and several secretaries. Still other members were of the lower class, a bricklayer and several domestic servants. Thus the ritual corps ranged from affluent middle to lower class. As is true in the general population, and in Umbanda centros as well, most, though not all of the middle-class participants at this centro were *brancos* (whites), while lower-class participants included a greater number of *mulatos* and *pretos* (blacks).[9] A similar social range is reflected in this centro's clientele, judged on the basis of such external markers of social position as manner of speech, clothing, jewelry, and manner of transportation (arrival at the centro in expensive cars or by taxi).

Another centro of this type, located in a specially constructed building in a middle-class suburban neighborhood, had been run for many years by an engineer employed in an important managerial position in one of Brazil's largest factories. Other affluent middle-class members of the ritual corps included his son, also an engineer preparing to take over the direction of the centro when his father retired, and two friends, one a wealthy banker, and the other a highly placed civil servant. Also among those in the ritual corps were an accountant, a *despachante* (bureaucratic middleman), a retired barber, a shopclerk, the wives of a grocer and a minor public functionary, a stonemason, a telephone lineman, an electrician, a taxi driver, a retired (female) textile worker, a floorwasher, several female domestic servants, and a *biscateiro* (a marginally employed odd-jobber). Thus, in this centro as in the other, the ritual corps was socially very diverse, as was the clientele.

A more homogeneous middle class centro, again in a redecorated rented suburban house, was run by a high-ranking military officer who taught at the military academy. The ritual corps here was composed almost entirely of army officers and their wives, almost all of whom were school teachers. However, as in the other centros mentioned, the clientele varied from middle class (friends and colleagues of the members of the ritual corps) to lower class, and one of this latter group, a domestic servant, was preparing at the time of my research to begin training as a medium.

Some middle-class centros undoubtedly do restrict their attendance, and may thus preserve a more homogeneous social composition. However, even when attendance is restricted to family members and acquaintances it need not necessarily prohibit a multi-class composition. I attended one session run by a chefe who was the daughter of one of Rio's millionaire families. It was held in the consulting clinic of her husband, a medical doctor and high-ranking officer in the naval reserve, who was also a member of the ritual corps. After the medical equipment had been moved out of the way, the Caboclos descended to her, three members of her family, two of her husband's business colleagues, his medical assistant, and a household servant. The clientele here was limited to invited relatives and acquaintances.

A few centros have become very large and offer extensive social welfare services. One, a huge, multi-story building located on a central city thoroughfare, was run by a retired military officer who held services every night of the week, and maintained a ritual corps of some 1,500 mediums. These ranged from affluent middle-class men and women to the poorest residents of several nearby favelas, including the one in which I lived. Participants from this favela explained to me that they came here in preference to the centros in the favela because the *ambiente* (atmosphere and surroundings) was better, the people *mais elevado* (of higher social status), and because of the social welfare services it offered. In fact, this centro maintained medical and dental clinics, a pharmacy where medicines donated by pharmaceutical firms were distributed free, and from time to time clothing and food donated by the members also were distributed. In addition, it ran an orphanage housing some forty children, which occupied an upper floor of the building. These charitable activities were organized and run by a large volunteer administrative staff, made up mainly of the husbands and wives of mediums.

Between the extremes of very poor and predominantly affluent middle-class centros are found a great many others, probably the great majority, which are located in working-class or lower middle-class neighborhoods and whose members come predominantly from these sectors. Such centros are composed of domestic servants, factory workers, shopclerks, and low-ranking civil servants. One I attended was run by a worker in a munitions factory, and the ritual corps also included his wife, his daughter, one of his fellow workers, four other factory workers, two machinists and their wives, two low-ranking civil servants, a detective, an army sergeant, two saleswomen (one retired), a manicurist, a clotheswasher, and two domestic servants.

These examples illustrate both the range of class composition in Umbanda and the tendency toward multi-class participation in Umbanda centros, the significance of which will be considered below. According to my selected survey, these examples are more or less representative of the class composition found in Umbanda centros in Rio at that time. During this period I was also able to do some research in other cities, and was able to confirm the presence of a similar range of participants and of multi-class centros in the city of São Paulo, in smaller cities in the interior of São Paulo state, such as Taubaté and Guaretinguetá, in Porto Alegre, the capital of the southern state of Rio Grande do Sul, and in other cities in the interior. The presence of middle-class participants in Umbanda has also been confirmed by researchers in the northern city of Belém (Leacock and Leacock 1972; Vergolino e Silva 1976). My own ongoing research in Campinas (an industrial city about an hour away from São Paulo) presently in its preliminary stages, indicates considerable lower- and middle-class participation in Umbanda, and at the same time has revealed some middle-class adherents as well as the active involvement on the part of at least a few members of the local social elite.

I am not trying to argue here the numerical predominance of middle class participants in Umbanda. In Rio, and elsewhere in Brazil, the majority of members are probably lower class. I want only to indicate that persons of the middle classes participate extensively in all aspects of Umbanda activities. In the survey which I made of members of the ritual corps in fourteen Umbanda centros my aim was limited to obtaining a representative sample of the range of variation in size, location, ritual orientation, and socioeconomic composition among Umbanda centros. A random sample would undoubtedly have included a larger proportion of centros primarily composed of lower-class membership. However, at the time of my research, a random sampling of centros was not possible since the boundaries of the sampling universe could not be ascertained.[10]

I will discuss very briefly some of the data from this survey (see Brown 1974) since it demonstrates the range of socioeconomic differences and thus supports my central argument. The sample (N = 403) deals only with members of the ritual corps (chefes, mediums, and ritual helpers) in these fourteen centros, since these were judged to be the most committed to Umbanda practices and beliefs. For the purposes of analyzing this sample, respondents were first classified into middle class and lower class on the basis of the broad occupational distinction between non-manual and manual labor. Here, I followed the approach used by Soares (1966; 1968) and Adams (1967).[11] According to this distinction, the respondents in the sample fall more heavily into the middle class (57 percent) than into the lower class (43 percent). When class is correlated with income, the lower class is composed almost equally of individuals who earn the minimum wage or less (the minimum wage in Rio de Janeiro in 1969, when the sample was taken, was Crs 156, or US $39 per month, just under US $480 per year), and those who earn somewhere between $40 and $100 per month ($480 to $1,000 per year). The middle-class group contains only two individuals who earn the minimum wage or less. The salaries in this group fall into the categories of $40 to $100 per month (35 percent), $100 to $200 per month (27 percent), and $100 per month or more (37 percent), ranging up to a maximum of $30,000 per year.

Correlating social class with education, the 35 percent of the sample who had not completed primary school were almost exclusively found within the lower-class group, while of the 44 percent of the sample who had some high school, and the 22 percent who had further specialized training in normal or technical school, or in college, almost all were in the middle-class group. Thus, the distinction between manual and non-manual labor in this sample appears to correlate significantly with income and education as well.

The sample was then classified into occupational sectors. Thirty-eight percent identified themselves as housewives and 3 percent as full-time students. These individuals were subtracted from the sample, which then included only those employed in or retired from paid labor. Of the remaining middle-class group, 42 percent was involved in commerce, 25.4 percent in the civil servive, 20 percent in the professions, most of them teachers, and 13.5 percent in the military officer corps. The lower-class group showed an almost equal distribution between skilled labor (47 percent) and semi- and unskilled labor (53 percent). The great majority of these individuals were either self-employed or employed in small shops, and very few in large factories. The possible implications of these sectoral percentages will be discussed below.

Another aspect of the sample which is indirectly related to social class concerns participation by sex. I. M. Lewis has suggested that low status possession religions often have a predominance of female adherents although they may include low status males as well (1971:88). The female/male ratio of 2:1, which appears to be relatively constant in Umbanda and is confirmed as well in the sample, would suggest that Umbanda falls into this category. However, a number of factors again make such a simplistic classification untenable. While female participants are almost evenly divided between middle and lower classes, male participants are located primarily in the middle class, where the number of male participants is double that found in the lower class. In other words, male participation increases with higher social status. Also, while the 2:1 ratio holds generally in Umbanda, some centros in fact have a predominance of male participants. Thus, with respect to the greater overall numbers of female participants, it could be suggested that, given the considerable amount of time demanded of active participants in the centros (often several hours two or more times a week), men as a group are more likely to be restricted from participation in Umbanda by long and set working hours dictated by their employment than are women, many of whom are housewives.

It is also significant that while females predominate numerically, males tend to predominate in leadership positions. Despite their smaller numbers there appear to be more male than female chefes. In my sample, for example, eight of the fourteen chefes are men. Men are also found almost exclusively at the higher positions of leadership and influence in Umbanda federations. Moreover, active participation of men in Umbanda is not a recent phenomenon, but dates to the early days of Umbanda in Rio in the period around 1930. During this time, the first group to self-consciously and actively promote Umbanda as a religion, and to codify its practice and ideology, were a group of men from the middle class. These men, and others who have since joined or competed with them, founded what are today the largest and some of the best known centros in Rio. Their influence, through their own activities and their connections with directors of radio programs, journalists and politicians, has been extremely important in gaining both publicity and legitimacy for this religion. Thus the fact that Umbanda is a religion of spirit possession does not imply in this case either marginality or the low social status of its participants. Individuals who participate actively in possession roles include significant numbers of successful and even prominent individuals from the middle classes.

I want to mention here another aspect of multi-class participation in Umbanda centros which relates back to the discussion of the relation between ritual setting, ideology, and social class. Differences were noted in the discussion on ritual between the more controlled, sedate settings and the more colorful, expressive ones. Similarly, in the area of ideology the more intellectualized, "scientific" orientation was seen to contrast with the more magical one. It would be easy to assume that the more sedate rituals and intellectual orientation correlate with middle-class participation and that the more expressive, magical orientation is found within the lower class. This assumption has some basis in fact, since historically the more middle class orientation has derived from Spiritism which, as has been seen, is a more middle-class religion. In fact, the early middle-class leaders of Umbanda were former Kardecists and were responsible for developing the more Kardecist-oriented form of Umbanda. The more lower-class orientation is historically linked to the Afro-Brazilian tradition which, as has been seen, was lower class.

Today, however, while there is still some degree of truth to these class correlations, the multi-class composition of the centros confounds such neat correlations. While the majority of the wealthier centros may adopt the more middle-class ritual setting and ideological orientation, lower-class participants in these centros participate in middle-class Umbanda, while individuals of the middle class who attend lower-class centros, among which the Afro-Brazilian orientation is more frequent, participate in this more lower-class orientation. Founders of new centros have generally undergone long training as mediums and tend to follow the orientation of the chefes under whom they have received their training. Thus, for example, in the first centro described above, in the favela, the ceremony was of the more sedate, middle-class type, although the ritual corps were lower class. The chefe had first attended a Spiritist centro, then had become a medium in a wealthy centro outside the favela which practiced a middle-class form of Umbanda, and when she founded her own centro she followed the same orientation. The reverse of this situation also occurs, and individuals from the middle class open centros with a strongly Afro-Brazilian orientation.

In other words, social class is not a reliable gauge of the ritual and ideological orientation of the participants at any particular centro, nor does knowledge of the particular ritual setting and ideological orientation followed by a specific centro allow for an accurate prediction of the social class of the participants. Multi-class centros appear to result from two quite different principles of attraction: one of prestige and the availability of social services, which frequently attracts lower-class individuals to wealthier centros, and one to which I referred earlier as força or power, which might perhaps be labeled "supernatural charisma." This is attributed to certain spirit consultants and may be, but is not necessarily, present in the individual medium outside of his or her possession role. Força may operate in all centros, of whatever social class, and it draws individuals to the centro on a basis which does not obey class principles. It is capable, as has been seen, of drawing wealthy clients to poorer centros. One final aspect of multi-class participation in Umbanda concerns the lack of connection in Umbanda centros between the ritual status hierarchy and the secular social class hierarchy. This results in frequent instances of ritual inversions of the secular class relations between individuals. Members of the lower class often achieve high ritual rank within middle-class centros and ritually dominate others of higher socioeconomic status within the ritual corps. And the same applies to relations between members of the ritual corps and clients. For example, it is common to see a poor black medium possessed by a high-ranking Caboclo or Preto Velho receiving homage and extremely deferential behavior from wealthy, white clients. The hierarchy of status and role based on spiritual powers which dominates Umbanda rituals denies the significance of class differences among the participants, and of class boundaries between them as well.

## Discussion

It should now be clear that the social composition of Umbanda does not permit its classification as a lower-class religion and that in many

respects Umbanda diverges from the expectations of class participation in religious phenomena generated by the three-class model. I
want to discuss the bi-modal model of Brazilian social structure and
reexamine Umbanda within this framework.

Scholars agree that Brazilian class structure differs significantly
from that of Western Europe and the United States. Industrialization
in the presence of an already industrialized world, foreign powers and
with high internal rates of population growth, has resulted in the perpetuation of an extremely uneven income distribution and low rates
of social mobility within the context of an increasingly strong and
centralized state.[12] A relatively closed small elite continues to control
the essential economic resources of Brazil and exercises an important
degree of control over political institutions as well. Counterpoised
against this small elite are the overwhelming majority of Brazilians
who form the lower classes or "masses," and who have virtually no
control over economic resources and comparatively little control over
the political apparatus although, because of their numbers and their
poverty, they represent a continual political threat.

The middle class, so important in the Euro-American sphere,
remains, for the period under discussion, relatively small, lacking
ideological cohesion, and composed of interest groups representing
different occupational sectors with different social origins. These different groups tend to act independently of each other, and to be prag-
matic in their economic interests and political behavior, sometimes
showing patterns of sectoral, rather than class alliance with either the
elite or the masses. In fact, there is not a cohesive, bounded and self-
conscious middle class in Brazil, but instead a series of often distinct
groups who, while defining themselves as middle class, often fail to
share political and economic interests.

Some researchers have argued the relevance of a three-class
model for Brazil, considering the middle class or "middle sectors" a
significant and independent group on the basis of economic position,
life style, and self-identity (see, for example, Wagley 1968:196; Germani 1973:115). Many others, however, have treated these middle
groups as pragmatically dependent in both political and economic
terms on various sectoral alliances, and particularly, at their lower
levels, as dependent on the government bureaucracy. Rather than a
middle class acting in terms of its own class interests, these scholars
have tended to emphasize the disaparateness and relative power-

lessness of the Brazilian middle class as a class. This has facilitated the use of a model which distinguishes two main loci of power: one centered in the increasingly powerful industrial elite, the other in the lower classes which remain in a position of political and economic dependence, although it is clear that they represent a potential source of power. This model, with variations, has been followed by many Brazilian social scientists (see Fernandes 1973; Ianni 1963; Jaguaribe 1968; Saes 1974) and by other Brazilianists such as Leeds (1965) and Adams (1967).

Discussions of the mechanisms by which this system operates have frequently emphasized the importance of vertical rather than horizontal relationships between individuals and groups in urban areas, and stressed patronage ties as an important means of gaining access to employment and urban services and in the workings of politics. With increasing state power and the penetration of more rationalized forms of bureaucratic organization in government and in industry, employment opportunities still frequently rely on personal ties of patronage rather than on impersonal, objective criteria, and this is true also of access to urban services. Cardoso (1964) for example, has described the continuing importance of patronage among industrialists. Leeds (1965) has discussed the ways in which Brazilian businessmen create *igreginhas* (''little churches'') of followers which are used and manipulated in business maneuverings with equals and superiors. Jaguaribe (1968) has dealt with numerous forms of patronage at various levels of the government bureaucracy, and the proletariat and the lower classes have often been similarly described as searching for *''o bom patrão''* (the good patron), sometimes to improve, but often simply to maintain their tenuous positions (Jaguaribe 1968; Leeds and Leeds 1970; Touraine 1961).

In urban politics, politicians serve clienteles composed of various interest groups, and approach the voters with populist appeals. Promises to serve the interests of the various groups are accompanied by the use of political middlemen to secure the votes of individual clienteles. Since the lower-class electorates far outnumber those of the middle and upper classes, middle-class politicians are heavily dependent on seeking lower-class followers as sources of political support.

The result is a structure which often relies for its operation on the creation of vertical relations between individuals with differential access to resources and political power. The strength of these vertically oriented structural ties has been cited as inhibiting the development of both solid, cohesive, horizontal, social strata or classes at all socioeconomic levels of the population, and in the pre-1964 period of coherent national political parties (see Lopes 1966; Jaguaribe 1968).

This does not imply a lack of status consciousness among Brazilians of different socioeconomic strata; in fact, quite the opposite holds. As in most systems with low rates of social mobility, status consciousness is very marked in Brazil. Thus, for example, people who consider themselves members of the middle class often reveal a considerable degree of social prejudice against ideas and forms of behavior considered lower class. But however great the degree of such prejudices, indications are that, for many Brazilians, the socioeconomic and political necessities of daily living still frequently require the formation of patronage relationships with individuals of lower as well as of higher statuses. It might even be suggested that the high degree of status consciousness in Brazil is to some degree a reflex of the dependence on vertical ties, and of the need to reaffirm individual status in the face of the numerous personal dependency relationships which may be required for the maintenance of social position.

The reexamination of Umbanda in relation to these aspects of patronage in Brazil reveals that, as in Brazilian society, patronage is a central idiom in Umbanda ritual, ideology, and social relations. Umbanda ritual and ideology present an image of human beings as fragile creatures whose daily existence is constantly threatened and frequently disrupted by supernatural figures and forces beyond their direct control. They depend upon benevolent supernaturals for general protection against these forces and for specific intervention in the crisis situations which they often provoke. Their position with respect to these benevolent spirits is one of clients to patron, clients who seek favors and protection from a powerful patron, rendering in return homage and loyal support.

Consultas may be seen as ritual dramatizations of the search for and transaction of supernatural patron–client relations. Individuals from Umbanda congregations seek out Caboclo or Preto Velho spirits of their choice, from whom they ask favors, and to whom in return they pay ritual homage and bring prestige. The numbers of clients waiting to consult with particular spirits and the consequent size of the spirits' clienteles are important marks of their status. Furthermore, clients seek out specific spirits, with whom they frequently establish long term relations, even following the spirit consultant to another centro if the medium who receives this spirit should make such a change. Mediums in the ritual corps, on the other hand, have a dominant patron spirit among those they receive, although the chief spirit received by the chefe of the centro, with whom the members of the ritual corps have their consultas, is a more powerful patron. This spirit is often referred to as well as the patron spirit of the centro.

The dual Catholic–African divinities described above are, as in folk Catholicism, in turn still more powerful but more distant patrons in a heavenly patronage hierarchy. Umbandistas petition them and pay them homage, but deal more directly with their subordinates, the Caboclos and Pretos Velhos, whose availability and willingness to serve humankind is demonstrated by their appearance in Umbanda centros.

In the centros themselves, other aspects of patronage relations may be found. Centros are generally composed of small groups organized around the dominating figure of the chefe, and their activities are directed toward providing solutions, both spiritual and material, to the problems of their members. Chefes are the chief source of spiritual aid, and, as mentioned above, they act as the focal points for the redistribution of the resources available in the centros to those who seek them. Chefes may thus be seen in patronage roles as the leaders of clienteles, providing aid and favors to their supporters who reciprocate with respect, homage, and loyal support in the form of regular participation and capable performances of their ritual duties. These, in turn, enhance the reputation of the centros and attract larger clienteles, generating prestige which ultimately devolves upon the chefe.

The internal exchanges within these clienteles favor the redistribution of secular resources and favors from wealthier to less wealthy members. This is particularly evident in the wealthy, multiclass centros, and I even encountered several instances of patron–client relationships which had developed between chefes and poor members of the ritual corps. Such chefes also frequently arrange employment, loans, and living accommodations or hospitalization for poorer members of their clienteles. Other versions of this material redistribution also occur even in very poor centros, where wealthy clients show their gratitude for the spiritual help received by financial donations to the centro. Chefes in poorer centros may join an Umbanda federation which offers legal aid or medical services to the clienteles of its member centros, or they may gain access to favors through forming alliances with politicians. These latter activities link individual centros into wider patronage networks and into the formal political process.

The prestige and influence which chefes gain through these redistributive activities often extend outside their centros. Depending on their location and the degree of neighborhood participation in their centros, chefes may gain influence as local community leaders, or may even become famous enough in the city to become the subjects of lengthy illustrated articles in major weekly magazines. In the area of urban politics, Umbanda chefes and their clienteles are a source of special interest to politicians striving to establish personal relationships with the voters as a means of securing political support. Politicians visit Umbanda centros especially at election time, hoping to make brief appeals during the public rituals as defenders of Umbanda, and, if possible, to engage the chefes as *cabos eleitorais* (local ward heelers). In this capacity, chefes attempt to influence their members' voting behavior in return for favors to themselves and to needy members of their clienteles. Chefes react variably to these offers, but I met many who had served or were serving as cabos eleitorais, and several elected politicians in Rio and other Brazilian cities are known to be heavily supported by Umbanda voters. Some Umbanda chefes have attempted to utilize their clienteles as *trampolins* (launching pads) for their own political careers, and although unsuccessful at this local level, they have been successfully elected by extending their patronage connections through leadership in Umbanda federations and through participation in Umbanda radio programs. Thus, Umbanda centros participate in and extend the possible arenas for the vertical exchange of goods and services within Brazilian society, with material goods and services moving downwards in return for homage, loyalty, prestige, and political support.

Active participation in such secular patronage exchanges tends to point up the dependence of the lower class on the resources and contacts of the middle class, and may involve only a minority of Umbandistas. However, the idioms of patronage and personal dependence which are stressed in Umbanda ritual and ideology reach all Umbandistas, since they are the modes through which spiritual aid is obtained and exchanged. It is important in this context that Umbanda is an indigenous Brazilian religion. Some of its middle-class leaders have been overtly interested in politics and appear to have a vision of the political viability of a religion which draws heavily upon symbols and ritual practices which already have wide appeal within the lower classes (see Brown 1977). Their reworking of these elements within a more sedate and intellectualized setting, and their efforts at publicizing this image of Umbanda have made it more respectable and legitimate for members of the middle classes.

But this alone does not explain the fact that today large and increasing numbers of individuals from the middle class continue to seek out Umbanda for help and choose to contribute their own time and resources within Umbanda centros. The great majority of these participants have no such political interests in Umbanda. Their participation would seem to argue that the sense of dependence and the need for patronage which are emphasized in Umbanda are meaningful and attractive to a significant number of solidly middle-class Brazilians. This interpretation seems problematic if the Brazilian middle class is conceived according to the Euro-American three-class model as stable and autonomous in the socioeconomic and political spheres. Yet if it is viewed as relatively powerless, non-cohesive, and lacking in autonomy, the attraction of its members to a religion such as Umbanda may be seen as emerging from the desire to symbolically represent and respond to this sense of powerlessness and dependence.

It is suggestive that the occupational sectors most often represented among Umbandistas—middle management, small commerce and civil service among the middle class, and among the lower class the self-employed and those employed in small shops—are among the sectors where patronage remains most significant. There appear to be relatively few workers from industry and especially from large industry, a sector where patronage might be expected to be less strong. It might be hypothesized that Umbanda's appeal will continue to be greatest in occupational sectors where patronage ties remain most important. If this is true, it would provide a suggestive basis for contrast between Umbanda and another recently popular religion, Pentecostal Protestantism which, unlike Umbanda, appears to place a greater emphasis on horizontal ties and rational bureaucratic organization (Fry and Howe 1975). These two authors have suggested that preferences for one or the other of these religions by individuals of similar socio-economic backgrounds may be based on differences in their life experiences.

The continuing sense of dependency and the importance of patronage ties within sectors of the middle class may provide some basis for understanding middle-class participation in Umbanda. But it does not explain why status conscious middle-class individuals choose to participate together with members of the lower class in a lower status religion. It is hard, for example, to imagine comparable members of the American or Western European urban middle class participating together with individuals from the lower class in a religion whose ritual and ideology have a lower-class image. At least at present, the degree of ideological and social cohesion within the middle class, and the strength of the class boundaries between middle and lower classes in these countries would seem to militate strongly against such participation.

In Brazil, however, if we accept the bi-modal model, the middle class is not viewed as being cohesive, nor as behaving economically or politically as a class. Thus, while the status boundaries between the middle and lower classes may be very strong in Brazil, the boundaries between their economic and political modes of action are less well-defined, and in fact may be no stronger, or less strong, than such boundaries between different sectors within the middle class. In other words, status boundaries are not necessarily reinforced by clear differences in spheres of economic and political behavior. It might then be argued that a phenomenon which has occurred frequently in the Brazilian political process, the formation of coalitions which are vertically rather than horizontally or class oriented, is occurring as well in the area of religion. Such coalitions do not imply the unity of all of the political or economic interests among the groups involved, but rather their perception of a common interest in achieving a single specific goal. Umbanda might then be considered as a religious coalition, not one formed within the general boundaries of social class, but within vertical sectors of the population whose perceptions of a common position and common interests coincide and find expression in one aspect of their lives—their participation in religious activities. The goal in this case is that of obtaining and dispensing spiritual and material aid.

If Umbanda is thought of in this manner, then certain areas of Umbanda ideology and symbolism take on a new meaning. The idioms of dependence and patronage appear as features shared by individuals of different social classes who, through Umbanda, experience both the dominant and subordinate aspects of patronage. They participate either directly (if they receive high-ranking spirits) or indirectly, as observers, in the roles of patrons, and all enact dependency roles as clients.

Umbanda's nationalistic emphasis takes on new significance as well. Umbanda provides symbols of Brazilian identity which transcend class differences, possessing potential appeal to both middle and lower classes, although they may be experienced differently by these two groups. The nationalist potentialities represented in Umbanda are very similar to those often utilized in Brazilian politics, where nationalism is a central ideological issue and is often used deliberately for its ability to appeal to voters across class boundaries.

Furthermore, Umbanda ritual and ideology emphasize a hierarchical system based on access to supernatural rather than to secular sources of power, and this acts to downplay the importance of class differences among participants. In fact, Umbanda ritual activities commonly produce inversions of secular social status, thus obscuring, neutralizing and even denying the secular hierarchy of social classes. In its emphasis on aspects of ideology which operate across class boundaries and deny the significance of class differences, Umbanda ritual and ideology appear to provide an ideal model of a vertically oriented sectoral coalition of a type which has often characterized populist politics. As Weffort notes: "populism as a social and political fact acts to mystify the differences between class and ideology . . . it manifests itself always as a mass phenomenon, or as a personal relation between a leader and an agglomerate of individuals." (1965:41)

Umbanda, in other words, is an indigenous Brazilian religious movement which appears to have taken its form from Brazilian politics and indigenous structural and ideological features of Brazilian life.[13] It would appear to demonstrate a potential of indigenous religious movements discussed by Peter Worsley (1957) in another context: that of overriding important secular social boundaries between groups and drawing their members into common participation in a religious context. However, unlike the Melanesian situation discussed by Worsley, the groups are in this case composed of different social strata.


## Notes

1. Bastide (1951b, 1960) and Camargo (1961a; 1961b) had already recognized the participation of the middle classes in what were considered to be "higher" forms of Spiritism, and had noted as well marginal "lower middle class" participation in Umbanda.

2. From this point I will restrict myself to a discussion of middle-class participants in Umbanda. Although I have some fragmentary evidence of "upper-class" women who may participate, it has not yet been verified, and presents an area for further investigation.

3. Unfortunately, due to the frequency of social denial of participation and dual religious participation, and to the use of written questionnaires as a method for taking this census, the figures which result are totally inadequate as a measure of Umbanda's popularity. The 1972 census, for example, listed only 303,000 Umbandistas nationally.

4. The chefe may also be known by the terms familiar in many regional Afro-Brazilian cults as *mãe* or *pai de santo* (mother or father in sainthood) and the mediums as *filhas* or *filhos de santo* (daughters or sons in sainthood).

5. This includes as well those with illnesses, the great majority of whom have either previously consulted with doctors or are presently doing so.

6. Another category of spirits, the Exús, who also give consultas in some Umbanda centros, should perhaps be included here. However, these ambiguous spirits, who work either for evil or for good ends, depending on the payment, are considered here as being less central to Umbanda than the Caboclos and Pretos Velhos.

7. The works of Allan Kardec, the name under which the founder wrote, were translated into Portuguese during the nineteenth century and continue to be very popular sellers.

8. This term in Brazil refers generally to people who have dark skin and African facial and hair characteristics rather than, as in the United States, to all African-descended non-whites. Although color categories are not a determinant of social class in Brazil, there is a very high correlation between darkness of skin and low social position (see Wagley 1952; Fernandes 1969).

9. It should be noted, however, that mulatos and pretos of the middle class do participate in Umbanda, not, as previously thought, abandoning this symbol of lower class African culture, as suggested by Hutchinson (1957) and Pierson (1942).

10. No even minimally adequate listing of Umbanda centros existed, nor could I sample a particular neighborhood, since outside of the centros themselves many people denied participating in Umbanda.

11. It should be noted that both of these authors consider this to be the only significant class boundary in Brazilian society.

12. Fishlow (1972), for example, shows that inequalities in income distribution for the period 1960–1970 increased rather than declined. The classic study by Hutchinson (1960) on social mobility is still considered relevant for the present Brazilian situation.

13. In retrospect, with populist politics and patronage now in apparent decline in Brazil, it is interesting to speculate as to whether Umbanda, too, will wane, or whether the idiom of dependence which pervades it may find another and equally significant reference point in the dependence of both individuals and sectoral interests on an increasingly powerful state.

*This paper demonstrates Umbanda's wide appeal and argues that simple categories of social class and religion must be dropped.*

# FOURTEEN

# The Function of Middle-Class Extended Family Networks in Brazilian Urban Society

## Charlotte I. Miller

THE STUDY OF modern, industrial, and largely urban societies has challenged the anthropological tools of the past, at a time when the number of such societies and their proportion of the world's population is increasing. Contemporary Brazil represents the change from a largely agrarian, rural society to a largely industrial, urban society. As a result, it is an ideal setting for research by anthropologists on the phenomenon of urbanization and its impact on social structure.

Anthropologists of urbanization phenomena, whether in Brazil or in other societies, have struggled with attempts to define their units of study without losing the essentially humanistic, informant-oriented approach of the participant-observer community study method. Yet traditional concepts of community neighborhood and other territorially defined units are less relevant in the urban setting. Even the concept of social structure as a relatively fixed set of relationships between behavior and social institutions loses much of its heuristic value when applied to the analysis of large urban or metropolitan living patterns. Urban and metropolitan residents communicate and interact with many unrelated people, in groups or singly, in various locations frequently far from the urbanite's place of residence. In studying the impact of urbanization on social structure in Brazil, geographic mobility and ease of communication become very important factors, even when researching kinship patterns and family relationships which occur within the residential unit.

The idea that a particular kinship relationship involves a particular interaction pattern does not hold true for all cases of urban kinship relations; all relatives of the same degree do not receive the same treatment. As a result, doubts have been raised about the usefulness of traditional modes of kinship analysis in such societies. As Talcott Parsons points out, the relatively static concept of "corporate kin group," exemplified by the lineage or clan, as "firmly structured units of the social system" does not give much insight into family life and kinship patterns in complex societies (1971:120). On the other hand, the equally static concept of "isolated nuclear family," an ideal type which Parsons hoped would give more insight into kinship patterns in complex societies, has been found to ignore certain important links among wider kin groups, as indicated by the research of Litwak, Bott, and others (Litwak 1960; Bott 1957). In order to study how individuals actually behave with their kin, anthropologists have turned to the concept of personal kinship network, which traces for each ego all of the perceived ties he or she has with kin. This network sometimes excludes kin who are as closely related to ego as those who are included.

The personal network concept is very useful in the study of urban family and kinship ties, especially in Brazil, where the word for family, *família*, is not exclusively used for the co-resident household of husband, wife, and children. It may also refer to a person's sibling group, one's family of orientation, especially in contrast to one's affines, one's whole extended family or some part of it, or a woman's husband and children. Males, in fact, never refer to their wives and children, that is, their family of procreation, as their família, preferring to call them "woman and children" (*mulher e filhos*).

Another term which exists in Brazilian Portuguese, *parentela*, refers to all of one's relatives, much like the English term *kindred*. Although this term is not widely used, parentela refers to an ego-focused set of living kinspeople, which may, but does not always, include affinal and fictive kin as well as consanguineal kin. It includes only consanguineal kin who are known and who have established a relationship with ego or who have had a relationship established for them. In other words, the parentela may be seen as a network of people with whom ego has actual or potential interactions. This perception corresponds closely with Hubbell's definition of personal kinship network (1973:2).

In urban Brazil, as in most societies, whether simple or complex, the socialization of infants and young children is under the control of parents and other closely related kin. Due to the increasing social mobility and achievement orientation which is occurring in Brazil, the moral, economic and emotional support of the kinship group is extremely important to many members of the middle class. No public or private agencies, associations or institutions in any complex society have been able successfully to supplant the humane, personalized, and sensitive treatment of family and kinship.

In Brazil, the sector of the social structure which includes agencies, secondary associations, institutions, and bureaucracies is enormous, growing in importance due to the specialization of functions and diversity of economic opportunity associated with Western capitalism. However, in comparison with parallel United States institutions, certain functions have not been significantly bureaucratized and institutionalized in Brazil, including child care, information sharing, and employment referral. At the same time, the functioning of many Brazilian agencies is permeated with kinship links. Often those agencies and institutions which do exist have become conduits for kinship networks in providing services which are the province of voluntary associations in the United States and Western Europe.

Some social scientists have argued that the importance of kinship in modern Brazil derives from urbanization prior to industrialization, i.e., from a pre-industrial stable, two-class system of "haves" and "have-nots." Brazil is today in the process of becoming an industrial society, with the accompanying growth of an important middle sector (Rios 1964:39). The major cities already show the increased complexity and diversity brought about by increase in real income, growing ease of communications and transportation, specialization of labor (with large growth in industrial, white collar, bureaucratic, and commercial sectors) and social secularization. It is important to note, however, that the bureaucracies, agencies, and associations in urban Brazil have not kept pace with industrialization, and that they themselves tend to play a more limited role in influencing and controlling individual attitudes and behavior than do the kinship networks. In fact, familial networks are constantly taking on new urban functions in Brazilian cities, especially among the members of the middle and upper classes.

The metropolitan area of Belo Horizonte, the capital of the state of Minas Gerais, is an excellent site for the study of the relationship between urbanization, social structure, and family. Not only is Belo Horizonte the center of a recently urbanized metropolitan area, but it also is located in a region of Brazil which is reputed to have a strong historical tradition of familialism in the heritage of its rural people (Wagley 1971:47). In the twenty years between 1950 and 1970, the population of the city has quadrupled; current estimates place it at 1.5 million. Originally an administrative and commercial center for the state, Belo Horizonte is now a center for iron, steel, mineral extraction and processing, petroleum, textile, and construction, as well as a host of light industries which provide food, drink, furnishings, clothing, and other consumer goods for the constantly growing population of the region. Civil service and utilities have expanded needs for white collar and professional workers, and the liberal professions have increased to service the larger population.

In Belo Horizonte, there is an identifiable strata which can be called a middle class, based on the criteria of income level, occupational prestige, educational level, life style, and attitudes. The level of income of members of this class allows them to have domestic servants (housekeepers, maids, laundresses, and nurses for children) as well as such technological amenities as automobiles, televisions, and telephones, all accoutrements of "modern" life beyond the reach of the lower classes. Both men and women tend to want satisfying and interesting careers which have relatively high pay. They value being close to the members of their families and the places in which they grew up, and they view the city as being a better, more healthful place than the *interior*.[1] They view themselves as being self-initiating in career choices, but they know and depend on the personal evaluation of administrators (often through family members) to help them succeed in their professional lives, rather than on stringent rules or bureaucratic edicts. In their personal lives, their attitudes toward marriage reflect change from traditional Brazilian patterns. Marriage is deferred until after education, and employment is secured for both men and women. Many hold egalitarian sex-role ideals, usually members of households where women contribute substantially to the income. Younger women feel free to have non-domestic roles. The attitude that marriage should not deny a woman a career, but that the career should be balanced with the woman's primary responsibilities of running the home is common, especially among women themselves. At the same time, the idea that a woman should commit herself to full-time child rearing, consumerism, and domestic duties is quickly becoming obsolete. Furthermore, the notion that the woman should always accede to her husband's demands has given way to the concept of "give and take" and mutual understanding in marriage.

Attitudes on childrearing approximate Herbert Gans's model, developed for working-class Italian Americans, of the adult-directed pattern (Gans 1962:54).[2] The parents see themselves as under the obligation to provide healthful and beneficial living conditions for their children, but unlike members of the U.S. middle class, they do not center family decision-making around considerations of what is best for children at the expense of what is perceived to be best for the adults. They come closer to the views of middle classes in other industrialized countries in the primacy attached to secondary and university education, seeing it as a prerequisite for satisfactory professional lives. Child rearing practices, therefore, are aimed at developing "good personal adjustment," providing play and enrichment opportunities for children (art, music and foreign language acquisition) and teaching them to make good choices which might affect their own and their family's futures. Children, for example, are strongly urged to avoid doing proscribed things "because it would dishonor the family." Learning that family members are key contacts for gaining and maintaining status in the society begins at a young age. Children receive guidance, attention, gifts, and punishment from various relatives. Childhood romances between cousins are common and are encouraged by adults, although cousin marriage is exceedingly rare in the urban setting, a change from the agrarian generation now in middle and old age.

Six large kinship networks or parentelas, studied in Belo Horizonte, exemplify the perceptions and problems of this middle strata. Three were developed around men and three around women, using the techniques of participant-observation, informal interviewing, and the collection of life histories.

## The Subjects

The six men and women were diverse in age, place of birth, and occupation. All were born in the state of Minas Gerais, and they ranged in age from 24 to 60. Of the three females, Sandra, 24; Edite, 35; and Conceição, 50, only one was born in Belo Horizonte (Edite). Sandra was born in a farm village near Belo Horizonte, and Conceição in a mining town. Conceição is the owner-principal of a private day school. Edite is a psychologist for a state agency. Sandra is a full-time housewife with a young baby. None of the three males, João, 32; Otávio, 60; Paulo, 45, were born in Belo Horizonte. João was born in a small farm service town, Otávio in a small resort city, and Paulo on a rural farm. João has lived in Belo Horizonte since childhood. Otávio and Paulo came to the metropolis upon marriage and have been resident for thirty-one and twenty years respectively. João is employed as a teaching supervisor of a large foreign language school, although he was trained as a lawyer. Otávio is a retired bank executive who works part time as a bureaucrat in a state agency. Paulo is a supervisory engineer for an electric power company. The spouses and fathers of most of the egos had occupations of similar prestige. These occupations included economist, state politician, civil engineer, accountant, judge, veterinarian, grocer, teacher, medical doctor, tax collector, librarian, social worker, and rancher.

## The Parentelas

All the egos were asked to list all their known kin, consanguineal, affinal, and fictive. They were also asked about these kinspeople's residence, occupation, age, terminology of address (kinship terminology, first name, surname, nickname) and any additional information or anecdotes about them which the informants cared to volunteer. Three categories of kin seemed to appear: 1) activated kin, those about whom ego had complete or almost complete information; 2) non-activated kin, those about whom ego had minimal information (but had means of getting more information, usually through a contact person); 3) dormant kin, those about whom ego had no information other than the fact that they existed and were related (having no means or desire of obtaining more information). Including just the activated and non-activated kin in the definition of parentela, the parentelas ranged in size from 125 to 263 members. Within the activated subgroup, each ego identified a smaller subgroup with whom he or she had at least weekly contact, numbering from 15 to 30 persons. In the six networks studied, these kinspeople with whom weekly contact was maintained included the following categories of relatives, in order of frequency: spouse, own children, mother, father, mother-in-law, father-in-law, parents' siblings and their spouses, grandparents, first cousins, spouse's siblings and their spouses, own siblings and their spouses, nieces and nephews. Fictive kinship ties rarely brought new members into the parentelas by the mechanism of godparenthood, *compadrio,* established at religious ceremonies such as baptism and marriage. Such fictive kin were usually taken from the consanguineal and affinal kin, rather than from outside the group. The baptismal godparents of ego's own children, when taken from the consanguineal or affinal kin group, were included in the activated group, as were ego's own baptismal godparents. But there were only two cases of this in the six parentelas studied.

In order to test whether this degree of frequency of contact between ego and various members of his or her activated kin subgroup was common among the middle strata, a questionnaire survey of 365 high-school seniors was administered:[3] 110 were found to be in the middle class, and another 119 were found to meet many of the criteria for membership in this class. This high number is indicative of the greater attendance of secondary educational facilities by the middle class, who probably constitute no more than 10 percent of the population of the city. Of the 110 middle-class students, 25 were found to be upper middle class in terms of higher levels of consumption, greater status of parental occupations, and higher prestige of residential zone. Of the upper middle class group, 80 percent stated that they had weekly contact with family members outside the nuclear family (defined for this age group as parents and siblings). Of the remainder within the middle-class group, 69 percent said that they had similar contacts.

In the in-depth study of the parentelas it was found that contacts on this level of frequency were usually in the areas of business arrangements, professional consultations, shared home life, patronage of services (other than professional services), exchange of information and gossip by telephone or by personal visits, family gatherings, and regular babysitting services. Most of this contact was selective, based on the nearness of the residence of the person and the affective and economic dependencies which had been built up over the years, rather than strictly on the kinship category, although such contact was less frequent with cousins than with other relatives.

Clear illustrations of this intense type of contact may be found in the typical daily activities of given individuals. Sandra, her husband, and baby live with her parents, her seven younger siblings, and her mother's sister. On a daily basis, due to a shared home life, she has intimate contact with these twelve alters. The home is above her father's grocery where various other kin members come to shop, since they get a discount from him. These kinspeople include two of her father's brothers, another sister of her mother and some of their children. Since Sandra's father is upwardly mobile, his middle-class status contrasts with that of many members of the parentela. Nevertheless, he maintains contacts by giving discounts and favors to his kin despite the fact that this behavior would seem to inhibit his mobility. Sandra explains that the relatives, although they pay less than others, are more reliable customers who honor their debts and bring a significant amount of business to the store. Sandra, one of her sisters, and her two brothers all help out in tending the store.

In the case of Edite, her home is residence for herself, her husband, and three daughters. It is next door to her husband's parents' home, which also houses her husband's younger brother and his wife of three years. Her husband's other brother and wife live across the street. Thus, on a daily basis, she has contact with ten alters based on a type of common residence. Edite visits her own parents on her way to work, since she picks up her father and drives him to work every day. In her parents' home, she also sees her own godmother (her mother's sister), who lives there, and often sees a cousin who lunches there. In addition, every Sunday, she and her husband go to visit his mother's sister, her husband, and their nine children, one of whom has an infant son who also resides there. Another example is the case of João who has an apartment for himself, his wife, and their 5-year-old daughter. They take their daughter to either João's parents' or his wife's parents' for child care daily. João said that it is essential that this child care be allotted to the two sets of grandparents with an even hand, or jealousy would arise. There are still two young brothers and

*The statistical, no attribute to values*

a young female cousin from the country living in João's parents' home. Every Saturday or Sunday, however, many of João's brothers and sisters and their spouses and children get together at the parental home for a family gathering. There are eight brothers and sisters living in their own homes, six of whom are married with one to four children, and two of whom are in religious orders. João's wife's parents also have the custom of weekend family reunions. As a result, the scheduling has to be carefully planned so the young couple does not hurt the feelings of one family or the other. João says that problems arise when an important celebration such as a birthday or the anniversary of one set of parents comes on a weekend, causing conflict with the schedules of the other. The other three parentelas have similarly intense weekly contact with a core of activated kin.

With regard to less frequent parentela contact, egos tend to cite first cousins and more distantly related cousins as well as genealogically closer relatives who live further way. These contacts often are for the purpose of obtaining aid in crisis situations such as illness, marital breakdown, or trouble with the law, as well as for the procurement of employment, personal favors, especially in facilitating bureaucratic functions, and attendance at ritual events such as weddings, wakes, and funerals. There is an expectation that if an individual visits a distant place where he or she knows kin of any degree, he or she will be obliged to visit those kin, or at least call them on the phone. Paulo, for example, said that when he goes to São Paulo on business there are a number of first and second cousins he would be expected to visit. This requires that he make his business trips lengthy enough to include family visiting. Since he cannot always do that, he often stays in a hotel and avoids his cousins because of the obligations involved. If he visits one whom he favors, this fact would get back to the others. Conceição, however, told of going to Rio de Janeiro and visiting various relatives without the pressure of time, and of finding the experience very enjoyable.

Another clear way to exemplify the extent of intra-parentela contact is to look at a typical week in the functioning of a network. On Monday morning, Edite gets up at seven A.M. to supervise the cook in preparing breakfast and to aid the children in getting ready for school. Her husband and children leave for work and school at eight A.M. She drives her children to school, stopping at her parents' house nearby to pick up her father to take him to work. While at her parents' house, she greets her mother and her unmarried aunt who is also her godmother and the godmother of her youngest child. After delivering her children to three separate schools and her father to his office, she does the grocery shopping and returns home to instruct the cook about preparing *almoço*, the noon meal. Her husband picks up the children after their four-hour school day and brings them home for almoço. He reports that his younger brother came to his office seeking information about a better paying job. Edite leaves for work, stopping briefly in the driveway to chat with her husband's mother about the latest news from her husband's sister in Porto Alegre. She drops her children off with her mother, greeting her cousin Jorge, a medical student who has almoço there every day.

These patterns repeat themselves on a daily basis throughout the week. Tuesday night is the youngest daughter's birthday party. There are approximately 75 guests, about half of whom are children who are entertained in the backyard by a magician hired for the occasion. The adults, almost all of whom are kin, remain in the sitting rooms, drinking, talking, eating, and smoking. Thursday, Edite's husband is asked by his mother to send some money to his sister who is having financial difficulties. Friday, Edite is asked by her mother-in-law to talk to her younger son and his wife who live at home about their family responsibilities. Her mother-in-law frequently does this because Edite is a psychologist, and her advice is respected by other members of the family. Saturday, Edite, her husband and the three children go to their club where they see Edite's brother, his wife, and their three children, as well as several cousins. They spend all their time at the club with these kin. Sunday, Edite and her husband visit his mother's sister (leaving the children with his mother). This aunt has always served as seamstress to the family, making dresses for special occasions. Edite says that the family always uses her services because her pension is small.

As can be seen from this review of a week's activities, the variety of intra-parentela contacts are great. Edite's and her husband's families serve many important functions in their lives, and they are well aware of this significance.

In Brazil, then, kinship obligations are not rejected in urban settings, especially by the middle classes. Such ties are not seen as burdensome, time-consuming, and expensive luxuries; they are not perceived as standing in the way of personal advancement and monetary gain. In Belo Horizonte, associations and agencies devoted to child care are few and poorly administered. The institution of babysitting for wages is unknown. Formal procedures and requirements for obtaining credit are extremely complicated and aimed at barring as many as possible from access to it. Hotels are expensive, especially when compared with the real income of most middle-class members. Rental housing is difficult to find and quite expensive. Rules against nepotism in employment rarely exist and are usually ignored if they do. The administration of justice is notorious; penal institutions are stratified in terms of treatment of prisoners according to class. The number of hospitals and medical personnel is small in proportion to the needs of the population. As a result, facilities are strained, and hospital care is often of poor quality. Bureaucratic procedures such as getting a driver's license, licensing an automobile, obtaining a visa, renting a post office box, getting a marriage license, and many others are designed to be obstacles to the uneducated and the unsponsored.

The attitude that kinship obligations are burdensome was not consistently found among the parentelas studied. Paulo's case was not a rejection of all kin ties, but only of the relatively unproductive, spatially distant ones. The attitude of egos and alters interviewed was that the maintenance of kinship ties tends to be looked to for psychological, political, symbolic, and economic benefits. The egos and other members of the networks studied expressed the idea that the demands kin make can sometimes be annoying, but can also bring great prestige and potential power. The maintenance of non-activated kin ties means for many the assurance of potential sources of help. The elderly in Brazilian middle-class life usually do not experience the stinging effects of being considered useless as do so many elderly in the United States. The Brazilian elderly are regularly and dutifully visited by their children and grandchildren, nephews and nieces, and many other kinds of relatives who ask them for all kinds of advice and help: where to buy and how to finance a car, requests for letters of reference to real estate rental agencies, help getting a job, and so on. Many of these powerful elderly people are difficult to get along with, but the power they wield is formidable.

One retired colonel of the military police was an especially difficult individual who had opinions on every issue and listened only rarely to anyone else. When talking to Americans, he would expound on racism in the United States and the Brazilian "economic miracle.'' One of his grandchildren noticed that an American guest was not able to get away gracefully and diverted him to another subject. Later, his daughter-in-law laughed about how pompous he was and how he always managed to dominate those around him. But she quickly stated, in a very loyal fashion, that he had been very helpful in getting names of academicians and intellectuals (friends of the family) removed from military blacklists which had impeded their obtaining visas. He also had used his influence to get his daughter's husband out of jail in another state. She had respect for his power.

In many respects, middle-class Brazilians strive to achieve a level where they can be thought of as helpful and useful to their kin. One of the colonel's sons turned down a job which would have tripled his salary because it would have required him to move away from the family home and the helpful influence of his father.

Part of the reason for the great importance of kinship ties in Brazilian society today is the usual failure of its bureaucracies to work in rationally designed ways, but there is no doubt that they can work very efficiently for those who are related to the right people. Kinship networks, furthermore, function to create barriers to the mobility of members of lower strata, since their access to such networks is sharply limited by intra-class endogamy. Bureaucratic organizations work, but only for certain groups with "key contacts" within administrative structures. Kinship, in middle class families, provides these contacts. Among the Brazilian middle class, networks therefore, function as mutual aid associations,

*Charlotte Miller writes about the nurture of family then my nature of middle class. Isolates do not fall of our likes or values.*

## Notes

1. The interior here refers to smaller cities, towns, and villages as well as rural open country.

2. These attitudes and behavioral indicators and those which follow were obtained from life histories of men and women as they told their biographies in non-directed interviews in which they were simply asked to relate the story of their lives and how they felt about themselves.

3. Although the term high-school senior is not used in Brazil, it is used here to indicate students in their last year of *colégio*.

# PART IV

# Political Organization

POLITICAL ORGANIZATION IS only one component, albeit an important one, of social organization. Although it may be analyzed as a separate unit or series of units, it does not and cannot stand alone. It is inextricably linked to and enmeshed with religious traditions and institutions, education, economics, social status, and the underlying values of society itself.

The contributions in this section illustrate these relationships, and again reveal a series of functional equivalencies and even structural parallels crosscutting all of Brazilian society. In terms of tribal organization, Daniel Gross tells us that too little emphasis has been placed on the relative ecological homogeneity of the region within which Central Brazilian tribes have developed. This homogeneity helps explain why similar patterns of warfare, population growth, and colonial expansion can be found in the entire region. Age, not lineality, has customarily been the basic organizing principle, and formally has been put into operation through constituted age sets and communal initiations. Gross also finds that Central Brazilian tribes commonly have one or more sets of dual divisions or moieties. These traditionally have been based on name transmission or age class and have served as units within which reciprocal services have been performed, labor has been exchanged, or marriage has been regulated.

Although Central Brazilian societies are frequently spoken of as possessing "dual organization," for Gross the most important duality is the dichotomy between two basically seasonal forms of organization. He finds that Central Brazilian villages will expand, contract, or even move according to the season of the year. Thus there are such things as "rainy season moieties," and these customarily crosscut loyalties and affiliations based on other principles. Even the household, the unit generally looked upon as the basic unit of subsistence production and consumption, is divided several ways by ceremonial memberships and obligations.

Since age is an important organizing principle in Central Brazilian villages, the age set is a common structural arrangement. It is built around groups of boys or men of approximately uniform age ranges who are initiated jointly, and who often form corporate groups for warfare, house building, clearing and harvesting of gardens, and ceremonial management. The village, made up of a number of these age sets, is a fluid unit that can easily absorb additional members without major friction or disturbance.

While Central Brazilian Amerindian villages have often reached considerable size, this has always been a seasonal matter only, and probably reflects adaptation to warfare and resource fluctuation. In general, the villages of Central Brazilian Amerindians have remained politically autonomous and have been units in which centralized politics, social classes, craft specialization, and a priesthood have not developed. The crucial variable has probably been the fact that these villages are broken up year after year, only to be formed again, often with different constituents.

Although units such as these Central Brazilian villages are today fast disappearing, the type of rather loose affiliation they represent remains in many segments of Brazilian society. Shirley's discussion of law in rural Brazil documents, for example, how flexible handling of the country's legal structures can go hand in hand with complex reciprocities, both symmetrical and asymmetrical. Sidney Greenfield follows with a more global discussion of reciprocal exchanges, arguing that, through the patron–client relationship, the life of the local community is articulated quite adequately with the institutions of the larger society. In exchange for goods and services needed at the local level, votes and support flow up and out in an elaborate but functional symbiosis.

The classic strengths of anthropology are to look at the two ends of the human spectrum, i.e., to focus, on the one hand, on the details of the micro situation and, on the other hand, on the overview of the macro system. In Brazil, anthropologists have focused almost exclusively on the little community. They have, in the words of Forman and Riegelhaupt, authors of the final contribution to this section, looked at the country "from the bottom up." The patron-client tie has been a major concern. Yet this tie is merely one dimension of a complex system.

Although most patron–clientship has been studied at the local level, it does not germinate at that level. Rather, it derives from the nature of power in the nation as a whole and, more specifically, from the granting of land in autonomous economic and political units by Portuguese colonial governments. The power structure set into motion by this colonial situation allowed for only a modicum of competition, at times was blindly authoritarian, and nearly always was closed to entry by the peasantry. This is not to say that the peasant was not incorporated in any way into the political regime, however. At first he was involved as a dependent, then as a client, and today as a "self conscious and self interested member of the electorate" bypassing not only the patrons, but even the electoral machinery set up by those patrons.

Until the 1930s, Brazil was dominated by undifferentiated elites. However, with the Vargas regime, three new sectors appeared: an articulate urban middle class demanding electoral and political reform, a bourgeois industrialist group promoting economic nationalism, and an urban proletariat. These three have coalesced into a new and important political mass that has seriously disturbed traditional political relationships in the Brazilian countryside.

The first anthropologists to study contemporary Brazilian rural life carried out their work just as these three new sectors were emerging. Much of their concern over patron–client relationships would thus seem to stem from the fact that their work coincided with a national struggle between centralists and localists. What few of these anthropologists realized was that the forces they saw at work were but one point along a great historical continuum.

Forman and Riegelhaupt argue that anthropologists need to be less myopic in the future. They must be wary of "reading the past from the ethnographic present." In Brazil, peasants have seldom, if ever, been out of step with the national system. Micro-studies of such groups, the speciality of many anthropologists today, may be justified, but only if they are placed within the broader context of national and international power structures, i.e., within the framework of larger historical analysis.

In political structures, just as in social structure itself, there is a certain continuity in the Brazilian tradition that links tribal with contemporary and urban societies. Political power in Brazil has been and continues to be fluid, far more so than political power in Brazil's mother country, Portugal. Leaders come and go, loyalties wax and wane, traditional structures change and adapt. Patron-clientism exists, that cannot be denied, but it is far from being all encompassing or all explanatory.

Today, in Brazil, divergent forces are at work. The urban middle class, the new industrial elite, the urban proletariat, the rural peasant, and even the tribal Indian all have an impact on national policy. To neglect any would be to fail to understand the whole. And to force any into a static mold would be to betray the dynamism of the constantly emergent society.

# FIFTEEN

# A New Approach to Central Brazilian Social Organization

Daniel R. Gross

THE NATIVE PEOPLES of Central Brazil pose formidable problems to ethnologists.[1] These groups—predominantly Gê speakers[2]—once spent much of the year dispersed into small nomadic foraging units, subsisting on wild plants and animals. Yet their social organization appears to be more elaborate than that of the fully sedentary horticulturalists of the tropical forests of the Amazon basin. For all their social elaborateness, Central Brazilians are politically egalitarian. Like most hunter–gatherers they have no high chiefs, full-time religious or craft specialists, and no segment holds a monopoly over resources or the use of force. These societies, whose subsistence systems led ethnologists to classify them as "marginals" (Steward 1946; Wissler 1917; Cooper 1942) nevertheless boasted startlingly elaborate organizational structures.

In 1971 I conducted preliminary field research among the Western Gaviões (Timbira) funded by a grant from the Research Foundation of the City University of New York. I read an earlier version of this paper at the Annual Meeting of the American Anthropological Association in Mexico City, November 1974.

In developing the ideas in this paper, I received much helpful criticism from the following persons: Ellen Basso, Daniel Bates, Francis Conant, Gertrude Dole, Silêde Gross, Michael Harner, Marvin Harris, Jennifer Hunt, Conrad P. Kottak, Nancy Flowers, Susan Lees, David Maybury-Lewis, Júlio Cesar Melatti, Burton Pasternak, Madeline Ritter, Anthony Saeger, Judith Shapiro, Patricia Townsend, Dennis Werner, and George Zarur. I thank them all for their generous assistance but none of them should be held responsible for any of the shortcomings of this essay; indeed, several of them persist in disagreeing with me on various points.

**321**

This apparent paradox drew some Boasians to use Central Brazilians as an example of the non-correspondence of cultural complexity with subsistence techniques, thus defying evolutionary generalizations. Alfred Kroeber, for example, suggested that the organizational complexity of Central Brazilians was due to a propensity of some peoples to whimsically elaborate on their social structure, concluding, "many of these institutions are what I have called them—true luxury products. They serve some function, but it may be a minor one among major possible ends which are left unprovided for. A great deal of the total picture suggests the play of earnest children, or the inventive vagaries of fashion" (1952:224). Other ethnologists suggested that the Gê must be descended from some higher, more complex civilization which, perhaps, had class stratification (Lévi-Strauss 1944; Haeckel 1938; Zuidema 1969). But these explanations have not been supported with evidence and, fittingly, they have gained few adherents.

The myth of Central Brazilian "marginality" was not laid to rest until 1959 when Steward and Faron reclassified them as "Hunters and Gatherers Turned Farmers" (1959:369ff; see also Bamberger 1968), although they presented no evidence for a recent adoption of horticulture by these societies. All of Nimuendajú's richly detailed monographs on Central Brazil described developed horticultural practices, including the use of a cultivar ( Cissus sp.) unknown outside this region (Nimuendajú 1939, 1942, 1946:57–64). Students of Central Brazilian societies owe much to this passionately devoted German ethnographer who took an indigenous name and who spent his life in the defense of the natives against the "neo-Brazilians." Many of his numerous writings were translated into English by Robert Lowie; they are generally descriptive and reflect the bias of historical particularism.

Claude Lévi-Strauss did field work among the Bororo and Nambikwara, but much of his writing on Central Brazil is based on secondary sources. He suggested that "dual organization" in Central Brazil is a deceptive overlay which masks with egalitarian and reciprocal structures, social institutions which are actually complex and hierarchical. Among the Central Brazilians, Lévi-Strauss found evidence for the existence of fundamental oppositions in human thought, such as between nature and culture (1944, 1963).

More recently, a number of ethnologists have trained their attention on the Central Brazilian groups, under the supervision of David Maybury-Lewis of Harvard and Roberto Cardoso de Oliveira of the University of Brasília. A series of field studies was undertaken during the 1960s and new data are now available which correct and extend earlier accounts. They add to our knowledge of Central Brazilian kinship, marriage, social dynamics, naming, ceremonialism, etc. The authors of these studies tend to be revisionists with regard to Lévi-Strauss' structuralism. Maybury-Lewis (1965) seems to have knocked some major struts from under Lévi-Strauss' "discovery" of triadic, non-reciprocal structures among the Sherente. J. C. Crocker (1969) has reinterpreted the Bororo data and presents a picture of dynamic but equilibrated balance between reciprocal (egalitarian) and hierarchical aspects of Bororo social organization. As yet, little comparison has emerged in the work of this group, although a collective volume is in press (Maybury-Lewis 1979). Most of the studies emphasize the individual and particular characteristics of each society by trying to reduce the elements of social organization into a logical set of principles for each one. In short, their work seems aimed at explicating how each group functions within a well ramified structural functional framework, as opposed to explaining why they share so many characteristics in common, or what accounts for the differences among them.

Maybury-Lewis has written a very detailed study of the Shavante (1974) focusing mainly on social organization. In a brief section at the end of the book, he proposes an "ideal type model" of Shavante social structure, rooted in a dichotomy between two native concepts which is reflected in most aspects of social organization. The age-set system, however, fails to conform to the model. This exception is dealt with by declaring that the age-set system is, "in a sense, a subordinate institution" (1974:299). The author goes on to note some broad similarities among Central Brazilian groups, concluding that "these societies are not so much representatives of distinct types of social organization as variations on a single sociological theme" (1974:303). He points to differences in degree of factional strife and the presence or absence of institutionalized sex antagonism against a common background of uxorilocality:

The common element in all of these situations is the strain and ambiguity inherent in the male role. I would suggest that this role conflict is related to the valuing of bellicosity and the institutionalization of aggression, and that it is in this set of factors that an explanation of the high incidence of factionalism among the Shavante, Sherente, and Kayapó should be sought (1974:308–309).

This style of inquiry leads us to reflect long and deeply on the meaning of these various institutions among these societies. But to treat one aspect of social organization as "subordinate," while emphasizing another as central strikes one as arbitrary.[3] With such an approach, it is difficult for outsiders to assess the value of rival explanations of particular features of Central Brazilian culture. What are needed are public criteria which permit tests of particular hypotheses.

My orientation leads me to reopen the questions of why the Central Brazilians are so distinctive as a group, how their unique institutions may have evolved, and what factors may have selected for them, in an evolutionary sense. I shall look for answers to these problems in the influence of the natural habitat, warfare patterns, population pressure, and colonial expansion. It is remarkable how little of the research so far done on Central Brazilians emphasizes the relative ecological homogeneity of the region within which they occur (an exception is E. Becker 1965).

There is a close correspondence between the distribution of most Central Brazilian societies and the limits of a floristic province covering much of Brazil's central plateau known as *cerrado* (Eiten 1972).[4] The cerrado takes a number of forms, ranging from relatively open grasslands to high canopy forest, but taken as a whole it is distinctive from and intermediate between other well-known floristic provinces of Brazil: the mesophytic evergreen forest (*mata*) of the Amazon valley and the thorny *caatingas* of the interior northeast. The cerrado is not a savanna since it invariably occurs on well-drained soils. Nor does it represent an early or arrested stage of succession in a tropical forest series but rather has its own distinctive climax forms. It occurs in zones with tropical temperatures and rainfall ranging from 800mm to 2,000mm annually, but where there is a prolonged and severe dry season. In addition, cerrados occur on deep, well-drained soils derived from very old parent material, which are very low in nutrients, low in humus, acidic, and possessing a low but permanent water table. Cerrado vegetation is semi-deciduous, generally perennial and tends to assume tortuous shapes in contrast to the long straight trunks of trees in the mesophytic forest. Little has been written about the fauna of the cerrados, but it appears that many of the same species found in the Amazon valley are present, although perhaps in different numbers and with different habits owing to the lack of cover and different vegetation. The cerrado is interlaced by narrow bands of gallery forest, or mesophytic forest, close to watercourses and on valley floors where soil nutrients and moisture permit (Eiten 1972). The cerrados offer natural forage to cattle, but only the gallery forests can be effectively planted in food crops without mechanized cultivation and fertilization.[5]

Among the groups occupying the Central Plateau of Brazil south of the Amazon are the following: (Gê speakers) Timbira (including Krahó, Pukobyé, Ramkókamekra Apânyekra, Krĩkati, Western Gaviões), Apinayé, Kayapó (including Gorotire, Xikrin, Kubenkankren, Txukarramãe, Mekrãnhoti et al.), Suyá, Kreen-Akrore, Erigbatsa, Sherente and Shavante; (probable Gê speakers) Nambikwara, Karajá, Bororo; (Tupians) Mundurucú and Tapirapé. These groups share many of the following characteristics:

1. scheduling of activities (cf. Flannery 1968) and residence according to season; nomadic hunting and gathering part of the year in the cerrados and horticulture in fixed riverine villages for the remainder of the year;
2. circular or semi-circular plans in village gathering;
3. uxorilocal extended family households;
4. elaborate ceremonial and sport activities, pitting part of the village against the other;
5. stress on age as an organizing principle, often with formally constituted age sets, communal initiations, etc.,
6. one or more sets of dual divisions or moieties based on name transmission, age class, or other criteria which function to stage ceremonies, perform reciprocal services, cooperate in labor, or regulate marriage;
7. the proliferation of special societies recruited by name transmission or other criteria with primarily ceremonial responsibilities;
8. institutionalized sex antagonism; and
9. relatively large villages in comparison to other tropical lowland societies in the Amazon basin.

In the next section, I shall describe what appear to me to be the principal problems of Central Brazilian ethnology from an ecological perspective. Following that, I propose a model of Central Brazilian adaptation which I believe helps to explain some of the similarities and differences described above.

## The Problems Presented by the Central Brazilians

The major problem of Central Brazilian ethnology is to account for the extraordinary degree of organizational complexity among them. The distinctiveness of Central Brazilians is seen most clearly when they are compared with most ethnographically known societies of the tropical rain forest in the Amazon and Orinoco basins. The latter groups generally live in smaller villages, depend more heavily on horticulture, are more sedentary (cf. Carneiro 1968), and exhibit less richness and elaborateness of social structure than Central Brazilian societies. Many of the tropical rain forest groups inhabit *malocas* (or large communal dwellings). When the village splits up, it usually is the result of a more or less permanent rift. They lack the degree and frequency of ceremonialism, sporting events, sex antagonism, and age organization common in Central Brazil.

While generally more elaborate than Amazonian groups, the Central Brazilians vary amongst themselves in degree of elaborateness. For example, while all of the Central Brazilian societies have formally constituted age sets and some kind of formal friendship between individuals, several of them lack the non-descent "moieties" which are a much referred to feature of these groups. Another kind of difference is more qualitative, e.g., where age sets carry out the functions in one society which are played by men's societies in another. There would appear to be a continuum among Central Brazilian groups in regard to degree of elaboration. It is important to determine whether this variation may be scaled consistently along a single dimension, and if so to find the source of this variation.

The second major problem in Central Brazilian ethnology is the unusually large size reported for village aggregates. Among the Gê, for example, the following observations have been reported:

Kreyé village (no date): 400 to 500 inhabitants (Nimuendajú 1946:16).
Pukobyé villages (1858): 100, 800 inhabitants and two of 600 inhabitants each (Nimuendajú 1946:18).
Pokekamekra village (1814): 400 to 500 adults (Nimuendajú 1946:7).
Apinayé villages (1822–1840): 1,000, 1,300, 500, 1,400 (Nimuendajú 1939:7).
Bororo village (1888): 350 (formerly up to 1,000) (Steinen 1894, cited in Lowie 1946b:419).

How were such large villages supported? How long could such large agglomerations remain in one place? What were their sources of calories and protein and how reliable were they? A number of studies concerning lowland tropical South American societies have suggested that agricultural productivity and protein availability placed relatively low ceilings on the maximum size of tribal villages (Meggers 1954; Lathrap 1968; Gross 1975; but see Carneiro 1961, 1968).

The unusually large size of Central Brazilian villages also poses interesting sociological problems. Many students of South America have observed that, in the lowlands, large communities, lacking centralized political controls, tend to be unstable and are likely to fission as a result of feuding and/or adultery (Carneiro 1961, n.d.; Chagnon 1968b). If we assume this as a baseline of egalitarian, lowland villages in South America, i.e., as the usual condition, then we must ask what were the selective pressures which favored larger villages and what were the mechanisms which counteracted any centripetal tendencies in these villages. Finally, were the larger aggregates as durable or as fixed in composition as smaller groups?

## A Model of Central Brazilian Adaptation

The following is a model of the seasonal cycle and cultural adaptation of several Central Brazilian societies which yields testable hypotheses and at least partially answers the questions posed in the last section. The model relates organizational complexity and multiple cross-cutting associations to relatively extreme seasonal pulsations, fluctuation in village composition, competition, and warfare.

During much of the year, Central Brazilians used to split up into relatively small, highly mobile foraging groups to exploit the wild food resources of the *cerrados*. These groups, composed of clusters of households, made successive camps together, generally remained independent of other foraging groups, and returned only occasionally to the base village. During these periods, lasting from weeks to months, the foraging groups may have felt vulnerable to attack because of their small size; they scanned the horizon for smoke from unfriendly fires and generally avoided contact with strange groups

(Maybury-Lewis 1974:53–59). As the harvest season approached, each group began to move towards the village site where gardens had been planted months earlier, sending scouts ahead, perhaps to determine whether the crops were ripe (Nimuendajú 1939) or to determine whether hostile groups had occupied the site in their absence. Most groups have partly or completely abandoned trekking, but some, more distant from the leading edges of the expanding Brazilian frontier, continue the practice, e.g., the Mekrãnhoti.

Cultivation is restricted to the rainy season and can be practiced only in the limited area of gallery forests along major streams where the soil is moist and fertile enough to be tilled by hand. The size of the population and the duration of village life were limited by the production of the gardens. Most central Brazilian societies extended the clearings each year, leaving their second- or third-year swiddens to be reclaimed by forest. Thus, a single village must have much more land at its disposal than it requires for cultivation in any given year (Carneiro 1961). This need is accentuated by the narrowness of the gallery forest; thus cerrado dwellers are even more likely than people of the tropical forests to move their villages to be closer to garden sites.

There was considerable variation in degree of dependence upon horticulture for subsistence among the central Brazilian groups, ranging from relatively low for the Nambikwara and Shavante, to very high for the contemporary Canela (Timbira). There is also variation in the crop mix with greater dependence on bitter manioc varieties among the more highly sedentarized groups like the Canela.

During the period of sedentary residence, ceremonials take place, sports activities—particularly log races—are held, and there is frequent dancing at dusk, at sun-up, or both. Several authors report that no sooner has one ceremonial been staged than preparations for another begins, although there apparently is no fixed annual cycle of ceremonials for most groups.

Several ethnographers have reported that Central Brazilians represent their social structure by reference to the village circle. The residential houses, forming the rim, are generally fairly large (averaging perhaps 50m$^2$), lodging an extended uxorilocal family group. Nowadays they are of rectangular post-and-lintel, thatch-covered construction, but formerly they were smaller in a round, beehive shape. The ring of houses is the domestic sphere where such activities as cooking, eating, child care, and most sleeping occur. The center of the village is likely to be a public or ceremonial plaza, scene of dancing, oratory, and a meeting place for men (Da Matta 1973). The ideal village plans of informants include locations for moieties or other divisions, men's societies, age classes, and often a structure designated as the men's house (bachelor's hut or flute house). There may be regularity in the location of each extended family group on the village periphery (Nimuendajú 1946:37–38, 40; J. C. Crocker 1969:46; Maybury-Lewis 1974:172), relating to ceremonial organization.

This arrangement permits each household, the smallest indivisible unit of economic function, to take a co-equal place in village life. Each such unit is equidistant from the center or public sphere. Additional arrivals can be accommodated by fitting them into the circle or even by forming a second concentric ring of houses (Lévi-Strauss 1963:138).

The utilization of different habitats during periods of maximum resource availability in each is the key to understanding the scheduled dispersal of Central Brazilians. Partial dependence on horticulture enabled a much larger population to exist than one which depended on hunting and gathering alone. Many Central Brazilian groups are apparently descended from groups which had a considerably higher commitment to foraging in the past than recently. It seems possible that a gradual evolutionary change was taking place from precontact times to the recent past in which groups expanded into the mixed niches which they occupied until very recently. Other pressures may have induced these groups to depend more heavily upon horticulture and thus to sedentarize more fully than before.

Autonomous foraging groups could have established their gardens in isolated locations along a given stream, thereby founding numerous "strip" settlements. But this apparently did not occur in Central Brazil. Instead, each year, several foraging groups joined and formed a single nucleated settlement, often quite large. It must be kept in mind that larger villages present organizational problems to people without rulers (Oberg 1955). Large settlement populations probably required higher subsistence effort and created greater potentiality for adultery, aggression and factional disputes. In view of these higher "costs," what plausible reasons could have existed for establishing such large villages?

The "model" described so far is based entirely upon selected but well documented facts of Central Brazilian life. What follows requires a departure to plausible speculation regarding the causes of certain institutions. I suggest that large size village aggregates are favored by warfare or unreliable resource fluctuation. High risk of attack by formidable enemies would favor formation of large settlements as a deterrent. Similarly, the risk of occasional crop failures or game fluctuations could favor the occasional formation of large aggregates in locations where resources have not failed in a given season. Either factor might also tend to select for aggregates whose composition is itself unstable. In other words, I suggest large village aggregates occurred under force of conditions which were, to some extent, peculiar to the cerrado region. An alternative hypothesis could be that the large aggregates were formed in order to carry out social and ceremonial activities too grandiose to realize in small, foraging bands. In other words, the ceremonialism becomes the cause.

The organizational complexity and ceremonials of Central Brazil are very costly in terms of human energy and depletion of natural resources. My argument assumes that people would not engage in such costly activities unless there were some substantial benefit vis-à-vis survival, but not that this benefit was necessarily perceived as such by the actors themselves. Even in the absence of this assumption, I believe my hypothesis valid, because little of the social elaborateness reported for village aggregates is present in the small foraging units, and ceremonialism appears to atrophy in villages which become severely depopulated (Wagley 1940; J. C. Lave, personal communication; D. Gross, field notes). Conversely, villages which are reconstituted of refugee groups may revive their ceremonial life (Nimuendajú 1939; Gross, field notes).

Little is known about the stability of resources upon which human populations depend in Central Brazil. Garden productivity is a primary factor in determining the permanance of villages. Central Brazil characteristically has a severe dry season of several months. The risk of a crop failure because of the delayed onset of rains would therefore appear to be higher than in the forests to the north where rainfall is more evenly distributed.[6] Localized crop failures might force affected villages to take refuge at another site where gardens were producing. The Sherente have a tradition of a great fast held to ward off droughts, and their oral history recalls periods of serious privations from drought (Nimuendajú 1942:93–94). The great fast is one of the principal occasions on which several villages aggregate into a larger unit (1942:10).

Warfare may also have played a substantial role in selecting for large villages due to the greatly increased threat of attack during the sedentary period because flight to avoid attack is an undesirable tactic which is related to the high investment in gardens, and villages situated along rivers are easy to locate, particularly by groups traveling by canoe along the river. It is noteworthy that most of the Central Brazilian groups made little or no use of riverine resources (the exceptions are the Bororo and the Karajá). For the most part they lacked water craft and fishing techniques. In this manner, Central Brazilians avoided competition with other groups which may have exploited riverine resources along the same rivers where the Central Brazilians farmed. It seems plausible that other societies dominated the rivers and river banks during much of the pre-contact and early contact period. These could have been intruders traveling seasonally upstream (southward) from the lower course of the Amazon where there lived densely populated, politically centralized groups (Meggers 1971:121–36). The alternative is to assume that the rich fisheries of the Xingú, Araguaia, and the Tocantins with their tributaries were simply left untapped by native peoples. Archaeological studies may some day provide partial evidence for seasonal fishing trips into Central Brazil by Amazonians, and for warfare with other societies relying on gallery forests for gardens. Elsewhere in lowland South America, warfare and the threat of attack favor the dispersal of groups into small villages (Chagnon 1968b; Carneiro 1964). But this option was not open to Central Brazilians since suitable garden land was available only along the highly exposed river banks. Thus large villages were formed as defense or deterrence against armed attacks. A similar observation has been made for comparable conditions in New Guinea in a recent study by P. Townsend (1974).

While the suggestion that Central Brazilians fought riverine intruders is conjectural; there is hard evidence that all Central Brazilian societies were heavily committed to warfare as a way of life. Every major ethnographic source about Central Brazil refers to some form of inter-tribal warfare, and most give details regarding the organization of warfare. As suggested below, age sets are particularly important in the mobilization of warriors, and ritual observances concerning killing have been described for several groups. It is difficult to determine the relative extent of intra- versus inter-tribal warfare since the political or linguistic boundaries between "tribes" are impossible to define. Nimuendajú describes many instances of hostilities between linguistically related and proximate Timbira groups in addition to struggles between Timbira groups and the Tupian Guajajara (Tenetehara) (1946:149ff). The only remaining question is whether Central Brazilian groups practice warfare or feuding within village aggregates. Again, the answer appears to be affirmative in most groups for which data are available. As one indicator of this, at least one segment of all the major Central Brazilian groups has been described as having split off from another village, not only among the factious Shavante (Maybury-Lewis 1974) and Kayapó (Banner 1953) but also the allegedly solidary Timbira (Gross field notes, Melatti 1972:8–9). There is, then, no lack of evidence about the existence of both internal and external warfare on a significant scale among all Central Brazilian societies.

Large, seasonal settlements thus may reflect adaptation to warfare and resource fluctuation. Unlike the large villages which formed permanently among the Amazon River, in the Antilles and elsewhere in the tropical lowlands, the Central Brazilian villages remained politically autonomous and did not develop centralized polities, social classes, craft specialization, a priesthood, etc. This was probably because the large aggregates were broken up year after year, only to be formed again, perhaps with different constituents. Centralized political controls did not emerge as they might have in fully sedentary settlements of comparable size and stable composition. Neither was kinship a sufficient organizing principle especially if the composition of village aggregates fluctuated frequently.

The annual aggregation of disparate, economically autonomous, kin-based social units into a larger but unstable village presented clear dangers. A way had to be found to avoid the explosive rivalries, potential violence, and schisms so common even in relatively small South American Indian villages. Elaborate village plans, cross-cutting moieties, social divisions, age sets, sporting events, frequent dances and ceremonials, and special ties between individuals may have served as cultural means for effectively integrating the semi-autonomous foraging units (and later refugee groups) into large unified village units. These mechanisms provided for the regulation of conflict among component units; the mobilization of warriors for defense and raiding; and the coordination of cooperative activities such as surround hunting, housebuilding and garden clearing. In addition, these social units could serve to equitably distribute food and other resources throughout the group; regulate marriage in a manner which maximizes intergroup cohesion and exchange; and institutionalize dyadic relationships which serve as channels for exchange of resources with groups in other areas.

Central Brazilian societies are frequently spoken of as possessing "dual organization." To me, the most fundamental dualism in these societies is the dichotomy between the two seasonal forms of organization. It is not that dualism is reflected symbolically in social structure, but rather that two sets of structures exist to deal with different problems at different times. Within the aggregated village, this dichotomy is expressed as a distinction between the constituent foraging units (household clusters based on kinship, forming irreducible units of economic cooperation) and "ceremonial corporations" which incorporate households and their members into a more encompassing organization (J. C. Crocker 1973:30). In the same paper, Crocker compares household exchanges among Central Brazilian groups:

The general tendency seems to be toward a pooling of resources within the household, coordination of division of labor among its members, and a stress on residential self-sufficiency. But along with this ecological autonomy there comes an emphasis on exchanges among separate households, often in multilayered ceremonial contexts. . . . the extensity of such exchanges varies from society to society. I estimated that during the dry season, the period of relative prosperity, the typical Bororo household consumed less than half of the food it itself has produced. . . . [A]ll the ethnographers in this region stress the economic, political and ritual importance of these inter-household transactions . . . in most cases the ceremonies which are the occasion for these prestations are associated with the particular type of public collectivity recognized by the society. (J. C. Crocker 1973:30)

Roberto Da Matta (1973:278–79) refers to the same dichotomy in more purely structural terms:

As with the other Northern Gê, the social universe of the Apinayé divides itself into two complementary antithetical areas: the domain of everyday relations, primarily concentrated in the nuclear and extended uxorilocal families, located in residential groups on the periphery of the village; and a ceremonial or public domain, institutionally expressed by ceremonial groups.

And in an intriguing paper, Anthony Seeger (1974) demonstrates how leadership is similarly dichotomized between ceremonial roles (leading songs and dances, etc.), and political roles (representing interests of particular extended family groups or factions, etc.) in a number of Gê-speaking societies, including the Suyá.

The integrative functions listed above may be fulfilled by a number of the complex social and ceremonial structures reported among Central Brazilian societies. Following are a few examples. It is difficult to exemplify a structure which minimizes or regulates conflict since, if it functions, conflict will not be visible. However, internal strife is found among some Central Brazilian groups, most notably the Shavante, Sherente, and the Kayapó (Maybury-Lewis 1974:305). Nevertheless, an adult male Canela (Timbira) might hesitate to initiate a conflict with another man because the latter would almost certainly be a member of his own "exogamous moiety," age set, Plaza Group, Men's Society, or Rainy-season "moiety" all of which have different, cross-cutting principles of recruitment. And it might be difficult to garner support in such a conflict because of the division of loyalties of other individuals, preventing the formation of conflict groups along territorial or kinship lines. Uxorilocal residence also serves to break up potential agnatic alignments among brothers and other agnates by sending them off to different households (cf. Ember and Ember 1971; Divale 1974). Even the household, generally the basic unit of subsistence production and consumption, is divided several ways by ceremonial memberships and obligations.

Age sets, which are practically universal for Central Brazilian males, are a prime example of this kind of structure. These are groupings of boys or men of approximately uniform age ranges who are initiated jointly, and who often form a corporate group who cooperate in warfare, house building, clearing, and harvesting of gardens, and always in ceremonial affairs. The age set cuts across any other kinship or locality principle and establishes a bond of solidarity among men who have endured a lengthy and sometimes arduous initiation together. In a recent cross-cultural study, Madeline Ritter

(1974) provided evidence that age sets function to integrate societies for the purpose of warfare when there is a pattern of seasonal aggregation and dispersal as in the case of Central Brazil. Age sets do not conflict with or replace descent groups but provide a potentially more encompassing principle of organization.

"Dual organization" and other non-kin based societies may also function in this context. Membership in one or another society or dual division often depends on an arbitrary principle, often a name bestowed by a relative or ritual kinsmen of ego's parents. Frequently the boys' names are bestowed by maternal uncles and girls' by paternal aunts (Nimuendajú 1946; Lave 1968; Bamberger 1974). Groups formed by name bestowal generally cross-cut kin- or locality-based groups (cf. Ortiz 1969:132–33). The arbitrariness of these principles is the key to their regulatory function. On the one hand, an abstract set of rules governs participation in social and ceremonial units which override principles based on a kinship metaphor. On the other, these systems permit manipulation such as the reassignment of individuals to specific ceremonial units whose numbers are depleted, thereby maintaining balance.

Garden produce and other food is distributed about the village through the social networks created by various rules. Among several Central Brazilian groups, for example, a married hunter is obliged to contribute game to both his wife's households and to sisters'/mother's household as well. Among the Timbira, young men are required on several occasions to present food gifts to members of the council, composed of older men who have "graduated" from the age-set system (Nimuendajú 1946). Finally, we must note numerous structures such as formal friendships which link individuals and which may serve to provide access to resources in another area or refuge from enemies when the necessity arises (Nimuendajú 1946:100ff). An informant among the Western Gaviões recalled his father's taking him to another village as a child and introducing him to a man, saying "This is my friend. If ever you need anything here, you can come to this house, for it is just like your house."

An especially important feature of Central Brazilian village organization is the capacity to absorb additional members into the village scheme, apparently without perturbing the general structure of the village. Louise Sweet suggested that a similar flexibility exists among Bedouin Camel pastoralists in an unreliably fluctuating environment (1965). There are a number of examples of this in Central Brazil. Maybury-Lewis states that any Shavante village "automatically grants asylum to refugees or seceders from other groups . . . no matter how unwelcome individuals or groups may be to the dominant lineage" (1974:205). Other groups have apparently incorporated outsiders into their ceremonial structure. For example, of the six Plaza Groups among the Timbira, five are named for animals, and a sixth is called by a term translated as "Alien Tribe (Nimuendajú 1946:77). Nimuendajú speculates that these Plaza Groups are derived from "clans formerly localized within the village" (1946:90). Among the Sherente, two clans, one in each patrimoiety, were said to be "alien tribes" added after the formation of the original four clans, "but even nowadays, these clans are not quite reckoned as peers" (Nimuendajú 1942:20). Lave (1968), Nimuendajú (1939), and Melatti (1972) report for the Krĩkati and Apinayé and Krahó respectively, that the villages they studied were composed of remnants of diverse groups apparently with no impairment of ceremonial structure. In my brief work with the Gaviões, I found that two groups, formerly separated by a wide distance, had been brought together on the same reservation by the National Indian Foundation (FUNAI). They soon began jointly to carry out ceremonial activities, log races, archery contests, etc.

Aggregation from diverse roots figures importantly in a Bororo origin myth paraphrased by J. C. Crocker:

Long ago . . . the ancestors of each clan lived in their own region very distant from the areas occupied by the progenitors of the other clans. They fought bitterly within each group and with each other on the few occasions they chanced to meet. Some informants treated these groups as separate tribes; characterizing them as speaking distinctive languages, practicing different and equally barbarous customs, and being no more than so many varieties of wild beast. . . . This chaos was ended and social order established through the deeds of two culture heroes . . . who instituted the village plan, the system of ritual prestations between the clans, the major ceremonials and the clans' ownership rights. Each tribe was transformed into an exogamous clan and related to other clans through a moiety system. (1969:50–51)

Crocker treats this tale as a charter for the Bororo village structure in which humans are brought from a state of nature to a state of culture through the civilizing influence of the culture heroes. I feel that it may be just as valid to treat this account as a partial history of actual events although I regard it as unlikely that two individuals were responsible for creating so many institutions by themselves. In my view, the Bororo may be depicting their origin as a society in terms of a concrete process which was repeated time and time again in Central Brazil among several different societies. The view of Crocker's Bororo informants is remarkably close to my own: the village plan serves to limit conflict and to regulate exchange.

## Recent Factors Favoring Organizational Ela ration

We are accustomed to considering acculturation as a process of accommodation to or adoption of foreign culture traits by one society in contact with another. In the case of the Central Brazilians, however, I think it is possible that many indigenous elements of culture have been intensified as a result of contact with Western culture. This form of acculturation is known to have occurred on the Great Plains of North America with the adoption of the horse and also on the Pacific Northwest Coast. It seems plausible to me that the most elaborate efflorescence of Central Brazilian culture occurred in the recent past and as part of an adaptive process responding to changes brought about by European and Brazilian invaders.

The nature of contact with Brazilian society varies considerably from one Central Brazilian society to another. The Shavante were in a virtual state of war with Brazilian intruders until about twenty years ago (Maybury-Lewis 1974), while the Canela (Timbira) have been in peaceful contact for over a century. Virtually all Central Brazilian groups were affected long before direct contact with Western culture, however, as a result of epidemics of introduced diseases. Some of the mechanisms by which direct and indirect contact with Westerners may have intensified Central Brazilian culture patterns are suggested below. There are a number of items which lend credibility to this hypothesis:

1) As suggested above, the large size of Central Brazilian villages may have been a response to the threat of attack from intruders traveling upstream from the Amazon. But these intruders may have been other Brazilians in the sixteenth to eighteenth centuries since the latter penetrated the interior largely via waterways.

2) The dislocations, wars, and epidemics brought by the arrival of Europeans in Brazil may have been a powerful spur to migrations,

placing greater population pressure on certain regions. Such pressure might well have favored intensification and expansion of horticulture. Two loan items assisted in this regard: the basketry manioc press borrowed from the Tupians (Nimuendajú 1946:58), and the copper griddle for toasting manioc flower, obtained from Euro-Brazilians. Both these implements permitted expanded utilization of the high-yielding "bitter"manioc varieties, the large scale production of dry manioc flour, and even trade in flour which was practiced by the Mundurucú (Murphy 1960), and the Canela (Nimuendajú 1946:61). Trade for European goods was another motivation for more permanent riverine settlements. The intensification of horticulture could have had a deviation amplifying effect since it permitted larger settlements of longer duration which would in turn lead to more intensification of horticulture. The dislocations and migrations caused by contact may have created more refugees and placed a premium on the ability to absorb them.

3) Cattle introduced by Brazilians may have competed with native grazing species, and even degraded the habitat forcing Central Brazilian peoples to reduce their dependence on hunting in relation to horticulture.

4) Finally, we may point to a change in the house styles as symptomatic of the increasing sedentarization and thereby aggregation of Central Brazilians. Nimuendajú observed only large rectangular houses in the Timbira and Apinayé villages (1946, 1939), but the smaller beehive shaped hut was remembered by informants and still used as a shelter on hunting treks. Maybury-Lewis observed the transition among the Shavante from one house style to another. Only the older style is found among the Nambikwara. Flannery (1972) has pointed to a statistical correlation between small, circular houses and nomadism, and large, rectangular houses with sedentism.

North American ethnography provides a remarkable parallel to the Central Brazilian situation. There, on the Great Plains, several tribes practiced seasonal aggregation and dispersal in accordance with the buffalo herding cycles. The Plains groups, having adopted the horse, roamed the plains in small bands for much of the year, gathering together into one large village during the summer and early fall when the buffalo congregated into large herds requiring large scale organization for collective hunting. Albers and Parker (1971) have summarized the outcome succinctly:

The buffalo hunt itself required coordinated activities and a carefully delineated division of labor; while in the camp circle, rivalries and arguments between autonomous bands had to be curtailed and adjudicated by new social control measures. The new adaptive structures transcended the organizational capacities of the nomadic band and the relatively amorphous social structure of hunters and gathers.

Unlike the situation in horticultural societies, however, new structures were not organized on the basis of kinship. Clan organization was absent, except among the Crow. As Oliver indicates, kinship as the basic organizational device would conflict with the flexibility and mobility needed for the exploitation of the True Plains environment. Instead, the True Plains societies developed a series of non-kin organizational devices, the major ones being governing councils, religious sodalities, and warrior societies. (221)

The Cheyenne provide a particularly interesting comparison to Central Brazilian groups. They practice uxorilocality but reckon descent bilaterally. During the period of aggregation, the bands all take up positions in a large circular village within which order is maintained by men's warrior societies. The Cheyenne warrior societies are not age graded (they are in other Plains groups) but they do cross-cut the constituent bands. Several of the Cheyenne Warrior societies have female associates not unlike those of the Timbira. A council of chiefs oversees all tribal affairs and ceremonial life is quite elaborate during the great buffalo hunt (Hoebel 1960).

Perhaps other parallels exist, particularly in Africa among pastoralists who also farm. I believe that prehistoric examples may also be found of this sort of dual strategy, especially during early stages of development of horticulturalists, e.g., in the Tehuacán valley (Mac-Neish 1964). The process probably has a long trajectory, perhaps stretching back to the pre-contact period. A sufficient perspective will be achieved only when archeological studies reveal the human activities over the past 500 years in the region.

## Testing the Model

The model presented here may not apply in every respect to all Central Brazilian societies, since it is designed primarily to highlight and to explain the similarities among them and to relate these features to adaptation to external features. The model also suggests some of the causes of variation among Central Brazilians. It should be emphasized, however, that the model does not purport to render every detail of Central Brazilian society intelligible. For example, in each of the societies discussed there occur certain dual structures in social organization which are imbued with symbolic meanings expressed in the form of contrasting colors, compass points, heavenly bodies, etc. While these are of great intrinsic interest and significance, this investigation does not propose to deal with phenomena at the symbolic level. The model should yield testable hypotheses which may account (probabilistically) for some variation among Central Brazilians. The principal variables to which the model draws attention are the form and complexity of social organization, subsistence variables, and the size, duration and stability of settlement composition. The model suggests a number of interacting conditions which may individually or jointly favor the formation of relatively large, seasonal village aggregates. These are the high frequency and/or intensity of inter-village warfare, the unreliability of some critical resource, especially garden produce, and, secondarily, the degree of dependence on horticulture for subsistence and the degree of dependence upon high-yield, slowly maturing crops.

A major problem in dealing with the complex and interacting variables delineated is that of lag. The process of cultural elaboration due to contact has now given way to assimilation. Today, nearly everywhere, Central Brazilian lifeways are disappearing. Some of the societies of Central Brazil have apparently displayed a trajectory, passing through several stages varying with the degree, directness, and type of contact with expanding Brazilian society. Each stage may have involved particular adaptive response processes which partially determined the responses of the next stage (see Oliver 1968). The Shavante, for example, may have reached a relatively high peak of elaboration prior to 1850 when they were a branch of a larger society including the contemporary Sherente (Maybury-Lewis 1965). Since 1850, however, they appear to have undergone a degree of simplification since they migrated to a more remote and less productive habitat where they depended heavily on foraging and met infrequently with outsiders until the 1950s.

An objection may be raised that I have selected particular aspects of culture from particular societies because they conform to my general model of Central Brazilian society and that therefore I cannot claim to have "tested" the model. This statement is true. The purpose of the foregoing is primarily to demonstrate the plausibility of the model proposed. There is not sufficient space here, nor data available, to conduct a satisfactory test of the particular hypotheses derived from the model.[7] Nor has it been my aim to present a "full" account of any Central Brazilian society as a "complete system" (Lave 1973:315). I regard such a goal as illusory, since investigators disagree regarding the boundaries of what conventionally constitute "complete" systems. It is much more profitable, in my view, to concern ourselves with the plausibility of theories and the empirical validity of particular hypotheses than to argue whether a given account is complete or incomplete. This essay is not intended to be the last word on Central Brazilian social organization, but rather to stimulate further investigation into the conditions which favored the rise of these societies.[8]

## Notes

1. It is a particular pleasure to be able to pay homage to Charles Wagley with this essay, since it is largely the result of some suggestions he made to a fledgling graduate student at Columbia University in 1964. In need of a term paper topic, I solicited his suggestions. He thought it would be interesting for me to deal with the problem of the extraordinarily large settlements of the Eastern Timbira and other Gê-speaking peoples of Central and Eastern Brazil. For theoretical inspiration he referred me to Julian Steward and Kalervo Oberg, and he himself guided me and encouraged me in a most constructive fashion. While he might not agree with every aspect of the approach taken in this paper, Charles Wagley's research and writing have for me always served as a model of the finest ethnology has to offer, rich in detail, always clear, and with a pervasive humanity which brings groups like the Tapirapé to us in a way which preserved them as integral human beings.

2. Most of the groups considered are speakers of the Gê family of languages (Loukotka 1968), or are identified by the controversial Greenberg (1960) classification as "Macro-Gê." But some speak Tupian or "isolated" languages. The Tupian-speaking Mundurucú, for example, share men's houses, men's cults, circular villages, uxorilocality, and moieties with the other Central Brazilian groups. While adaptive radiation from a single historical base may account for some of the similarities among Central Brazilian groups, we cannot ignore the possibility of parallel evolution as accounting for part of the similarities as well. Hence my preference for the term "Central Brazilian" over "Gê."

3. Particularly so when one considers that age organization is among the most common features of social organization in Central Brazil.

4. The Gavião-Timbira and some Kayapó groups presently live in evergreen forest areas, although they appear to have migrated from the cerrado to the jungle fairly recently.

5. Some authors find the cerrado to be a "harsh" environment, while others (e.g., Bamberger, 1968) emphasize the abundance of resources. Ecological analysis calls for more precise statements regarding the density, distribution, seasonality and other aspects of resources as well as the potential competitors for a given niche, etc.

6. While perhaps less severe than in the semi-arid *sertão* of Northeastern Brazil, droughts do occur with great regularity in Central Brazil. Known as *veranicos*, these short interludes during the rainy season can devastate an entire crop, especially the shallow root systems of hand-cultivated, unfertilized fields. See Wolf (1975) for a discussion of water stress on crops in Central Brazil.

7. Much of the recent research among the Gê has yet to find its way into print. I was publicly chided at the Mexico City presentation of this paper for failing to cite from privately circulated, unpublished manuscripts dealing with the Gê. I have not had access to many of these manuscripts, but a few which I have seen seem to offer support for the interpretations offered here. I hope that the students of Central Brazil will speedily make them available through publication so that readers of this essay can judge for themselves.

8. The author and four associates have recently completed over one year of field research among four Central Brazilian societies, the Bororo (Maria Francisca A. Leoi), Mekrānhoti (Dennis Werner), Canela (Madeline Ritter), and Shavante (Nancy Flowers) under a grant from the National Science Foundation with supplementary funds from the City University of New York. The research is aimed primarily at testing some of the hypotheses put forward here. The analysis of field data is now underway and we hope that our first results will be available in 1979.

# SIXTEEN

# Law in Rural Brazil

## Robert W. Shirley

THE BRAZILIAN JUDICIAL system in many ways parallels patterns of other social organizations in the country. In law, as in many other things in Brazil, there is a sharp distinction between rural and urban—a distinction which is partly maintained between the poor and middle classes in the cities. Although this paper concentrates on the operation of a single administrative system, the judiciary, it must be noted at the outset that, by anthropological definition (e.g., Hoebel 1954:18–28), there are really several different systems of law in Brazil, all of which are important for a thorough knowledge of the dynamics of the social structure.

This fact has created a series of conceptual problems in the study of law in the country. Brazil has long been noted as a nation where the formal legal system, despite a number of very capable jurists, is considered largely separated from the realities of social power. Many people have felt that the formal institutions are either extremely weak, especially in the rural zones, or are arbitrary and undisciplined. The judicial system has thus largely been ignored by social scientists in and of Brazil. Yet the judiciary offers a powerful lens through which one can examine the enforcement of social control, politics, and social dynamics. The struggle between local and centralized institutions of law enforcement is one of the great themes of history and has been especially acute in Brazil. Here, as in other countries, the central power of the nation has gradually come to dominate, and this growing force of the state is one of the most important his-

343

torical processes of the country. The full story of this centralization is too long to develop here (see Faoro 1975), but it would seem that the judicial institutions have had an important role to play in it.

To understand the process it is important to use modern theories of law (such as those of H. L. A. Hart 1961 and Paul Bohannan 1957) which take into account both existing norms (substantive law) and the mechanisms which enforce them (procedural law). Also valuable is the view of Eugene Ehrlich (1975) which sees law as infusing all, or almost all, of the institutions of society in a series of hierarchical levels, each of which has its own norms (laws) and institutional patterns to enforce these norms.

Many different sets of "law making" and "law enforcing" institutions exist in Brazil. Since we are here interested in rural-urban interrelations, it will suffice to distinguish three: popular "folk" law or custom; the laws of the landed aristocracy, the *coroneis;* [1] and, the urban national law of the government and courts.

These different patterns have interacted and intertwined in various ways in Brazilian legal history. It is not always easy to say which was more important, although an interesting degree of parallelism was obtained by the cultural fact that most forms of Brazilian law are derived from the same source: traditional Portuguese custom. The Código Filipinas, the patterns of Portuguese customary law collected by Philip II of Spain when he ruled the country, served in effect as the Civil Code of Brazil until 1914.

The different forms of law in Brazil operate in different types of communities which vary radically depending upon size, communications, economic base, and regional and ecological variation. We might first note the values and practices—customs—of the isolated peasantry (using the term loosely as an economic category) in much of rural Brazil. These people, for the most part, live far from the town, in loose aggregations of houses (called *bairros* or neighborhoods) scattered along a path or river (see Candido 1964; also Gabriel n.d.). The peasant village as a concentrated community rarely occurs in Brazil (see Wagley 1971:135–37; Smith 1972:433). These independent peasants, with possession or at least access to their lands, are a class frequently ignored in the literature. Juridically, however, they are interesting because they have a proud and distinct customary legal pattern in such matters as marriage, inheritance, and land tenure (Moura 1973) as well as their own forms of dispute settlement. Law enforcement institutions in these communities tend to be informal, based upon reciprocal obligations of communal labor and family pressures (see Caldeira 1956). This relates to Malinowski's (1959) famous theory of reciprocity as the basis of law although, in the last analysis, the possibility of retaliation or feuds was an important juridical factor in these communities, with the family acting as enforcement agency—another common pattern (Barton 1919).

Local leaders, often religious or commercial, exist in these communities and help solve difficult disputes. Interestingly in some areas, notably in the center and south of Brazil, these people are increasingly seeking the official judicial figures for decision making and dispute solving on an informal basis, a good sign of popular confidence in such figures.

The other great informal, unwritten, "traditional," pattern of law in rural Brazil is the law of the coroneis—the great landowning commercial elite—living on their plantations (*fazendas*) with their dependents and sharecroppers. For these dependent families, millions of rural Brazilians, the first and final jural authority was the landowner (*fazendeiro*), who could bring to bear both economic and physical sanctions (through hired gunmen) on a reluctant peasant or client. Among themselves, however, this elite elaborated a system of norms which could be fairly stable, based on family ties, mutual economic cooperation and the high risks involved in feuds between powerful landed families (Jorge Amado 1965). These families were, and in some areas still are, the juridical apparatus for much of rural Brazil, often in competition with that of the national state.

Finally there is the national, or urban law, developed by the government officials, written and explained in exhaustive detail in the various legal codes, their many modifications, and the numerous explanations and elaborations made through the written decisions (*jurisprudência*) of the courts. This law is at the top of the hierarchy and is, at least in theory, the law of the land, to be enforced by the great judicial apparatus of the states and nation of Brazil. Moreover there is always the risk of conflict between this and the other informal legal systems.

To examine urban law it is essential to understand the role of the town (*cidade*) in Brazilian life. The word *cidade* denotes a formal administrative unit with a concentration, however small, of urban people, urban activities, and urban services. They are centers for local and national commercial activity as well as for the operation of local, state, and national bureaucracies; the linking institutions between the rural population and the state, national, and international societies (Shirley 1971).

The town is fundamentally the smallest urban unit and therefore usually contains representatives of several urban bureaucratic institutions, i.e., one or more schoolteachers, a parish priest, state and federal tax collectors, a judge, a state attorney, and a police *delegado*,[2] usually supported by several state or federal policemen. It is thus in the town, if it is the center of a judicial district—(*comarca* in Portuguese) that written and unwritten law meet.

It is essential to note that Brazil as a nation belongs to the great Romano-Germanic (David and Brierley 1969:21–118) or Civil Law Tradition (Merryman 1969). This historical fact sets the form of the urban judicial system and has great cultural and social repercussions. In this tradition there is supposed to be a very sharp division between those who make and those who apply the laws. Laws are codified and elaborated in great detail by the central government and are to be applied formally and rigorously by the judicial authorities. In this tradition the entire formal legal system is highly professional and fully centralized. The judges, and often other officials as well, are career professionals appointed with life tenure (given proper behavior) by the executive power. Their role is not to make law or find law, but simply to apply the codes as written by the legislative power. This at least is the central philosophy. In fact, although a judge has little discretionary power in theory, he has a very great deal in actual practice. Hence the development in Brazil of many volumes of jurisprudência—guides to decision making developed by the higher courts.

Almost all legal cases in Brazil, at least those that are formally brought to court, are tried by career judges. The basic, first instance decision is made by one professional acting alone. Since this concentration of power in one individual creates serious possibilities of error or corruption on the part of the judge, the tradition allows for an appeal to be made in any case to a higher tribunal. Here, in the second instance, the case is reexamined by several senior career judges who are able to study and correct the decisions of their junior colleagues. The latter's opportunities for promotion depend upon these higher courts, and their success in their careers, at least in theory, depends upon how carefully they apply the law, in other words, their degree of conformity to the state laws. Finally, a case may be appealed still further to the Federal Supreme Court (STF, Supremo Tribunal Federal) if constitutional issues are involved.

A judicial district in Brazil is known as a comarca and contains, at a minimum, one professional judge (*juiz de direito* or judge of law) and one state attorney (*promoter público*).[3] By the author's calculation, in 1972 there were about 1,713 comarcas in Brazil. A comarca may have more than one judge, however. The city of São Paulo is a single comarca with over 155 specialized *varas* (literally a rod or sceptre, but in this case meaning a judgeship or judicial place). Within Brazil there are some 2,552 varas, but even this does not really indicate the total number of career judges (juizes de direito) since a vara may have one or more auxiliary or substitute judges in the larger cities. On the other hand, the judicial positions in some of the smaller, poorer districts, for reasons which will be explained, are chronically vacant. It has been estimated that there are some 4,000 professional judges in Brazil including those in the appeals courts and the federal courts. Even that figure leaves a ratio of only one judge to settle the legal problems and disputes for every 25,000 people, a fact which may explain a great deal about the delays and difficulties of Brazilian justice.[4]

Location theory, that is the theory which attempts to explain the location of hamlets and towns on the basis of modes of transportation and various socioeconomic needs (see Christaller 1954), has considerable utility in Brazil, where one finds that the many small neighborhoods are tied socially and economically to a cidade, usually the center (*sede*) of a municipality (município). Several small rural municipalities usually are, in turn, linked to a regional center of some 20,000 to 100,000 people, and several of these to a major city, usually the capital of a state. At the very highest level are the great national and international metropolises of Rio de Janeiro and São Paulo. The complexity of Brazilian community patterns, from scattered bairros of a few dozen families to great cities of several million inhabitants, implies a variety of judicial patterns and agents. The hierarchy of importance of Brazilian towns is reflected in the judicial systems of the states. Brazil has thousands of urban establishments (cidades) with populations ranging from one thousand to well over six million. In every state the judicial districts (comarcas) are classified according to their importance and population. These classifications are known as *entrâncias,* in a sense, career levels. The smallest, most isolated districts are grouped in the first entrância, larger towns in the second, etc. The final entrância, the last career stage for a judge is almost always in the state capital.

A judge in Brazil, after he graduates from law school, usually must undergo an initial testing period as a substitute judge (*juiz substituto*). Only after successfully passing this stage does he receive tenure of office and begin his life career as a professional state judge of law. Normally he starts out as the only judge of a district of the first entrância—that is in one of the smallest, poorest towns in the state—and from there, should he wish, he is promoted through the entrâncias to a position in the state capital. A judge can stay in a small district for many years, however, if he is not ambitious, until he rises through seniority.

The state of São Paulo has four entrâncias, Amazonas two, and Maranhão five. A judge of competence who has not made serious errors of judgement or important enemies will, at the end of his career, probably be appointed to the Tribunal de Justiça (the state Supreme Court) as a *desembargador* (literally, one who dispatches or untangles disputes, a state superior court justice). As such he will join the exclusive organization which controls the entire judiciary of the state, including the promotion, demotion, and correction of other judges. Promotion of the judiciary in Brazil is done through an interesting pattern of alternation by merit and seniority, a system which solves a host of difficult personal and political problems within the judiciary, as it allows able young professionals to advance rapidly, yet in the long run keeps no one down. The superior court judges also have a key role in selecting their own replacements since they make up the lists of three people who they think deserve to enter the tribunal by merit. Final selection, however, is made by the state governor (note Scheman 1962). Thus, although the judiciary is independent to a fair degree of the other branches of the government, there is still a political element involved in the development of judicial careers.

The human result of such a system of entrâncias and promotion is the fact that almost every Brazilian judge has been forced to live, at least for a year or two, in one of the smallest and most backward towns of his state. In such rural comarcas, even the federal laws are largely enforced by the state officials who actually become temporary federal officials for such cases. Some judges love working in the small towns—with the feeling of importance that it gives—and others detest it, but at least they have seen and dealt with problems of the rural population first hand. This fact does help reduce the austere and severely formal operation of Brazilian procedural law. Powerful and distinguished Superior Court justices of the state of São Paulo recalled, in interviews, that they had traveled about their first comarcas by horseback, in an era when automobiles were unknown in the rural zones. If one wants to know what the law says, he seeks a law professor; if he wants to know what the law does, he had best seek a judge. Only in the superior courts, with the second judicial decision, is there a return to dealing with purely written information, and even here there is an effort by many justices to go beyond the written law to understand the people involved in the case, especially in a criminal case.

A major factor which makes the study of the Brazilian judiciary extremely complex, and has adverse effects upon its operation, is the fact that each Brazilian state has its own judiciary. This means that there are now over twenty separate judicial systems, each with its own tribunal of justice and patterns of judicial correction and appeals. Each state is also free, at the present writing, to establish independently the number of comarcas, judges, judicial salaries and career requirements. This fact has meant great discrepancies in the past as well as in the present. This is especially marked in salary levels where, for example, a judge in São Paulo may earn up to seven or eight times what his counterpart earns in the northeast. It also presents an unusual picture of a federalized Civil Law Pattern, an odd contradiction.

There are, moreover, two major exceptions to the general pattern of the Civil Law tradition in Brazilian Law. The first is the institution of the jury which was borrowed, with considerable modifications, from the Anglo-American legal tradition in the early part of the last century (1832). Its function in Brazil, however, has been very different from that of England and the United States. In the latter countries, the jury of peers was established as an individual defense against arbitrary acts of Royal judicial officials (Maitland 1897), whereas in the former, the jury has served largely to protect local interests and elites from the authority of the written laws and the professional judiciary (see Carvalho Franco 1969; or Chandler 1972:79–102). Gradually, through successive historical changes, however, the role of the jury in Brazil has been reduced to the point where it exists only for trials of homicide or attempted homicide. It currently seems to have an important service in modifying the rigor and austerity of the penal code.[5]

The second major exception is the series of special federal courts, military, labor, and electoral. These were established in the days of the Estado Novo of Getúlio Vargas to take precedence over the state courts in these matters, and have been maintained up to the present. The labor courts are of special interest since they deal directly on a regular basis with the lower working class. Further, in striking divergence from the civil law tradition, they are not made up of a single professional judge who applies the law strictly and formally, but consist of councils (juntas) of conciliation as well as judgement. Labor law in the first instance is made up of these councils (Juntas de Conciliação e Julgamento) which consist of one professional federal judge as president, and two "class representatives" (vogais, pl. of vogal), one each of labor and management. These representatives (vogais) are elected by the workers' and employers' unions respectively to represent their interests and conciliate disputes within the labor courts. The very name of "Council of Conciliation and Judgement" suggests a break with civil law patterns since their basic role is not strict interpretation of the codes and laws, but rather the resolution of disputes between employee and employer through conciliation and compromise, though with decision making power through the laws if necessary. (The corporate ideology of the Estado Novo is here manifest—labor and management should work together for the good of the nation, with the state [the judge] as arbitrator.) Although majority vote carries in the juntas, it should be noted that the tradition of appeal still exists in labor law, and decisions at the first instance by the councils can be overturned by a regional appeals court (TRT = Tribunal Regional de Trabalho), where professional judges outnumber the "class" representatives. Thus, in their judgements, the juntas stay fairly close to the labor laws which were put together in 1943 in the Consolidação das Leis do Trabalho (Consolidation of the Labor Laws), although there have been a great number of modifications since that year (Campanhole 1974). In procedure, the labor courts follow the pattern of the civil codes, though more efficiently than the regular courts. A further appeal is also possible to the superior labor court (TST = Tribunal Superior de Trabalho) in

Brasília. Although these labor courts are the most modern in the country (the Brasília court has even put its judgements on a computer) the immense volume of work, some hundreds of thousands of cases per year, has caused a crisis in the handling of them.

Other cases handled by the federal courts involve any electoral disputes or doubts handled by federal electoral judges, also with appeal possible to the Regional Electoral Tribunals (TRE) and the Superior Electoral Tribunal. There exists also a series of federal military courts which judge in the first instance through a council of two military officers and a civilian judge. These were originally established to handle cases which involved military problems and personnel, but their jurisdiction currently includes any case which is seen as involving national security. In keeping with Brazilian tradition, there are a series of higher military appeals tribunals as well.

This, then, is a brief and rough sketch of the formal system of the application of written urban laws in Brazil. It was noted above, however, that in reality there exist several patterns of informal law and law enforcement in Brazil. To obtain some idea of how these elements interact in the rural setting, I have reconstructed an interview with "Dr. Clovis," a judge in one of the rural districts. This form of presentation in some ways reflects the way in which the data were collected. The formal data are all published, whereas the rest were mainly obtained through interviews and observation. I have tried to sum up much of the latter material in the form of a single interview. "Dr. Clovis" is, of course, a fictionalized character, an amalgam of several judges I have known in São Paulo and elsewhere, but his statements are all taken from many personal interviews.

The scene is a town of about 15,000 people well in the interior of Brazil in one of the less developed states. The day is warm and rather humid. The Forum, the focus of all legal proceedings and center of the judicial district, is located on a small secondary plaza away from the central Catholic church. It is a two-story building in an imposing but undistinguished style which has been remodeled several times since the comarca was established at the end of the empire. The first floor houses the various registry offices, whereas the judge's offices and the jury room, with its inevitable crucifix and state and national flags, are located on the second. Not many people are about: a policeman looking at, but not really directing, traffic; a few women shopping; a number of clerks and store owners sitting just outside their shops awaiting customers; two or three town beggars lounging in the plaza; and a couple of small boys in ragged clothing playing with a soccer ball. Several cars, trucks, and horse driven carts go by without stopping.

I am with the judge, Dr. Clovis, who drives up in his three-year-old Volkswagen just before the afternoon court session begins. Despite the heat, the judge is the only one in the plaza wearing a suit and tie, a formality which he dislikes but feels is important to his position. Dr. Clovis is in his thirties, intelligent, and ambitious. He lives in the comarca, as he must by law, and he supplements his not very generous judge's salary by teaching, the only other job he can legally hold as a professional judge. He is a professor of social science and practical law in a faculty of a nearby city. This is the second district he has served in, as he was promoted by merit to the second entrância the year before. As we walk up the steps of the Forum, an old black woman in a torn white dress tugs at his sleeve. He stops, fumbles in his pocket for a few coins to give her, and tells her that she really shouldn't beg on the steps of the Law Court. She mumbles something which sounds like a blessing and shuffles off, having decided it would be too risky to try to tap me as well.

Inside the Forum we are surrounded by several people, mostly lawyers asking favors for their clients. The local state attorney, sporting a large ruby ring, the sign of his law degree, is there, and I am introduced to him, as well as to an elegantly dressed man in a grey silk suit who is the local court notary and head of the land registry office. He is also, the judge mentions later, one of the largest of the local landowners, and earns many times the judge's salary. Everyone, however, shows Dr. Clovis immense deference, tinged with a bit of nervousness, for here is the man, despite his youth, who really makes legal decisions in the district.

The afternoon session is short. The parties in a land dispute case arrive with their lawyers and witnesses. One of the older lawyers attempts to lecture the judge and is quickly put down. There is no doubt who is in command of the case, despite the fact that the local lawyer has been practicing in the town for twenty years.

After the session we go back to the judge's private office to discuss the session and other matters. I want to know if things are always this slow in the comarca.

"Yes," Dr. Clovis replies, "this district is really very peaceful.

The region is poor so there aren't many severe disputes over land and relatively little crime. There are a couple of civil cases a week to decide, and occasional violence breaks out, though even this has declined considerably, since the elections are no longer as important as they once were.'' In general he feels that this is a good thing, but for him personally it is a problem since judges in his state collect a percentage of trial costs; a quiet comarca means a reduced income.

"Do you realize," he says, "that some judges here earn more from court costs than they do from their own salaries, and they have refused promotions because it would mean such a financial sacrifice?''

I object, noting that the state of São Paulo eliminated the collection of court costs in 1921 and that the Brazilian Constitution of 1969 (Art. 114 II) actually forbids it.

"Come now," he says, "of course I know that, so does the Tribunal of Justice, so does everybody, but São Paulo is a rich state and we are a poor one; their salaries are three or four times ours. If you were to eliminate the collection of court costs here, half of our judges would quit, and then where would you be? Someday maybe they will pay us enough that we can eliminate costs without a problem.''

Leaving the case study for a moment, one should remember that the traditional pattern of social organization and social order in the Brazilian interior had very little to do with the laws and codes created in the capitals. It was fundamentally a system created and enforced by the landed elite or by local leaders.

Many jurists consider such a social pattern, run by great families or by patriarchial whim, not to be a legal order at all, but it would be an error to call it complete anarchy or lawlessness. In the view of the anthropologist, the rural Brazilian system had its own framework, rules, and definitions. It was the second traditional pattern, the law of the *coronel* or the great landowners, decidedly a form of social order and organization, even if lacking written laws. Several travelers in the interior of Brazil in the last century commented on the security of the countryside for those who had the friendship of the local elite. Those who did not often did not return.

The whole pattern of *coronelismo*—rule by the landed aristocracy—is very well documented and will be only briefly summarized here (see Leal 1948; Faoro 1975; and Vilaça and Albuquerque 1965). The power of the Brazilian elite came basically less from its military strength than from its commercial position. The coronel was a trader, patron, and commercial middleman, linking the folk of the interior with the international economy. He had a monopoly on their contact with the outside world, bought their production and sold them the manufactured and trade goods they needed, including tools and arms. The wealth thus obtained enabled him to influence the political and military institutions of the state (Leal 1948). His position thus had tremendous strength and flexibility, and made him virtual lawgiver to the local people.[6] It should be noted, however, that this great pattern of local social control and law known as coronelismo was in constant tension and occasional conflict with the central government and the structure of urban—codified—law.

The relationship between the landed elite, the coroneis, and the administrative system of the central government forms a major theme in Brazilian history (see Faoro 1975). The judiciary was a central factor in this interplay since it was the professional judge (juiz de direito) who was the principal agent of the central government, responsible for bringing urban law and the law codes to the sertão, the backlands. The struggle has ebbed and flowed, with local independence reaching high points during the early years of the empire and the old republic (1891–1930) and centralization increasing greatly toward the end of the reign of Dom Pedro II and from the 1930s to the present time.

The degree to which the judiciary really acted as enforcement agents for the central government, or were co-opted into the local power structure, is a matter for considerable debate. There is good evidence (from the Imperial Government Reports—Relatórios) that the administrative machinery of the empire became fairly effective from about 1850 to 1880 and then began to decline. It must be noted that during the empire (1822–1889) the judiciary was fully centralized at Rio de Janeiro, with judges being sent to all parts of Brazil at government order and paid from the imperial treasury. The decentralization of the judicial system in the early years of the republic (after 1892) was a tremendous blow to the national administration and judicial power, since it allowed each state to develop its own judiciary. This put the enforcement of national urban law and the selection and promotion of judges into the hands of state governments usually dominated by the rural elite who were, at best, much weaker and poorer than the Brazilian national government.

It is interesting to note the mechanisms which were used by the coroneis to control the judiciary even in São Paulo, one of the richest and most powerful state governments. It is clear from the biographical data of the members of the Tribunal of Justice (desembargadores) that many judges came from, or married into, powerful landed families of the state (Shirley, n.d.). This insured that the elite could obtain scarce legal talent and gave the judge powerful political support for his advancement.

During both the empire and old republic, moreover, the landed patriarchate had ways of dealing with judges who threatened them too strongly and who could not be bought off. In the struggle between local political leaders and the state judges, according to Julio Cesar de Faria (1942), it was usually the judge who lost, at least in this epoch, the old republic.

Assassination, however, was rare. Killing a professional judge in Brazil under any circumstances is a profoundly serious matter since it arouses the whole judiciary and legal profession. In the entire history of the São Paulo State Judiciary since 1889, there are records of only one judge assassinated in the line of duty, although there was an attempt on the life of the president of the Tribunal of Justice, Inácio Arruda, in 1902 (Faria 1942:131–34). On the other hand, there were many other ways that local political chiefs could get rid of a bothersome judge. Most of the older, and many of the contemporary laws of judicial organization, including that of the empire, have a clause to the effect that a judge could be transferred from his district if his presence threatened public order and stability. Further, it is almost certain that any judge who opposed the local politicians would automatically threaten public order and stability, or at least it might appear so. Thus many judges were transferred out of districts where they were really trying to impose urban law on the law of the coroneis.

Since 1946, however, the position of the judiciary has been strengthened considerably in relation to the local landowners, at least in the majority of states, but the struggle still continues.

Returning to Dr. Clovis: "Most of us at some time or another," he says, "have had real fights with landowners over various issues and we usually win, but if it happens too often, or if we pick a fight with a really powerful politician, things may be different. The Tribunal of Justice here isn't interested in heroes or martyrs and it doesn't want to offend the politicians who determine its budget. So if something like that comes up, the tribunal usually finds a vacant district in a better location or arranges a quick promotion. There are a dozen or so such districts in the northern part of the state which have not had judges in years,[7] partly because living conditions in some of these little towns are terrible. Who wants to bring up his children in a place where there is no electricity, poor schools, the water is dangerous to drink, and where malaria and Chagas' disease are common? But also these are regions where the old coroneis are still in control, or want to stay in control, and if a judge has any pride and honesty at all, he is soon going to get into a fight with them, and that is a real struggle. They control public opinion there, and have influence in the state capital as well, and the judge will have everything from his sexual habits to his personal honesty impugned, and is it worthwhile to make all those sacrifices for that? At what we earn? That's why no one goes to those districts.''

I ask Dr. Clovis about acts of violence toward the judiciary and in general.

"Killing a state judge is not very common,'' he replies. "I can recall hearing about three or four cases in all in this state. But you should remember that the Tribunal of Justice will usually transfer a judge whose life is threatened. It's those empty districts again. Here we have a handful of homicide, that is jury, trials a year, but I have a colleague who took over a comarca in the northwest of the state and found a backlog of fifty murder cases, going back years, waiting for a jury.''

Since there is not too much violence against judges, I ask him about corruption in the judiciary. Are the judges who are not threatened, bought?

"Look,'' he says, slightly nettled, "everyone has a price, you have a price; we all do if it's high enough; judges are human. You Americans probably think of Brazilian judges as a group of Latin bureaucrats who can be bought and sold every day. That's just not true. Take São Paulo, for example. The Paulista judiciary is considered incorruptible, and there are good reasons for that. The judges there receive good salaries, even by your standards, and they have a lot of pride, a tradition. Even more important, though, is the fact that the Tribunal of Justice there is tough; decisions are constantly reviewed, and their *corregedor* (corrector) of justice is very active; he makes trips to the interior several times a year. So if one wants to buy justice in São Paulo, he would have to pay not only one judge but all 36 superior court justices at the same time. Imagine the cost. Even here, where our salaries are low, the Tribunal much less active, and the temptations greater, I doubt if more than one judge in ten has ever accepted bribes, and even then the Tribunal often finds out and it blocks their careers. We work hard. People don't usually enter the judiciary to make money; there are lots of easier ways to do that for a lawyer. Once in a while a major scandal breaks out over a judge who is really venal, and the people get upset. Then the Tribunal of Justice acts, and our corregedor holds a court of inquiry. There have been several judges forceably retired because of that. They should be thrown right out, but that would create too much publicity, so the Tribunal prefers to give them an early retirement with pension and forget about them."

I ask the judge if he thinks that the judiciary has had some effect in breaking down local power and the coronelismo.

"We have had some effect," he replies cautiously, "especially in the south and São Paulo where politics isn't dominated by the big landowners. But don't forget that in this generation there have been immense economic and cultural changes as well in Brazil. People here now can leave the countryside to find jobs in the industrial cities, and they do. Also transportation and communication have improved greatly so that nearly every farm hand can buy a little transistor radio. Personally," he says, "I doubt if the judiciary has done much more than keep up with the changes of the times in the country as a whole."

Another topic which recently has taken on importance in the rural zones of Brazil is that of Labor Law. The original Consolidação das Leis do Trabalho (Consolidation of Labor Laws) was promulgated in the waning days of the Estado Novo of Getúlio Vargas. This law was almost a labor code which established the rights and duties of both labor and management.[8] It set up minimum wages and hours, holidays, rest periods and working conditions. It was, however, designed almost exclusively for the urban worker. Rural laborers, especially sharecroppers, were expressly excluded (Art. 7-b) from the consolidation. Moreover, the judicial apparatus established to enforce the laws, the Councils of Conciliation and Judgement, were established originally only in the state capitals and other large cities. The number of these has gradually increased from a few dozen in 1943 to 262 in 1973. The emphasis is still on protecting the urban worker, however, with 32 councils in São Paulo and 25 in Rio de Janeiro. In fact, since only 144 cities in Brazil have their own councils, this leaves 92 percent of the 1,713 comarcas of the country dependent upon the local state judge to enforce the federal labor laws. It is, moreover, exactly these isolated and more rural judicial districts which have the majority of the rural workers.

The problem was not important to the judiciary as long as the rural workers were excluded from the jurisdiction of the laws. But gradually over the past thirty years the rural worker has gained more and more formal legal rights. A major step was made with the Estatuto do Trabalhador Rural (Statute of the Rural Worker)—Lei No. 4.214 of March 2, 1963 (Sampaio, 1964). This law gave the rural worker, whether compensated in either money or kind (i.e., share-croppers) a series of rights which they did not have before, among others the minimum wage, holidays, adequate working and living conditions ("depending upon regional standards") and the specific right to form rural unions (sindicatos).[9] The enforcement provisions were rather vague, however. The statute was to be enforced by the Labor Courts, mainly located in the big cities: "by jurisprudence, by analogy, by equity, and other principles and norms of law. . . . But always in a manner that no class or private interest will prevail over the public interest." The statute was not strongly enforced for a time, however, due to the manner in which the military coup of 1964 created major political changes in the federal government.

It was only in 1973[10] that almost all of the rights and obligations of the Brazilian consolidation of Labor laws were extended to the rural worker, giving him stability of employment and social security, among other things, and putting the political weight of the Federal government behind the judicial system to enforce the laws.

I ask Dr. Clovis the degree to which such labor laws are enforced in the rural areas.

"That varies a great deal," he replies. "Many rural people are afraid of judges and government people in general. But very recently some of them are beginning to find out that they do have legal rights, and I will enforce them; I don't care what the landowners think. When a worker brings a case to me he usually wins effortlessly; the laws are very clear. So we're getting more such cases as the workers find out that they have a judge who will defend their rights. On the other hand, there are many judges here who don't like to take on labor cases. A judge doesn't make much out of it, after all, and he usually alienates many powerful people in the community who don't want to give the workers the minimum wage and all their back pay as well.''

"There is another factor here," he comments a little bitterly. "The rural workers in this region are really very poor; they simply do not have much in the way of reserves of any kind, and they may have large families as well. So if one of them brings a case against his employer, however justified, to me, he will probably lose his job, despite the fact that firing him is illegal too. What's worse, he'll get known as a troublemaker so others won't hire him either. Let's say that he brings the case to me and wins; I order that he gets what is legally his and be rehired. But the landowner has money and a lawyer and the worker doesn't. The landowner appeals to the Regional Tribunal and maybe even goes to Brasília. He will almost surely lose in both places, but in the meantime this poor farmhand, who probably has a wife and five kids to support, is sitting out there in the plaza with no job and no income for two years while his case grinds through the appeals courts. There aren't too many workers who can face that, and that's why there aren't as many labor cases as there should be. Still, things seem to be getting better for the rural worker here.''

I want to know why he should say something like that.

"Well," Dr. Clovis says, "not so much due to our work as judges as due to the fact that there is currently a large demand for agricultural products, and a shortage of field hands, since so many men have left to work in the cities. So the landlords have simply had to give their workers some extra advantages. Even so, there are very few workers who have simply what they are properly entitled to by law.''

I ask what he sees for the future.

"Who knows," he says, "things are changing. The government may reform the whole judicial system. In the meantime, one does one's best.''

*Superb article on legal systems, + the regulation in Brazil*

# Notes

1. *Coronel*, pl. *coroneis* is a name often given to the great landowners in Brazil, i.e., those who were wealthy enough to buy commissions in the national militia during the empire (1821–1889) and old republic (1890–1930) (see Leal 1948).

2. It is interesting to note that in civil law countries, i.e., countries with codified laws, such as Brazil or France, the delegado, the head of the local police, is really a delegate of the central police authority, an agent of the executive power of the state. This contrasts with the constable in common law countries such as England and the United States, who is considered simply a private citizen paid to do a job—law enforcement. This has several corollaries such as the fact that a policemen can be sued like any other citizen in Common Law countries, nor is his sworn testimony any stronger in court than that of any other citizen. This is quite the opposite in the Civil Law tradition (Banton 1969).

3. The Brazilian institution of the Ministério Público has no real counterpart in Anglo-American law. The promotor of justice (promotor público) represents the state government in trials, but is not a district attorney or prosecutor. He prosecutes, defends, is supposed to look after the weaker parties, and in general "supervises" the legal process. This may include the gathering of evidence, sometimes at considerable personal risk. Hence the translation here of "state attorney" (see David and de Vries 1958:20 on the French Ministère Public).

4. Such number games should be treated with caution. The United States, with double the Brazilian population, had only 5,087 state judgeships in 1969 (Glick and Vines 1973:37). It should be remembered that the role of the judge is extremely different in the two systems.

5. A Brazilian jury trial, to one who is accustomed to American procedure, seems rather strange, though not illogical. There are only seven jurors, selected from a group of about forty regular candidates, usually middle-class civil servants. All evidence and testimony are taken before the beginning of the trial by the presiding or auxiliary judge of the jury in association with the state attorney (promotor público) and in the presence of the defendant and his lawyer. Comments and expert opinions (*laudos*) by the police are also taken and dictated by the judge into the official trial record. This record forms the basis of all the trial evidence and is read orally in whole or in part by the promotor público (wearing a red sash and black robes) and the defense attorney, depending upon their utility to the side of the case which they want to present, and accompanied by whatever oratorical devices seem necessary. No direct evidence or witnesses are presented to the jury nor does the jury have powers as a body to request reviews. Only the judge can order evidence taken or reexamined. In the trial, after the presentation of both sides of the case, the members of the jury retire to a special room where each member votes individually without discussion among themselves, "each in his own conscience," about the case. Majority vote carries.

6. One story, from Pernambuco, can illustrate this point (Nery n.d.:45): Chico Heráclio was the most famous coronel of the Northeast. In Limoeiro, he was the boss; ruler of earth, fire, and air. One obeyed or died. . . . It was a festival day in Limoeiro. The city soccer team was playing against that of Garanhuns for first place in the intermunicipal championship of the state. Coronel Heráclio arrived dressed all in white, seated himself on a wicker chair, and the play commenced.

The first quarter and the second quarter, nothing—zero to zero. Five minutes before the end of the game, the referee, who had come all the way from Recife, marked a penalty against Limoeiro. The local fans went crazy and poured onto the field. The referee, afraid of being lynched, ran to the side of Coronel Heráclio. The coronel lifted his cane. Everything stopped.

"What is it, Mr. Referee?"

"It's over a penalty which I just marked, coronel."

"What is this thing, this penalty?"

"It's when a player makes a foul in his own side."

"Then what happens?"

"Ah, coronel, the ball stays there where it's marked in front of the goal, and an opposing player has a chance to kick. With only the goalkeeper to stop him."

"And he scores, Mr. Referee?"

"Generally he does, coronel. It's very hard to stop a penalty kick."

"Very good, Mr. Referee. Your explanation is quite clear. And I'm not going to interfere with your authority. Since this thing—this penalty has been called, we'll do just what the rules of soccer say. Just that you, sir, instead of putting the ball in front of the goal of Limoeiro, do me the favor instead of putting the ball on the other side and let a player from this city kick."

"But coronel, that's against the law."

"Just so, it's just a little favor for me. Here in Limoeiro I am the law."

Limoeiro won!

7. Since 1970 the Tribunals of Justice—Superior Courts—of each state have had the capacity of determining the number and location of the judicial districts of the state. The result has been that many districts long vacant have been consolidated with others. The Tribunal of the state of Minas Gerais, for example, in the most extreme case, abandoned 60 comarcas in the reorganization of 1970. In many Northeastern states, the majority of districts of the first entrância are missing a professional judge, a state attorney or both. The influence of local officials such as the notary (escrivão) or justice of the peace (juiz de paz) over legal matters may increase notably in the absence of a professional judge, and in some states, the justice of the peace, a locally elected official, may in many ways substitute for the state judge in the latter's absence. There is also the subtle social fact that the sheer authoritative presence of a professional judge may affect the actions of the local elite toward less arbitrary behavior.

8. *Decreto Lei* No. 5.452 of May 12, 1943.

9. All Brazilian workers under the Constitution and Consolidation can belong to a sindicato, or union, registered and regulated by the federal government. This fact, and its history, is, in itself, a fascinating topic which cannot be adequately developed here (see Rodrigues 1968).

10. With Lei 5.889 of June 8, regulated by Decreto 73.626 of February 12, 1974.

# SEVENTEEN

# Patron–Client Exchanges in Southeastern Minas Gerais

## Sidney M. Greenfield

THE FOLLOWING PAGES examine aspects of the social life of southeastern Minas Gerais, Brazil.[1] The objective is to show how exchanges of the type that have come to be referred to as patron–client (Boissevain 1966; Foster 1963; Galjart 1964, 1967; Hutchinson 1966; Kaufman 1974; Kenny 1960; Powell 1970; Silverman 1965; Strickon and Greenfield 1972; Wolf 1966b), integrate persons, kinship groups, and other units of the local community with the institutions of larger Brazilian society. The data to be presented specifically relate a crisis in small town family life to the formal educational system of the state of Minas Gerais, to the political system, and to the flow of resources into the local community in exchange for qualitatively different resources from within.

Patron–client relations have come to be associated with exchanges of the asymmetrical type that see individuals with unequal access to, and control over, resources exchanging the different commodities they have with others, with each of the parties striving to maximize his or her own situation (Barth 1966; Strickon and Greenfield 1972). In the process of negotiating and making the exchanges, social relations are developed that then are characterized as being of the patron–client type.

To illustrate this process, some case materials collected while doing research in the *município* (county) of Paraízo will be pre-

362

sented.[2] From the descriptions a web of social relations, generally characterized as being of the patron–client type, will be analyzed in an effort to present the relationships and the asymmetrical exchanges on which they are based, as illustrative of the ways in which the life of the local community is articulated with the institutions of the larger society.

## Paraízo and the Zona da Mata

The local community in which the people whose behavior is to be presented and analyzed below live is called Paraízo. Paraízo is a small município of 105 square kilometers located in the Zona da Mata of the state of Minas Gerais. There were approximately 5,500 people living in the município at the time the research was conducted.

The município is located in the mountains between 800 and 1,000 meters above sea level. It is approximately equidistant between Rio de Janeiro, the former federal district, on the coast and Belo Horizonte, the state capital. In the mid-1960s it took approximately eight hours to go by road from Paraízo to Rio and some six hours to get to Belo Horizonte.

Geographically the area is an extension of the Paraíba valley. It was settled in the nineteenth century as the cultivation of coffee moved northward into Minas Gerais. The topography of the region is mountainous, dominated by old, eroded hillsides that, although not especially high, are quite steep. The landscape, for example, generally rises to a peak rapidly only to drop sharply some fifty to one hundred meters to a shallow trough. Then, after forming a narrow valley cut by a stream, the land rises precipitously to another peak, only to drop again forming another trough in what gives the feeling of being an endless sea of hills and valleys.

Coffee was planted on the sides of the steep hills. To facilitate its cultivation, most of the hillsides and mountain tops were cleared of the luxuriant native woods that give the name to the Zona da Mata. As the years passed, the rains leached and eroded the soils, leaving them deficient and limited in fertility.

When coffee declined as a cash crop, foodstuffs were planted in greater quantities; today corn, beans and rice are the primary crops raised in the município, although some coffee still is being grown. Agriculture, however, no longer is as profitable as it once was. Instead, the entire Zona da Mata is in the process of being transformed into a cattle region. But Paraízo, since its roads are poor and do not connect with the major highways built by the state and federal government, is too far away from the markets for beef and dairy products to partake in the profits that are rapidly transforming other parts of the region.

In Paraízo agriculture still dominates the economy. And since the land is poor, for the most part, so are the people. The community we are discussing is a poor one in which only limited resources are produced locally. The "extras" that make life more satisfying, as we shall see, are obtained from outside the local community. The means of obtaining them are the exchanges that are the basis of relationships of patronage and clientage.

## A Domestic Crisis in the Resende Family

Pedro and Maria Resende were a young, recently married couple who live in the *município* of Paraízo. At the time I first met them Pedro was 21 years old and Maria was 18. They had been married for approximately two years and were the parents of a 6-month-old child named Ana. Pedro and Maria both were children of several generations of land-owning elite of the community.[3]

When I first encountered them Pedro and Maria were in the midst of the first major crisis in their married life. The crux of the problem related to Maria's employment. Prior to marrying at the age of 16, she had completed the secondary course at the newly established school in Paraízo. Shortly after the wedding there was an opening for a substitute teacher in the state-supported primary school in the municipal center. Maria applied for the position which, after her appointment, was made into a permanent post.

At the time Maria had no great desire to teach. Instead, she wanted to have a baby. Like most of the daughters of the elite families in Paraízo she had hoped to become pregnant on her honeymoon. When she did not, she became concerned and sought help. First she spoke to her friends who offered her a combination of advice, treatment, and remedies. When she still did not conceive she went to a physician, the customary next step when home remedies do not work.

Within three months of the wedding Maria was pregnant. In that time, however, she did many things as her frustration and the fear of being barren preyed on her mind. One of the things she did was to accept the position as teacher at the school in the *sede*, or seat of the município.

Pedro, although the son and heir of a landowner, had no land of his own. His inheritance was being held for him by his mother who retained legal title. When he married at the age of 19 he also had but minimum personal wealth and resources. When he returned from his honeymoon, therefore, as was the custom of the children of local elites, he took his bride to live in the *fazenda* house in which he had been raised. When Maria accepted the post as a teacher, however, the couple no longer could reside in the country; they needed a home in town.

Maria went to her mother-in-law to explain the situation and to ask for help. Dona Dulce responded by offering the couple the use of her home in town which she and her children used only on weekends. Since Pedro could travel to the land from town while Maria could not commute to school from the country (she had a fixed work day while he did not) the couple took up residence in the municipal center where they were joined on weekends and holidays by Pedro's mother and his siblings.

All went well until Maria's fears about not being able to become pregnant proved to be unfounded. But by that time she had decided that she liked teaching, and even more, she liked the income, benefits, and independence the civil service position of *professora* afforded her. She decided, therefore, to continue working after the baby was born.

She had no problem arranging for a maternity leave from school when the time of birth approached. But after the baby was born she could return to work only if she could arrange for someone to care for the child during school hours. As was common practice, she turned to her mother who also lived in the town. Maria then decided that it would be more convenient if she, Pedro, and the baby went to live in her parents' home. Her father, however, in uncharacteristic fashion, since most fathers with the means will provide a home for and look after their married daughters, declared that the house was too small for them all. There was room for Maria and the baby, to be sure, but if they were to be a family with Pedro, he insisted, they would have to find another place and someone else to care for the child.

When they moved back to Pedro's mother's house, Maria went to her mother-in-law to say that she needed someone to care for the child or else she could not work. Dona Dulce then had Pedro arrange for a spinster aunt to live with them. The arrangement did not last long since the aunt found the weekends with Dona Dulce and her children to be too much for her. When she left, Maria took the child and moved in with her parents again.

In anger Pedro went to the home of his in-laws and, in a display of force, carried his young wife and child back to the fazenda in the country. He followed this action by sending a message to the head of the school stating that Maria no longer would be working there. Maria's mother, however, on her behalf, asked the director of the school to hold the position open for a while, which she did.

Although Maria returned to the fazenda with her husband she did not hesitate to inform her friends and relatives as to how poorly she was being treated. But the villain as she told the story—to anyone willing to listen, including me—was her mother-in-law and not Pedro.

Just prior to taking his wife and child home by force, Pedro had started an affair with the wife of a young sharecropper living on the family's land. The woman, of course, had little choice when approached by the man who was her *patrão* (boss).[4] If she rejected him, Pedro would tell her husband the opposite. The husband, when the story became public, as it certainly would, would be branded as a cuckold. He then would have no choice but to abandon his disgraced wife, or to move elsewhere, giving up his home and the crops he had planted. In either case the woman would be worse off than she would be in Pedro's bed.[5]

Maria soon learned of the affair from the maid of a friend. Her first reaction was to turn to Pedro's younger brother, Tarcísio, requesting him to accompany her in trying to catch the couple in the act. Tarcísio instead advised his brother to be a little more discrete. Maria, however, went after the young woman with a torrent of accusations. When she defended herself against the charges, in an unusual display of courage, there was a great scene. Pedro, of course, was nowhere to be seen during the confrontation.

From the time he started the affair with the sharecropper's wife, Pedro had not slept with Maria. In anger and frustration Maria complained not only to her friends, but to Pedro's brothers and to her mother-in-law.

"Last year," she burst forth bitterly one afternoon to my research assistant, who had been her *madrinha de casamento* (maid of honor), "I was married, and this year I am single." She then went on to tell how in her innocence she almost had accepted Pedro's suggestion, made after the spinster aunt had left, that the young woman come to live with them to take care of the child while Maria worked. Her only objection at the time, she added emphasizing how innocent and foolish she had been, was that she preferred not to have her child looked after by a stranger.

In the expression of her anger it is significant to note that again Maria's hostility was directed less against Pedro than against her mother-in-law. As she perceived the situation, Pedro's behavior was to be expected, given the circumstances. The problem was the circumstances which neither she nor Pedro could control. The person who could change them was her mother-in-law. What Maria wanted was for Dona Dulce to provide a house for the couple plus someone, preferably one of Pedro's kinswomen or *comadres*,[6] to care for the child. Then, as Maria read the situation, she and Pedro could live happily and he would have no need for the sharecropper's wife. True he might pass an occasional afternoon with her, or some other wife or daughter of a landless, dependent family, but this would affect neither Maria nor her relationship with Pedro. The difficulty, according to Maria, was that Dona Dulce was being niggardly in refusing to provide the conditions that Maria believed were essential for her happiness. Dona Dulce, of course, objected to being expected to pay out of her own pocket for a home and a servant for her son and daughter-in-law.

Maria then stopped speaking to Dona Dulce. Instead, she talked about her—only negatively—to her friends and relatives in the hope that her complaints might bring some public pressure to bear on her mother-in-law. To a degree this strategy proved to be successful as we shall see below.

Maria and Pedro were not speaking to each other and their marriage was at the point of being dissolved.

## The Resolution of the Crisis

Domestic crises like the one involving Pedro and Maria are usually resolved through the initiative of some elder person, usually a male, of great prestige and influence. For the local elite in Paraízo this is often the father, grandfather, or an uncle of the husband or wife who uses the occasion to demonstrate his influence and importance. Invariably he articulates a segment of a network of relationships he has built up over a lifetime to obtain the resources needed to resolve the problem that is at the heart of the crisis.

The scenario for domestic problems is for a man, chosen as an arbitrer, to sit down with the couple and have them make explicit the issues that separate them. He follows this with a lecture on the importance of the family, domestic morality, and the advantages of being able to work out problems cooperatively and in private. He then offers to make available the resources needed to resolve the problem that produced the crisis if the couple will forgive, forget and live, at least in the eyes of the community, a life that is a model of domestic harmony and bliss. In other words, in return for the help he will arrange, the couple must learn to keep their future disagreements to themselves and not make an issue of them in public.[7]

Pedro's eldest brother, João, took the initiative in resolving the problems of his brother and sister-in-law. João Resende, although only 26 years old himself, was the *prefeito* (mayor) of the município of Paraízo and an ambitious young man of growing stature and importance in the community. The previous year he had been the compromise candidate of the Partido Republicano (P.R.) and had won a hard fought victory.

João sat down with his brother and sister-in-law and started by delivering a sermon on the importance and sanctity of the family. Pedro and Maria, he observed, were young, but surely they realized the importance of the family as an institution. Their family likewise was important, and it had to be preserved. If they would patch up their differences, he promised, he would arrange a solution to the problem of Maria's employment.

First, he told his brother that, although acceptable in its place, his affair with the sharecropper's wife could not be permitted to interfere with his marital relationship and with his family life. He then was instructed to apologize to Maria for his injudicious behavior and to ask her forgiveness. Finally, he was told in no uncertain terms to reestablish his home with Maria.

Maria, for her part, was pleased to accept the apology and to be back with Pedro. The problem, however, still was between her employment and their place of residence. This was taken care of by João, with the help of state deputy António Vieira da Sousa.

Since Maria could not live in the country with Pedro and teach at the school in the municipal center, the solution arranged by João and António was to create a school where Maria was in the country. Within a month of the time Pedro had taken his wife from the home of his in-laws, therefore, a school had been established on the Resende fazenda. Maria in rapid succession was nominated and then appointed as its teacher. No new building had to be constructed. Instead, as was becoming common, one of the storerooms on the main floor of the two-story fazenda was cleared, cleaned and converted into a classroom. The students were the sons and daughters of the sharecroppers who lived on the lands belonging to the Resendes, plus others in the area who had had no school.

## Analysis

The school had been arranged by João Resende. João, as has been noted, had been a compromise candidate for his party in the elections of the previous year. The Partido Republicano had long dominated the political scene in Paraízo since the days of the old republic (1889–1930) when one of its own rose to the position first of governor of Minas Gerais and then president of the republic. João and Pedro's father had been a close friend and political associate of the former governor and president, and a coronel (literally colonel, but used to refer to a political boss) in the then district of Paraízo. He is reported to have provided a place for his distinguished friend to hide when he was being hunted by the police after the political coup of 1930.

The local leadership of the P.R. in Paraízo had been split on a candidate to run for the office of mayor. João's name had been suggested by António Vieira de Sousa, an attorney and retired sociology professor (see Greenfield 1972, 1977a) who recently had decided to run for political office. António had run for state deputy (*deputado estadual*) two years before, having lost by less than a dozen votes. In the hope of strengthening his voting base he had stepped into the deadlock in Paraízo and had convinced the aging party leaders to support the youthful João.

João's victory had strengthened not only his own political position, but also António's. The following year António was called to the state legislature to replace a colleague who had given up the seat for personal reasons.

As a retired professor, who had studied both in the United States and in Israel, António rapidly came to be accepted as an expert on educational matters. Soon he became liaison between his party, the P.R., which was a member of the majority coalition that controlled the state legislature, and the office of the secretary of education.

Minas Gerais, at the time, like the other states of Brazil and the federal government, was developing programs to reduce illiteracy. Schools were being built and teachers trained in a concerted effort to make available greater educational opportunities. António, among his many duties, recommended the locations at which the new schools should be placed and also nominated the teachers for the area he represented.

When told of the "problem" in Paraízo by João one afternoon in the state capital, he reacted by saying that he could resolve it. By establishing a school on the Resende fazenda and having Maria appointed as its teacher, he proposed, the couple would be able to live together on the fazenda. In this way, of course, António would ingratiate himself with the Resende family whose support he was counting on for the next elections to the state legislature.

António outlined his reasoning to me in the halls of the legislative chamber the following week. The state, he proposed, had to start creating schools somewhere. The greatest need was in the rural areas where illiteracy rates were the highest. Therefore, why not create a school on the Resende fazenda which was in the rural area and where the residents, with the exception of the Resendes and the other landowners, were illiterate? The argument was even more convincing when he added that the only cost to the state would be the salary and benefits of the teacher since the Resendes had offered to provide the space rent free.

The logic, I had to admit, was sound and consistent with the policy and the standards of the department of education. The school proposal was sound and Maria was a qualified teacher.

I accompanied António as he hand-carried the proposal, which had been approved by the leadership of his party and the coalition that controlled the legislature, to the office of the secretary of education. At each step in the bureaucratic progression needed to clear it before it could be signed by the secretary and the governor, prior to implementation, he expounded in flowery phrases on the educational benefits for the rural poor to result from the project. At each office the clerk, and others who read the proposal, commented unsolicitedly to me, who was known as António's friend, as to how sincere, hardworking, and dedicated António was. He was a wonderful man, I was told, dedicated to helping the poor and underprivileged. What Brazil needed, one senior official in the office stated, was more leaders like António.

The school in Paraízo was approved in July. To further ingratiate himself with the Resendes and their followers, António had the papers dated as of the previous January. This would provide Maria with back pay from January to July.

The local inspector, however, took exception to this action and reported it to her superior, who threatened to have the school on the Resende fazenda closed if the papers were not corrected. António, however, advised Maria, Pedro, João, and Dona Dulce to pay no attention to the inspector and her superior.

The local inspector, I was informed by António, was a political appointee, affiliated with the opposition, and unqualified for the post she held. She was out to make trouble for the members of António's faction because he had arranged for the daughter of his compadre, who also was a member of his faction and one of his *cabos eleitorais* (mobilizer of votes, see Greenfield 1977b), to take the course that would qualify her to be appointed in the place of the incumbent inspector. By the end of the year, Lydia, a member of the faction that included António, João Resende, and her father, would be replacing the complaining inspector.

To my surprise, no one took notice of the fact that in January, when Maria was placed on the state payroll as teacher in the not yet created school in the Resende fazenda in Paraízo, she was in the hospital giving birth to her daughter. When I mentioned it to António, he laughed and said that it did not matter.

The crisis in the Resende family then was resolved with the creation of the school and the appointment of Maria as teacher. By early September Pedro and Maria were back together and the affair with the sharecropper's wife had been forgotten. Maria, however, still had not forgiven her mother-in-law in spite of the fact that the older woman was taking care of the child during school hours.[8] But the important thing was that the marriage had been saved and the young couple were living together again in harmony.

The hero to the couple, and to the attentive members of the community observing each new development, had been João Resende. João had shown himself to be a man of force and ability, a true leader. He had made his brother and sister-in-law listen to reason and he had demonstrated that he had contacts and the ability to mobilize external resources in the solution of local problems.

Pedro summed this point up to me one afternoon when he confided, almost facetiously, "Eu não me casei com uma professora, mas agora estou fazendo uma professora a poder da política" (I did not marry a teacher, but now I am making a teacher politically). Politics had been the key to the solution to the problem.

It should be noted that, as Maria had defined the situation, it could have been resolved without external help if Dona Dulce had been willing to make available to Pedro what after her death would be his anyway. But instead, she chose what elsewhere (Greenfield 1972:92) I have referred to as "the rule that one never does locally what can be obtained as patronage from an agency or an individual at a higher level." Consistent with this principle she refused Maria's request and opened the door for someone, as it turned out her oldest son, to display publicly his connections and ability to tap external resources for the solution of local problems.

João then turned to António, as a member of his network at a higher level. António responded, as we have seen, by using his position as an educational expert in the state bureaucracy to arrange the school and the job that enabled João to return home with the means both to resolve the problem and to affirm his connections and influence.

António wanted to be elected on his own two years later to the assembly. To achieve this he needed votes. João Resende, as he grew in stature and importance in Paraízo, had an increasing number of dependents and supporters whose votes would go to António. To these would be added the votes of the dependents and supporters of an increasing number of leaders in other local communities who also had been helped by António. The total, hopefully, would be enough to secure the election. It was in his own best interest that António helped João to appear in Paraízo as a man with contacts and influence.

Without violating the spirit of the education program of the state António was able to have the school on the Resende fazenda created and Maria appointed as its teacher. By doing so he not only resolved the problem that had precipitated the crisis in the lives of Pedro and Maria; he also enabled João to show the members of the local community that he could get things done. That is, if they needed access to external resources to resolve any of their problems they could come to him because he had the contacts that would enable him to help them. In this way the network of persons to whom external resources would flow would be increased as would the number of voters to support João, António, and any other candidate for office they chose to support.

Finally, it should be added that the school on the Resende fazenda benefited not only Pedro and Maria. The people living in the neighborhood now had a school to which to send their children. To whom should they be grateful for the school? Certainly not to the state of Minas Gerais or any of the leaders they did not know and who, as they were convinced, did not care about them. Their school had been arranged by João Resende and António Vieira da Sousa, people they knew and who had helped them and would continue to do so.

Schools like the one on the Resende fazenda, it should be noted, were attended not only by children, but often also by adults unable to read and write. In the Zona da Mata illiterate laborers were encouraged to learn by their patrões; once they were minimally literate they were eligible voters. And for whom would the newly enfranchised laborers on the Resende fazenda vote? António Vieira da Sousa and João Resende knew the answer to that question and it provided further motivation for them to become involved in arranging the resources that resolved the problem of Pedro and Maria.

## Conclusion

The school on the Resende fazenda was not the only one arranged by António during his short term in office in the legislature of Minas

Gerais. Some dozen or more schools were created at his initiative on fazendas throughout the municipalities of the northern Zona da Mata that formed his electoral base. Each one, it turned out on examination, was on the land of someone who has served, or who had promised to serve as cabo eleitoral for António in the area. In each case a member of the family of the landowner, his wife, a daughter, or daughter-in-law was nominated and appointed teacher with civil service status.

Other schools also were created in the several municípios. Those in the towns had to be built which meant construction contracts, jobs, and other benefits for the local population. The state deputy played a significant role in determining who was to get the contracts and other benefits.

And schools were not the only resources being distributed by the state authority. Roads were being built, medical programs created, and development projects fostered. In each case decisions had to be made as to where the agencies of the state should begin. And in each case politicians at the state level made the decisions, but in terms of the series of exchanges with their cabos eleitorais in the local communities that maximized the chances of their being re-elected the next time around.

Individuals like Pedro and Maria Resende, along with their numerous less fortunate neighbors, who were the inhabitants of the local communities of the Zona da Mata, had numerous unresolved needs that regularly precipitated what for them were crises. Local leaders then would step in to resolve the problems by arranging the resources to satisfy the needs. Given the general poverty of the region, the number of problems and crises were considerable; but given the general poverty, the local leaders, although usually better off materially than most of the people, did not have the means with which to satisfy local needs. Although at times local resources were used in resolving some of the problems, for the most part, the local leaders appealed to for help, or who volunteered to provide it, would turn to someone at the state or national level with whom they had been making exchanges over the years. The resources, as in the case of the school arranged by António, then would flow into the local community from above by means of the intermediacy of the party in the state or federal capital and be funneled to the point of crisis by the local leader. With the problem resolved and the crisis over, the assisted party or parties would be indebted to the local leader directly and to the network of persons to whom he was articulated indirectly. The leader, in turn, would be indebted directly to the deputy, or other person or persons at the state or federal level who had arranged the resources.

Problems and crises are a part of life and can occur at any time. The debts incurred in this system of applying extra-local resources in resolving local problems and crises were paid, for the most part, at election time. In his capacity as cabo eleitoral, the local leader who had obtained the schools, the jobs, the medical supplies, the contracts, the roads, etc., would go back to those he had helped, and to others who might find themselves in need of his brokerage services in the future, and exhort them to vote for the state deputy, federal congressman, governor, or other office seeker who was a member of the network that had made available the resources (Greenfield 1977a). If their numbers were large enough, when added to the number of indebted dependents mobilized in other communities throughout the state or nation—depending upon the election—a candidate would be elected to office who now was indebted for his success to all those in his network who had contributed to his victory. As a result he would arrange resources in the future that in response to requests to filter up to him would flow down to local communities like Paraízo to resolve the problems of people like Pedro and Maria.

Most of the municípios of Brazil, like Paraízo, are poor. As a rule their local populations do not have the resources needed to take care of their own problems. The wealth of the society is being produced today, in ever increasing amounts, by the agencies and creations of government in the industrial sector of the nation. The new wealth is being distributed to a not insignificant extent by means of the exchanges that extend from local communities like Paraízo to the state and federal decision-making centers. The new wealth then is made available by political leaders like António to their cabos eleitorais in local communities. In return, votes and support flow up and out, through networks of persons involved in relations of patronage and clientage, to others at the state and federal level who exchange with still others, with the goods and services needed at the lower level flowing down and out in a delicate series of reciprocities that must be examined and understood at each level and in terms of each transaction.

In the preceding pages one case has been examined, illustrating the social relations and exchanges that brought a school to a rural neighborhood in the município of Paraízo as a solution to the domestic problems of a young couple. The problem, and the exchanges involved in its resolution, were typical of the patron–client type exchanges and of the flow of resources into and out of local communities like Paraízo that articulated the município and its inhabitants with Minas Gerais and national Brazilian society in the mid-1960s.

The exchange of favors for votes previously described, it should be obvious, is not unique to Brazil. To a degree, such exchanges are to be found in all systems of electoral politics including our own. What is distinctively Brazilian, however, is the degree to which transactional principles and the system of patron–client exchanges have been carried, both in interpersonal relations and in the articulation of local level populations with the developing institutions of national Brazilian society.

From the time of Getúlio Vargas, Brazil has gradually been transformed from an agrarian nation to an industrial one. The federal government, first under Vargas' direction, and then in the hands of his elected successors (and at present under the military), stimulated and mobilized the capital and expertise, and even organized industry. It also helped to create what elsewhere (Greenfield 1972 and 1977a) I have referred to as an industrial-service-welfare complex that has come to be the primary source of wealth in the nation.

In the years between 1945 and 1964 (actually 1968 when the federal congress was closed and the political system completely transformed) the resources of the industrial-service-welfare complex were harnessed to the electoral system. For most of Brazil's poor, and especially those in the economically depressed rural areas, there were few, if any, means for the resolution of their problems and the satisfaction of their needs and wants other than the resources of the new politically controlled sector of the economy.

Almost all transactions and interpersonal exchanges, or so it appeared, eventually came to be political, with votes (and offices which brought control of the industrial-service-welfare complex) exchanged for access to resources.

With goods and services flowing down and out from the federal and state capitals and metropolitan centers as favors, and votes moving up from the local communities, massive patronage networks were established that linked the residents of municípios like Paraízo to the decision-making centers of the state and the nation. The result was a distinctive patterning of transactions and patron–client exchanges that, among other things, articulated residents of local communities like Paraízo with the institutions and resources of national Brazil.

## Notes

1. My gratitude is expressed to Dr. Wagley, who first interested me in Brazilian society, and who in not so many words made me aware of relationships of patronage and clientage, the exchanges on which they are based, and the networks of social relations that stem from them. My thanks also are expressed to my many friends in Paraízo and elsewhere in Brazil for permitting me to share enough of their life to observe and examine them exchanging and implementing the relationships to be discussed in the paper. Special thanks are expressed to Dr. Arnold Strickon, who over the years has helped me to understand and to present in coherent form the data I collected in Brazil. My appreciation also is expressed to the Social Science Research Council, the Graduate School of the University of Wisconsin, and the Agency for International Development for the financial support that made the fieldwork in Minas Gerais possible. All views, interpretations, and conclusions herein contained are those of the author and not necessarily those of the supporting organizations.

2. Paraízo, literally Paradise, is a pseudonym, as are all names of persons and places used in the text.

3. I use the word *elite* to separate those who own land and their descendants from the majority of the population, who are landless. The reader should not assume, however, that the people referred to as elites are rich, influential, or powerful in the ordinary sense. That they are better off materially than their landless fellows goes without saying; but whatever wealth once was found in Paraízo is long since gone. In socioeconomic terms I am talking about the miserably poor and those who are slightly less so.

4. Although Pedro did not own the land lived on and worked by the sharecroppers, he administered it for his mother, who was the owner.

5. Pedro, it should be noted, had no commitment to the woman or to the relationship. He might, if he chose, show kindness and occasional material generosity, but nothing more could be required of him; if the woman became pregnant he would deny the affair and, to the world, the child would be that of the husband.

6. A man's kinswomen and comadres are included in the extension of the incest taboo. They therefore are the preferred categories of persons a wife turns to as help in her home. Since they are sexually taboo to her husband she considers them as safe and to be trusted in his presence.

7. For example, in one case a man in his mid-thirties, who was perhaps the most successful coffee merchant in Paraízo, but who was known to drink excessively in the dead season before the coffee harvest, and to chase women when drunk, was dis-

covered accidently by his wife in bed with the maid. The wife, who was the daughter of a leading political figure, was outraged. In anger she packed her bags and stormed out of the house, taking her children with her. The avalanche of accusations and threats hurled against her husband could be clearly heard in the main square of the town.

The following week the woman's father, now retired and living in Rio de Janeiro, returned to the município, whose political independence he had been instrumental in gaining, and where he had served as the first prefeito (mayor) and still was active, serving on the governing council of the Partido Republicano (P.R.)

After reproaching his son-in-law for unpardonable indiscretion, he turned to his daughter to expound on the theme of marital responsibility. His point was that the maid had meant nothing to his son-in-law, who still loved his wife and children. True he had behaved foolishly, but that was no reason for their home to be destroyed. His daughter, he counseled, should learn to overlook such occasional affairs by her husband. Men do such things, he stated, especially strong men with leadership ability, but it is not to be taken seriously. The unity and survival of the family, he concluded, was more important.

He then chastized the son-in-law for showing such bad taste. If he wished to enjoy a servant, or the wife or daughter of a poor family, he could do so, but he should make the effort to find someplace other than the bed he shared with his lawful wife to have his affairs. What had been immoral about this situation, he stressed as he elaborated a philosophy of domestic morality, was not the affair with the maid, but the defiling of the marital bed. If his son-in-law must indulge himself in the future, as most men must, he continued, he should do so where and when there was no chance of his wife and children learning about it.

He then turned to his daughter and added that as a mature and sensible wife and mother, if she did learn of another such indiscretion in the future—conducted in secret—she should respond to it as she would respond to a piece of unfounded and malicious gossip.

In summary, he told the couple that their home was sacred and that they both should return to it in harmony. The daughter was then advised that if she did not go back to her husband, her father would neither take her in with him nor provide for her materially. She would have to find some other means of support for herself and her children.

The son-in-law was instructed to apologize and ask his wife to forgive him. He then was told to re-establish his household with his wife as its center. If not, he was warned, the coffee growers, who still were dependent on the father-in-law and his political associates for loans and for political favors, would be doing business with another merchant. Finally, in recognition of the fact that the basis of the problem was the son-in-law's drinking when he had little to do and was bored, the father-in-law informed his children that he had arranged a position for the son-in-law as inspector of construction projects for the município. The duties could be performed in the dead season before the coffee harvest. Not only would the son-in-law have the additional income and prestige, but he would be hard at work in the future during the times he previously drank and chased women to pass away the empty hours. By the time I arrived in the community the Ladeira's gave the appearance of being a devoted couple with a model household.

8. Pedro would take the child to his mother in the morning and pick her up when classes were over.

# EIGHTEEN

# The Political Economy of Patron-Clientship: Brazil and Portugal Compared

## Shepard Forman and Joyce F. Riegelhaupt

THIS PAPER EXAMINES a local level political phenomenon, patron–clientship, from the perspective of the political economy of the nation–state. Deliberately historical and comparative in its orientation, it is an analytical attempt to bridge the gap between macro- and micro-political analysis by focusing on the changing nature of the specific institution of patron–clientship within successive Brazilian and Portuguese political regimes. The Brazilian–Portuguese comparison has been selected because our individual studies of these two societies have led us to discuss these issues in an explicitly comparative way.[1] Moreover, the initial development of the municipal system in both countries as part of an expanding national bureaucracy in fourteenth-century Portugal (Johnson 1972) and seventeenth-century Brazil (Russell-Wood 1974) provides us with a similar institutional base which then experienced subsequent centuries of socio-economic and political modification. It is in this context in Brazil that patron–

An earlier version of this paper was delivered by Riegelhaupt at the Anthropology Colloquium of the City University of New York in February 1976. In addition to comments and criticisms received at that time, we are also grateful to Daniel Levine and Mark Rosenberg for their comments.

clientship has flourished in certain epochs and, in others, has been relatively diminished. Now, with the institutionalization of an authoritarian state, it may be in the process of disappearing entirely, much as it has been absent during Portugal's recent political history.


## The Background

Decades of anthropological work in Brazil and Mediterranean Europe have resulted in a number of ethnological studies which have been most successful in pointing up the extreme complexities of these societies. Paradoxically, the greater part of the anthropological endeavor systematically has been to reduce this complexity, to define a research strategy within which anthropologists could feel comfortable. The effect, a rather natural one given the history of the discipline, was to focus on the little community. Anthropologists thought, at first, that a series of community studies in different regions of a nation-state would provide a good picture.[2] Later by shifting the focus slightly to the various micro-economic environments, especially in Brazil through studies of fishing (Forman 1970; Kottak 1966), sisal (Gross 1970), or coffee (Margolis 1973), the portrait would be completed. We knew where, if not how, these communities fit into the nation, and efforts were focused on the nature of the communities (their styles of life) or on the micro-economies themselves. Occasionally, the linkages between community and nation were looked at but rarely, if ever, were the processes that integrated system and sub-systems over time examined.[3]

This attention to the community and to the sets of relationships and events that occurred within its boundaries is understandable within the context of anthropology. Within the emerging field of political anthropology, the principle paradigms were derived from African and South Asian contexts, where British social anthropologists had long been at work (Bailey 1963; Evans-Pritchard 1968; Leach 1965; Turner 1957). There, attention was also devoted to the community, and to the sets of relationships and events that could be observed within its boundaries. Typologies of political "systems" were elaborated (Fortes and Evans-Pritchard 1961) and local "arenas" were defined (Swartz 1968; Swartz, Turner, and Tuden 1966). The behaviors and decisions which went on within these were analyzed at

considerable length and in great detail (Bailey 1969).[4] Given the colonial system under which such studies took place, the nature of the
attachments of local communities or units to the colonial structures
were considered an inappropriate subject for study. Moreover, such
studies would have belied the anthropological myths about primitive
isolation and holistic tribal societies.

American anthroplogists' interests, after World War II, turned to
seeking "baseline understandings" for programs that ultimately, if
not always explicitly, envisioned social, economic, and political
"modernization" as their goals. These studies organized politics on a
dualistic basis in which the local level was seen as more or less "integrated" into a state system over time in a classically unilinear direction. The end-in-view was "modern society." This view allowed
social scientists to draw circles of encapsulation or boundary lines
within which the study of "conflict," often reduced to the notion of
local level factionalism, was pursued (Nicholas 1965). Such an approach is, however, a distortion of the realities of developing societies, since it accepts a dual society or "separate systems" model as
its point of departure and minimizes the historical differences between states.

As a corollary, the "dual" analysis of political activity directed
the researcher to the junctures, or linkages, at which the assumed
separate systems appear to come together. The result has been to
focus down on the behaviors of actors as the sources for the penetration of the state into the bounded local arena. These actors have been
called alternately "hingemen" (Redfield 1960), "agents" (Nash
1965), "culture brokers" (Geertz 1960; Wolf 1956); and particularly
in the Brazilian and European contexts "patrons" (Foster, 1963,
1965; Leeds 1964; Wolf 1966a, 1966b). With these persons have
come the invariable host of "followers" or "clients" (Galjart 1964;
Gellner and Waterbury 1977). This concept of patron-clientism has
come to characterize for much of Brazilian and South European ethnography the totality of political life. The behavioral propensities of
the actors have been scrutinized as sets of dyadic interactions which
organized into networks, and hierarchies are then said to be the so-
cial/structure and political system of the nation-state (Leeds 1964).
They are also used as the bases for innumerable conclusions regarding Brazilian and Latin "political culture" (Forman 1977; Levine
1974).

Studying the points of juncture in politics—the patron-clients, the mediators, the agents—is akin to studying the activities of the marketplace as though they constituted the totality of the peasant economic system. As we have pointed out elsewhere (Forman and Riegelhaupt, 1970), in order to fully comprehend the nature of the peasant economic system in Brazil, we must know the overall structure of production and market relations in the nation (or region) as a whole and how they have changed over time. Likewise, in order to understand the nature of political relationships at the local level, we must elaborate in a general way the actual power relations, codified in the state and modified at the local level. Only then can we know the extent and significance of political action in specific localities.

While patron-clientship might well be used to describe the kinds of linkages that exist between villages and wider socioeconomic and political systems, the "joining" of separate systems through mediators of one sort or another fails to adequately describe the nature of integration within unitary and total systems, that is, systems of which "backwater," agrarian communities are an integral part.

Patron-clientship and factionalism (as part of that system of clientship), which are the focus of anthropological attention on Brazilian politics, do not have their germination at the local level. Their interpretation solely as local level phenomena has led to distortions and subsequent expectations about the degree of competition and openness in the political system as a whole (Love 1970). In reality they represent forms of local mobilization and control within a system which has been only semi-competitive at best and, at its worst, has been markedly authoritarian and largely closed to meaningful participation by the peasantry (Forman 1977).

It is not surprising that some political scientists have borrowed the concept of patron–client relationships—a set of relatively "harmless" observations about one type of hierarchical dyadic interaction— as a base on which to construct a new paradigm, which they believe serves as an explanatory model for certain kinds of political systems and political change (Kaufman 1974; Powell 1970; Scott 1972a, 1972b). Unfortunately, in so doing the political scientists (and some anthropologists) have transmuted a valid observation of a behavioral manifestation at the local level into an explanation of a political system writ large.

Patron-clientship is a structural and cultural phenomenon which neither generates a political system nor, by itself, adequately begins to describe one. In fact, these relationships acquire different forms and functions in each historical epoch as the constellation of social, economic, political and ideological elements that nurture them are themselves transformed. They are nothing more/nothing less than one mode of integration between social classes, the form and content of which varies considerably over time (Forman 1975; Scott, 1972a, 1972b; Silverman 1965).

In our view, *patron–client ties* (when they can be identified empirically at all) *are merely diagnostic elements of a total political system*. To equate peasant politics with forms of patron–clientism generally is a misreading of the historical process, as we believe a rereading of the Brazilian and Portuguese materials will show. The best way to demonstrate this point is to examine the changing nature of municipal and village politics in the context of national regimes, and to do so comparatively.[5] In the historical narrative that follows, we will concentrate largely on Brazilian materials, and call on data from Portugal, in order to demonstrate that what we are seeking is an understanding of the systematic nature of processes through time rather than a description of a series of responses that might simply be written off as culturally unique. For example, a series of comparisons between the two cases would allow us to document the fact that the nature of peasant articulation varies with different kinds of regimes, whether feudal, absolutist, populist, liberal democratic, authoritarian, totalitarian, etc., and precludes the argument that in any event what we are describing are simply Luso-Brazilian "cultural" responses.[6]

It is a serious mistake to simply collapse historical time and posit a set of "traditional" relationships—like patron–clientship—as a timeless baseline against which to measure change.[7] What is required for an understanding of that set of relationships is an examination of differentiation in the elite sectors of the social system and the changing constitutional basis for a polity at different points in time. To our mind, the system of decision-making and manner of resource distribution within the nation is far more critical than the content of the specific exchanges that are generated at the local level. Patron-dependency, patron-clientship, brokerage—these forms of exchange represent the mode of resource dispersal within the political system at specific points in time.

In the Brazilian case, for example, sets of historical transformations lead from patron-dependency (when the peasant is forced to enter into a set of exchanges with a given patron) to patron–clientship (when the peasant is presented with a choice, however limited, among potential "benefactors" who offer him differential returns for services rendered) (de Kadt 1970:23; Hutchinson 1966). Patron–clientship only becomes generalized in Republican Brazil when electoral politics begins to infuse the political system with a degree of relative competition. In brief, the very appropriateness of a patron-client model of political behavior is, as we will demonstrate, limited by the presence of certain types of electoral systems characterized by elite interest conflict.

Anthropologists should view political history as a continuum of processes in which structures and events confront each other to produce sequentially different configurations. The nature of peasant articulation in the state system varies with different kinds of regimes, whether liberal democratic, authoritarian, fascist, socialist, or feudal. The critical question that the anthropologist can answer is: what is the impact of different kinds of political systems—for example, limited parliamentary representative regimes vs. bureaucratic nonrepresentative regimes—on political action and behavior at the local level?

This is not the place to undertake a thorough and complete analysis of Brazilian and Portuguese political history.[8] What we shall do is examine briefly the ways in which successive regimes have incorporated the peasantry into the polity and the particular forms that incorporation has taken at the local level.[9] What will become clear is that patron-client relationships and the bases of their legitimacy change as the form of incorporation itself is altered in response to the national and international situation. Again, this is more than simply saying that patron-clientship is regime-specific or that it characterizes certain kinds of political systems. On the contrary, we must focus our analysis on the political economy of the state and its attendant regime as the comparisons with Portugal will readily show.

## Peasants in the Brazilian Political Process

The key to the nature of peasant participation in successive Brazilian regimes lies in an understanding of the national political economy. Throughout the historical development of the Brazilian system, the dominant theme has been one of centralization vs. local autonomy in which different elite sectors compete for control at the center and at the periphery. This problem of the locus of power, initially posed in the granting of land in autonomous economic and political units by a distant metropolitan power has, for centuries since, pitted centralists against localists in a protracted struggle for control over the administrative and legal apparatus of the municipality, the province, and the nation-state. Inevitably, the Brazilian masses, both rural and urban, have been included in this national political struggle. The nature of that inclusion, however, is understandable only in relation to a second, corollary theme, namely that of elite vs. mass. The interplay of these two fundamentals of Brazilian political history—centralization vs. local autonomy and elite vs. mass—are the principles around which the successive regimes have been ordered.

Brazilian elites, whether agrarian or commercial, always adopted a tutelary and paternalistic attitude in their political struggles. Despite a series of liberal constitutions modeled along French, English, and American lines, participatory democracy in Brazil has remained illusory. Inclusion and exclusion more readily describe the process of manipulation of the Brazilian masses by the real participants in this basically authoritarian political system. The patriarchs of the colonial period, the ennobled coffee bourgeoisie of the empire, the ruling oligarchs of the old republic and the agro-industrialists of the new republic, used the rural masses in a variety of ways in their quest for power (either in the form of local autonomy or as control over the legally constituted authority in their respective municipalities). These elites extended and retracted the electoral system in relation to the changing economic and social fabric of Brazilian society.

Examination of the historical record makes it clear that patron–clientship did not emerge unchanging out of a traditional set of relationships which characterized the colonial period. Rather, the plantation system itself was part of a colonial political economy that underwent considerable transformation as changes occurred in Brazil's relationship to the world economy. Thus, with the passage of time, the loci of seignorial power shifted from sugar planters to coffee barons and then, critically, into the hands of urban industrial elites. With each shift, the peasant was incorporated differentially into successive political regimes, first as dependents, then as clients, and finally as a self-conscious and self-interested electorate which began to bypass not only the patrons, but even the electoral machinery which those very patrons had established. The peasant political movements that developed during the 1950s and 1960s were not simply traditional responses to a new set of patrons as some analysts argue (Galjart 1964; Leeds 1965), but a part of the process of "massification" which began in the Vargas Estado Novo (Forman 1971).

The homogeneity of agrarian elite interests that characterized the struggle for local autonomy against a distant monarchy during the colonial period (sixteenth and seventeenth centuries) was transformed under the empire (1822–1889) as regional interests began to respond differentially in their own quests for power and privilege within a newly centralized regime. In each of Brazil's vast regions, agrarian elites sought hegemony over their own domains and decision-making power over their own economic and social interests. Until the first explicit threat to their discretionary power was posed, there was no need to incorporate the masses into the political process. The patrons had no clients; they had dependents. These dependents did not operate directly in the political system, but were mobilized as seignorial henchmen for the elite actors in the local political arena.

Under the empire, defense of agrarian interests was assured by rural elite infiltration of the imperial bureaucracy. However, the advent of the Republic and its extreme federal system in the late nineteenth century permitted the landed classes to exercise their influence directly from their rural bases. The privilege of so doing was provided for in the Republican Constitution of 1891 which yielded up all crown lands, control over tax revenues, and local militias to the individual states (Vieira da Cunha 1963). Moreover, the provision for direct elections of all local, state, and national offices, along with a literacy requirement for suffrage, effectively concentrated power in the hands of the rural elites who could call upon a political electorate (Azevedo 1950). The urban middle class, whose demands had led to the expansion of the electoral system, was momentarily satisfied by a rapid growth in the military and civilian bureaucracy which established a system of clientage characterized as the "Cartorial State" (Jaguaribe 1969). The extension of this clientage system into the municipalities provided the rural oligarchy with a critical new resource (positions in the bureaucracy) in its struggle for power.

The First Republic (1891–1930) was a compromise in every

sense, a calculated trade-off, fully elaborated in the "politics of the governors" in which state governors and the President of the Republic agreed to accept each others' authority in their respective domains. With congressional support for the president's foreign policy assured, there was a *de facto* return to provincial autonomy and a guarantee of federal patronage in the states, including the right of regional elites to appoint public functionaries at state and municipal levels (Love 1971). The currency in this exchange was votes, and the electorate soon began to expand in relation to demand. In a single party system in which the presidential office alternated between the two states with the largest electorate, direct suffrage and absolute majorities were simple electoral mechanisms to affirm the choice of presidential successors (Oliveira Vianna 1933).

The kingpin in obtaining presidential votes and electing a compatible congressional majority was the *coronel*, who mobilized the electorate. The coronel was by no means the "traditional" plantation owner transformed, nor was his "following" the same as on the colonial estate, those personal fiefs of aristocratic potentates "which possessed all of the conditions of sovereign power" (Oliveira Vianna 1933:226). By controlling bureaucratic sinecures at the local level, the resources for clientelism were placed firmly in the coronel's hands. By expanding municipal revenues in public works, the coronel built his reputation as a local benefactor, thereby ensuring himself a following. His attributes of leadership were enhanced by the political bargaining at the state level in which a dependent municipal electorate became the counter in a straightforward exchange of vote totals for political spoils. While at the national level, competition for control over the decisional apparatus of the political economy was an important factor, local conflict was of little importance. The state oligarchy watched dispassionately as local rivals fought for the right to supervise the municipal electoral machinery, since it hardly mattered to them which local notable actually delivered the votes in state elections.[10] The resources which did flow into the countryside thus generated the factionalism that anthropologists so often describe as characteristic of Brazilian politics (Gross 1973; Nicholas 1965). This factionalism, too, is a function of national political machinations and the scale of rural Brazilian society at a time when relatively undifferentiated elites rivaled each other for the attentions of political oligarchs at the state level.[11]

In this system, local balloting was rarely seriously contested, since alliances between municipal chieftains and state oligarchs were usually effected before the voting actually took place. A minority opposition, eager for some share of the favors dispensed for electoral support of congressional candidates, occasionally tried to collect some votes to use in bargaining at election time. However, they were merely competing for the privilege of adhering to the ruling oligarchy in the state, not trying to elect a rival slate to state office. The hallmark of this coronelista system and the "politics of adherence" that characterized it was the simple aggregation of votes. The idea of actually winning elections occurred only at the end of the Vargas dictatorship when, in the Second Republic (1945–1964), the competition between numerous parties in hotly contested elections, particularly at the local level, made electoral victory the *sine qua non* for the receipt of political spoils (Jaguaribe 1969). Such competition was no more a continuity of traditional factionalism than were the coroneis mere latifundistas transformed.

Again, the importance given to electoral politics and the changes it fostered at the local level can only be understood in the context of changes at the national level. Paradoxically, the semi-competitive political system (Schmitter 1971a) which made the município a hotbed of political electoral activity during the Second Republic actually was significantly developed within the apparent authoritarian constraints imposed by the Vargas Revolution and the extension of the syndicalist New State. The Estado Novo (1930–1945) saw the emergence on the Brazilian scene of new sectors which challenged the agrarian elites' manipulated hegemony in the countryside. During the Vargas years, three new sectors appeared on the Brazilian political scene: an articulate urban middle class demanding electoral reform, "honest" politics, and a vastly enlarged state bureaucracy, a bourgeois industrialist group that ushered in an era of development based on an ideology of economic nationalism, and an urban proletariat that coalesced into a new and critically important political mass. These new groups altered the balance of power in the nation and established new ground rules for a highly competitive political system that eventually seriously threatened political relationships as they had come to be established in the rural areas.[12]

The rigid control of the Vargas years masked, but failed to subvert, the fundamental struggle between centralists and localists in the

Brazilian polity although, for a time, it managed to bridle the masses, particularly the urban masses, by a paternalistic and tutelary extension of syndicalist authority (Lopes 1966; Wiarda 1969). When the Constitution of 1946 reopened the political arena, the system was so full of inherent conflict that it led to its own demise within two short decades. While populist leaders appealed to the new urban masses in successive and successful campaigns for the presidency, rural elites continued to manipulate a relatively diminished rural electorate for control of the Congress, thereby creating a governmental impasse between an executive branch oriented to national industrial growth and a legislature still geared to regional and predominantly agrarian interests (Furtado 1965b).

Anthropologists witnessed these two decades of competition in the Brazilian countryside. Yet the activity they observed and recorded was nothing more than a fleeting moment in the long development of the political system. The Constitution of 1946 encouraged the proliferation of parties at the national, state, and local levels (Soares 1967), but these were little more than vote-getting mechanisms which operated primarily at election time. Unlike the old Republican Party, a multiplicity of parties was organized so that the various aspirants could have vehicles necessary to run for office. They openly competed for political power by securing and extending their followings through bureaucratic sinecures and other forms of patronage. These parties were responsive to the needs of the political leadership they were organized to serve, but quite unable to meet the growing demands of the electorate they helped to create (Forman 1975).

The clientist politics that pervaded the Second Republic were based on relationships between two individuals, the elector and the candidate—more often the candidate's broker—who distributed spoils in exchange for votes. The simple aggregation of vote totals on electoral lists no longer guaranteed support from a state oligarchy as it had in the old republic. There was no longer an entrenched superpatron in the statehouse to whom the coronel-in-power could simply adhere. It was now necessary for local political competitors to procure votes that would win municipal elections and contribute to their party's victory in the state as well, since the government in power would not likely honor its obligations to a município whose political chieftains were members of an opposition party.

At the municipal level, two competing factions serving the interests of rival local notables—sometimes new commercial elites opposing the landowning "native sons"—organized along party lines as well. Political parties became the instruments for access to municipal resources. For the peasantry, dependency became clientship as they and other rural workers were offered a choice between competing patrons. However, the very competition which the system allowed contributed to its downfall as peasants and agricultural workers began to pursue an alternate model to the monopoly power of the coronel. As objects of competitive vote-seeking at the local level, peasants and agricultural workers were subject to a variety of messages, promises, and payoffs. They soon became convinced that the vestiges of paternalism were no longer viable, and that the party structure was not geared to meet their demands. Peasants and rural workers began to bypass the patrons and the electoral system as manifest in increasing absenteeism at the polls and in their adherence to a variety of peasant and rural syndicalist movements (Forman 1971).

Thus, the process of inclusion of peasants into the national Brazilian polity over time contributed to a radical transformation of interclass relationships, from patron-dependency to patron–clientship, from intra-party factional conflict to party mobilization and ultimately to class-based organizations which bypassed the party structure and gathered a momentum which for a time seemed to threaten the very basis of the Brazilian political system. That is, until the "Revolution of 1964" once more made "exclusion" and centralization the dominant themes of Brazilian politics.

## The Peasantry in the Portuguese Political Process

We will now briefly sketch the nature of peasant political participation, or the lack of it, in Portugal in relation to the dominant themes that emerge from our analysis of Brazilian political history. Our point is to demonstrate that the failure of patron–clientship and factionalism to fully develop in Portugal is directly related to the political economy there and to the structure of the national political system in which the homogeneity of the elite sector played a paramount role. The fact that patron–clientism seems to arise at particular places and particular times, supports our contention that it is a response to the exigencies of electoral politics and elite competition for votes.

Portugal has not undergone the degree nor the rate of structural differentiation that characterizes Brazil. At the same time, the Portuguese political system developed and maintained a high degree of centralization from the start, despite the presence of an ideology of "municipalismo." While the very smallness of continental Portugal may very well have mitigated demands for local autonomy, it is probable that an integrated set of kinship and other ties among elites effectively tied periphery to center on critical issues. Furthermore, unlike the shifting locus of authority in colonial Brazil, Lisbon has always been the center of Portugal's bureaucratic structure. The stranglehold that the capital has over the rest of the country never really weakened, either in the Republic (1910–1926) or during the Estado Novo (1926–1974), or even today as post-Revolutionary Portugal demonstrates.

In such circumstances, elite objectives have rarely required the competitive mobilization of rural and urban workers alike. Rather a Bonapartist exclusion model prevailed throughout most of Portuguese history. In the 1870s–80s, a tutelary and paternalistic attitude emerged as part of a newly articulated "republican" political philosophy among intellectual elites who spoke about what would be good for *o povo* (the people), but politics remained very much an elite and urban affair. With perhaps one short-lived exception, political spoils and patron–clientship did not become characteristic of a system of competitive vote-getting in which different and opposed elite sectors sought to mobilize supporters in the cities and in the countryside in hard fought electoral campaigns. Hence, the paradox which led to the demise of the party system in Brazil was not built into the expansion of the party system in Portugal. The circumstances surrounding the imposition of authoritarian rule under Salazar, then, differ markedly from those which led to the 1964 military coup d'etat in Brazil. Nonetheless, the net effects in the countryside of the extension of the administrative state may well turn out to be the same (Forman 1975). We will return to this particular issue in the conclusions. For the moment, we turn to a brief history of peasant political integration in Portugal.[13]

The earliest possibilities for peasant participation in the political process in Portugal only occurred with the advent of the Constitutional Monarchy as a result of the Liberal Revolution of 1820, an event to which the peasantry was largely indifferent (Silbert 1968:38). Still, Liberalism in Portugal hardly represented a demand for democracy or popular sovereignty. Rather, the "democratic burst" which overthrew the absolutist monarchy was encouraged by the loss of the Brazilian colony and the ensuing crisis suffered by northern Portuguese commercial and professional elites. Although an extended franchise was envisioned, the first constitution adopted a system of indirect suffrage, and subsequent decrees significantly limited the size of the electorate. Until 1851, however, Portugal was torn by a series of civil wars and uprisings (1823, 1832–34, 1838, 1846–47). However, with the exception of the uprising of 1846–47, all of these were predominantly conflicts in which the urban and rural bourgeoisie, the clergy, and the nobility aligned and realigned their forces in an attempt to maintain the existing social structure under the aegis of the constitutional monarchy. The transformation of church and mortmain lands into private property in 1834 enabled commercial elites to purchase these lands, thereby establishing a class of rural capitalists tied to the nobility through a series of mutually consistent interests. These groups combined to defeat a nascent urban middle class in the "Setembrist" uprising of 1836, instituting a period of laissez-faire capitalism which dominated Portuguese economic policy for a century thereafter.

Laissez-faire capitalism, an increasing penetration of urban bourgeoisie interests into rural society, a campaign for agrarian individualism, and British trade domination, all contributed to the impoverishment of the peasantry and other rural workers. It is not surprising then that these rural peoples rose up across the country in the movement of Maria da Fonte and the unsuccessful Patuleia uprising of 1846–47 (Riegelhaupt 1976).

These peasant uprisings, despite their temporal proximity to the Revolutions of 1848 which swept through Western Europe, more closely resemble the eighteenth-century French Revolution and earlier nineteenth-century European revolts. They coincided with attempts to change the administrative and land tenure system and with the introduction of new agricultural techniques throughout much of Portugal (Riegelhaupt 1976). New methods of crop rotation, the introduction of cattle raising and dairy farming as well as farm machinery and chemical fertilizers were hallmarks of a new capitalism which increasingly affected patterns of land tenure, specifically communal land rights. North of the Tagus River land enclosures led to a process of parcelization which within a few decades resulted in the *minifúndia* which continue to characterize northern Portuguese agriculture even today. In the Alentejo to the south, large landholdings were consolidated and vast areas left uncultivated (Halpern Pereira 1971:137–38). It was an alliance of the rural bourgeoisie with the commercial elites of Lisbon which effectively put down the Patuleia uprising (with British intervention) and successfully blocked any program of agrarian reform in Portugal until recent years.

After the Patuleia, Portuguese political life continued to be marked by exclusion of the masses, despite some initial concessions in the decrees of 1851 which led to a slightly increased electorate. The rural bourgeoisie, members of the liberal professions, and the commercial elites of the growing cities of Lisbon and Porto were organized into two parties which manipulated elections so as to assure their control of the legislature. This two-party system, a semi-developed British parliamentary model, sufficed to alternate incumbents in office in a system of *rotativismo* which makes evident the factional rather than sectoral nature of Portuguese politics at the time. No significant rural-urban cleavage took place which required rural elites to enter the political arena as self-interested competitors. Government policies effectively curtailed peasants' access to education (hence literacy) and consequently to enfranchisement. Hence, "mass participation" never occurred, and under both the Constitutional Monarchy (1821–1909) and the First Republic (1910–1926) "towns had a greater significance than rural areas in legitimate and conscious balloting" (Oliveira Marques 1972:161).

Toward the end of the nineteenth century, a system of *caciquisimo* seems to have emerged in various rural regions as issues of protectionism effected the expansion of wheat production, particularly in the Alentejo. This surge of political patron–clientelism, as in the Brazilian case, was directly related to the desire of landowners to have a sympathetic voice in the National Assembly. In Portugal it reached its apex in those zones where there were resources for patrons to control and peasants able to vote. What is critically different from the Brazilian context, however, is the fact that "cacique" control in Portugal seems to have occurred only in certain areas, like the Alentejo, and that it was a relatively short-lived phenomenon. Although controlled, rigged elections and governmental dispersing of bureaucratic sinecures also characterized the Portuguese constitutional monarchy, the limited nature of the electorate confined most patterns of patronage to cities and towns. This urban preponderance occurred in a country that was, in fact, heavily rural.

Perhaps the most significant political act on the part of the Portuguese peasantry from the last quarter of the nineteenth century through the 1930s was their migration into the urban centers of Lisbon and Porto and their emigration out of the country. Between 1878 and 1890, Lisbon's population doubled and more than one-eighth of the nation's population was located in the capital and Porto. While it is not possible to give exact figures for emigration, Orlando Ribeiro estimates that between 1890–1940, 1.2 million Portuguese left the country (Serrão n.d.:39).[14] The national political and economic problems, many of which underlay this vast movement of the population, led intellectuals, statesmen, and philosophers alike to the "myth of Republicanism" (Wheeler 1972).

Republicanism in Portugal takes on a special form. Initially acceptable to the ruling elites as an alternative to socialism and anarchism, it became identified with nationalism and the removal of foreign control over the nation and her African colonies. It also became synonymous with anticlericalism and "good government," which in turn meant a decentralization of political control from Lisbon back into the countryside and an end to bureaucratic corruption.

The sixteen chaotic years of the First Portuguese Republic (1910–1926), despite a profusion of elections, continued the previous pattern of excluding the peasants from participation. While the overthrow of the monarchy had involved the mobilization of the urban masses, including recent rural migrants, the rural masses were themselves scarcely heard from. Once more, under the First Republic, despite the rhetoric, educational policies and a literacy requirement for voting resulted in a decidedly restricted electorate. Republican ideals did begin to filter into the countryside as the myriad of small-town local newspapers make evident; however, the vast majority of peasants and agricultural workers were illiterate, and it is difficult to know in exactly what form these ideas were communicated to them. A series of rural strikes in the Alentejo attests to the politicization of rural workers there, a singular event in Portuguese rural history (Cabral 1974:433). Thus, in the Alentejo where clientship, through the equation of large-scale estates, landless laborers and the need for votes, had been most highly developed, class-based politics began to emerge (Cutileiro 1971:217).

With the advent of Salazar in 1928 and the subsequent imposition of the Constitution of the Estado Novo (1936), the very concept of competitive political activity—whether for the peasantry or a restricted electorate—was removed from Portuguese life. Landlord-laborer strife, as well as industrial strife, was inimical to a societal model of "harmony" which denied the existence of class conflict. Rather, a Catholic corporativist model became the ideological center of a political system which discouraged participation, encouraged political apathy, restricted educational opportunities, and institutionalized a non-party party (Riegelhaupt in press).

For almost fifty years, until April 1974, Portugal was governed as an authoritarian political system with no "liberal" pretensions. This highly centralized state needed no local level participation or concurrence. It governed from the center, distributing sufficient resources to the populace so as to maintain order. A system which set low and achievable goals, it made few promises and through extensive censorship effectively controlled the spread of different messages to the countryside. At the local level, both peasant and shopkeeper were harassed by an overwhelming number of administrative rules and regulations, enforced by an ubiquitous rural police force (and paid informers) which served to keep the population in check. The direct penetration of the state into many aspects of local life cut the peasant off from the local elite and vice versa. Even in the regions like the Alentejo where the political economy under the Constitutional Monarchy and the First Republic permitted the development of patron-clientism (through a combination of votes, jobs, and land), the peasantry was completely cut off from access to the political arena. Under the Estado Novo, even those rural elites who had encouraged clientship saw less and less advantages to having followers since their interests were accommodated by policies which provided a protected and stabilized economic environment (Cutileiro 1971:222, 241).

Thus, vertical ties presented to us as characteristic of peasant sociopolitical organization—those enduring dyadic ties and their emergent corollaries of networks, action sets, and coalitions—ceased to have any meaning or function for the peasant, within the Portuguese political system. Moreover, the Estado Novo specifically excluded interest-based party organizations, leaving the government to function without any form of local level participation except for acquiescence. Salazar's corporatist authoritarian state did not substitute "party patronage" for the "patron–client" system as posited by developmental models of southern European politics (Weingrod 1968). Acquiescence was enforced by a repressive, if not exceedingly oppressive, political climate and the possibilities for emigration. Administration replaced politics for both the peasantry and the elite.

If then, the process of inclusion of peasants into the national Brazilian polity over time led to a radical transformation of interclass relationships, from patron-dependency to patron–clientship, to a short period of class-based conflict, the Portuguese peasantry, for the most part, experienced neither the reality nor the model.

## Conclusion

Thus far, we have not discussed the current regimes in Brazil and Portugal, nor have we suggested the possible effects that these regimes might have in the countryside. In relation to Portugal, the dramatic events of the years since the April Revolution of 1974 make predictions unwarranted and highly speculative in any case. Elsewhere, Forman has discussed the apparent immediate result of the imposition of centralized, authoritarian rule in Brazil in 1964, noting that the direction which the military regime was then taking pointed to certain identifiable outcomes in the countryside (1975). Namely, he argued that the discussion of elite competition through the nullification of simultaneous and closely linked elections at local, state, and national levels, coupled with strict fiscal controls at the center and the consequent dissolution of the spoils system, militated against forms of local level competition which previously had resulted in widespread patron–clientism.[15] That process of extension of the administrative state was dubbed the "portugalization" of Brazil (Schmitter 1971b). To invert the analogy, within a few months of the Portuguese Revolution of 1974, there was a clear possibility that it could have undergone a process of "Brazilianization." Direct mobilization around basic socio-economic issues and competition among varying party alignments and sectors of the military could have led to a new form of authoritarian response.[16]

It is hardly the moment to engage in any form of academic opportunism. Yet, the logical conclusion of this paper is to suggest that the authoritarian political system of Brazil and the emergent political system of Portugal provide new opportunities for the analysis of peasant political participation (Forman 1977). As we have briefly shown, pat assumptions about peasants' behavioral propensities (i.e., toward clientelism or dependence) or cultural "traditions" mask the complexities of the political process in agrarian-based societies. The nation-state in these two cases did not encapsulate some previously closed local level political system. Rather, the state provided the system within which local participation could and did take place. The nature of the state political system, the position of that state within the world economy, elite interests, the structure of the local economy as well as local society are all vital aspects for the study of local level politics.

Anthropologists must be wary of reading the past from the ethnographic present. We are perhaps most guilty of presenting a timeless "traditional" cultural system which other social scientists now routinely feed into their developmental analyses as the antithesis of "modernization." Yet, in societies like Portugal and Brazil, peasants have not been out of step with the national political system. On the contrary, they have occupied an important position within the larger system, a position which is quite capable of change. Rather than studying the points of juncture between the local level and the larger system, the analyst of local level politics must begin to develop a set of tools which encompass both peasants and local elites within the framework of the larger polity over time. We must study conflict and power not merely in the limited arena of the endless "factional" disputes of Brazilian elites, for example, but within the broader structure of resource dispersal within the national (or regional) political system. Perhaps the proper place for anthropologists to begin their investigation of politics might be to ask a set of interrelated questions:

1. What are the "legitimate" political goals as derived from the dominant ideologies available within the system?
2. What modes of organization are possible, and how are they effected at various levels of the political system (thus relating land tenure, market products, and resource allocation to type of oligarchic structure)?
3. What is the nature of demands on the system at these different levels and how are they met?
4. If they are not met, what alternate forms of political expression are available and what forms do they take in action?

Too much of "local level" politics and particularly Brazilian patron–client/factionalism literature reads like the "formalist" literature on "prestige" economies of tribal peoples. Basically positivistic, the political anthropology of peasant societies—like economic anthropology—has concentrated primarily on exchange between patrons and clients, emphasizing the utilitarian and voluntaristic aspects of decision-making, even when the relationships involved are so asymmetrical as to reduce almost entirely the element of significant choice. The subject of local level politics is not simply coterminous with patrons and clients. Our analysis of peasant participation and mobilization in recent centuries in both Brazil and Portugal shows that the resources available to peasants in their relationships with local elites and to local elites in their quest for power vary as the larger political system operates to include or exclude the rural masses. In both cases, the variations in the structuring of electoral politics was a key factor in understanding peasant political organizational choices. Yet, as Riegelhaupt has shown elsewhere (in press), the apathy of Portuguese peasants under the Salazar regime was not evidence of an inherent "apoliticalness" of the rural masses, but an official demobilization of the people. With the first post-Revolutionary elections in 1975, the previous apathetic and "politically incapable" Portuguese electorate turned out in record numbers. In fact, a full 93.7 percent of the electorate voted.[17] Moreover, from all the reports, rural people voted independently with no evidence of votes being purchased, rigged, or manipulated.

Still, it should be obvious from the argument of this paper that the subject of politics cannot be reduced to voting and elections, and it is not our intention to end on that kind of note. Rather, the point to be made is that only by combining an adequate understanding of the structure of the national political system and the political economy of the state along with regional variations, will we be able to fully grasp the alternatives available to the rural populace. A series of careful studies at the grass-roots level which place an anthropological microanalysis of municipal power structures into an historical macroanalysis should provide not merely the evidence for comprehending the net effects of different kinds of regimes on forms of political participation but also the insights necessary to understand and compare the more subtle and elusive meanings of freedom, liberty, welfare, repression, justice, and all of the other hallmarks of contemporary political systems.

# Notes

1. There is danger in this comparison of which we are well aware. Namely, that some analysts would argue that much of what we are going to discuss below is in fact a result of an all pervasive "Iberic" cultural tradition in which Brazil and Portugal both share. We find the use of the concept of culture in this sense by political scientists in their catchall phrase of "political culture" incorrect, since it tends to parallel the "culture and personality" school's attempts to psychologize about total systems. If any concept of culture is useful in a comparative political framework it is Geertz's view that culture refers to symbols and their meanings that inform behavior and not to the actual behavioral manifestations (such as patron–clientism, factionalism, corruption, etc.) themselves. If culture is viewed in this way, European/Latin American comparisons can be highly instructive, in part because of the importance since the eighteenth century of similar political theories of the state. A Brazilian/Portuguese comparison is made even more interesting since Mediterranean European and Latin American polities have also experienced similar patterns of relationship to Northern European states, as Wallerstein has recently described (1974).

2. A series of community studies in the 1950s under the direction of Charles Wagley set the program for a decade of research. See, for example, Harris 1956, Hutchinson 1957, Wagley 1953. Parallel work among Brazilian anthropologists is best represented by Willems' earlier classic study of Cunha (1947) restudied by Shirley in the mid-1960s (1971). Leed's research on cacao pioneered subsequent localized historical accounts of particular economic phenomenon (Leeds 1957). The community study approach also characterizes much of the anthropological work on Mediterranean Europe. For a discussion of these studies see Davis 1977.

3. A prime example of the anthropological study of the nation state is Wagley's fine discussion of Brazil (1971). Epstein (1973) offers one of the few accounts of the integration between community and state in his study of Brasilia.

4. A recent attempt to modify this approach and collapse the macro- micro-distinction into a single behavioral arena is to be found in Vincent 1977.

5. Given the realities of the Brazilian polity (or polities) over the centuries, the best arena for anthropological inquiry is the município, the local administrative center and its surrounding hinterland. For it is actually over the disposition of resources among commercial (later industrial) and agrarian elites that the battle between the forces of centralism and localism is fought, and it is over control of these resources, once dispersed, that local political struggles take place. It is at this juncture, where electoral politics and spoils come together, that patrons and clients enter Brazilian ethnology. A focus on the município allows a special vantage point, then, from which both the micro-level and the macro-system can be examined.

6. For a discussion of the concept of "political culture" in the Brazilian context, see Forman 1977.

7. Forman was himself guilty of an evasion of 450 years of Brazilian political history when he wrote:
"Traditionally, the Brazilian peasant participated only vicariously in the political process by exchanging his vote for the favor of a patrão. He was insulated from the pressures of the outside world by the attitude of noblesse oblige of the plantation master. Communication was unidirectional, passed down along the rigid lines of the social hierarchy. Alternative courses of action for the rural masses were few. Grievances could only be aired to the patrão or through open rebellion." (1971:5)

Such a characterization fails both to describe the "traditional" system and the historical processes of change and integration.

8. Detailed discussions about the nature of Brazilian and Portuguese regimes have been made elsewhere individually (Forman 1975; Riegelhaupt 1976, in press).

9. The outstanding study of municipal politics in Brazil is Leal 1948. For an interesting account of four recent coroneis, see Vilaça and Albuquerque (1965). A number of studies of local politics have appeared in the *Revista Brasileira de Estudos Políticos.*

10. Della Cava describes how local coroneis vied with one another for the privilege of supporting the state oligarchy in Ceará—which simply waited for a victor to emerge—and to the victor belonged all the electoral spoils. (1970:94–95; 142)

11. It seems to us, at a glance, that factionalism best describes the infighting between rivals who recruit individuals into groups or units of a certain scale, but that social differentiation and the emergence of different "interest groups" may well produce a form of competition more akin to sectoral clashes that have gone unnoticed in studies of rural Brazil.

12. Schmitter (1971a:29–30) suggests that the system moved from semi-competitive (competition at the local level) to fully competitive (competition at the local and national levels) during the Goulart regime. It is at this juncture that the distinction between "factionalism" as rivalry and sectoral competition should be explored.

13. The anthropologist attempting to analyze nineteenth-century rural Portuguese society is working in very poorly understood terrain. Only in recent years has work been undertaken as evidenced in the writings of Serrão, Halpern Pereira, Vitor de Sá, Villaverde Cabral, Silbert and, in this country, Douglas Wheeler.

14. In 1890, Portugal's population was 4.6 million (Serrão 1971:799); in 1940, it was 7 million. (Serrão n.d.:91)

15. This does not mean that the government does not permit the continuance of rivalrous factions at the local level in some places as long as they pose no threat to the imposed administrative structures. This, in fact, may account for the disagreements between Forman and Gross (1973).

16. One need only mention the Spinolista attempt from the Right on March 11, 1975 and the abortive Leftist activities of November 25, 1975.

17. In the elections of 1975, suffrage was extended to all males and females over the age of 18. Registration was 6,177,698, of whom 5,666,696 voted. In contrast, in the last election of the Estado Novo in November 1973, in which one list of candidates was presented, only 2,096,020 were registered voters. (The franchise was limited by sex, age, and literacy requirements.) The actual number of votes cast was 1,393,294 for a turnout of 66.5 percent of the eligible voters. From one regime to another, the franchise was expanded by 66 percent and there was an increase of 75.4 percent in the number actually voting (Instituto Nacional de Estatística 1974; see also "Os resultados oficiais das ultimas eleições," *O Seculo,* November 11, 1973).

# Glossary of Portuguese Terms

| | |
|---|---|
| *agrópolis:* | planned towns of about 300 people along the Trans-Amazon Highway. |
| *agrovila:* | planned nucleated village settlement along the Trans-Amazon Highway. |
| *almoço:* | lunch, the noon meal. |
| *ambiente:* | atmosphere. |
| *aviamento:* | a system of trade in the Amazon Basin in which goods were exchanged for raw forest products, usually latex. |
| *bairro:* | neighborhood. |
| *barraco:* | wooden shack. |
| *biscateiro:* | someone who is marginally employed doing odd jobs. |
| *branco:* | white, a white person. |
| *broca:* | (*Hypothenemus hampei Ferrari*) a coffee pest which burrows into the beans. |
| *caatinga:* | low, thorny scrub forest of the northeast interior. |
| *caboclo:* | anyone of part Indian descent; a rustic backwoodsman. |
| *cabos eleitorais:* | local ward heelers. |
| *cachaça:* | a crude Brazilian rum. |
| *caipira:* | backwoods rustic, peasant. |
| *caridade:* | charity. |
| *carta patente:* | a written document issued to Indian chiefs recognizing their authority. |
| *casa matriz:* | maternal home, home of orientation. |
| *cerrado:* | "closed" savannah. |
| *chefe:* | chief, leader. |
| *cidade:* | city, town. |
| *cidade cogumelo:* | literally "mushroom city"; a city that grows up very rapidly. |
| *coalhada:* | curds. |
| *colégio:* | high school. |

| | |
|---|---|
| *colono:* | worker paid on a monthly basis to care for a set number of coffee trees. |
| *comadre:* | literally "co-mother"; the relationship between a child's godmother and its parents. |
| *comarca:* | judicial district. |
| *compadria:* | godparenthood, also called *parentesco.* |
| *consulta:* | spiritual consultation. |
| *copa:* | community kitchen. |
| *coronel* (pl. *coroneis*): | wealthy landowners who bought commissions in the national militia during the Empire and Old Republic; local political power. |
| *coronelismo:* | rule by *coroneis.* |
| *cortiço:* | slum at the outskirts of a city. |
| *cruzeiro:* | Brazilian monetary unit. In 1978 one cruzeiro equaled about U.S. $0.6. (U.S. 6 cents). |
| | |
| *delegado:* | head of the local police, delegate, representative. |
| *deputado estadual:* | state representative. |
| *desconfiança:* | suspicion, mistrust. |
| *despachante:* | literally "dispatcher"; a bureaucratic middleman. |
| *drogas de sertão:* | literally "drugs of the backland"; refers to all manner of wild forest products. |
| | |
| *edilidades:* | Indian town councils created during the colonial period. |
| *elemento de côr:* | color factor. |
| *empanemado:* | having bad luck. |
| *entrância:* | career level. |
| *espera:* | waiting point where hunters remain near plants known to be attractive to game animals. |
| *espigões:* | colloquialism for high-rise condominiums. |
| *Espiritismo:* | Spiritism, also known as *Kardecismo,* a form of Spiritism derived from France. |
| *Estado Novo:* | "new state"; refers to the Getulio Vargas regime. |
| | |
| *família:* | family. |
| *farinha:* | manioc flour. |
| *farinha puba:* | coarse manioc flour. |
| *favela:* | a shantytown; often refers to the hillside shantytowns of Rio de Janeiro. |
| *fazenda:* | a large landholding, a ranch. |
| *fazendeiro:* | the owner of a *fazenda.* |
| *feira:* | market. |
| *filha (filho) de santo:* | literally "daughter (or son) of the saint"; a medium in an Afro-Brazilian or Umbanda cult. |
| *filhos:* | sons, children. |
| *força:* | force, power. |

*frequesia:*  parish town established in the Amazon region during the Colonial period.

*guerras justas:*  lit. "just wars."

*homens de côr:*  men of color.

*igrejinhas:*  little churches.

*juiz de direito:*  judge of law, a professional judge.
*juiz substituto:*  substitute judge.
*jurisprudência:*  written court decisions.

*latifúndia:*  a large landholding.
*latifúndista:*  owner of a *latifúndia.*
*laudos:*  expert opinions.
*lingua geral:*  an inter-tribal lingua franca based on Tupi-Guaraní.

*madrinha:*  maid of honor in a wedding ceremony.
*mãe de santo:*  literally "mother of the saint"; a leader of an Afro-Brazilian or Umbanda cult.
*mais elevado:*  of higher social status.
*maloca:*  communal Indian dwelling.
*mata:*  forest; evergreen forest of the Amazon Basin.
*mazombismo:*  an attitude that denigrates all that is Brazilian and admires all that is European.
*mazombo:*  individual with a *mazombismo* outlook.
*mediunidade:*  inherent potential mediumship.
*mestiço:*  an individual of Indian-white ancestry.
*minifúndia:*  small landholding.
*mulher:*  woman, wife.
*município:*  county.

*oure verde:*  lit. "green gold," a euphemism for coffee during periods of high prices.

*pãe de santo:*  literally "father of the saint," the leader of an Afro-Brazilian or Umbanda cult.
*panema:*  bad luck.
*parentela:*  large extended networks of kin related both consanguineally and affinally.
*parentesco:*  godparenthood; also called *compadria.*
*passe:*  a ritual cleansing in Umbanda ceremonies.
*patrão:*  employer, boss, patron.
*paus finos:*  thin trunked forest growth.
*pesqueiros:*  broad ecological zones of the ocean floor; particular fishing spots.

| | |
|---|---|
| *pessoa de côr:* | person of color. |
| *ponto:* | Umbanda hymn. |
| *potreiro:* | small enclosed pasture for draft and saddle animals. |
| *prefeito:* | mayor. |
| *preto:* | black, a black person. |
| *primo irmão:* | lit. "brother cousin"; first cousin. |
| *professora:* | teacher. |
| *promotor público:* | public prosecutor. |
| | |
| *redução* (pl. *reduções*): | Jesuit mission. |
| *remoso:* | dangerous. |
| *requeijão:* | homemade cheese. |
| *rurópolis:* | planned cities of 1,000 or more families along the Trans-Amazon Highway. |
| | |
| *saveiro:* | fishing boat. |
| *sede de município:* | county seat. |
| *sertanejo:* | a backlander; a native of Brazil's arid northeast. |
| *sessões:* | Umbanda religious sessions. |
| *sindicato:* | labor union. |
| | |
| *terra firme:* | uplands away from the main rivers of the Amazon Basin. |
| *terra roxa:* | a deep red porous soil particularly well-suited to coffee cultivation. |
| *terreiro:* | Umbanda cult centers; also called *centros espírites*. |
| *timbó:* | poisonous vine used to stupefy fish in the Amazon Basin. |
| *trampolin:* | launching pad. |
| *travessão* (pl. *travessões*): | narrow dividing road. |
| *tropas de resgate:* | "rescue missions," a euphemism for slave raids during the colonial period. |
| | |
| *Umbanda:* | a form of Spiritism with Afro-Brazilian and Indian elements that has gained wide popularity in Brazil. |
| *Umbandista:* | member of an Umbanda cult. |
| *urucu:* | (*Bixa orellana*), a pigment used in body painting among many Brazilian Indians. |
| *usina:* | a modern heavily capitalized sugar mill and, by extension, the lands pertaining to it. |
| *usurário:* | money lender. |
| | |
| *vara:* | literally, a rod or sceptre; a judgeship or judicial place. |
| *vinho:* | wine. |
| *vogal* (pl. *vogais*): | class representative in judicial proceedings. |

# REFERENCES

Abernethy, Thomas P.
1922 *The Formative Period in Alabama: 1815–1828.* Montgomery: Boston Printing Company.
1961 *The South in the New Nation: 1789–1819.* Baton Rouge: Louisiana State University Press.

Adams, Richard N.
1967 "Political power and social structures." In Claudio Veliz, ed., *The Politics of Conformity in Latin America,* pp. 15–42. New York: Oxford University Press.

Albers, Patricia and Seymour Parker
1971 "The Plains Vision Experience: A Study of Power and Privilege." *Southwestern Journal of Anthropology* 27(3):203–33.

Aldersheim, Úrsula
1962 *Uma Comunidade Teuto-Brasileiro.* Rio de Janeiro: Centro Brasileiro de Pesquisas Educacionais, INEP, MEC.

Allen, M. R.
1967 *Male Cults and Secret Initiations in Melanesia.* New York: Cambridge University Press.

Allen, William L. and James B. Richardson III
1971 "The Reconstruction of Kinship from Archaeological Data: The Concepts, the Methods, and the Feasibility." *American Antiquity* 36(1):41–53.

Amado, Jorge
1965 *The Violent Land.* Samuel Putnam, trans. New York: Knopf.

Andrade, Mário de
1928 *Macunaíma.* 1st ed. São Paulo: Eugênio Cupolo.

Araujo Lima, Alceu Maynard
1961 *Medicina Rústica: Piaçabuço Vale do São Francisco.* São Paulo: Companhia Editôra Nacional.

Armillas, Pedro
1957 *Programa de Historia de la América Indígena: América Pre-columbina.* Vol. 1. Washington: Pan American Union.

Aubert, Vilhelm (ed.)
1969 *Sociology of Law.* Baltimore: Penguin.
Azevedo, Fernando de
1950 *Brazilian Culture.* New York: Macmillan.
Azevedo, Thales de
1953 *Les Elites de Couleur dans une Ville Brésilienne.* Paris: UNESCO.
1963 *Social Change in Brazil.* Gainesville: University of Florida Press.
1975 *Italianos e Gauchos.* Porto Alegre: A Nação/Instituto Estadual do Livro-DAC/SEC.
Baena, Antonio L. Monteiro
1969 (orig. 1838) *Compêndio das Eras da Província do Pará.* Belém: Universidade Federal do Pará.
Bailey, Frederick George
1963 *Politics and Social Change: Orissa in 1957.* Berkeley: University of California Press.
1969 *Strategems and Spoils: A Social Anthropology of Politics.* New York: Schocken.
Baldus, Herbert
1970 *Tapirapé, Tribo Tupí no Brasil Central.* São Paulo: Companhia Editôra Nacional.
Bamberger, Joan
1968 "The Adequacy of Kayapó Ecological Adjustment." Paper presented at the 38th International Congress of Americanists, Stuttgart.
1974 "Naming and Transmission of Status in a Central Brazilian Society." *Ethnology* 13(4):363–78.
Banner, H.
1953 "A casa dos homens Gorotire." *Revista do Museu Paulista* 6:455–59.
Banton, Michael
1969 "Law Enforcement and Local Control." In Vilhelm Aubert, ed., *Sociology of Law,* pp. 127–41. Baltimore: Penguin.
Barandiarán, Daniel
1967 "Agricultura y recolección entre los indios Sanemá-Hanoama." *Antropológica* (Venezuela) 19:24–50.
Barata, Frederico
1952 "Arqueologia." In Rodrigo Melo Franco de Andrade, ed., *Artes Plásticas no Brasil,* pp. 13–74. Rio de Janeiro: Graf Ouvidor.
Barnes, John
1962 "African Models in the New Guinea Highlands." *Man* 62(1):5–9.
Barth, Frederik
1966 *Models of Social Organization.* Occasional Paper No. 23. London: Royal Anthropological Institute.
Barton, R. F.
1919 *Ifugao Law.* University of California Publications in American Archaeology and Ethnology No. 15. Berkeley: University of California Press.
Bastide, Roger
1944 "Estudos Afro-Brasileiros." *Revista do Arquivo Municipal* 98:83–103.

1945 *Imagens do Nordeste Místico em Branco e Preto*. Rio de Janeiro: Gráfica 'O Cruzeiro'.

1951 "Religion and the Church in Brazil." In T. Lynn Smith, ed., *Brazil: Portrait of Half a Continent*, pp. 334–55. New York: Dryden Press.

1958 *Le Candomblé de Bahia (Rite Nagô)*. The Hague: Mouton.

1960 *Les Réligions Africaines au Brésil: Vers une Sociologie des Interpénétrations de Civilisations*. Paris: Presses Universitaires de France.

1970 *Le Prochain et le Loitain*. Paris: Editions Cujas.

Bastide, Roger and Florestan Fernandes

1951 *Brancos e Negros em São Paulo*. São Paulo: Companhia Editôra Nacional.

1955 *Relações Raciais Entre Negros e Brancos em São Paulo*. São Paulo: Editôra Anhembi Ltda.

1971 "O preconceito racial em São Paulo." In Roger Bastide and Florestan Fernandes, eds., *Brancos e Negros em São Paulo*, pp. 271–300. 3d ed. Companhia Editôra Nacional.

Bates, Henry Walter

1962 (orig. 1864) *The Naturalist on the River Amazons*. Berkeley: University of California Press.

Bateson, Gregory

1958 *Naven*. Stanford: Stanford University Press.

Becker, E.

1965 *Ecological Systems in the Amazon*. M.A. thesis, University of Chicago.

Bettelheim, Bruno

1954 *Symbolic Wounds*. Glencoe, Ill.: The Free Press.

Billington, Ray Allen

1967 "The American Frontier." In Paul Bohannen and Fred Plog, eds., *Beyond the Frontier*, pp. 3–24. Garden City, N.Y.: Natural History Press.

Biocca, Ettore

1970 *Yanoáma: the Narrative of a White Girl Kidnapped by Amazonian Indians*. New York: Dutton.

Black, Francis

1975 "Infectious Diseases in Primitive Societies." *Science* 187:515–18.

Blaut, James M., Ruth Blaut, Nan Harman, and Michael Moerman

1959 "A Study of Cultural Determinants of Soil Erosion and Conservation in the Blue Mountains of Jamaica." *Social and Economic Studies* 8:402–20.

Bohannan, Paul

1957 *Justice and Judgement Among the Tiv*. New York: Oxford University Press.

Boissevain, Jeremy

1966 "Patronage in Sicily." *Man*, n.s. 1(1):18–33.

Borges Pereira, J. B.

1967 *Côr, Profissão, e Mobilidade: o Negro e o Rádio de São Paulo*. São Paulo: Livraria Pioneira Editôra-Editôra da Universidade de São Paulo.

## 408   REFERENCES

Bott, Elizabeth
   1957 *Family and Social Networks: Roles, Norms, and External Relationships in Ordinary Urban Families*. London: Tavistock.
Bowman, Isaiah
   1931 *The Pioneer Fringe*. Special Publication 13. New York: American Geographical Society.
Brazilian Studies
   1975 *The Politics of Genocide Against the Indians of Brazil*. Toronto.
Brown, Diana DeG.
   1974 *Umbanda: Politics of an Urban Religious Movement*. Ph.D. dissertation. Columbia University
   1977 "O papel histórico da classe média na Umbanda." *Religião e Sociedade* 1(1):31–42.
Cabral, Manuel Villaverde
   1974 *Materiais para a História da Questão Agrária em Portugal: Seculos XIX e XX*. Porto: Editorial Inova.
Caldeira, Clovis
   1956 *Mutirão: Formas de Ajuda Mútua no Meio Rural*. São Paulo: Editôra Nacional.
Camara, José Gomes B.
   1964–1973 *Subsidíos Para a História do Direito Pátrio*. 5 vols. Rio de Janeiro: Livraria Brasiliana.
Camargo, Candido Procopio Ferreira de
   1961a *Aspectos del Espiritismo en São Paulo:* Friburgo: Oficina Internacional de Investigaciones Sociales de FERES.
   1961b *Kardecismo e Umbanda*. São Paulo: Livraria Pioneira Editôra.
Campanhole, Adriano
   1974 *Consolidação dos Leis do Trabalho*. 36th ed., Rio de Janeiro: Editôra Atlas.
Candido, Antonio
   1964 *Os Parceiros do Rio Bonito*. Rio de Janeiro: José Olympio Editôra.
Cardoso, Fernando Henrique
   1962 *Capitalismo e Escravidão no Brasil Meridional: o Negro na Sociedade Escravocrata do Rio Grande do Sul*. São Paulo: Difusão Europeia do Livro.
   1964 *Empresário Industrial e Desenvolvimento Econômico no Brasil*. São Paulo: Difusão Européia do Livro.
   1972 *O Modelo Político Brasileiro e Outros Ensaios*. São Paulo: Difusão Européia do Livro.
Cardoso, Fernando Henrique and Otavio Ianni
   1960 *Côr e Mobilidade em Florianopolis: Aspectos das Relações Entre Negros e Brancos numa Communidade do Brasil Meridional*. São Paulo: Companhia Editôra Nacional.
Carneiro, Edison
   1937 *Negros Bantus*. Biblioteca de Divulgação Científica. Rio de Janeiro: Editôra Civilização Brasileira.
   1948 *Candomblés da Bahia*. Bahia: Publicação do Museu do Estado.

Carneiro, Robert L.
  1960 "Slash and Burn Agriculture: A Closer Look at Its Implications for Settle-
       ment Patterns." In Anthony F. C. Wallace, ed., *Men and Cultures*, pp.
       229–34. (Selected papers of the 5th International Congress of Anthropo-
       logical and Ethnological Sciences). Philadelphia: University of Pennsyl-
       vania Press.
  1961 "Slash and Burn Cultivation Among the Kuikuru and Its Implications for
       Cultural Development in the Amazon Basin." In Johannes Wilbert, ed.,
       *The Evolution of Horticultural Systems in Native South America: Causes
       and Consequences*, pp. 47–67. Antropológica (Venuzuela), Supplement
       2.
  1964 "Shifting Cultivation Among the Amahuaca of Eastern Peru." *Volker-
       kundliche Abandlungen*, Hannover, 1:9–18.
  1968 "The Transition from Hunting to Horticulture in the Amazon Basin." In
       *Proceedings of the International Congress of Anthropological and Ethno-
       logical Sciences*. Tokyo: Science Council of Japan.
  1970 "A Theory of the Origin of the State." *Science* 169:733–38.
  n.d. "A Computer Simulation Model of Population Growth in the Amazon
       Basin." Manuscript.
Carvajal, Gaspar de, Alonso de Rojas, and Cristobal Acuna
  1941 *Descobrimento do Rio das Amazonas*. C. de Melo Leitão, ed. and trans.
       São Paulo: Editôra Nacional.
Carvalho Franco, Maria Sylvia de
  1969 *Homens Livre na Ordem Escavocrata*. Instituto de Estudos Brasileiros.
       São Paulo: Universidade de São Paulo.
Castro, Josué de
  1967 *Geografia da Fome*. São Paulo: Editôra Brasiliense.
Cecchi, Camilo
  1959 "Determinantes e características da emigração italiana." *Sociologia*
       21(1). São Paulo.
Chagnon, Napoleon
  1968a *Yanamamö: The Fierce People*. New York: Holt, Rinehart.
  1968b "Yanamamö Social Organization and Warfare." In M. Fried, R. Mur-
        phy, and M. Harris, eds., *War: The Anthropology of Armed Conflict and
        Aggression*, pp. 109–59. New York: Natural History Press.
  1968c "The Culture-Ecology of Shifting (pioneering) Cultivation among the
        Yanamamö Indians." *Proceedings of the VIII International Congress of
        Anthropological and Ethnological Sciences*. (Tokyo) 3:249–55.
  1973 *Studying the Yanamamö*. New York: Holt, Rinehart.
  1975 Unpublished lecture. Lehman College, New York, February 17, 1975.
  1977 *Yanamamö: The Fierce People*. 2d ed. New York: Holt, Rinehart, and
       Winston.
Chagnon, Napoleon, James V. Neel, Lowell Weitkamp, Henry Gershowitz, and
Manuel Ayres.
  1970 "The Influence of Cultural Factors on the Demography and Pattern of
       Gene Flow from the Makiritare to the Yanoama Indians." *American Jour-
       nal of Physical Anthropology* 32:339–50.

# 410    REFERENCES

Chambliss, William J. and Robert B. Seidman
    1971 *Law, Order, and Power*. Reading, Mass.: Addison-Wesley.
Chandler, Billy Jayne
    1972 *The Feitosas and the Sertão dos Inhamuns*. Gainesville: University of Florida Press.
Chavez, J. M., E. Pechnick, and I. V. Mattoso
    1949 "Estudo da constituição química e do valor alimentício da pupunha (*Guilielma speciosa* Mart.)." *Arquivos Brasilienses de Nutrição* 6(3):185–92.
Christaller, Walter and August Lösch
    1954 *The Economics of Locations*. New Haven: Yale University Press.
Ciriacy-Wantrup, S. V.
    1963 *Resource Conservation, Economics and Policies*. Revised ed. Berkeley: University of California Press.
Coale, Ansley
    1974 "The History of the Human Population." *Scientific American* (September), 231:41–51.
Cohn, David L.
    1956 *The Life and Times of King Cotton*. New York: Oxford University Press.
Comitas, Lambros
    1962 *Fishermen and Cooperation in Rural Jamaica*. Ph.D. dissertation, Columbia University.
Conklin, Harold
    1957 *Hanunóo Agriculture: a Report on the Integral System of Shifting Cultivation in the Philippines*. Rome: Food and Agriculture Organization. Forestry Development Paper No. 12.
Cooper, John M.
    1942 "Areal and Temporal Aspects of Aboriginal South American Culture." *Primitive Man* 15(1–2):1–38.
Costa, Esdra Borges
    1960 *Cerrado e Retiro: Cidade e Fazenda no Alto São Francisco*. Rio de Janeiro: Comissão Nacional do Vale do São Francisco.
Costa Pinto, Luis A.
    1953 *O Negro no Rio de Janeiro: Relações de Raça numa Sociedade em Mudança*. São Paulo: Companhia Editôra Nacional.
Coutinho, Afrânio
    1969 *An Introduction to Literature in Brazil*. Gregory Rabassa, trans. New York: Columbia University Press.
Craven, Avery
    1925 *Soil Exhaustion as a Factor in the Agricultural History of Virginia and Maryland, 1606–1860*. University of Illinois Studies in the Social Sciences, vol. 13, no. 1. Urbana: University of Illinois Press.
Crocker, J. Christopher
    1969 "Reciprocity and Hierarchy Among the Eastern Bororo." *Man* 4(1):44–58.
    1973 "Marital Discord and Household Dynamics Among the Eastern Bororo." Paper presented at the 72d Annual Meeting of the American Anthropological Association, New Orleans.

Crocker, William H.

1961 "The Canela since Nimuendajú: a Preliminary Report on Change." *Anthropological Quarterly* 34(1):69–84.

1964 "Conservatism Among the Canela: An Analysis of Contributing Factors." In *Actas y Memorias* (35th Congreso Internacional de Americanistas, Mexico, 1962), 3:341–346.

1971 "Observations Concerning Certain Ramkókamekra-Canela (Brazil) Indian Restrictive Taboo Practices." 3:337–39. In *Verhandlungen*, 38th Internationalen Amerikanisterkongresses, Stuttgart-München, 1968. München: Klaus Renner.

1972a "The Non-Adaptation of a Savanna Indian Tribe (Canela, Brazil) to Forced Forest Relocation: An Analysis of Factors." In *Anais*, 1:213–81. Encontro Internacional de Estudos Brasileiros, September 1971. São Paulo: Instituto de Estudos Brasileiros 21.

1972b "Canela Kinship: What Principles They Utilize and Some Factors in Change." Paper presented at the 71st annual meeting of the American Anthropological Association, Toronto.

1973 "Canela Marriage." Paper presented at the 72d annual meeting of the American Anthropological Association, New Orleans.

1974 "Extramarital Sexual Practices of the Ramkókramekra-Canela: An Analysis of Socio-Cultural Factors." In Patricia J. Lyon, ed., *Native South Americans: Ethnology of the Least Known Continent*, pp. 184–94. Boston: Little, Brown.

1977 "Canela 'Group' Recruitment and Perpetuity: Incipient 'Unilineality'?" In *Actes*, 2:259–75. 42d Congrès International des Americanistes, Paris, 1976. Paris.

1978 "Histórias das épocas de pré e pós-pacificação dos Ramkókamekra e Apâniekra-Canelas." *Boletim do Museu Paraense Emílio Goeldi*, pp. 1–30. n.s. Antropologia 68. Belem.

Cutileiro, José

1971 *A Portuguese Rural Society*. London: Clarendon Press.

Da Cunha, Euclides

1944 (orig. 1902) *Rebellion in the Backlands (Os Sertões)*. Samuel Putnam, trans. Chicago: University of Chicago Press.

Da Matta, Roberto

1971 "Uma breve reconsideração da morfologia social Apinayé." In *Verhandlungen*, 3:355–364. 38th Internationalen Amerikanisterkongresses, Stuttgart-München, 1968. München: Klaus Renner.

1973 "A Reconsideration of Apinayé Social Morphology." In Daniel R. Gross, ed., *Peoples and Cultures of Native South America*, pp. 277–91. New York: Natural History Press.

1976 *Um Mundo Dividido: A Estructura Social dos Índios Apinayé*. Coleção Antropologia 10. Petrópolis: Vozes.

David, René and Henry P. de Vries

1958 *The French Legal System*. New York: Oceana Publications.

David, René and John E. C. Brierley

1969 *Major Legal Systems in the World Today*. London: The Free Press.

Davis, Charles S.
1939 *The Cotton Kingdom in Alabama*. Montgomery: Ala.: State Department of Archives and History.
Davis, John
1977 *People of the Mediterranean*. London: Routledge, Kegan Paul.
Degler, Carl N.
1971 *Neither Black Nor White*. New York: Macmillan.
de Kadt, Emanuel
1967 "Religion, the Church and Social Change in Brazil." In Claudio Veliz, ed., *The Politics of Conformity in Latin America*, pp. 192–220. New York: Oxford University Press.
1970 *Catholic Radicals in Brazil*. New York: Oxford University Press.
Della Cava, Ralph
1970 *Miracle at Joazeiro*. New York: Columbia University Press.
de Sá, Vitor
1969 *A Crise do Liberalismo e as Primeiras Manifestações das Ideias Socialistas em Portugal (1820–1852)*. Lisbon: Colecção, n.s., section 7, no. 5.
Dickeman, Mildred
1975a "Demographic Consequences of Infanticide in Man." *Annual Review of Ecology and Systematics* 6:107–37.
1975b "Female Infanticide and Hypergamy: A Neglected Relationship." Paper presented at 64th annual meeting of the American Anthropological Association, San Francisco.
Diégues Júnior, Manuel
1973 "Populações rurais Brasileiras." Tamás Szmecsanyi and O. Queda, eds. In *Vida Rural e Mudança Social*. São Paulo: Companhia Editôra Nacional.
Divale, William
1974 "Migration, External Warfare, and Matrilocal Residence." *Behavior Science Research* 9(2):75–133.
Divale, William and Marvin Harris
1976 "Population, Warfare, and the Male Supremacist Complex." *American Anthropologist* 78(3):521–38.
Dole, Gertrude E.
1972 "Developmental sequences of kinship patterns." In Priscilla Reining, ed., *Kinship Studies in the Morgan Centennial Year*, pp. 136–166. Washington, D.C.: The Anthropological Society of Washington.
Dreyfus, Simone
1972 Introduction. *Journal de la Société des Americanistes* 61:9–16.
Dumond, Don E.
1975 "The limitation of human population: a natural history." *Science* 187:713–20.
Eaton, Clement
1949 *A History of the Old South*. New York: Macmillan.
1961 *The Growth of Southern Civilization*. New York: Harper and Row.

Eduardo, Octávio da Costa
1948 *The Negro in Northern Brazil: A Study in Acculturation.* New York: American Ethnological Society Monograph 15.
Eggan, Fred
1950 *Social Organization of the Western Pueblos.* Chicago: University of Chicago Press.
Ehrlich, Eugene
1936 *Fundamental Principles of the Sociology of Law.* Cambridge: Harvard University Press.
1975 *Fundamental Principles of the Sociology of Law.* 2d ed. New York: The ARNO Press.
Eiten, G.
1972 "The Cerrado Vegetation of Brazil." *Botanical Review* 39(2):201–341.
Eldredge, R. Niles
1963 "Some Technological Aspects of the Fishing Industry of a Town on the Northeast Coast of Brazil." Columbia-Cornell-Harvard-Illinois Summer Fields Studies Program in Anthropology. Manuscript.
Ember, Melvin and Carol Ember
1971 "The Conditions Favoring Matrilocal Versus Patrilocal Residence." *American Anthropologist* 73(3):571–94.
Epstein, David
1973 *Brasília: Plan and Reality: A Study of Planned and Spontaneous Urban Development.* Berkeley: University of California Press.
Evans, Clifford and Betty J. Meggers
1960 *Archaeological Investigations in British Guiana.* Bureau of American Ethnology Bulletin 177. Washington, D.C.: Smithsonian Institution.
Evans-Pritchard, E. E.
1968 (orig. 1940) *The Nuer.* Oxford: Oxford University Press.
Faoro, Raymundo
1975 *Os Donos do Poder.* New ed. Porto Alegre: Editôra Globo.
Farabee, W. C.
1917 *A Pioneer in Amazonia: The Narrative of a Journey from Manaos to Georgetown.* Philadelphia: Bulletin of the Geographical Society 15(2):57–103.
1918 *The Central Arawaks.* University Museum Anthropological Publication 9. Philadelphia: University of Pennsylvania.
Faria, Julio Cesar de
1942 *Juizes do Meu Tempo.* Author's ed.
Fernandes, Florestan
1949a *A Organização Social dos Tupinambá.* São Paulo: Instituto Progresso Editorial.
1949b "A análise functionalista da guerra: possibilidades de aplicação a sociedade Tupinambá." *Revista do Museu Paulista.* n.s. 3:7–128.
1952 "A função da guerra na sociedade Tupinambá." *Revista do Museu Paulista* n.s. 6:7–425.
1958 *A Etnologia e a Sociologia no Brasil.* São Paulo: Editôra Anhembi.

# 414 REFERENCES

1963 *A Sociologia Numa Era de Revolução Social.* São Paulo: Companhia Editôra Nacional.

1965 *A Integração do Negro na Sociedade de Classes.* 2d ed. São Paulo: Dominus Editôra.

1969 *The Negro in Brazilian Society.* New York: Columbia University Press.

1972 *O Negro no Mundo do Branco.* São Paulo: Difusão Europeia do Livro.

1973 *Capitalismo Dependente e Classes Sociais na América Latina.* Rio de Janeiro: Zahar Editôra.

1974 *Mudanças Sociais no Brasil.* 2d ed. São Paulo: Difusão Européia do Livro.

1975a *Sociedade de Classes e Subdesenvolvimento.* 3d ed. Rio de Janeiro: Companhia Editôra Nacional.

1975b *A Revolução Burguesa no Brasil: Ensaio de Interpretação Sociologica.* Rio de Janeiro: Zahar Editôra.

1977 *A Sociologia no Brasil: Contribução Para o Estudo de Sua Formação e Desenvolvimento.* Petropolis: Editôra Vozes.

Fishlow, Albert
1972 "Brazilian Size Distribution of Income." *The American Economic Review.* Papers and Proceedings 62 (2):391–402.

Fittkau, E. J. and H. Klinge
1973 "On Biomass and Trophic Structure of the Central Amazon Rain Forest Ecosystem." *Biotropica* 5:1–14.

Flannery, Kent V.
1968 "Archaeological Systems Theory and Early Mesoamerica." In Betty Meggers, ed., *Anthropological Archaeology in the Americas,* pp. 67–87. Washington, D.C.: The Anthropological Society of Washington.

1972 "The Origins of the Village as a Settlement Type in Mesoamerica and the Near East: A Comparative Study." In P. J. Ucko, R. Tringam, and G. W. Dimbleby, eds., *Man, Settlement, and Urbanism,* pp. 23–53. London: G. W. Duckworth.

Fleming-Moran, Millicent
1975 *The Folk View of Natural Causation and Disease in Brazil and Its Relation to Traditional Curing Practices.* M.A. thesis, University of Florida.

Fleming-Moran, Millicent and Emilio Moran
1975 "The Emergence of Social Classes in a Planned Egalitarian Society." Paper presented at the 74th annual meeting of the American Anthropological Association, San Francisco.

Fogel, Robert and Stanley Engerman
1974 *Time on the Cross.* Vol. I. Boston: Little, Brown.

Forman, Shepard
1967 "Cognition and the Catch: The Location of Fishing Spots in a Brazilian Coastal Village." *Ethnology* 6(4):417–26.

1970 *The Raft Fishermen: Tradition and Change in the Brazilian Peasant Economy.* Bloomington: Indiana University Press.

1971 "Disunity and Discontent: A Study of Peasant Political Movements in Brazil." *Journal of Latin American Studies* 3(1):3–24.

1975 *The Brazilian Peasantry*. New York: Columbia University Press.

1977 "The Significance of Participation: Peasants in Politics in Brazil." In John Booth and Mitchell Seligson, eds. *Participation and the Poor in Latin America*. New York: Holmes and Meier.

Forman, Shepard and Joyce Riegelhaupt

1970 "Market Place and Marketing System: Toward a Theory of Peasant Economic Integration." *Comparative Studies in Society and History* 12(2):188–212.

Fortes, Meyer and E. E. Evans-Pritchard, eds.

1961 *African Political Systems*. London: Oxford University Press.

Foster, George M.

1963 "The Dyadic Contract in Tzintzuntzan II: Patron-Client Relationship." *American Anthropologist* 65(6):1280–94.

1965 "Peasant Society and the Image of Limited Good." *American Anthropologist* 67(2):293–315.

Frazier, Franklin

1957 *Black Bourgeoisie*. Glencoe, Ill.: The Free Press.

Freyre, Gilberto

1956 (orig. 1933) *The Masters and the Slaves (Casa Grande e Senzala)*. 2nd ed. Samuel Putnam, trans. New York: Knopf.

1963 *New World in the Tropics*. New York: Vintage.

Fried, Morton H.

1957 "The Classification of Corporate Unilineal Descent Groups." *Journal of the Royal Anthropological Institute* 87(1):1–29.

1960 "On the Evolution of Social Stratification and the State." In Stanley Diamond, ed. *Culture in History*, pp. 713–31. New York: Columbia University Press.

Frikel, Protásio

1968 *Os Xikrín: Equipamento e Técnicas de Subsistência*. Museu Paraense Emílio Goeldi, Publicações Avulsas No. 7. Belém.

Frisch, Rose and J. MacArthur

1974 "Menstrual Cycles: Fatness as a Determinant of Minimum Weight for Height Necessary for the Maintenance or Onset." *Science* 185:949–51.

Fry, Peter Henry and Gary Nigel Howe

1975 "Duas respostas à aflição: Umbanda e Pentecostalismo." *Debate e Crítica* no. 6, pp. 75–94.

Furtado, Celso

1965a *The Economic Growth of Brazil*. Berkeley: University of California Press.

1965b *Diagnosis of the Brazilian Crisis*. Berkeley: University of California Press.

Gabriel, Chester Eugene

1970–1973 Personal communications.

Galeano, Eduardo

1968 "Brazil and Paraguay: Colony and Sub-Colony." *Monthly Review* 20(7):19–29.

Galjart, Benno
  1964 "Class and Following in Rural Brazil." *America Latina* 7(3):3–24.
  1967 "Old Patrons and New." *Sociologia Ruralis* 7(4).
Galvão, Eduardo
  1951 "Panema: uma criança do caboclo Amazônico." *Revista do Museu Paulista* 5:221–25.
  1953 *Cultura e Sistema de Parentesco das Tribos do Alto Xingú.* Boletim do Museu Nacional no. 14. Rio de Janeiro.
  1955a *Santos e Visagens: Um Estudo da Vida Religiosa de Itá, Amazonas.* São Paulo: Companhia Editôra Nacional.
  1955b "Mudança cultural no região do Rio Negro." In *Anais do 31st Congresso Internacional de Americanistas* 1:313–19. São Paulo.
  1959 "Aculturação indígena no Rio Negro." *Boletim Museu Paraense Emílio Goeldi,* no. 7. Belém.
  1960 "Areas culturais no Brasil, 1900–1959." *Boletim Museu Paraense Emílio Goeldi,* no. 8. Belém.
Gans, Herbert
  1962 *The Urban Villagers: Group and Class in the Life of Italian Americans.* New York: Free Press.
Gates, Paul W.
  1960 *The Farmer's Age: Agriculture, 1815–1860.* New York: Harper and Row.
Geertz, Clifford
  1960 "The Javanese *ki ja ji:* The Changing Role of a Culture Broker." *Comparative Studies in Society and History* 2:228–49.
Gellner, Ernest and John Waterbury, eds.
  1977 *Patrons and Clients in Mediterranean Societies.* Hanover, N.H.: Center for Mediterranean Studies of the American Universities Field Staff.
Germani, Gino
  1973 "Desenvolvimento econômico, urbanização, e estratificação social." In Luis Pereia, ed., *Urbanização e Subdesenvolvimento,* pp. 105–29. Rio de Janeiro: Zahar Editôra.
Gifun, Frederick V.
  1972 *Ribeirão Preto, 1880–1914: The Rise of a Coffee County or the Transition to Coffee in São Paulo as Seen Through the Development of its Leading Producer.* PH.D. dissertation, University of Florida.
Gist, Noel P.
  1940 *Societies: A Cultural Study of Fraternalism in the United States.* Columbia: University of Missouri Press.
Glick, Henry Robert and Kenneth N. Vines
  1973 *State Court Systems.* Englewood Cliffs, N.J.: Prentice-Hall.
Gluckman, Max
  1962 "Les rites de passage." In Max Gluckman, ed., *Essays on the Ritual of Social Relations.* Max Gluckman, pp. 1–52. Manchester: Manchester University Press.
Goffman, Erving
  1959 *The Presentation of Self in Everyday Life.* Garden City, N.Y.: Doubleday.

Goldman, Irving
    1948 "Tribes of the Uaupés-Caqueta Region." In Julian Steward, ed., *Handbook of South American Indians*, 3:763–98. Bureau of American Ethnology Bulletin 143. Washington, D.C.: Smithsonian Institution.
    1963 *The Cubeo: Indians of the Northwest Amazon*. Urbana: University of Illinois Press.

Goldwasser, Maria Julia
    1975 *O Palácio do Samba: Estudo Antropológico da Escola de Samba Estação Primeira de Mangueira*. Rio de Janeiro: Zahar Editôra.

Gray, Lewis C.
    1933 *History of Agriculture in the Southern United States to 1860*. Vol. 2. Washington, D.C.: Carnegie Institution.

Greenberg, Joseph H.
    1960 "The General Classification of Central and South American Languages." In A. F. C. Wallace, ed., *Men and Cultures*, pp. 791–94. Philadelphia: University of Pennsylvania Press.

Greenfield, Sidney M.
    1972 "Charwomen, Cesspools, and Road Building: An Examination of Patronage, Clientage, and Political Power in Southeastern Minas Gerais." In Arnold Strickon and Sidney Greenfield, eds., *Structure and Process in Latin America: Patronage, Clientage and Power Systems*, pp. 71–100. Albuquerque: University of New Mexico Press.
    1977a "Patronage, Politics and the Articulation of Local Community and National Society in pre-1968 Brazil." *Journal of Inter-American Studies and World Affairs* 19(2):139–72.
    1977b "El *cabo eleitoral* y la articulación de la comunidad local y la sociedad nacional brasileñas anteriores a 1968." In Esther Hermitte and Leopoldo Bartolomé, eds., *Procesos de Articulación Social*. Buenos Aires: Amorrortu Editores.

Gregor, Thomas
    1969 *Social Relationships in a Small Society: A Study of the Mehinacu of Central Brazil*. Ph.D. dissertation, Columbia University.

Gross, Daniel R.
    1970 *Sisal and Social Structure in Northeastern Brazil*. Ph.D. dissertation, Columbia University.
    1971 "Ritual and Conformity: A Religious Pilgrimage to Northeastern Brazil." *Ethnology* 10(2):129–48.
    1973 "Factionalism and Local Level Politics in Rural Brazil." *Journal of Anthropological Research* 29:123–44.
    1975 "Protein Capture and Cultural Development in the Amazon Basin." *American Anthropologist* 77(3):526–49.

Gross, Daniel R. and Barbara Underwood
    1971 "Technological Change and Caloric Costs: Sisal Agriculture in Northeastern Brazil." *American Anthropologist* 73(3):725–40.

Gusinde, Martin
    1961 *The Life and Thought of the Water Nomads of Cape Horn*. Vol. 2. New Haven: Human Relations Area File.

## 418 REFERENCES

Haeckel, J.
1938 "Zweiklassensystem Mannerhaus und Totemismus in Sudamerika." *Zeitschrift für Ethnologie* 70:426–54.
Halpern Pereira, Miriam
1971 *Livre Câmbio e Desenvolvimento Econômico.* Lisbon: Edições Cosmos.
Harris, Marvin
1956 *Town and Country in Brazil.* New York: Columbia University Press.
1974a *Cows, Pigs, Wars, and Witches.* New York: Random House.
1974b *Patterns of Race in the Americas.* New York: Norton.
1977 *Cannibals and Kings.* New York: Random House.
1979a *Cultural Materialism: The Struggle for a Science of Culture.* New York: Random House.
1979b "Protein and the Law of Diminishing Returns." *Natural History.* (In press.)
Hart, H. L. A.
1961 *The Concept of Law.* Oxford: The Clarendon Press.
Hoebel, E. Adamson
1954 *The Law of Primitive Man.* Cambridge: Harvard University Press.
1960 *The Cheyennes: Indians of the Great Plains.* Case Studies in Cultural Anthropology. New York: Holt, Rinehart.
Hofstadter, Richard and Seymour Martin Lipset
1968 *Turner and the Sociology of the Frontier.* New York: Basic Books.
Honda, E. M. S.
1972 "Peixes Encontrados nos Mercados de Manaus." *Acta Amazônica* 2(3):97–98.
Hubbel, Linda J.
1973 "The Mexican Middle Class as Perceived by Its Members." Paper presented at the 72d Annual Meeting of the American Anthropological Association, New Orleans.
Huntington, Ellsworth
1924 *Civilization and Climate.* New Haven: Yale University Press.
Hutchinson, Bertram
1960 *Mobilidade e Trabalho: um Estudo na Cidade de São Paulo.* Rio de Janeiro: Centro Brasileiro de Pesquisas Educacionais.
1966 "The Patron-Dependent Relationship in Brazil: A Preliminary Examination." *Sociologia Ruralis* 1:3–30.
Hutchinson, Harry W.
1957 *Village and Plantation Life in Northeastern Brazil.* Seattle: University of Washington Press.
Hutter, Lucy Maffei
1972 *Imigração Italiana em São Paulo, 1880–1889.* São Paulo: Instituto de Estudos Brasileiros da Universidade de São Paulo Publication No. 22.
Ianni, Constantino
1972 *Homems Sem Paz: Os Conflitos e os Bastidores da Emigração Italiana.* Rio de Janeiro: Civilização Brasileira.

Ianni, Otavio
1962 *As Metamorfases do Escravo: Apogeu e Crise da Escravatura no Brasil Meridional.* São Paulo: Difusão Europeia do Livro.
1963 *Industrialização e Desenvolvimento Social no Brasil.* Rio de Janeiro: Editôra Civilização Brasileira.
1968 *O Colapso do Populismo no Brasil.* Rio de Janeiro: Editôra Civilização Brasileira S.A.
1972 *Raças e Classes Sociais no Brasil.* 2d ed. Rio de Janeiro: Editôra Civilização Brasileira S.A.

Instituto Brasileiro de Geografia e Estatística (IBGE)
1972 *Anuario Estatístico do Brasil.* Rio de Janeiro: IBGE-Conselho Nacional de Estatística.

Instituto Nacional de Estatística
1975 *Eleição para a Assembléia Constituinte 1975.* Vol. 1. Lisbon: Ministério da Administração Interna.

Jackson, Jean E.
1975 "Recent Ethnography of Indigenous Northern Lowland South America." In Bernard J. Siegal, ed., *Annual Review of Anthropology,* 4:307–340. Palo Alto: Annual Reviews Inc.

Jaguaribe, Hélio
1968 *Economic and Political Development: A Theoretical Approach and a Brazilian Case Study.* Cambridge: Harvard University Press.
1969 "Political Strategies of National Development in Brazil." In Irving L. Horowitz, Josué de Castro, and John Gerassi, eds., *Latin American Radicalism,* pp. 390–439. New York: Random House.

James, Preston
1959 *Latin America.* New York: Odyssey Press.

Johnson, Allen
1971 *Sharecroppers of the Sertão: Economics and Dependence on a Brazilian Plantation.* Stanford: Stanford University Press.

Johnson, H. B.
1972 "The Donatory Captaincy in Perspective: Portuguese Background to the Settlement of Brazil." *Hispanic American Historical Review* 52(1):203–14.

Jorgensen, Joseph
1972 *Reservation Indian Society Today: Studies of Economics, Politics, Kinship, and Household.* Berkeley: University of California Press.

Jourard, Sidney
1971 *Self-disclosure.* New York: Wiley-Interscience.

Kaufman, Robert K.
1974 "The Patron-Client Concept and Macro-Politics: Prospects and Problems." *Comparative Studies in Society and History* 16(3):284–308.

Keesing, Roger M.
n.d. "Formal and Sociological Analysis of Ramkókamekra kinship." Manuscript.

Kenny, Michael
1960 "Patterns of Patronage in Spain." *Anthropological Quarterly* 33(1):14–23.
Kirchoff, Paul
1955 "The Principles of Clanship in Human Society." *Davidson Anthropological Journal* 1:1–11.
Kleinpenning, J. M. G.
1975 *The Integration and Colonization of the Brazilian Portion of the Amazon Basin.* Nijmegen: Institute of Geography and Planning.
Kloppenburg, Boaventura O. F. M.
1961a *Umbanda: Orientação para os Catolicos.* Rio de Janeiro: Editôra Vozes Ltda.
1961b *Ação Pastoral Perante o Espiritismo: Orientação para Sacerdotes.* Rio de Janeiro: Editôra Vozes Ltda.
Koch-Grunberg, Theodor
1909 *Zwei Jahre Unter den Indianern.* Reise in bordwest Brasilien, 1903–05, 2 vols. Berlin.
Kolata, Gina
1974 "Kung Hunters-Gatherers: Feminism, Diet, and Birth Control." *Science* 185:932–34.
Kottak, Conrad P.
1966 *The Structure of Equality in a Brazilian Fishing Community.* Ph.D. dissertation, Columbia University.
1967 "Kinship and Class in Brazil." *Ethnology* 6(4):427–33.
Kroeber, Alfred L.
1952 "The Societies of Primitive Man." In *The Nature of Culture,* pp. 219–25. Chicago: University of Chicago Press.
Kuper, Leo
1965 *An African Bourgeoisie: Race, Class, and Politics in South Africa.* New Haven: Yale University Press.
Landes, Ruth
1947 *The City of Women.* New York: Macmillan.
Lanternari, Vittorio
1963 *The Religions of the Oppressed: A Study of Modern Messianic Cults.* Lisa Sergio, trans. New York: Knopf.
Laráia, Roque de Barros and Roberto da Matta
1967 *Índios e Castanheiros: a Emprêsa Extrativa e os Indios no Médio Tocantins.* São Paulo: Difusão Européia do Livro.
Lathrap, Donald
1968 "The Hunting Economies of the Tropical Forest Zone of South America: An Attempt at Historical Perspective." In Richard B. Lee and Irven DeVore, eds., *Man the Hunter,* pp. 23–29. Chicago: Aldine.
Lave, Jean Carter
1967 *Social Taxonomy Among the Krĩkati (Gê) of Central Brazil.* Ph.D. dissertation, Harvard University.
1968 "Some Suggestions for the Interpretation of Residence, Descent, and Ex-

ogamy Among the Eastern Timbira.'' Paper presented at the 38th International Congress of Americanists, Stuttgart.

1970 "Trends and Cycles in Kr̃ikati Naming Practices.'' Manuscript.

1973 "A Comment on 'A Study in Structural Semantics: The Sirionó Kinship System.' ''*American Anthropologist* 75(1):314–17.

Leach, Edmund

1965 *The Political Systems of Highland Burma*. Boston: Beacon Press.

Leacock, Seth and Ruth Leacock

1972 *Spirits of the Deep: a Study of an Afro-Brazilian Cult*. New York: Doubleday Natural History Press.

Leal, Victor Nunes

1948 *Coronelismo: Enxada e Voto*. Rio de Janeiro: n.p.

Leeds, Anthony

1957 *Economic Cycles in Brazil: The Persistence of a Total Culture Pattern: Cacao and Other Cases*. Ph.D. dissertation, Columbia University.

1964 "Brazil and the Myth of Francisco Julião.'' In Joseph Meier and Richard Weatherhead, eds., *Politics of Change in Latin America*, pp. 190–204. New York: Praeger.

1965 "Brazilian Careers and Social Structure: A Case History and Model.'' In Dwight Heath and Richard Adams, eds., *Contemporary Cultures and Societies of Latin America*, pp. 379–404. New York: Random House.

1969 "Significant Variables Determining the Character of Squatter Settlements.'' *America Latina* 12(3):44–86.

Leeds, Anthony and Elizabeth Leeds

1970 "Brazil and the Myth of Urban Rurality: Urban Experiences, Work, and Values in 'Squatments' of Rio de Janeiro and Lima.'' In Arthur J. Field, ed., *City and Country in the Third World*, pp. 229–85. Cambridge: Schenkman.

Levine, Daniel

1974 "Issues in the Study of Culture and Politics: A View from Latin America.'' *Publius* 4(2):77–104.

Lévi-Strauss, Claude

1936 "Contribução para o estudo da organização dos índios Bororo.'' *Revista do Arquivo Municipal* 27:7–80. São Paulo.

1944 "On Dual Organization in South America.'' *América Indígena* 4(1):37–47.

1948 "La vie familiale et sociale des indiens Nambikwara.'' *Journal de la Société des Américanistes* 37:1–132.

1949 *Les Structures Elémentaires de la Parenté*. Paris: Presses Universitaire de France.

1961 *Tristes Tropiques*. Russell Wood, trans. New York: Criterion.

1963 *Structural Anthropology*. New York: Basic.

Lewis, I. M.

1971 *Ecstatic Religions: An Anthropological Study of Spirit Possession and Shamanism*. Baltimore: Penguin.

Lipkind, William
1940 "Carajá Cosmography." *Journal of American Folklore* 53(210):247–51.
1948 "The Carajá." In Julian Steward, ed., *Handbook of South American Indians*, 3:179–91. Bureau of American Ethnology Bulletin 143. Washington, D.C.: Smithsonian Institution.
Little, George F. G.
1960 *Fazenda Cambuhy: A Case History of Social and Economic Development in the Interior of São Paulo, Brazil.* Ph.D. dissertation, University of Florida.
Little, Kenneth L.
1949 "The Role of the Secret Society in Cultural Specialization." *American Anthropologist* 51(1):199–212.
Litwak, Eugene
1960 "Occupational Mobility and Extended Family Cohesion." *American Sociological Review* 25(1):9–21.
Lizot, Jacques
1970 "Compte rendu de mission chez les indiens Yanōman." *L'Homme* 10:116–21.
1971 "Aspects économique du changement culturel chez les Yanōman." *L'Homme* 11:32–51.
Loeb, E. M.
1929 *Tribal Initiations and Secret Societies.* University of California Publications in American Archaeology and Ethnology No. 25. Berkeley: University of California Press.
Lopes, Juarez Brandão
1966 "Some Basic Developments in Brazilian Politics and Society." In Eric Baklanoff, ed., *New Perspectives of Brazil*, pp. 59–77. Nashville: Vanderbilt University Press.
Loukotka, Cestmír
1968 *Classification of South American Indian Languages.* Reference Series, vol. 7. Los Angeles: University of California Latin American Center.
Lounsbury, Floyd. D.
1964 "A Formal Account of the Crow- and Omaha-Type Kinship Terminologies." In Ward H. Goodenough, ed., *Explorations in Cultural Anthropology*, pp. 351–93. New York: McGraw-Hill.
Love, Joseph L.
1970 "Political Participation in Brazil, 1881–1969." *Luso-Brazilian Review* 7(2):3–24.
1971 *Rio Grande do Sul and Brazilian Regionalism, 1882–1930.* Stanford: Stanford University Press.
Lowie, Robert H.
1920 *Primitive Society.* New York: Boni and Liveright.
1946a "The Northwestern and Central Gê." In Julian Steward, ed., *Handbook of South American Indians* 1:477–517. Bureau of American Ethnology Bulletin 143. Washington, D.C.: Smithsonian Institution.

1946b "The Bororo." In Julian Steward, ed., *Handbook of South American Indians* 1:419–34. Bureau of American Ethnology Bulletin 143. Washington, D.C.: Smithsonian Institution.

1946c "The 'Tapuya.' " In Julian Steward, ed., *Handbook of South American Indians* 1:553–56. Bureau of American Ethnology Bulletin 143. Washington, D.C.: Smithsonian Institution.

1949 "Social and Political Organization of the Tropical Forest and Marginal Tribes." In Julian Steward, ed., *Handbook of South American Indians* 5:313–50. Bureau of American Ethnology Bulletin 143. Washington, D.C.: Smithsonian Institution.

Lowry, Richie P.

1972 "Toward a Sociology of Secrecy and Security Systems." *Social Problems* 19:437–449.

MacKenzie, Norman, ed.

1967 *Secret Societies*. New York: Crescent Books.

MacNeish, Richard S.

1964 "Ancient Mesoamerican Civilization." *Science* 143:531–36.

Maitland, Frederick William

1897 *Domesday Book and Beyond*. Cambridge: Cambridge University Press.

Malinowski, Bronislaw

1959 *Crime and Custom in Savage Society*. Paterson, N.J.: Littlefield, Adams.

Margolis, Maxine L.

1972 "The Coffee Cycle on the Paraná Frontier." *Luso-Brazilian Review* 9(1):3–12.

1973 *The Moving Frontier: Social and Economic Change in a Southern Brazilian Community*. Latin American Monograph 11. Gainesville: University of Florida Press.

1977 "Historical Perspectives on Frontier Agriculture as an Adaptive Strategy." *American Ethnologist* 4(1):42–64.

1978 "Natural Disaster and Socioeconomic Change: The Case of Some Southern Brazilian Communities." Paper presented at the 77th annual meeting of the American Anthropological Association, Los Angeles.

Martin, Paul S.

1973 "The Discovery of America." *Science* 179:969–74.

Maybury-Lewis, David

1965 "Some Crucial Distinctions in Central Brazilian Ethnology." *Anthropos* 60(1–6):340–58.

1974 *Akwẽ-Shavante Society*. New York: Oxford University Press.

Maybury-Lewis David, ed.

1979 *Dialectical Societies*. Cambridge: Harvard University Press.

Meggers, Betty

1954 "Environmental Limitations on the Development of Culture." *American Anthropologist* 56(5):801–24.

1971 *Amazonia: Man and Culture in a Counterfeit Paradise*. Chicago: Aldine.

1974 "Environment and Culture in Amazonia." In Charles Wagley, ed., *Man in the Amazon*, pp. 91–110. Gainesville: University of Florida Press.

Meggers, Betty, Edward S. Ayensu, and W. Donald Duckworth, eds.
   1973 *Tropical Forest Ecosystems in Africa and South America: A Comparative Review*. Washington D.C.: Smithsonian Institution.
Meggers, Betty and Clifford Evans
   1957 *Archaeological Investigations at the Mouth of the Amazon*. Bureau of American Ethnology Bulletin 167. Washington, D.C.: Smithsonian Institution.
   1958 "Archaeological Evidence of a Prehistoric Migration from Rio Negro to the mouth of the Amazon." In Raymond H. Thompson, ed., *Migrations in New World Culture History*. Social Science Bulletin 27. Tucson: University of Arizona Press.
Meggitt, Mervyn
   1965 *The Lineage System of the Mae Enga of New Guinea*. New York: Barnes and Noble.
Melatti, Julio Cezar
   1970 *O Sistema Social Krahó*. Ph.D. dissertation. Universidade de São Paulo.
   1971 "Nominadores e genitores: um aspecto do dualismo Krahó." *Verhandlungen*, 3:347–353. 38th Internationalen Amerikanistenkongresses, Stuttgart-Munchen, 1968.
   1972 *O Messianismo Krahó*. São Paulo: Editôra Herder.
   1975 *Ritos de uma Tribo Timbira*. Brasília: Departamento de Ciências Sociais, Universidade de Brasília.
Merryman, John Henry
   1969 *The Civil Law Tradition*. Stanford: Stanford University Press.
Miller, Charlotte I.
   1975 *Middle Class Kinship Networks in Belo Horizonte, Minas Gerais, Brazil: The Functions of the Urban Parentela*. Ph.D. dissertation. University of Florida.
Ministério da Agricultura
   1972 *Altamira I*. Brasilia: INCRA.
Monbeig, Pierre
   1952 *Pionniers et Planteurs de São Paulo*. Paris: Librairie Armand Colin.
Moore, Oscar K.
   1962 *The Brazilian Coffee Economy*. Ph.D. dissertation. University of Florida.
Moran, Emilio F.
   1974 "The adaptive system of the Amazonian caboclo." In Charles Wagley, ed., *Man in the Amazon*, pp. 136–59. Gainesville: University of Florida Press.
   1975 *Pioneer Farmers of the Transamazon Highway*. Ph.D. dissertation. University of Florida.
   1976a "Manioc Deserves More Recognition in Tropical Farming." *World Crops*, 28(4):184–88.
   1976b "Food, Development, and Man in the Tropics." In Margaret Arnott, ed., *Gastronomy: The Anthropology of Food and Food Habits*, pp. 169–86. The Hague: Mouton.

Morren, George
1974 *Settlement Strategies and Hunting in a New Guinea Society.* Ph.D. dissertation. Columbia University.

Moura, Margarida Maria
1973 *Os Sitiantes e a Herança.* Dissertação de Mestrado. Museo Nacional da Universidade Nacional Rio de Janeiro.

Murdock, George Peter
1960 *Social Structure.* New York: Macmillan.

Murphy, Robert F.
1956 "Matrilocality and Patrilineality in Mundurucú Society." *American Anthropologist* 56(3):414–34.
1958 *Mundurucú Religion.* University of California Publications in American Archaeology and Ethnography, vol. 49, no. 1. Berkeley and Los Angeles: University of California Press.
1959 "Social Structure and Sex Antagonism." *Southwestern Journal of Anthropology* 15(1):89–98.
1960 *Headhunter's Heritage.* Berkeley: University of California Press.

Murphy, Robert F. and Buell Quain
1955 *The Trumaí Indians of Central Brazil.* American Ethnological Society. New York: J. J. Augustin.

Nash, Manning
1965 *The Golden Road to Modernity.* New York: Wiley.

Neel, James V. and Kenneth M. Weiss
1975 "The Genetic Structure of a Tribal Population, the Yanomama Indians." *American Journal of Physical Anthropology* 42(1):25–52.

Nelson, Michael
1973 *The Development of Tropical Lands.* Baltimore: Johns Hopkins University Press.

Nery, Sebastião
n.d. *350 Histórias do Folclore Político.* 2d ed. Edições Politika.

Newton, Dolores
1971 *Social and Historical Dimensions of Timbira Material Culture.* Ph.D. dissertation, Harvard University.

Nicholas, Ralph W.
1965 "Factions: A Comparative Analysis." In Michael Banton, ed., *Political Systems and the Distribution of Power,* pp. 21–61. London: Tavistock.

Nietschmann, Bernard
1973 *Between Land and Water.* New York: Seminar Press.

Nimuendajú, Curt
1939 *The Apinayé.* Anthropological Series No. 8. Washington D.C.: The Catholic University of America.
1942 *The Šerente.* Robert H. Lowie, trans. and ed. Publications of the Frederick Webb Hodge Anniversary Fund, 4. Los Angeles: Southwestern Museum.
1946 *The Eastern Timbira.* Robert H. Lowie, trans. and ed. University of Cali-

fornia Publications in American Archaeology and Ethnology 41. Berkeley: University of California Press.

1950 Reconhecimento do Rios Icana, Ayari, e Uaupés. *Journal de la Société des Americanistes* 39:125–82.

Nimuendajú, Curt and Robert H. Lowie
1937 "The Dual Organization of the Ramkókamekra (Canela) of Northern Brazil." *American Anthropologist* 39:565–82.

Nogueira, Oracy
1962 *Familia e Comunidade: um Estudo Sociológico de Itapetininga, São Paulo.* Rio de Janeiro: Centro de Pesquisas Educacionais, INEP.

Oberg, Kalervo
1955 "Types of Social Structure among the Lowland Tribes of South and Central America." *American Anthropologist* 57(3):472–87.

Odum, Eugene
1969 "The Strategy of Ecosystem Development." *Science* 164:262–70.

Oliveira, Roberto Cardoso de
1959 "A Situação Atual dos Tapirapé." *Boletim do Museu Paraense Emílio Goeldi.* Antropologia, no. 3. Belém.
1960 *O Processo de Assimilação dos Terena.* Rio de Janeiro: Museu Nacional.
1972 *O Índio no Mundo dos Brancos.* São Paulo: Livraria Pioneira Editôra.

Oliveira Marques, A. H. de
1972 *History of Portugal.* Vol. 2. New York: Columbia University Press.

Oliveira Vianna, Eliseu de
1933 *A Evolução do Povo Brasileiro.* São Paulo: Companhia Editôra Nacional.

Oliver, Symmes C.
1968 "Ecology and Cultural Continuity as Contributing Factors in the Social Organization of the Plains Indians." In Yehudi A. Cohen, ed., *Man in Adaptation: The Cultural Present,* pp. 243–62. Chicago: Aldine.

Ortiz, Alfonso
1969 *The Tewa World: Space, Time, Being, and Becoming in a Pueblo Society.* Chicago: University of Chicago Press.

Pan American Coffee Bureau
1964 *Annual Coffee Statistics.* No. 28. New York.

Parsons, Talcott
1971 "Reply to His Critics." In Michael Anderson, ed., *Sociology of the Family,* pp. 120–21. Hamondsworth, England: Penguin.

Pechnick, E. and J. M. Chaves
1945 "O acaí, um dos alimentos básicos da Amazonia." *Anais da Associação Química Brasileira* 4:169.

Pelto, Pertti J. and Gretel H. Pelto
1975 "Intra-Cultural Diversity: Some Theoretical Issues." *American Ethnologist* 2(1):1–18.

Perlman, Janice R.
1976 *The Myth of Marginality: Urban Poverty and Politics in Rio de Janeiro.* Berkeley: University of California Press.

Phillips, Ulrich B.
1929 *Life and Labor in the Old South*. Boston: Little, Brown.
Pierson, Donald et al.
1942 *Negroes in Brazil*. Chicago: University of Chicago Press.
1952 *Cruz das Almas: A Brazilian Village*. Institute of Social Anthropology. Washington D.C.: Smithsonian Institution.
Polgar, Steven
1975 "Population, Evolution, and Theoretical Paradigms." In Steven Polgar, ed., *Population, Ecology, and Social Evolution*, pp. 1–25. 9th International Congress of Anthropological and Ethnological Sciences, Chicago. The Hague: Mouton.
Powell, John D.
1970 "Peasant Society and Clientalist Politics." *American Political Science Review* 64:411–25.
Ramos, Arthur
1943–47 *Introdução a Antropologia Brasileira*. Vols. 1 and 2. Rio de Janeiro: Coleção Estudos Editôra de Casa do Estudante do Brasil, series B, 1.
Rappaport, Roy
1967 *Pigs for the Ancestors*. New Haven: Yale University Press.
Redfield, Robert
1948 *The Folk Culture of Yucatan*. Chicago: University of Chicago Press.
1960 *Peasant Society and Culture and the Little Community*. Chicago: University of Chicago Press.
Reichel-Dolmatoff, G.
1971 *Amazonian Cosmos*. Chicago: University of Chicago Press.
Reik, Theodore
1975 *Ritual: Four Psychoanalytic Studies*. Westport: Greenwood.
Reis, Arthur Cézar Ferreira
1940 *A Política de Portugal no Vale Amazônico*. Belém: n.p.
1943 *O Processo Histórico da Economia Amazonense*. Rio de Janeiro: n.p.
Renshaw, J. Parke
1969 *A Sociological Analysis of Spiritism in Brazil*. Ph.D dissertation, University of Florida.
Ribeiro, Darcy
1950 *Religião e Mitologia Kadiwéu*. Rio de Janeiro: Conselho Nacional de Proteção aos Indios, Publication No. 106.
1951 "Arte dos indios Kadiwéu." *Cultura* VI:145–94. Rio de Janeiro.
1955 "Os indios Urubús: ciclo anual das atividades de subsistência de um tribo da floresta tropical." *Anais do 31st Congresso Internacional de Americanistas*, pp. 127–55. São Paulo: Editôra Anhembi.
1956 "Convívio e contaminação." *Sociologia* 18(1):3–50. São Paulo.
1962 *A Política Indigenista Brasileira*. Ministério da Agricultura. Serviço de Informação. Rio de Janeiro.
1967 "Indigenous Cultures and Languages of Brazil." In Janice H. Hopper, ed. and trans., *Indians of Brazil in the Twentieth Century*, pp. 77–166. Washington, D.C.: Institute of Cross-Cultural Research.

## 428    REFERENCES

1970 *Os Indios e a Civilização*. Rio de Janeiro: Editôra Civilização Brasileira.
Ribeiro, René
1952 *Cultos Afrobrasileiros de Recife: um Estudo de Ajustamento Social*. Recife: Instituto Joaquim Nabuco.
1956 *Religião e Relações Raciais*. Rio de Janeiro: Ministério de Educação e Cultura.
Richards, Paul
1973 "The Tropical Rain Forest." *Scientific American* (December), 229:58–68.
Riegelhaupt, Joyce F.
1976 "Peasant Revolts in Portugal, 1846–1847." Paper presented at the annual meeting of the American Historical Association, Washington, D.C.
in press "Peasants and Politics in Salazar's Portugal: The corporate state and village 'non-politics' ". In Lawrence Graham and Harry Makler, eds., *Contemporary Portugal: The Revolution and its Local Antecedents*. Austin: University of Texas Press.
Rios, José Arthur
1964 *Campina Grande: um Centro Comercial do Nordeste*. Rio de Janeiro: Editôra Nacional.
Ritter, M. L.
1974 *The Conditions Favoring Age-Set Organization*. M.A. thesis. Hunter College of the University of New York.
Rodrigues, José Albertino
1968 *Sindicato e Desenvolvimento no Brasil*. São Paulo: Difusão Européia do Livro.
Ross, Eric
1978 "Food Taboos, Diet, and Hunting Strategy: The Adaptation to Animals in Amazon Cultural Ecology." *Current Anthropology* 19(1):1–36.
1979 "Reply to Lizot." *Current Anthropology*. (In press.)
Ruddle, Kenneth
1974 *The Yukpa Cultivation System: A Study of Shifting Cultivation of Colombia and Venezuela*. Ibero-Americana. Berkeley: University of California Press.
Russell-Wood, A. J. R.
1974 "Local Government in Portuguese America: A Study in Cultural Divergence." *Comparative Studies in Society and History* 16(2):187–231.
Saes, Decio
1974 *Classe Moyenne et Systeme Politique au Brasil*. Ph.D. dissertation. Paris: Ecole Practique des Hautes Etudes.
Sahlins, Marshall
1968 "Culture and Environment: The Study of Cultural Ecology." In Robert Manners and David Kaplan, eds., *Theory in Anthropology: A Sourcebook*, pp. 367–73. Chicago: Aldine.
Sampaio, Aluysio
1964 *Comentários do Estatuto do Trabalhador Rural*. São Paulo: Editôra Fulgor.

Schaden, Egon
1962 *Aspectos Fundamentais da Cultura Guaraní.* São Paulo: Difusão Européia do Livro.
Scheffler, Harold W.
1973 "Kinship, Descent, and Alliance." In *Handbook of Social and Cultural Anthropology,* pp. 747–793. John J. Honigmann (ed.). Chicago: Rand McNally and Co.
Scheffler, Harold W. and Floyd G. Lounsbury
1971 *A Study in Structural Semantics: The Siriono Kinship System.* Englewood Cliffs, N.J.: Prentice-Hall.
Scheman, Ronald
1962 "Brazil's Career Judiciary." *Journal of the American Judicature Society* 46(7):134–40.
Schilling, C. S.
1963 *Social Structure of the Eastern Timbira.* M.A. thesis, Yale University.
Schmitter, Philippe
1971a *Interest Conflict and Political Change in Brazil.* Stanford: Stanford University Press.
1971b "The Portugalization of Brazil?" In Alfred Stepan, ed., *Authoritarian Brazil: Origins, Policy, and Future,* pp. 179–232. New Haven: Yale University Press.
Schomburgk, Robert H.
1841 "Report of the Third Expedition into the Interior of Guyana." *Journal of the Royal Geographical Society* 10:159–90.
Scott, James
1972a "Patron-Client Politics and Political Change in Southeast Asia." *American Political Science Review* 66(1):91–113.
1972b "The Erosion of Patron-Client Bonds and Social Change in Rural Southeast Asia." *Journal of Asian Studies* 32(1):5–37.
Seeger, Anthony
1974 "Physical subsistence and knowledge: legitimacy of Suyá leadership roles." Paper presented at the 73rd Annual Meeting of the American Anthropological Association, Mexico City.
Serrão, Joel
n.d. *Emigração Portuguesa.* Viseu: Livros Horizonte 12.
Serrão, Joel, ed.
1971 "Demografia." *Dicionário de História de Portugal,* 1:795–800. Iniciativas Editoriais.
Service, Elman R.
1962 *Primitive Social Organization.* New York: Random House.
Seyferth, Giralda
1974 *A Colonização Alemã no Vale do Itajaí-Mirim.* Porto Alegre: Editôra Movimento.
Shapiro, Judith
1967 "Notes from Santa Teresinha." Manuscript.

1968a "Tapirapé kinship." *Boletim do Museu Paraense Emílio Goeldi*, Antropologia, no. 37. Belém.

1968b "Ceremonial Redistribution in Tapirapé Society." *Boletim do Museu Paraense Emílio Goeldi*, n.s. Antropologia, no. 38. Belém.

1971 *Sex Roles and Social Structure Among the Yanamama Indians of Northern Brazil*. Ph.D. dissertation, Columbia University.

Shirley, Robert W.

1971 *The End of a Tradition*. New York: Columbia University Press.

n.d. "The Judicial System of São Paulo State: A Historical Survey." Manuscript.

Silbert, Albert

1968 *Le Problème Agraire Portugais au Temp des Premières Cortes Liberales*. Paris: Presses Universitaires de France.

Silva, Fernando Altenfelder

1955 *Análise Comparativo de Alguns Aspectos da Estructura Social de Duas Communidades do Vale do São Francisco*. Curitiba: Faculdade de Filosofia, Ciências, e Letras, Universidade de Paraná.

Silverman, Sydel F.

1965 "Patronage and Community-Nation Relationships in Central Italy." *Ethnology* 4(2):172–89.

Simmel, Arnold

1968 "Privacy." In David L. Sills, ed., *International Encyclopedia of the Social Sciences*, 12:480–87. New York: Macmillan.

Simmel, Georg

1950 "The Secret and the Secret Society." In Kurt H. Wolff, ed., *The Sociology of George Simmel*, pp. 307–76. Glencoe, Ill.: The Free Press.

Simonsen, Roberto

1969 *História Econômica do Brasil (1550–1820)*. 6th ed. São Paulo: Companhia Editôra Nacional.

Sioli, Harold

1973 "Recent Human Activities in the Brazilian Amazon Region and Their Ecological Effects." In Betty Meggers, Edward S. Ayensu, and W. Donald Duckworth, eds., *Tropical Forest Ecosystems in Africa and South America*, pp. 321–34. Washington D.C.: Smithsonian Institution.

Siskind, Janet

1973 *To Hunt in the Morning*. New York: Oxford University Press.

Skidmore, Thomas E.

1974 *Black into White: Race and Nationality in Brazilian Thought*. New York: Oxford University Press.

Smith, T. Lynn

1972 *Brazil: People and Institutions*. 4th ed. Baton Rouge: Louisiana State University Press.

Soares, Glaucio Ary Dillon

1966 "Economic Development and Class Structure." In Reinhard Bendix and Seymour Martin Lipset, eds., *Class, Status and Power*, pp. 190–99. 2d ed. New York: Free Press.

1967 "The Political Sociology of Uneven Development in Brazil." In Seymour Martin Lipset and Stein Rubekan, eds., *Party Systems and Voter Alignments*, pp. 467–96. New York: Free Press.

1968 "The New Industrialization and the Brazilian Political System." In James Petras and Maurice Zeitlin, eds., *Latin America: Revolution or Reform?* pp. 186–201. Greenwich: Fawcett Publications.

Spix, Johann B. von and Karl F. P. von Martius

1824 *Travels in Brazil, 1817–1820*. 2 vols. H. E. Lloyd, trans. London.

Stein, Stanley

1957 *Vassouras:A Brazilian Coffee County, 1859–1900*. Cambridge: Harvard University Press.

Steinen, Karl von den

1966 (orig. 1894) *Among the Primitive Peoples of Central Brazil*. New Haven: Human Relations Area Files.

Steward, Julian

1949 "South American Cultures: An Interpretive Essay." In Julian Steward, ed., *Handbook of South American Indians*, pp. 5:669–772. Bureau of American Ethnology Bulletin 143. Washington, D.C.: Smithsonian Institution.

1955 *Theory of Culture Change*. Urbana: University of Illinois Press.

Steward, Julian, ed.

1946 "The Marginal Tribes." *Handbook of South American Indians*. Bureau of American Ethnology Bulletin 143. Washington, D.C.: Smithsonian Institution.

1948 "The Tropical Forest Tribes." *Handbook of South American Indians*. Bureau of American Ethnology Bulletin 143. Washington, D.C.: Smithsonian Institution.

Steward, Julian and Louis Faron

1959 *Native Peoples of South America*. New York: McGraw Hill.

Strickon, Arnold and Sidney M. Greenfield

1972 "The Analysis of Patron-Client Relationships: An Introduction." In Strickon and Greenfield, eds. *Structure and Process in Latin America: Patronage, Clientage and Power Systems*, pp. 1–17. Albuquerque: University of New Mexico Press.

Swartz, Marc. J., ed.

1968 *Local Level Politics: Social and Cultural Perspectives*. Chicago: Aldine.

Swartz, Marc J., Victor W. Turner, and Arthur Tuden, eds.

1966 *Political Anthropology*. Chicago: Aldine.

Sweet, Louise

1965 "Camel Pastoralism in North Arabia and the Minimal Camping Unit." In Anthony Leeds and Andrew P. Vayda, eds., *Man, Culture, and Animals*, pp. 129–52. Washington, D.C.: American Association for the Advancement of Science, Publication No. 78.

Sydnor, Charles S.

1948 *The Development of Southern Sectionalism, 1819–1848*. Baton Rouge: Louisiana State University Press.

Tavener, Christopher
1973 "The Karajá and the Brazilian Frontier." In Daniel R. Gross, ed., *Peoples and Cultures of Native South America*, pp. 433–59. New York: Natural History Press.

Terreiro Aranha, Bento de Fiqueirdo
1907 *Archivo de Amazonas*. Vols. I–II. Manaus.

Tiger, Lionel
1969 *Men in Groups*. New York: Random House.

Touraine, Alain
1961 "Industrialisation et conscience ouvrière à São Paulo." *Sociologie du Travail* 3(4):77–95.

Townsend, P. K.
1974 "Sago Production in a New Guinea Economy." *Human Ecology* 2(3):217–36.

Trujillo Ferrari, Alfonso
1960 *Potengi: Encruzilhada no Vale do São Francisco*. São Paulo: Editôra Sociologia e Política.

Turner, Frederick Jackson
1920 *The Frontier in American History*. New York: Holt.

Turner, J. B.
1967 *Environment and Cultural Classification: A Study of the Northern Kayapó*. Ph.D. dissertation, Harvard University.

Turner, Terence S.
1966 *Social Structure and Political Organization Among the Northern Cayapó*. Ph.D. dissertation, Harvard University.

Turner, Victor W.
1957 *Schism and Continuity in an African Society*. Manchester: Manchester University Press.

Valentine, Charles A.
1961 *Masks and Men in Melanesian Society*. Lawrence: University of Kansas Press.

Van Ginneken, J. K.
1974 "Prolonged Breastfeeding as a Birth-Spacing Mechanism." *Studies in Family Planning* 5:201–8.

Vergolino e Silva, Anaísa
1976 *O Tambor das Flores: Uma Análise da Federação Espírita Umbandista e dos Cultos Afro-Brasileiros do Pará*. Tese de Mestrado em Antropologia, Departmento de Ciências Humanas, Universidade Estadual de Campinas (São Paulo).

Veríssimo, José
1970 (orig. 1898) *A Pesca na Amazonia*. Belém: Universidade Federal do Pará.

Vianna Moog, Clodomir
1964 *Bandeirantes and Pioneers*. L. L. Barrett, trans. New York: George Braziller.

Vieira da Cunha, Mario Wagner
1963 *O Sistema Administrativo Brasileiro 1930–1950*. Rio de Janeiro: Instituto Nacional de Estudos Pedagógicos.

Vilaça, Marcos Vinicius and Roberto C. Albuquerque
  1965 *Coronel, Coroneis*. Rio de Janeiro: Edições Tempo Brasileiro.
Vincent, Joan
  1977 "Agrarian Society as Organized Flow: Processes of Development Past and Present." *Peasant Studies* 6(2):56–65.
Waddell, Eric
  1972 *The Mound-Builders*. Seattle: University of Washington Press.
Wagley, Charles
  1940 "The Effects of Depopulation upon Social Organization as Illustrated by the Tapirapé Indians." *Transactions of the New York Academy of Sciences*, series 2, 3(1):12–16.
  1943 "Xamanismo Tapirapé." *Boletim do Museu Nacional de Antropologia*, no. 3. Rio de Janeiro.
  1948 "Regionalism and Cultural Unity in Brazil." *Social Forces* 26:457–64.
  1951 "Cultural Influences on Population: A Comparison of Two Tupí Tribes." *Revista do Museu Paulista* 5:95–104. São Paulo.
  1952 "The Folk Culture of the Brazilian Amazon." *Proceedings of the 29th International Congress of Americanists*. Chicago: University of Chicago Press.
  1953 *Amazon Town: A Study of Man in the Tropics*. New York: Macmillan.
  1955 "Tapirapé Social and Cultural Change." *Anais do 31st Congresso Internacional de Americanistas* (1954), 1:99–106. São Paulo: Editôra Anhembi.
  1968 *The Latin American Tradition*. New York: Columbia University Press.
  1971 *An Introduction to Brazil*. Rev. ed. New York: Columbia University Press.
  1977 *Welcome of Tears: The Tapirapé Indians of Central Brazil*. New York: Oxford University Press.
Wagley, Charles, ed.
  1952 *Race and Class in Rural Brazil*. Paris: UNESCO.
  1974 *Man in the Amazon*. Gainesville: University of Florida Press.
Wagley, Charles and Eduardo Galvão
  1946a "O parentesco Tupí-Guaraní." *Boletim do Museu Nacional de Antropologia*, no. 6. Rio de Janeiro.
  1946b "O parentesco Tupí-Guaraní (considerações à margem de uma crítica)." *Sociologia* 8(4):305–8. São Paulo.
  1948 "The Tapirapé." In Julian Steward, ed., *Handbook of South American Indians*, 3:167–78. Bureau of American Ethnology Bulletin 143. Washington, D.C.: Smithsonian Institution.
  1949 *The Tenetehara Indians of Brazil*. New York: Columbia University Press.
Wagley, Charles and Marvin Harris
  1958 *Minorities in the New World*. New York: Columbia University Press.
Wallace, Alfred
  1899 *A Narrative of Travels on the Amazon and the Rio Negro*. New York: Ward, Lock.
Wallerstein, Immanuel
  1974 *The Modern World System*. New York: Academic Press.

Warren, Donald
  1968a "The Portuguese Roots of Brazilian Spiritism." *Luso-Brazilian Review* 5(2):3–33.
  1968b "Spiritism in Brazil." *Journal of Inter-American Studies* 10:393–405.
Weaver, Herbert
  1945 *Mississippi Farmers, 1850–1860.* Nashville, Vanderbilt University Press.
Weber, Max
  1958 (orig. 1920) *The Protestant Ethic and the Spirit of Capitalism.* New York: Scribners.
  1964 *The Sociology of Religion.* Boston: Beacon Press.
Webster, Hutton
  1932 *Primitive Secret Societies: A Study in Early Politics and Religion.* 2d ed. New York: Macmillan.
Wedgwood, Camilla H.
  1930 "The Nature and Function of Secret Societies." *Oceania* 1(2):129–45.
Weffort, Francisco
  1965 "Raizes sociais do populismo em São Paulo." *Revista Civilização Brasileira* 1(2):39–60.
Weingrod, Alex
  1968 "Patrons, Patronage, and Political Parties." *Comparative Studies in Society and History* 10:377–400.
Wheeler, Douglas
  1972 "The Portuguese Revolution of 1910" *Journal of Modern History* 44(2):172–94.
White, Benjamin
  1976 *Production and Reproduction in a Javanese Village.* Ph.D. dissertation, Columbia University.
White, Leslie
  1949 *The Science of Culture.* New York: Grove Press.
Whiting, J. W. M., R. Kluckhohn, and A. Anthony
  1958 "The Function of Male Initiation Ceremonies at Puberty." In Eleanor Maccoby, ed., *Readings in Social Psychology,* pp. 359–70. New York: Holt.
Wiarda, Howard J.
  1969 *The Brazilian Catholic Labor Movement: The Dilemmas of National Development.* Boston: University of Massachusetts Press.
Wilbert, Johannes
  1972 *Survivors of Eldorado.* New York: Praeger.
Willems, Emilio
  1940 *Assimilação e Populações Marginais no Brasil.* São Paulo: Companhia Editôra Nacional.
  1946 *A Aculturação dos Alemães no Brasil.* São Paulo: Companhia Editôra Nacional.
  1947 *Cunha: Tradição e Transição em uma Cultura Rural do Brasil.* São Paulo: Secretaria da Agricultura.
  1952 "Caboclo Cultures of Southern Brazil." In Sol Tax, ed., *Acculturation in*

*the Americas*, 2:231–43. Selected papers of the 29th International Congress of Americanists. Chicago: University of Chicago Press.

1966 "Religious Mass Movements and Social Change in Brazil." In Eric Baklanoff, ed., *New Perspectives on Brazil*, pp. 205–32. Nashville: Vanderbilt University Press.

1967 *Followers of the New Faith: Culture Change and the Rise of Protestantism in Brazil and Chile*. Nashville: Vanderbilt University Press.

1969 "Religious Pluralism and Class Structure: Brazil and Chile." In Roland Robertson, ed., *Sociology of Religion*. Baltimore: Penguin.

Wilson, Bryan

1973 *Magic and the Millennium: A Sociological Study of Protest Among Tribal and Third World Peoples*. New York: Harper and Row.

Wissler, Clark

1917 *The American Indian*. New York: D. C. McMurtrie.

1922 *The American Indian*. 2d ed. New York: Oxford University Press.

Wolf, Eric R.

1956 "Aspects of Group Relations in a Complex Society." *American Anthropologist* 58(6):1065–78.

1966a *Peasants*. Englewood Cliffs, N.J.: Prentice-Hall.

1966b "Kinship, Friendship, and Patron-Client Relations in Complex Societies." In Michael Banton, ed., *The Social Anthropology of Complex Societies*, pp. 1-22. London: Tavistock.

Wolf, J. M.

1975 *Water Restraints to Corn Productivity in Central Brazil*. Ph.D. dissertation, Cornell University.

Worsley, Peter

1956 "The Kinship System of the Tallensi: A Revaluation." *Journal of the Royal Anthropological Institute* 86(1):37–75.

1957 *The Trumpet Shall Sound*. London: MacGibbon and Kee.

Young, Frank W.

1965 *Initiation Ceremonies*. Indianapolis: Bobbs-Merrill.

Zerries, Otto

1968 "Some Aspects of Waica Culture." *Proceedings of the 31st International Congress of Americanists*, pp. 73–88. São Paulo.

Zuidema, R. T.

1969 "Hierarchy in Symmetric Alliance Systems." *Bijdragen Tot de Taal-Land en Volkenkunde* 11(1):134–39.

# INDEX